The Quintessential Quintuplets 8 is a work of
places, and incidents are the products of th
or are used fictitiously. Any resemblance to actual events, locales, or persons, living or dead, is entirely coincidental.

A Kodansha Comics Trade Paperback Original

Published in the United States by Kodansha Comics, an imprint of Kodansha USA Publishing, LLC, New York.

Publication rights for this English edition arranged through Kodansha Ltd., Tokyo.

First published in Japan in 2019 by Kodansha Ltd., Tokyo as *Gotoubun no hanayome*, volume 8.

ISBN 978-1-63236-919-2

Cover Design: Saya Takagi (RedRooster)

Printed in the United States of America.

www.kodansha.us

9 8 7 6
Translation: Steven LeCroy
Lettering: Jan Lan Ivan Concepcion
Editing: Nathaniel Gallant, Thalia Sutton
Additional Layout: Belynda Ungurath
Editorial Assistance: YKS Services LLC/SKY Japan, INC.
Kodansha Comics edition cover design by Phil Balsman

KODANSHA COMICS

Publisher: Kiichiro Sugawara
Managing editor: Maya Rosewood
Vice president of marketing & publicity: Naho Yamada

Director of publishing services: Ben Applegate
Associate director of operations: Stephen Pakula
Publishing services managing editor: Noelle Webster
Assistant production manager: Emi Lotto, Angela Zurlo

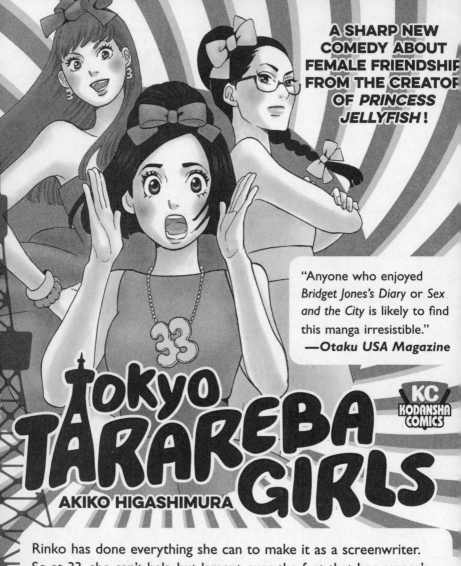

A SHARP NEW COMEDY ABOUT FEMALE FRIENDSHIP FROM THE CREATOR OF *PRINCESS JELLYFISH*!

"Anyone who enjoyed *Bridget Jones's Diary* or *Sex and the City* is likely to find this manga irresistible."
—*Otaku USA Magazine*

KC KODANSHA COMICS

Tokyo TARAREBA GIRLS

AKIKO HIGASHIMURA

Rinko has done everything she can to make it as a screenwriter. So at 33, she can't help but lament over the fact that her career's plateaued, she's still painfully single, and spends most of her nights drinking with her two best friends. One night, drunk and delusional, Rinko swears to get married by the time the Tokyo Olympics roll around in 2020. But finding a man—or love—may be a cutthroat, dirty job for a romantic at heart!

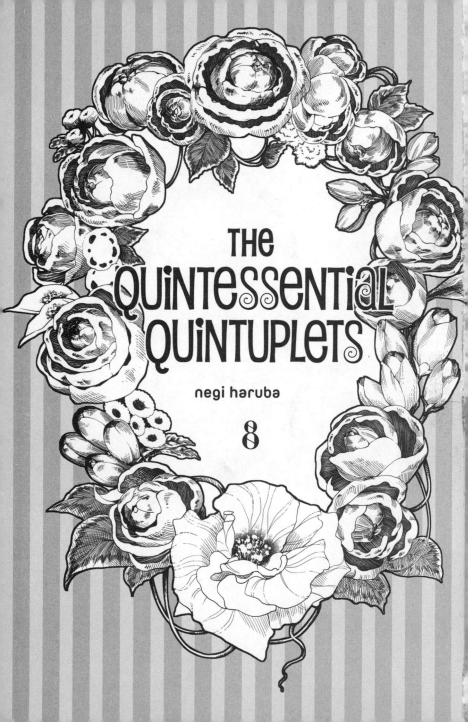

THE QUINTESSENTIAL QUINTUPLETS

negi haruba

8

Character intros

HIS FUTURE BRIDE IS ONE OF THE QUINTS!!

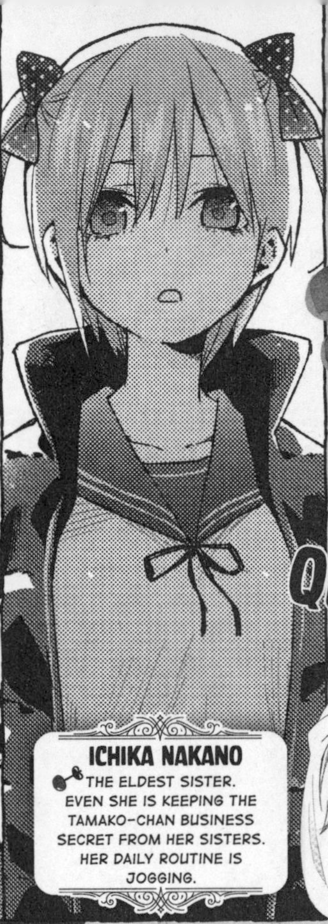
ICHIKA NAKANO
THE ELDEST SISTER. EVEN SHE IS KEEPING THE TAMAKO-CHAN BUSINESS SECRET FROM HER SISTERS. HER DAILY ROUTINE IS JOGGING.

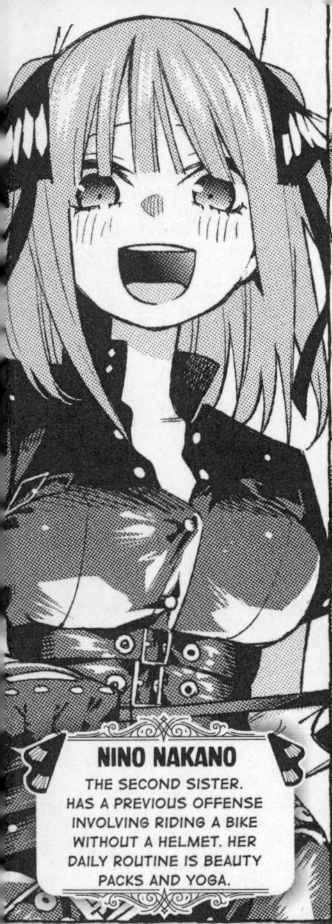
NINO NAKANO
THE SECOND SISTER. HAS A PREVIOUS OFFENSE INVOLVING RIDING A BIKE WITHOUT A HELMET. HER DAILY ROUTINE IS BEAUTY PACKS AND YOGA.

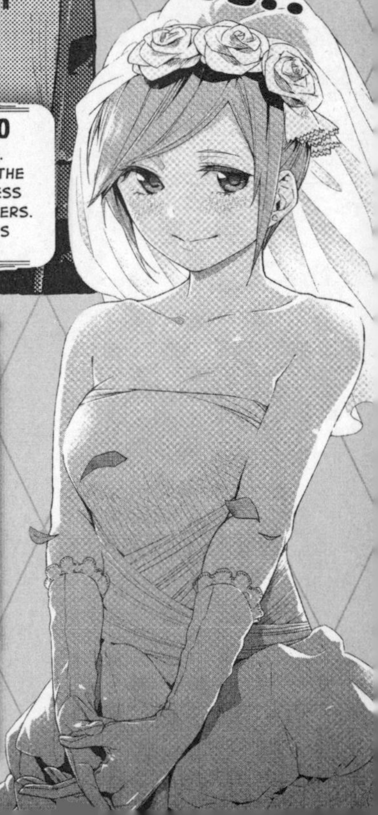

Quints Memo

- ☆ Hate to Study: If you try to teach them anything, they run.
- ☆ Potential Flunkers: Their score on Futaro's quiz was 100 points...between the five of them.
- ☆ On the Verge of Flunking: Had to change schools to avoid flunking out.
- ☆ Very Idiosyncratic: The five sisters each have their own intense quirks, so dealing with them won't be easy.

...Guide the five of them to graduation!!

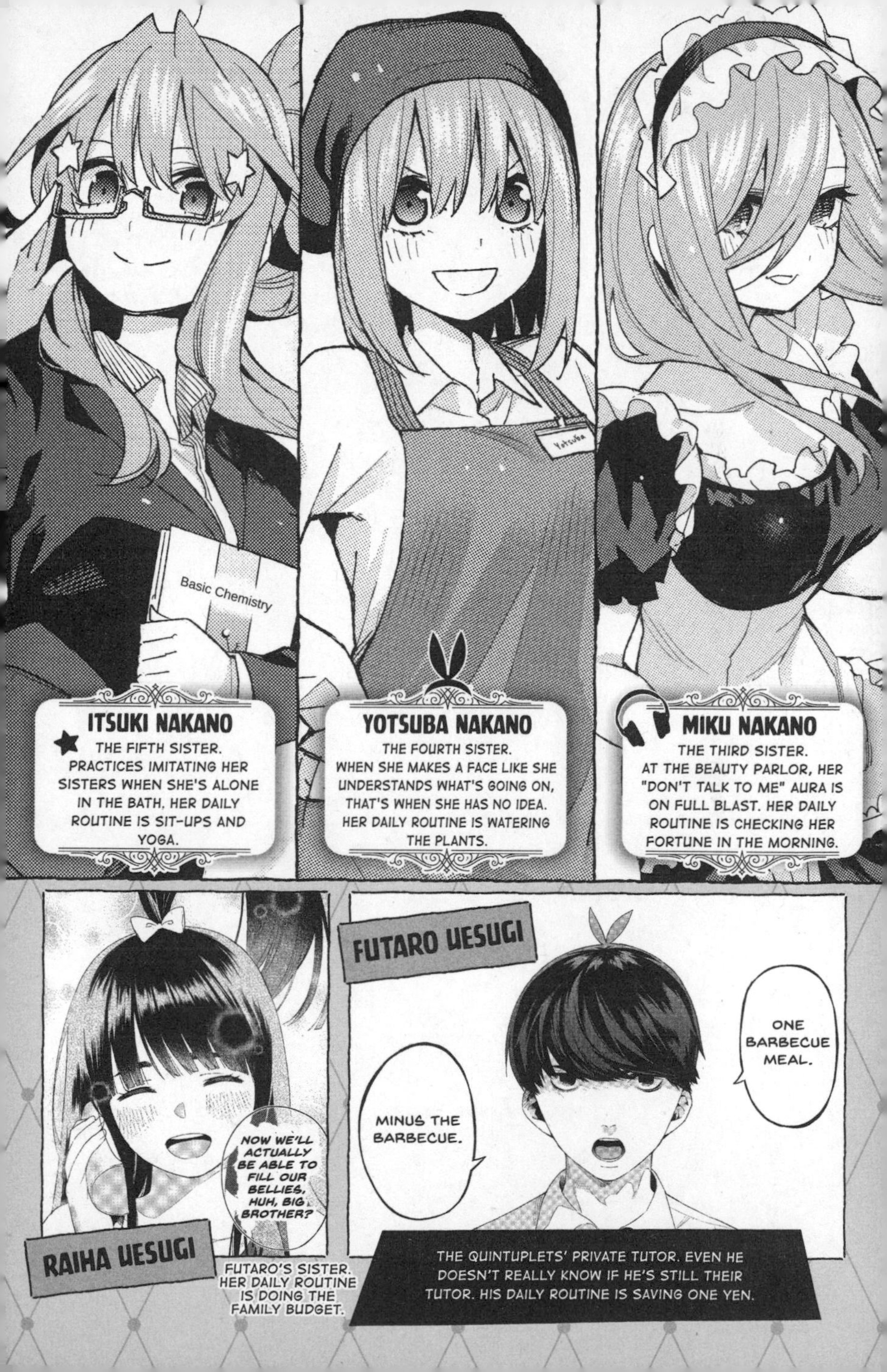
MIKU NAKANO
THE THIRD SISTER. AT THE BEAUTY PARLOR, HER "DON'T TALK TO ME" AURA IS ON FULL BLAST. HER DAILY ROUTINE IS CHECKING HER FORTUNE IN THE MORNING.
Yotsuba
YOTSUBA NAKANO
THE FOURTH SISTER. WHEN SHE MAKES A FACE LIKE SHE UNDERSTANDS WHAT'S GOING ON, THAT'S WHEN SHE HAS NO IDEA. HER DAILY ROUTINE IS WATERING THE PLANTS.
Basic Chemistry
ITSUKI NAKANO
THE FIFTH SISTER. PRACTICES IMITATING HER SISTERS WHEN SHE'S ALONE IN THE BATH. HER DAILY ROUTINE IS SIT-UPS AND YOGA.
FUTARO UESUGI
ONE BARBECUE MEAL.
MINUS THE BARBECUE.
THE QUINTUPLETS' PRIVATE TUTOR. EVEN HE DOESN'T REALLY KNOW IF HE'S STILL THEIR TUTOR. HIS DAILY ROUTINE IS SAVING ONE YEN.
NOW WE'LL ACTUALLY BE ABLE TO FILL OUR BELLIES, HUH, BIG BROTHER?
RAIHA UESUGI
FUTARO'S SISTER. HER DAILY ROUTINE IS DOING THE FAMILY BUDGET.

CONTENTS

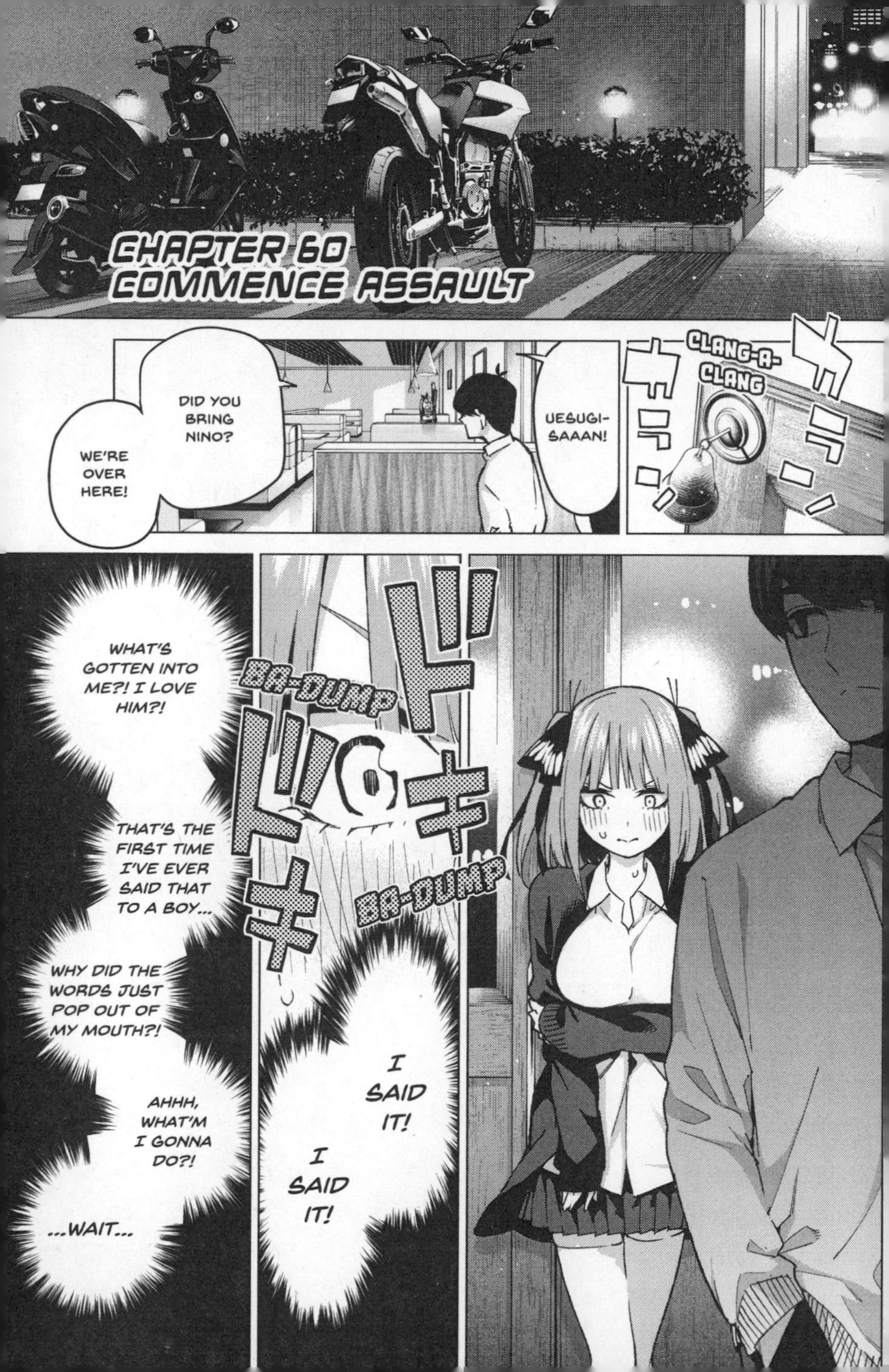
CHAPTER 60
COMMENCE ASSAULT
CLANG-A-CLANG
UESUGI-SAAAN!
DID YOU BRING NINO?
WE'RE OVER HERE!
BA-DUMP
BA-DUMP
I SAID IT!
I SAID IT!
WHAT'S GOTTEN INTO ME?! I LOVE HIM?!
THAT'S THE FIRST TIME I'VE EVER SAID THAT TO A BOY...
WHY DID THE WORDS JUST POP OUT OF MY MOUTH?!
AHHH, WHAT'M I GONNA DO?!
...WAIT...

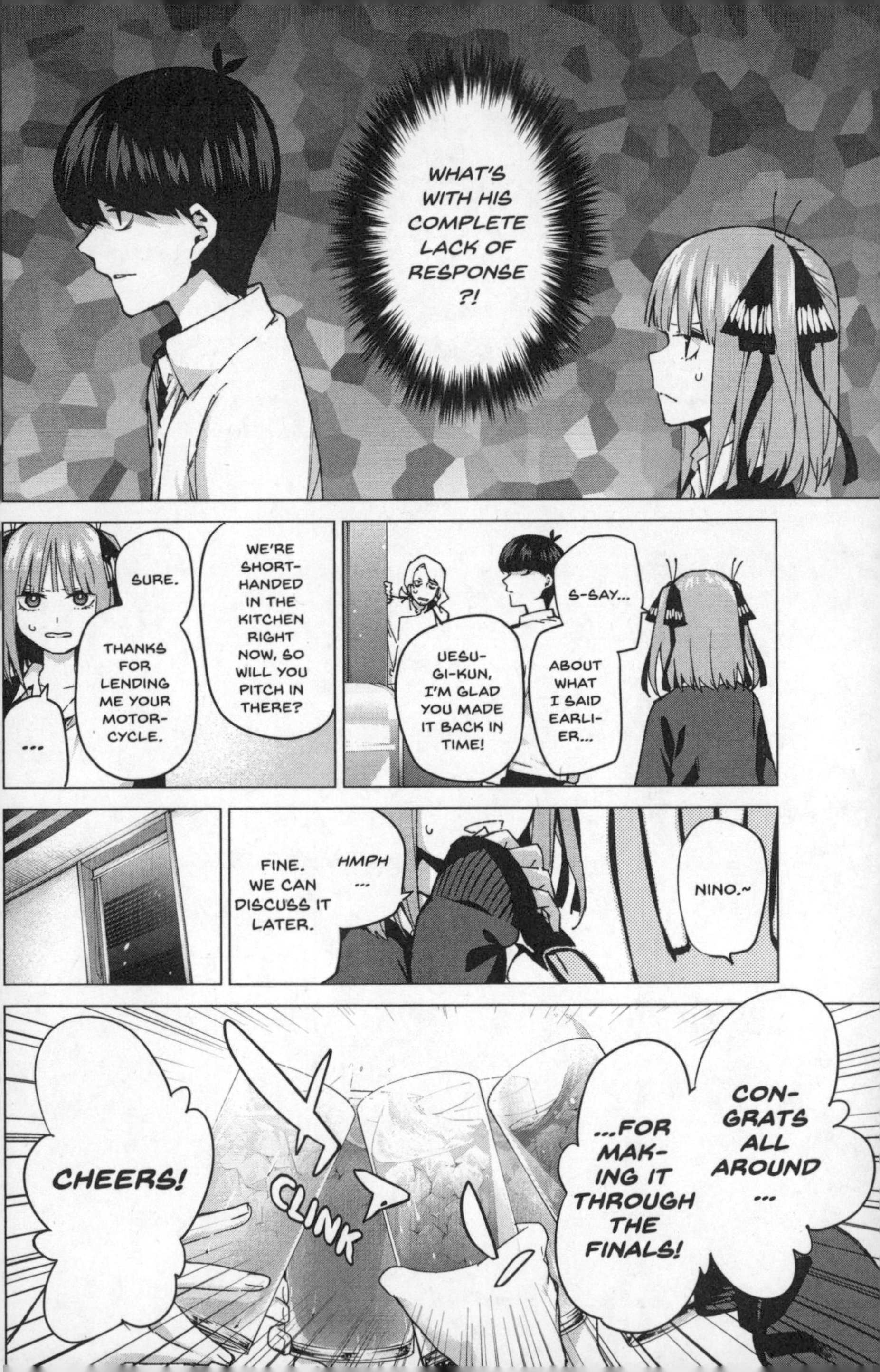
WHAT'S WITH HIS COMPLETE LACK OF RESPONSE ?!
S-SAY...
ABOUT WHAT I SAID EARLI-ER...
UESU-GI-KUN, I'M GLAD YOU MADE IT BACK IN TIME!
WE'RE SHORT-HANDED IN THE KITCHEN RIGHT NOW, SO WILL YOU PITCH IN THERE?
SURE.
THANKS FOR LENDING ME YOUR MOTOR-CYCLE.
...
NINO.~
HMPH ...
FINE. WE CAN DISCUSS IT LATER.
CON-GRATS ALL AROUND ...
...FOR MAK-ING IT THROUGH THE FINALS!
CLINK
CHEERS!

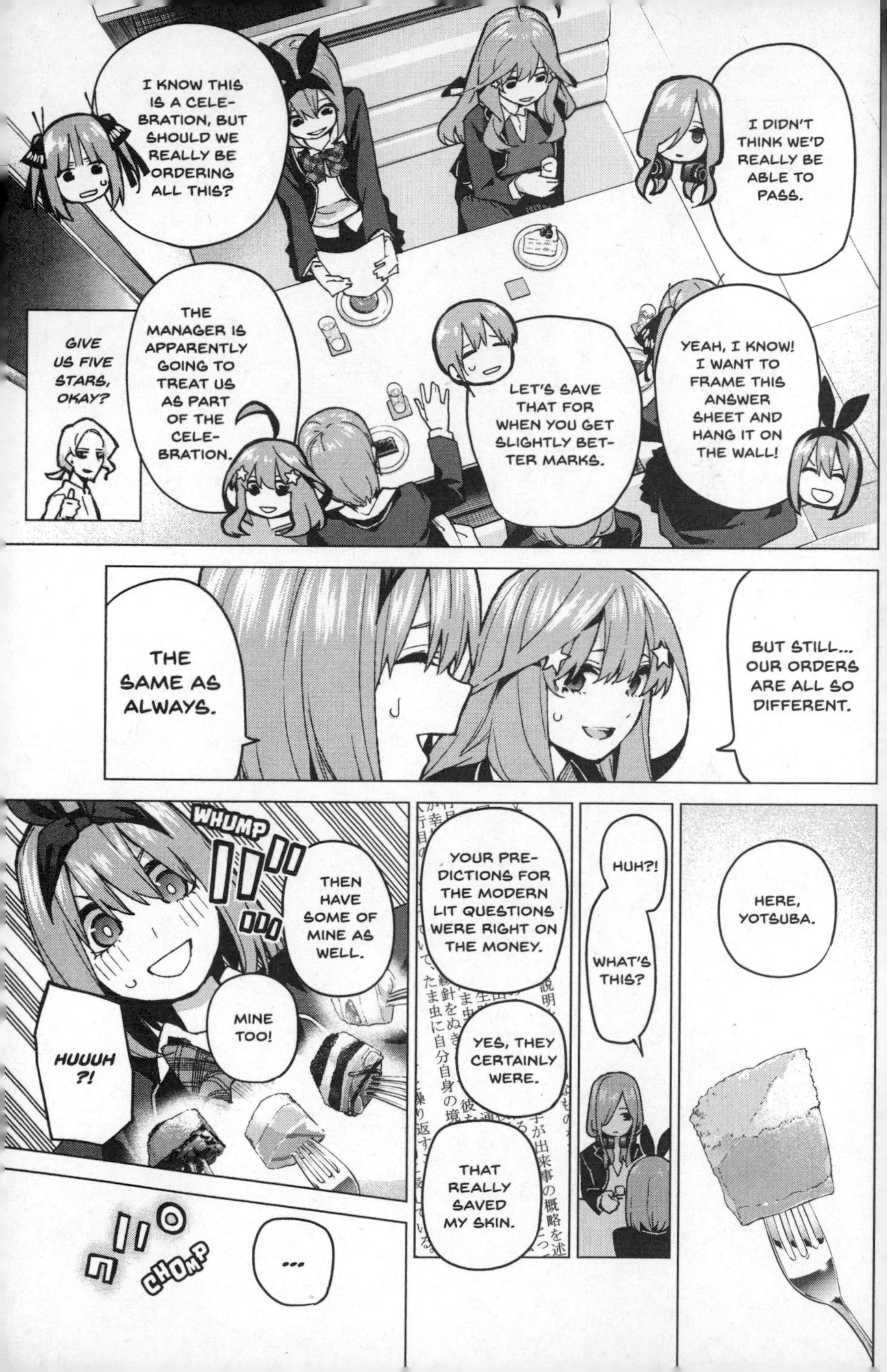
I DIDN'T THINK WE'D REALLY BE ABLE TO PASS.
I KNOW THIS IS A CELEBRATION, BUT SHOULD WE REALLY BE ORDERING ALL THIS?
YEAH, I KNOW! I WANT TO FRAME THIS ANSWER SHEET AND HANG IT ON THE WALL!
LET'S SAVE THAT FOR WHEN YOU GET SLIGHTLY BETTER MARKS.
THE MANAGER IS APPARENTLY GOING TO TREAT US AS PART OF THE CELEBRATION.
GIVE US FIVE STARS, OKAY?
BUT STILL... OUR ORDERS ARE ALL SO DIFFERENT.
THE SAME AS ALWAYS.
HERE, YOTSUBA.
HUH?!
WHAT'S THIS?
YOUR PREDICTIONS FOR THE MODERN LIT QUESTIONS WERE RIGHT ON THE MONEY.
YES, THEY CERTAINLY WERE.
THAT REALLY SAVED MY SKIN.
WHUMP
THEN HAVE SOME OF MINE AS WELL.
MINE TOO!
HUUUH?!
...
CHOMP

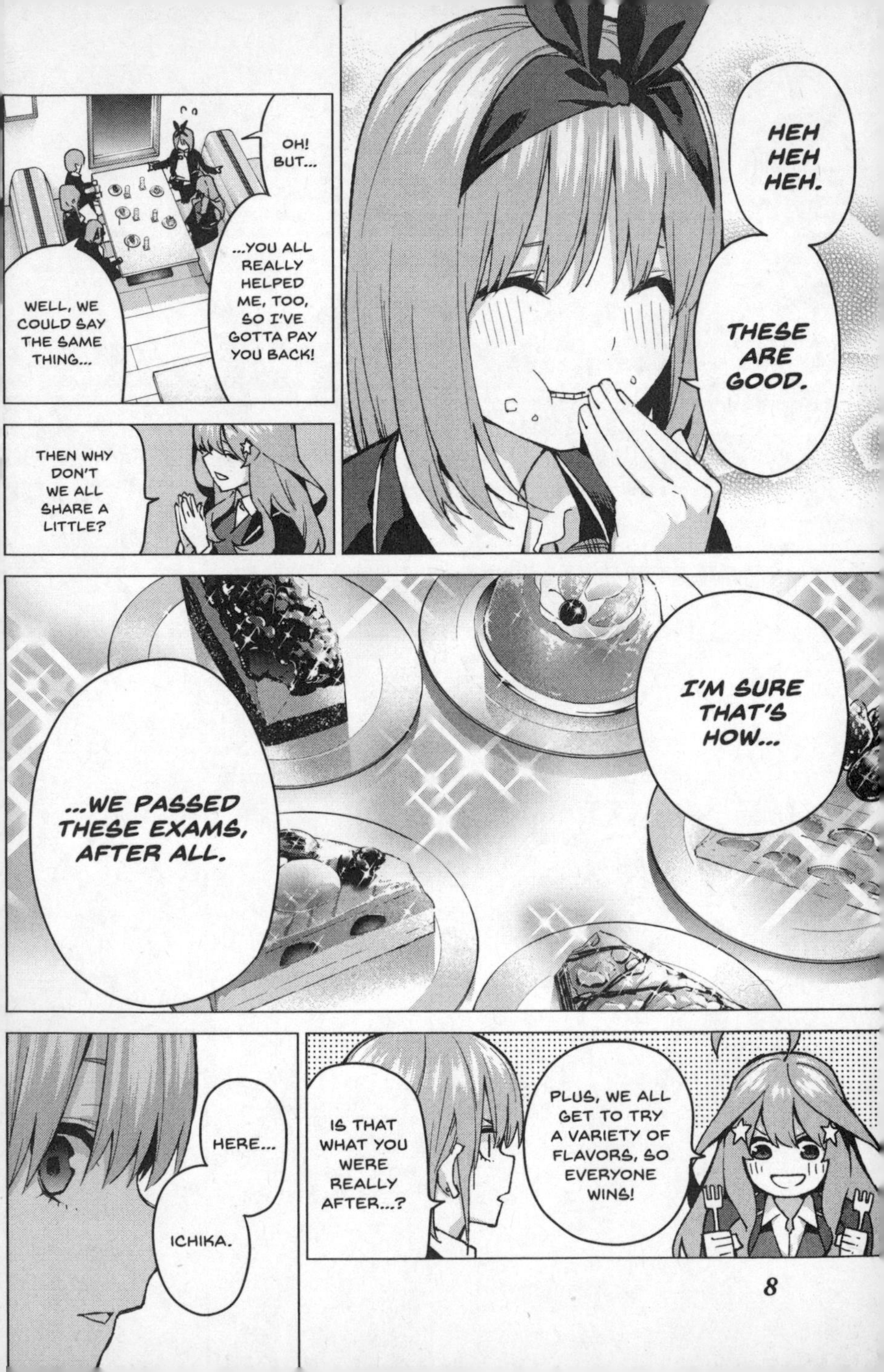
HEH HEH HEH.
THESE ARE GOOD.
OH! BUT...
...YOU ALL REALLY HELPED ME, TOO, SO I'VE GOTTA PAY YOU BACK!
WELL, WE COULD SAY THE SAME THING...
THEN WHY DON'T WE ALL SHARE A LITTLE?
I'M SURE THAT'S HOW...
...WE PASSED THESE EXAMS, AFTER ALL.
PLUS, WE ALL GET TO TRY A VARIETY OF FLAVORS, SO EVERYONE WINS!
IS THAT WHAT YOU WERE REALLY AFTER...?
HERE...
ICHIKA.

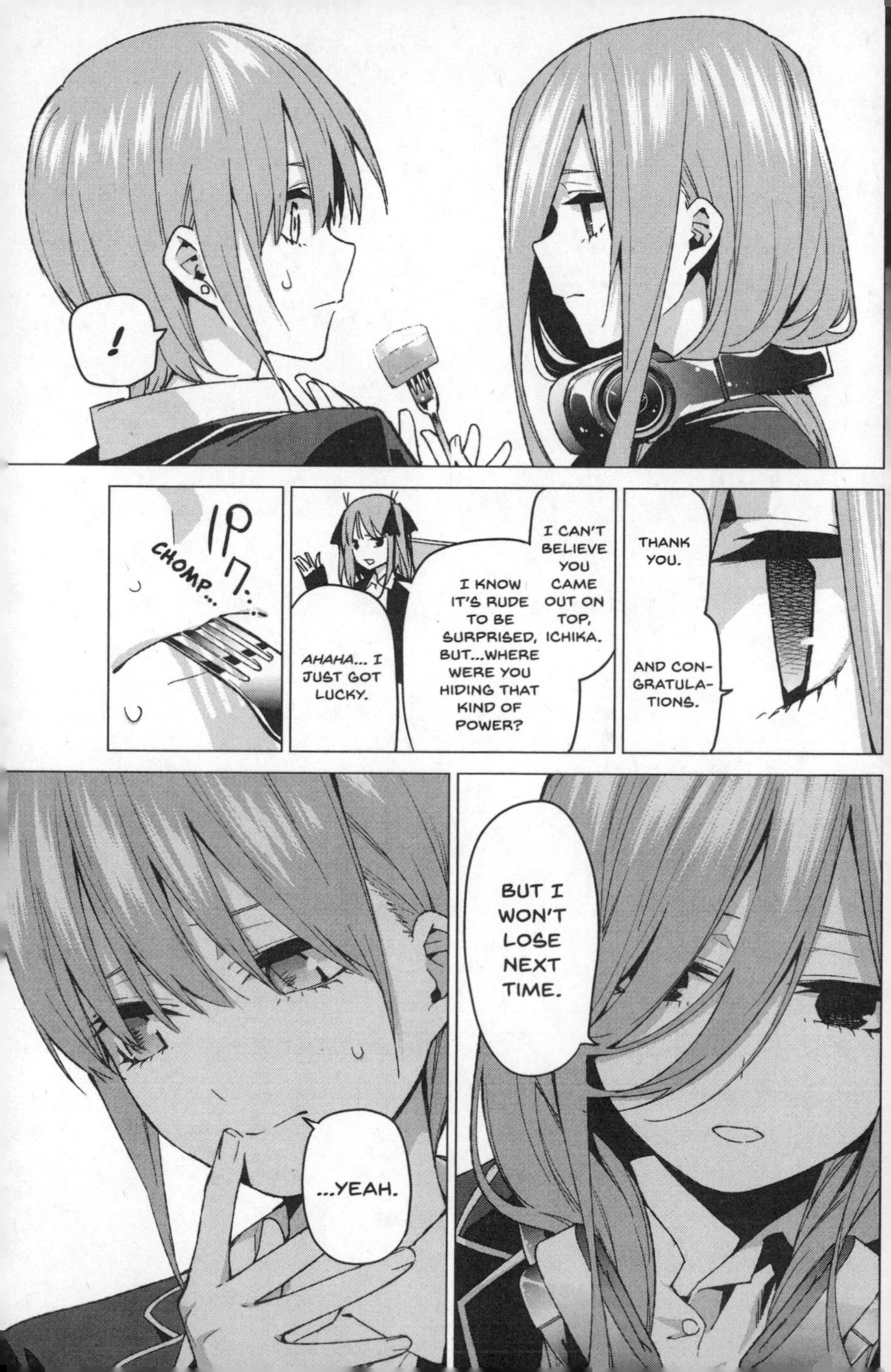

!
THANK YOU.
AND CONGRATULATIONS.
I CAN'T BELIEVE YOU CAME OUT ON TOP, ICHIKA.
I KNOW IT'S RUDE TO BE SURPRISED, BUT...WHERE WERE YOU HIDING THAT KIND OF POWER?
AHAHA... I JUST GOT LUCKY.
CHOMP...
BUT I WON'T LOSE NEXT TIME.
...YEAH.

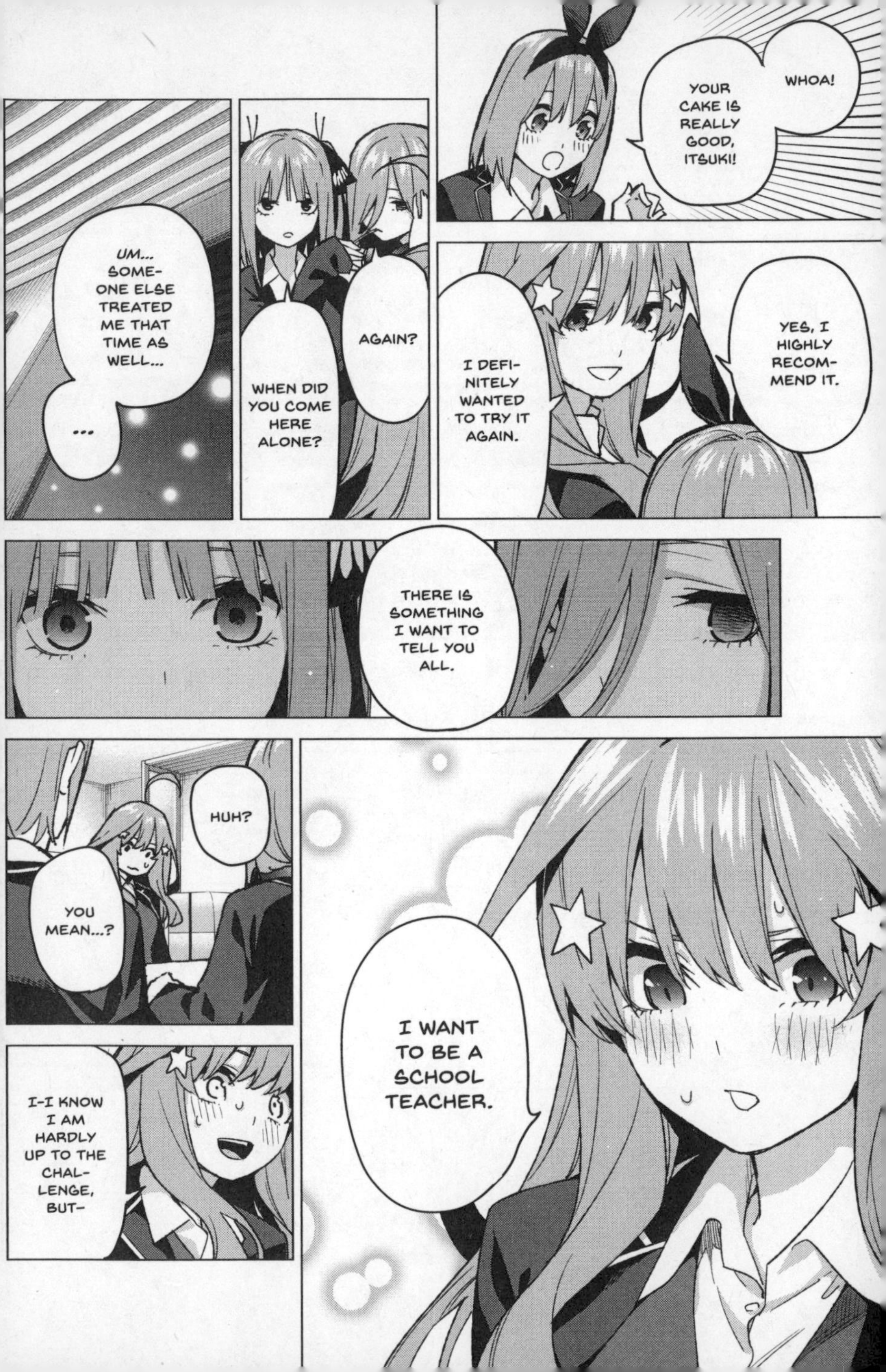
WHOA!
YOUR CAKE IS REALLY GOOD, ITSUKI!
YES, I HIGHLY RECOMMEND IT.
I DEFINITELY WANTED TO TRY IT AGAIN.
AGAIN?
WHEN DID YOU COME HERE ALONE?
UM... SOMEONE ELSE TREATED ME THAT TIME AS WELL...
...
THERE IS SOMETHING I WANT TO TELL YOU ALL.
I WANT TO BE A SCHOOL TEACHER.
HUH?
YOU MEAN...?
I-I KNOW I AM HARDLY UP TO THE CHALLENGE, BUT-

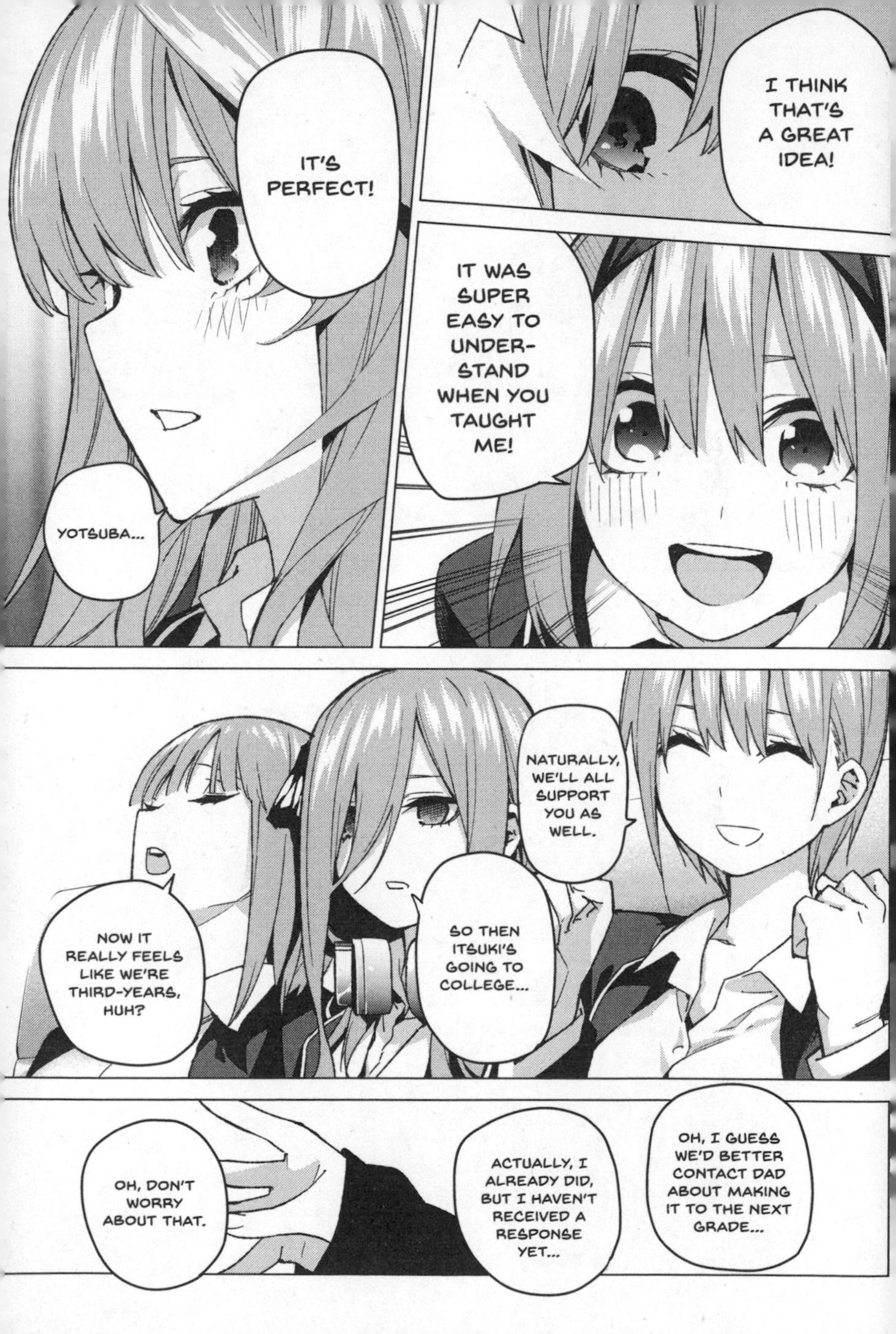
I THINK THAT'S A GREAT IDEA!
IT WAS SUPER EASY TO UNDER-STAND WHEN YOU TAUGHT ME!
IT'S PERFECT!
YOTSUBA...
NATURALLY, WE'LL ALL SUPPORT YOU AS WELL.
SO THEN ITSUKI'S GOING TO COLLEGE...
NOW IT REALLY FEELS LIKE WE'RE THIRD-YEARS, HUH?
OH, I GUESS WE'D BETTER CONTACT DAD ABOUT MAKING IT TO THE NEXT GRADE...
ACTUALLY, I ALREADY DID, BUT I HAVEN'T RECEIVED A RESPONSE YET...
OH, DON'T WORRY ABOUT THAT.

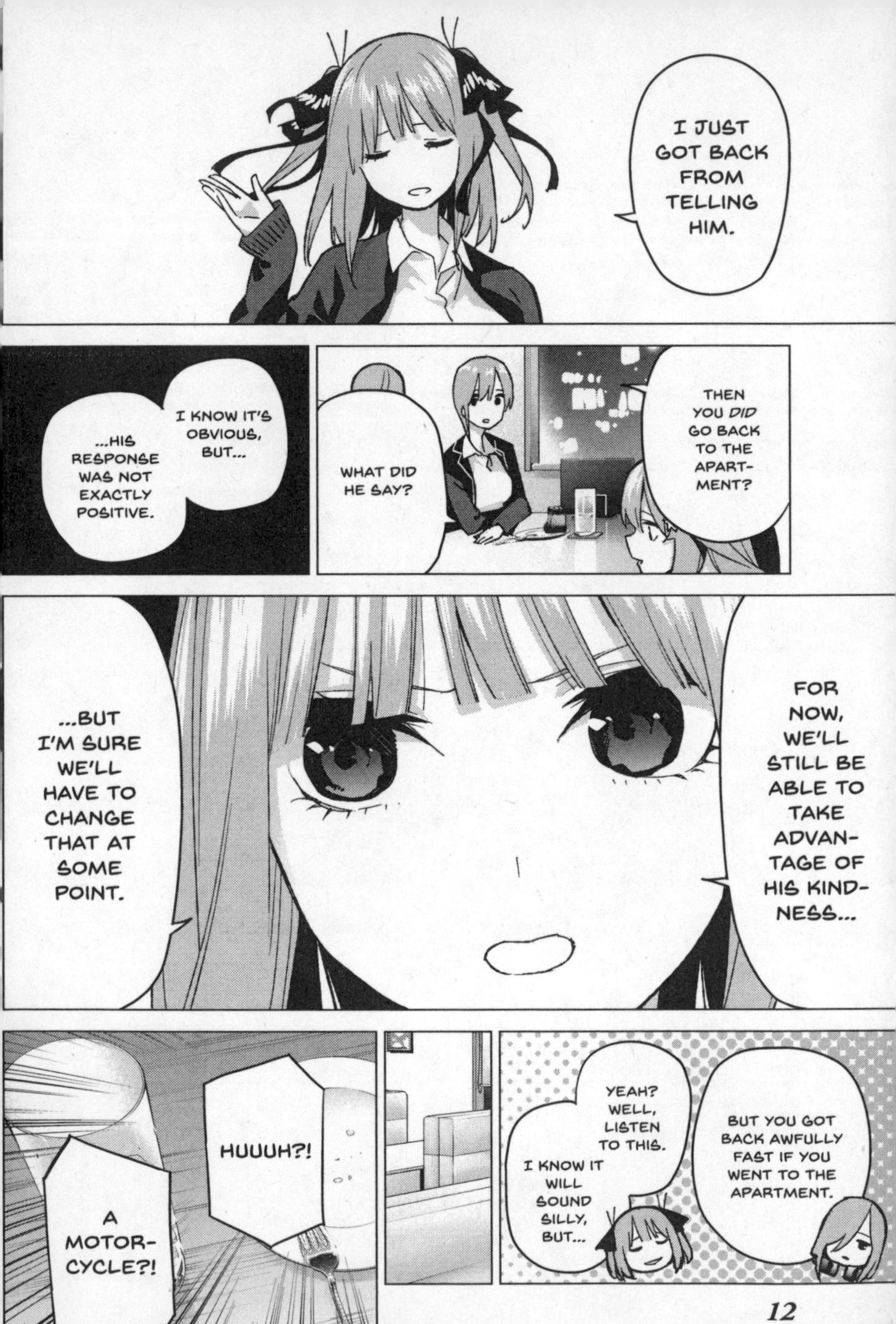
I JUST GOT BACK FROM TELLING HIM.
THEN YOU *DID* GO BACK TO THE APARTMENT?
WHAT DID HE SAY?
I KNOW IT'S OBVIOUS, BUT...
...HIS RESPONSE WAS NOT EXACTLY POSITIVE.
FOR NOW, WE'LL STILL BE ABLE TO TAKE ADVANTAGE OF HIS KINDNESS...
...BUT I'M SURE WE'LL HAVE TO CHANGE THAT AT SOME POINT.
BUT YOU GOT BACK AWFULLY FAST IF YOU WENT TO THE APARTMENT.
YEAH? WELL, LISTEN TO THIS.
I KNOW IT WILL SOUND SILLY, BUT...
HUUUH?!
A MOTORCYCLE?!

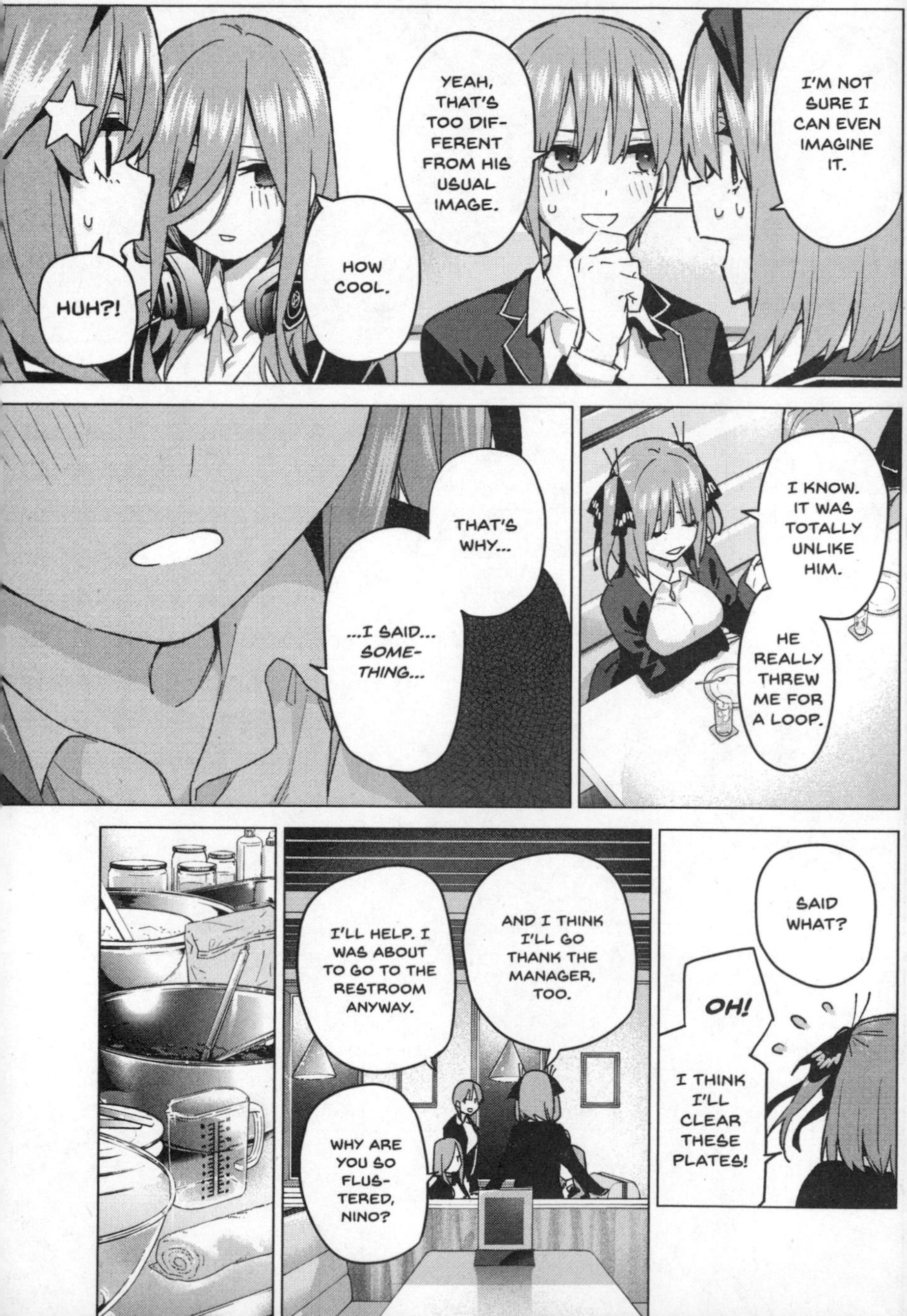
I'M NOT SURE I CAN EVEN IMAGINE IT.
YEAH, THAT'S TOO DIF-FERENT FROM HIS USUAL IMAGE.
HOW COOL.
HUH?!
I KNOW. IT WAS TOTALLY UNLIKE HIM.
HE REALLY THREW ME FOR A LOOP.
THAT'S WHY...
...I SAID... SOME-THING...
SAID WHAT?
OH!
I THINK I'LL CLEAR THESE PLATES!
AND I THINK I'LL GO THANK THE MANAGER, TOO.
I'LL HELP. I WAS ABOUT TO GO TO THE RESTROOM ANYWAY.
WHY ARE YOU SO FLUS-TERED, NINO?

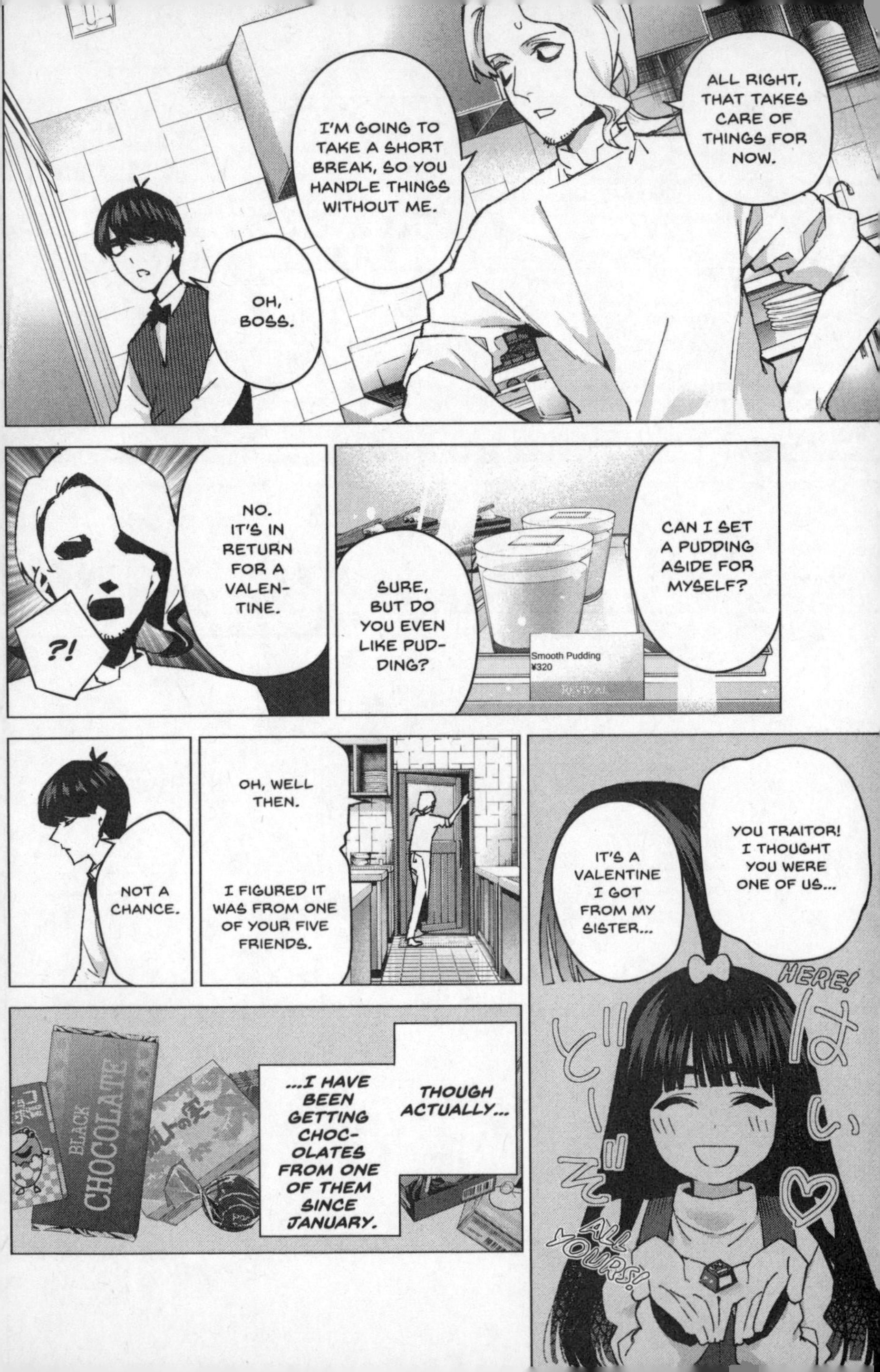
ALL RIGHT, THAT TAKES CARE OF THINGS FOR NOW.
I'M GOING TO TAKE A SHORT BREAK, SO YOU HANDLE THINGS WITHOUT ME.
OH, BOSS.
CAN I SET A PUDDING ASIDE FOR MYSELF?
SURE, BUT DO YOU EVEN LIKE PUDDING?
Smooth Pudding ¥320
NO. IT'S IN RETURN FOR A VALENTINE.
?!
YOU TRAITOR! I THOUGHT YOU WERE ONE OF US...
IT'S A VALENTINE I GOT FROM MY SISTER...
HERE!
ALL YOURS!
OH, WELL THEN.
I FIGURED IT WAS FROM ONE OF YOUR FIVE FRIENDS.
NOT A CHANCE.
THOUGH ACTUALLY...
...I HAVE BEEN GETTING CHOCOLATES FROM ONE OF THEM SINCE JANUARY.
BLACK CHOCOLATE

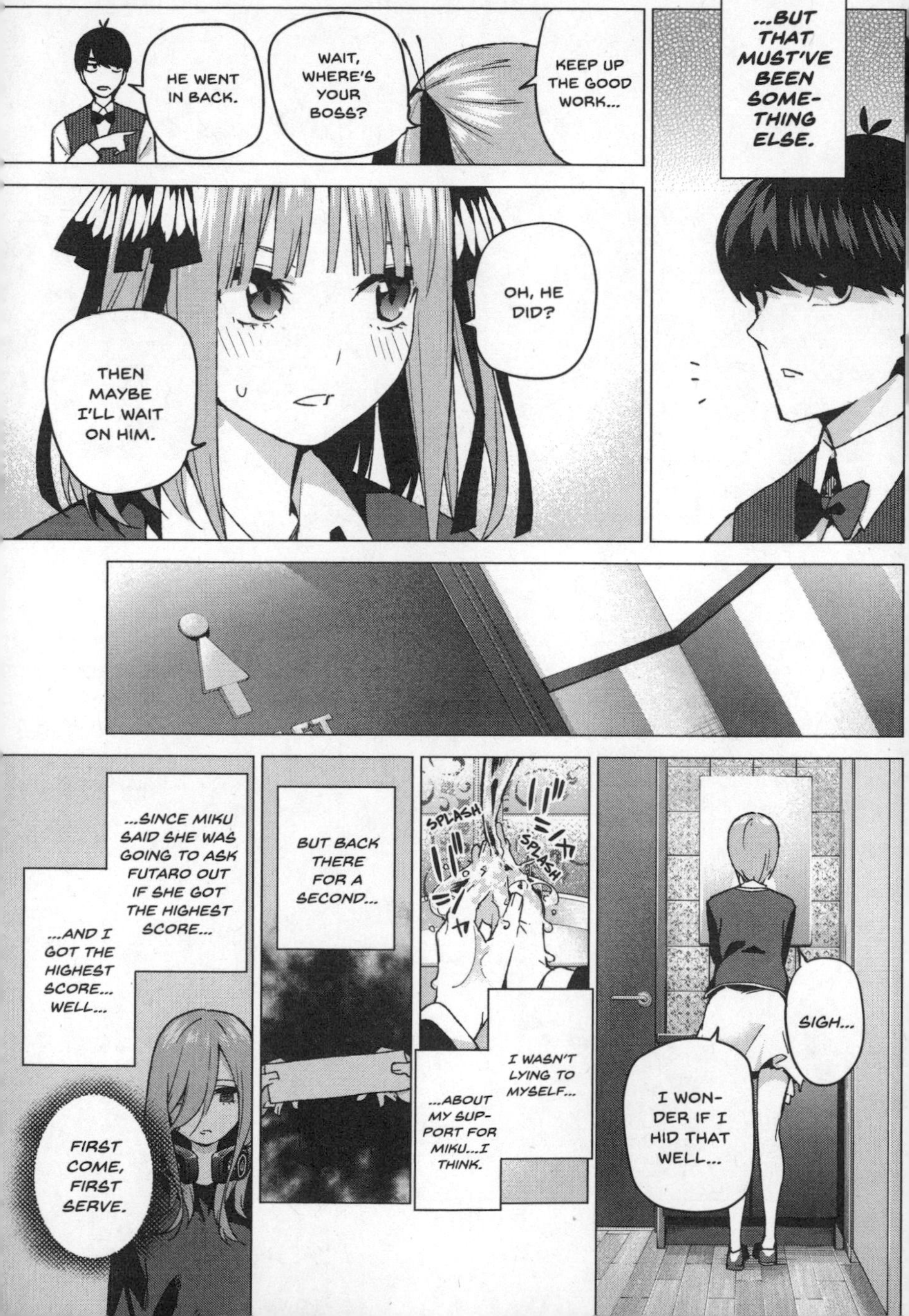
...BUT THAT MUST'VE BEEN SOME-THING ELSE.
KEEP UP THE GOOD WORK...
WAIT, WHERE'S YOUR BOSS?
HE WENT IN BACK.
OH, HE DID?
THEN MAYBE I'LL WAIT ON HIM.
SIGH...
I WON-DER IF I HID THAT WELL...
SPLASH
SPLASH
I WASN'T LYING TO MYSELF...
...ABOUT MY SUP-PORT FOR MIKU...I THINK.
BUT BACK THERE FOR A SECOND...
...SINCE MIKU SAID SHE WAS GOING TO ASK FUTARO OUT IF SHE GOT THE HIGHEST SCORE...
...AND I GOT THE HIGHEST SCORE... WELL...
FIRST COME, FIRST SERVE.

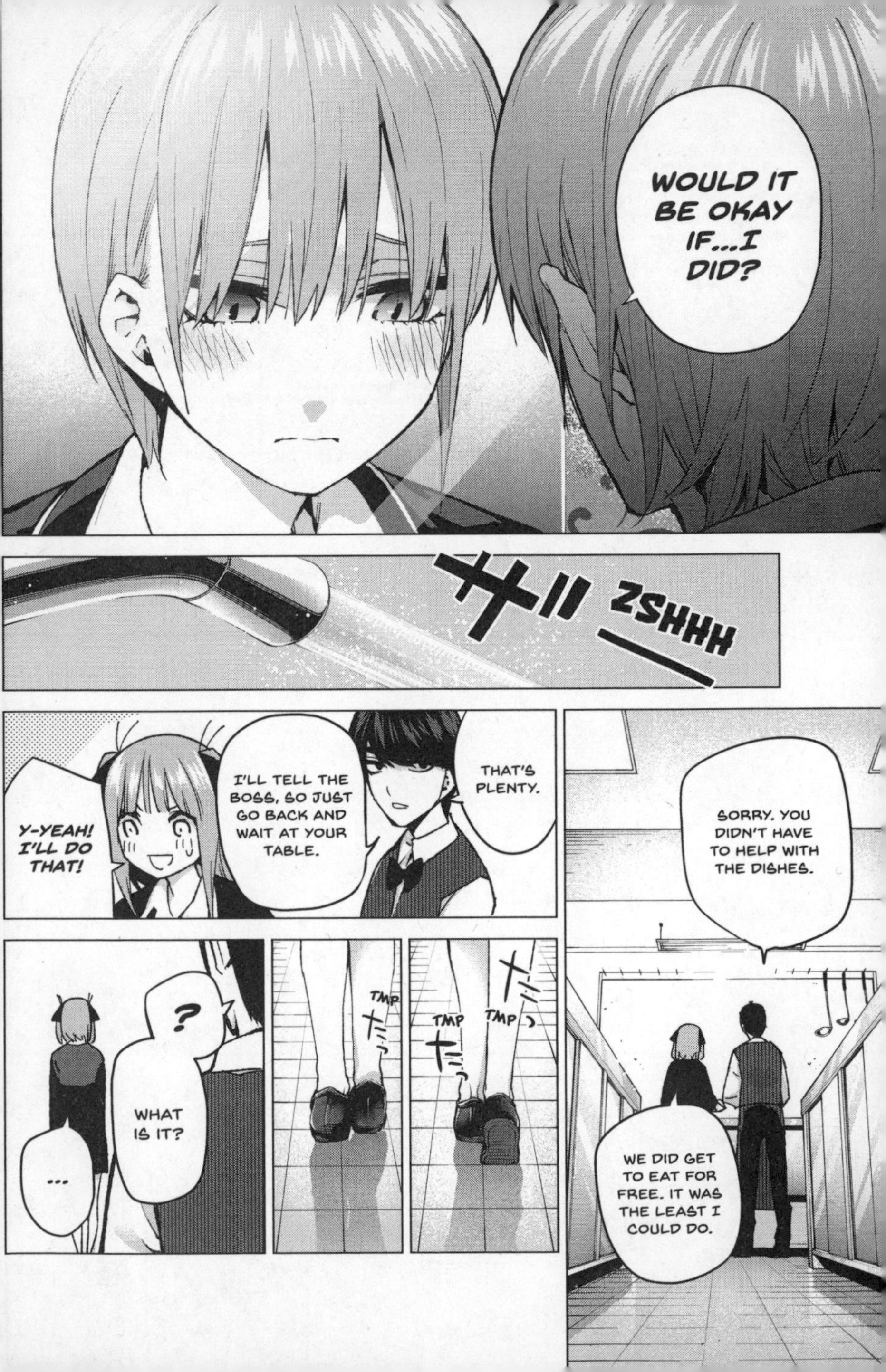
WOULD IT BE OKAY IF...I DID?
ZSHHH
SORRY. YOU DIDN'T HAVE TO HELP WITH THE DISHES.
WE DID GET TO EAT FOR FREE. IT WAS THE LEAST I COULD DO.
THAT'S PLENTY.
I'LL TELL THE BOSS, SO JUST GO BACK AND WAIT AT YOUR TABLE.
Y-YEAH! I'LL DO THAT!
TMP
TMP
TMP
TMP
?
WHAT IS IT?
...

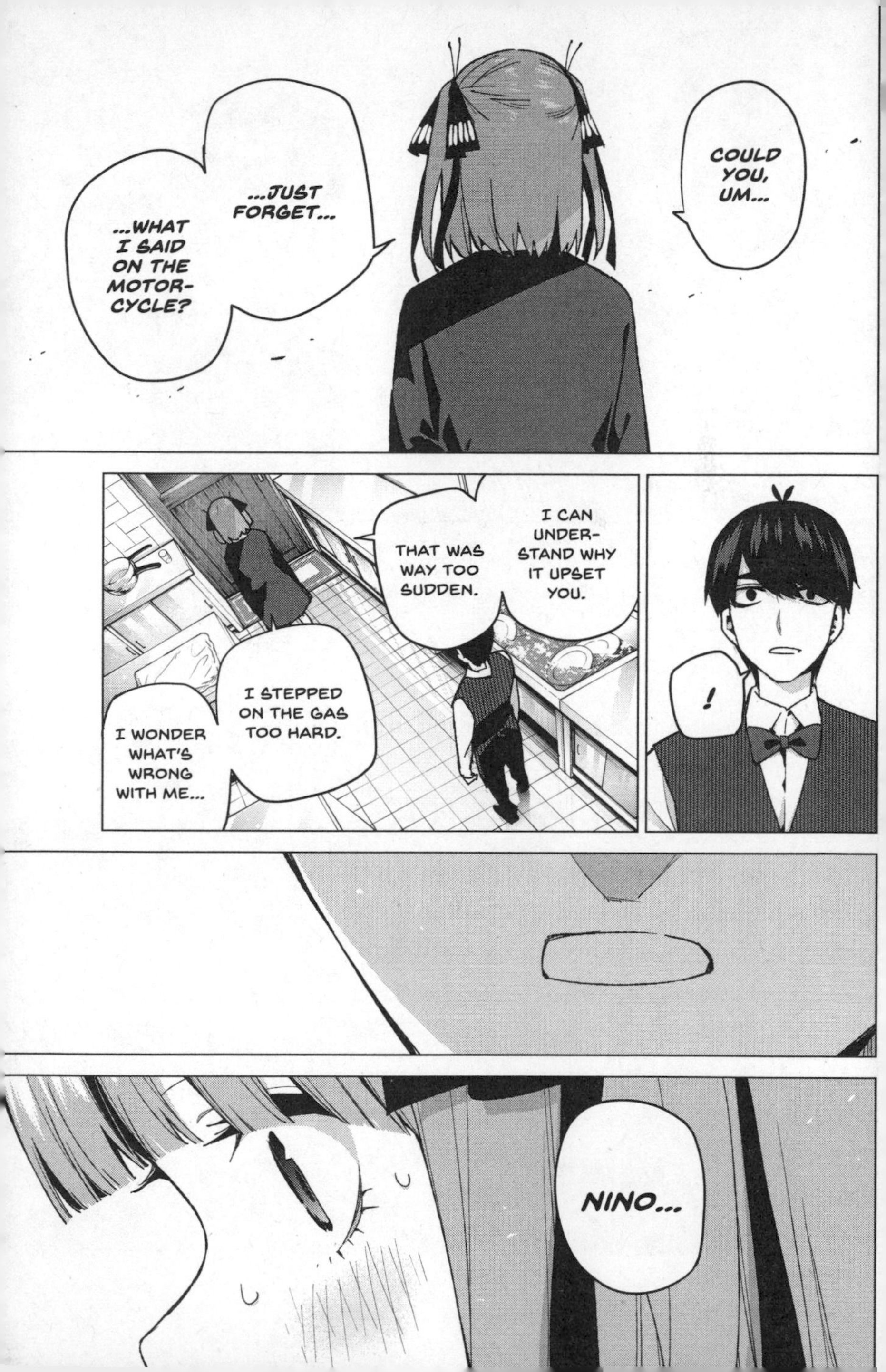
COULD YOU, UM...
...JUST FORGET... ...WHAT I SAID ON THE MOTOR-CYCLE?
!
I CAN UNDER-STAND WHY IT UPSET YOU.
THAT WAS WAY TOO SUDDEN.
I STEPPED ON THE GAS TOO HARD.
I WONDER WHAT'S WRONG WITH ME...
NINO...

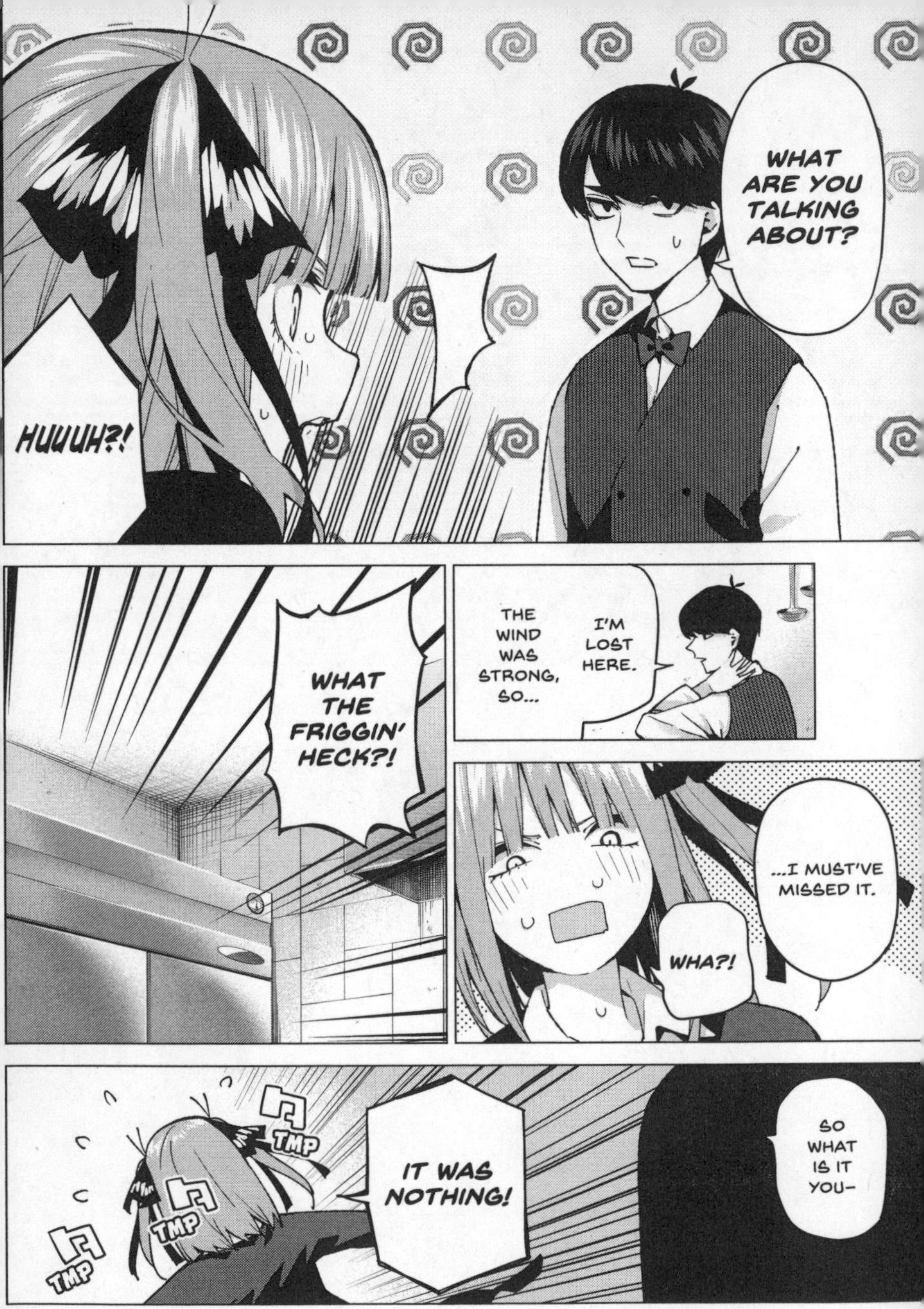
WHAT ARE YOU TALKING ABOUT?
HUUUH?!
I'M LOST HERE.
THE WIND WAS STRONG, SO...
...I MUST'VE MISSED IT.
WHA?!
WHAT THE FRIGGIN' HECK?!
SO WHAT IS IT YOU–
IT WAS NOTHING!
TMP
TMP
TMP

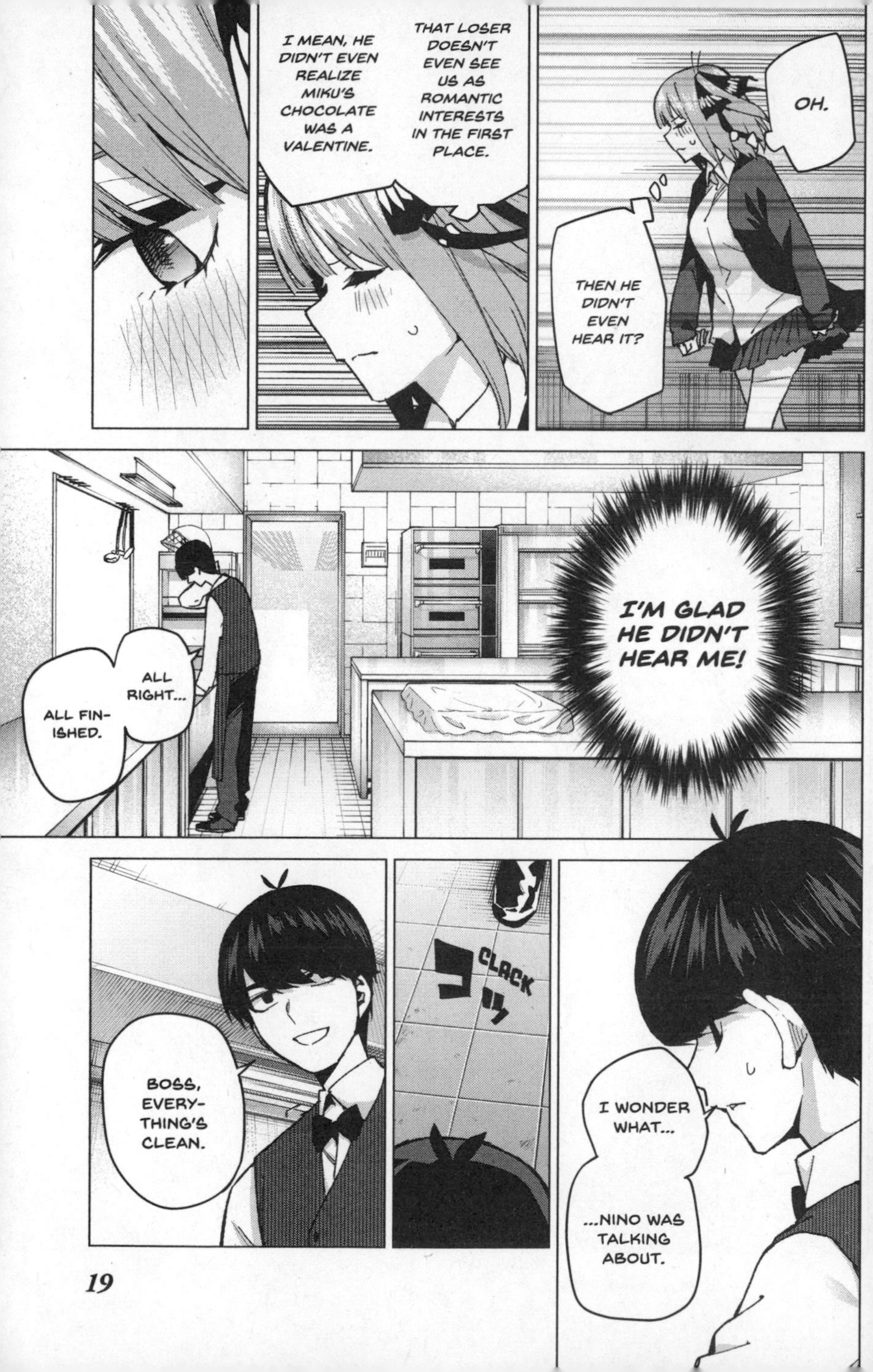
OH.
THEN HE DIDN'T EVEN HEAR IT?
THAT LOSER DOESN'T EVEN SEE US AS ROMANTIC INTERESTS IN THE FIRST PLACE.
I MEAN, HE DIDN'T EVEN REALIZE MIKU'S CHOCOLATE WAS A VALENTINE.
I'M GLAD HE DIDN'T HEAR ME!
ALL RIGHT...
ALL FIN-ISHED.
I WONDER WHAT...
...NINO WAS TALKING ABOUT.
CLACK
BOSS, EVERY-THING'S CLEAN.

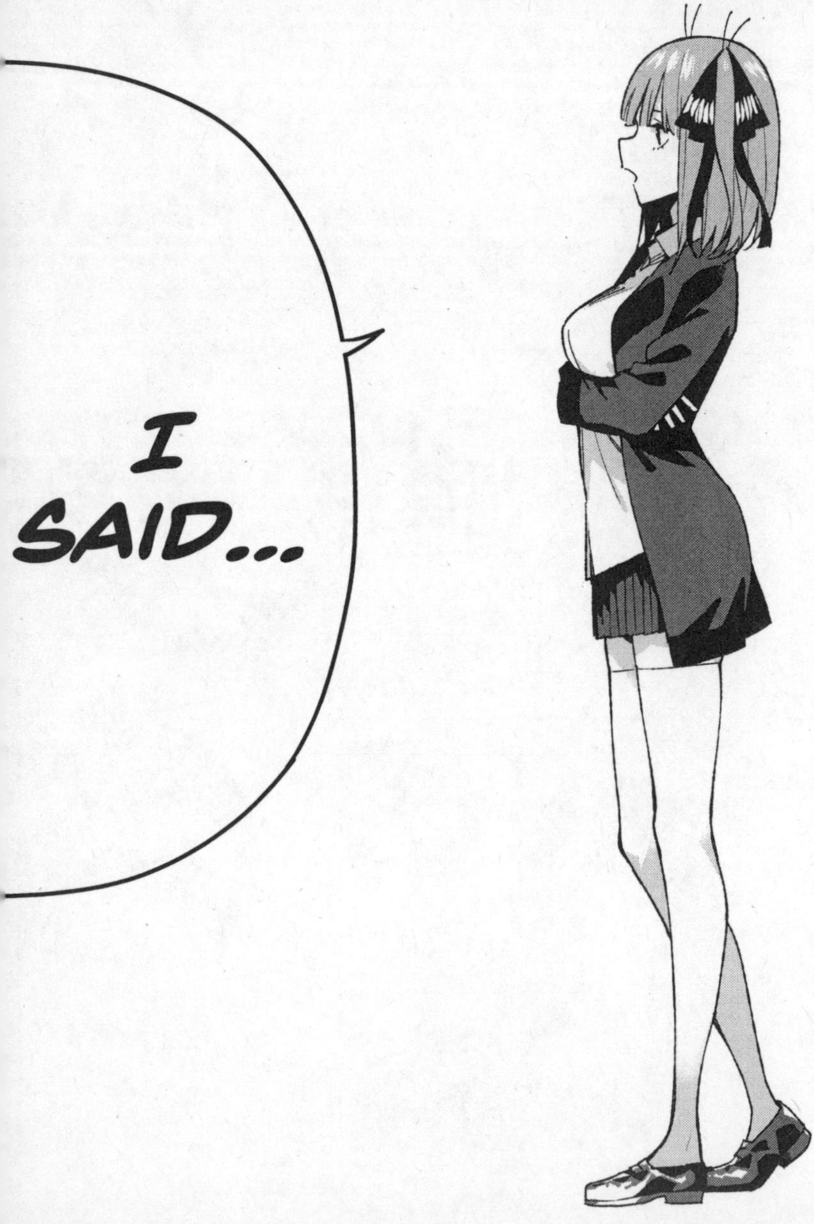
I SAID...

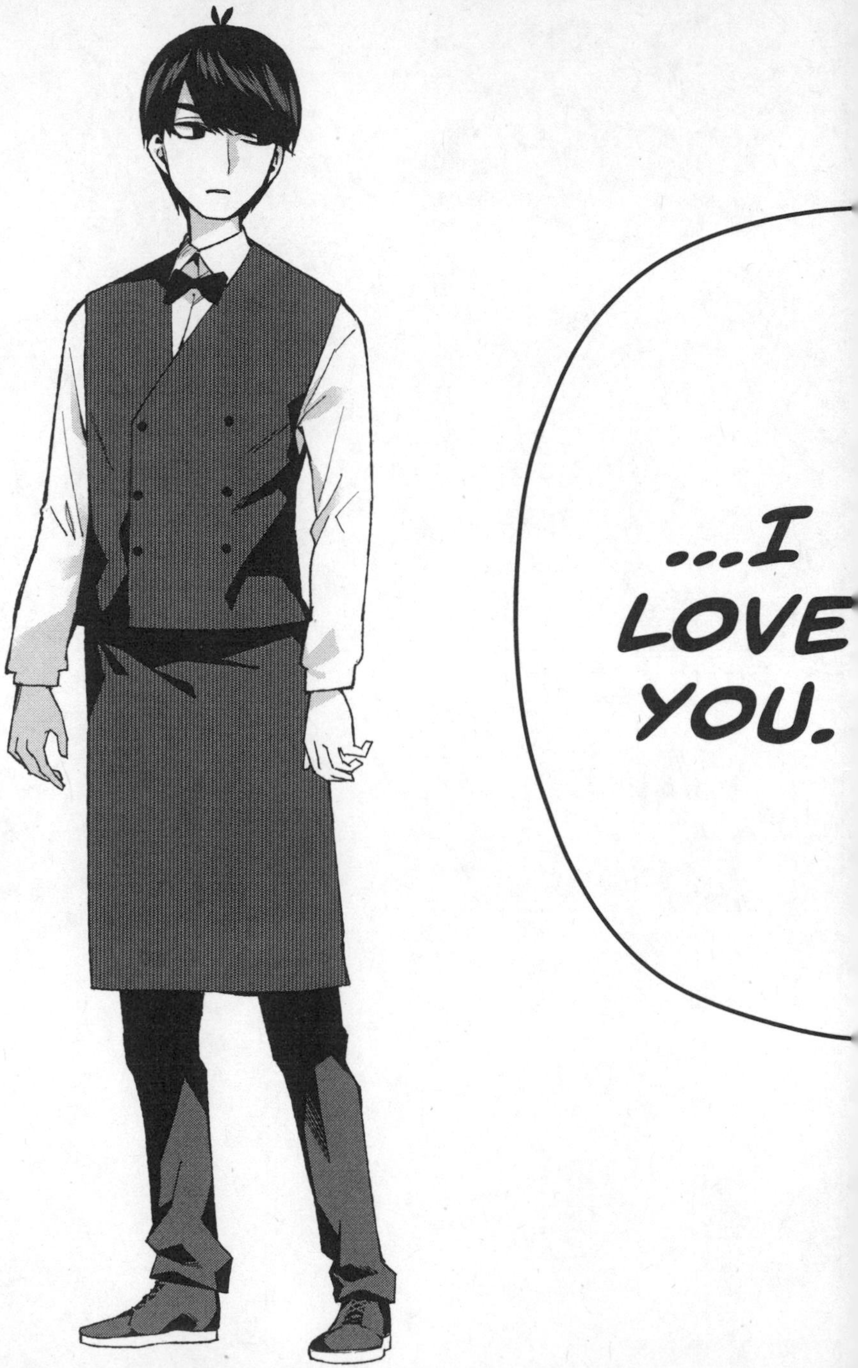
...I LOVE YOU.

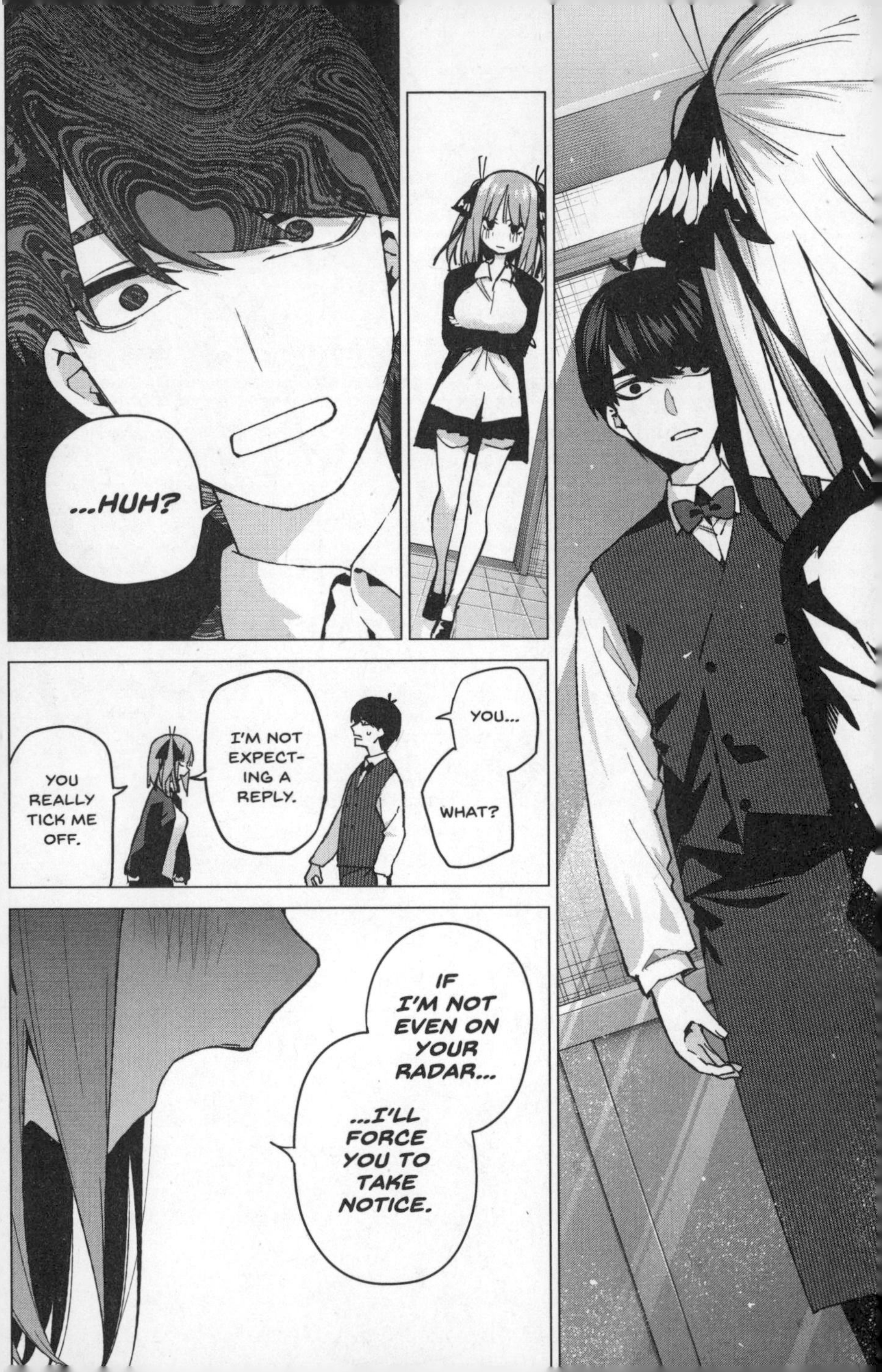
...HUH?
YOU... WHAT?
I'M NOT EXPECTING A REPLY.
YOU REALLY TICK ME OFF.
IF I'M NOT EVEN ON YOUR RADAR... ...I'LL FORCE YOU TO TAKE NOTICE.

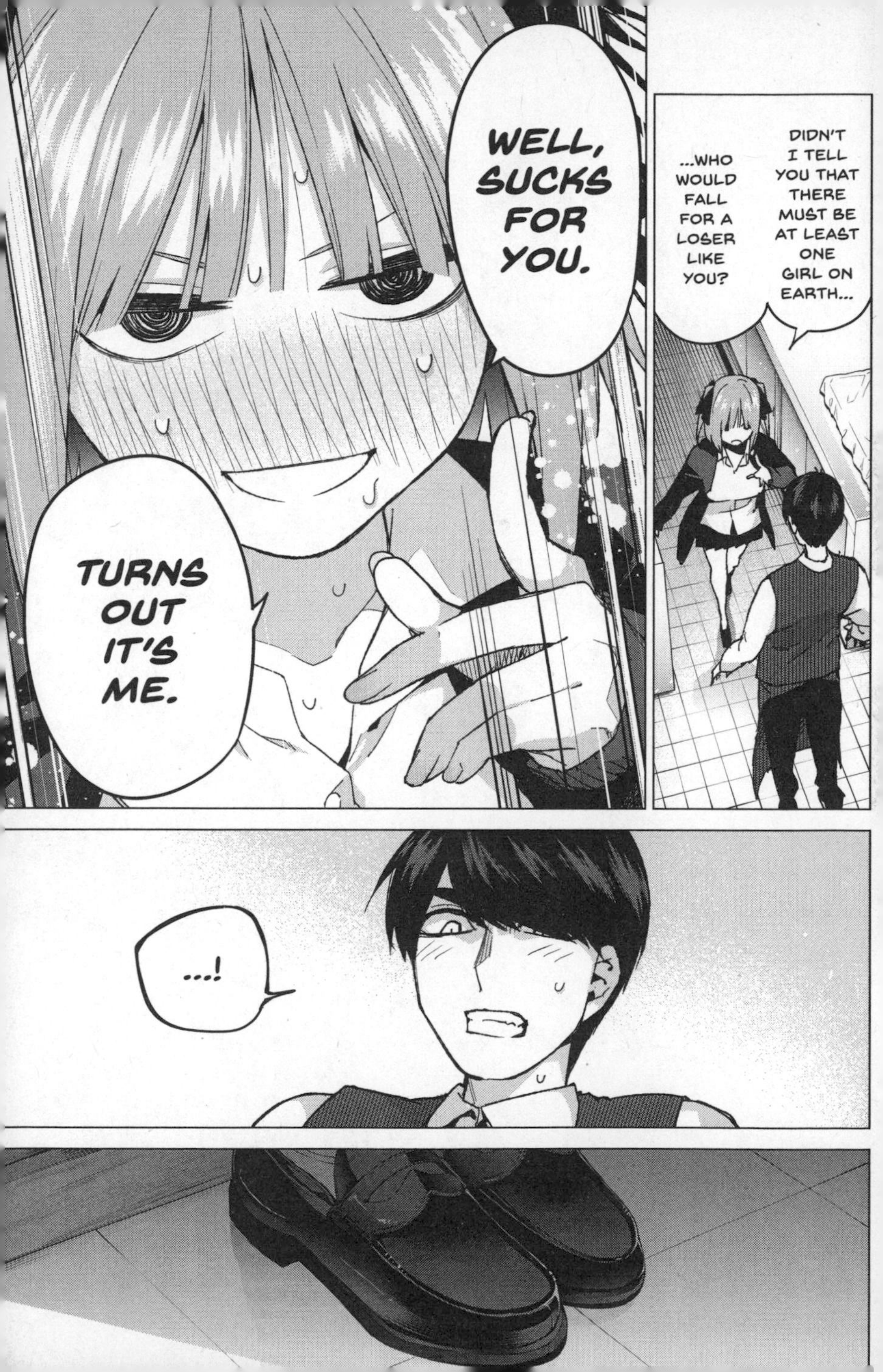
DIDN'T I TELL YOU THAT THERE MUST BE AT LEAST ONE GIRL ON EARTH...
...WHO WOULD FALL FOR A LOSER LIKE YOU?
WELL, SUCKS FOR YOU.
TURNS OUT IT'S ME.
...!

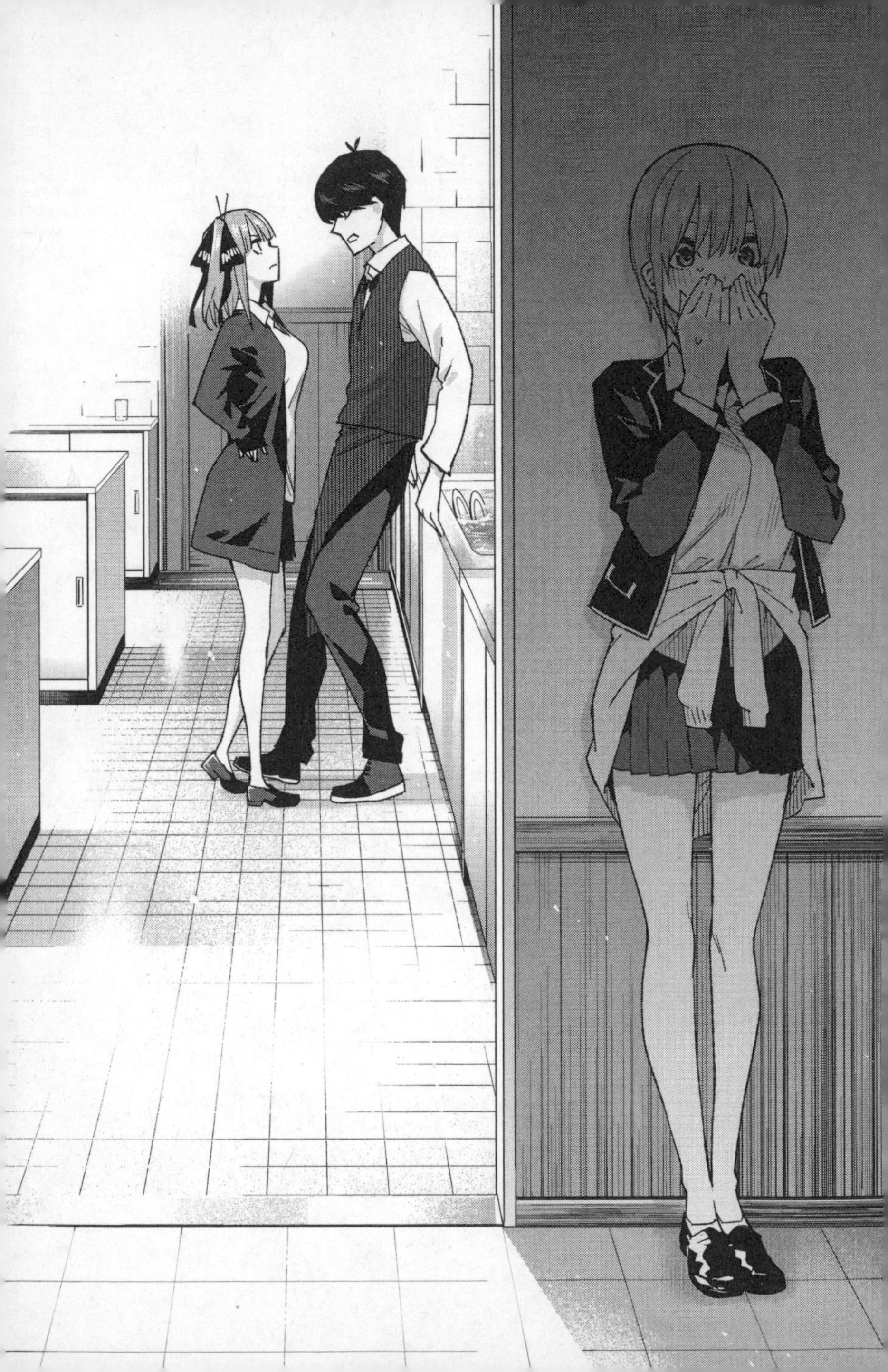

CHAPTER 61
SCRAMBLED EGGS ①

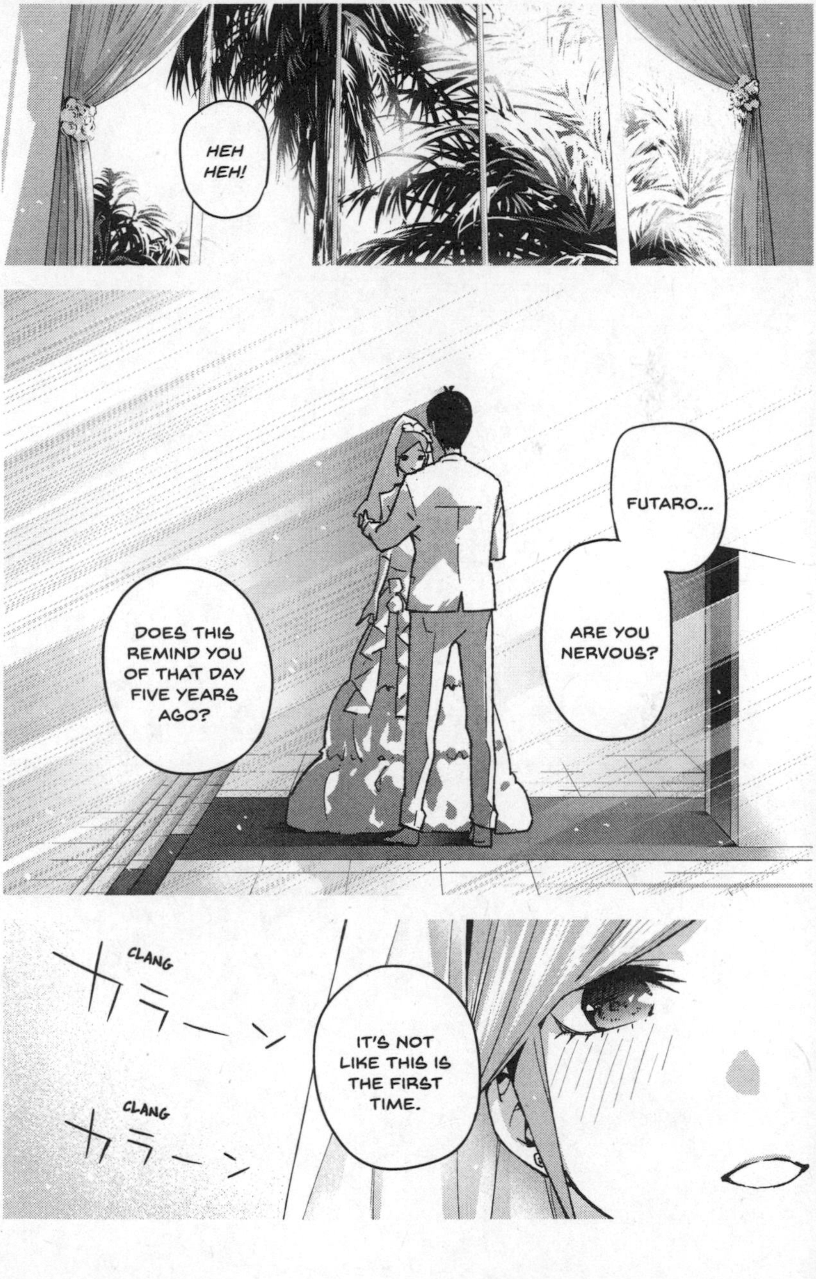
HEH HEH!
FUTARO...
ARE YOU NERVOUS?
DOES THIS REMIND YOU OF THAT DAY FIVE YEARS AGO?
IT'S NOT LIKE THIS IS THE FIRST TIME.
カラーン
CLANG
カラーン
CLANG

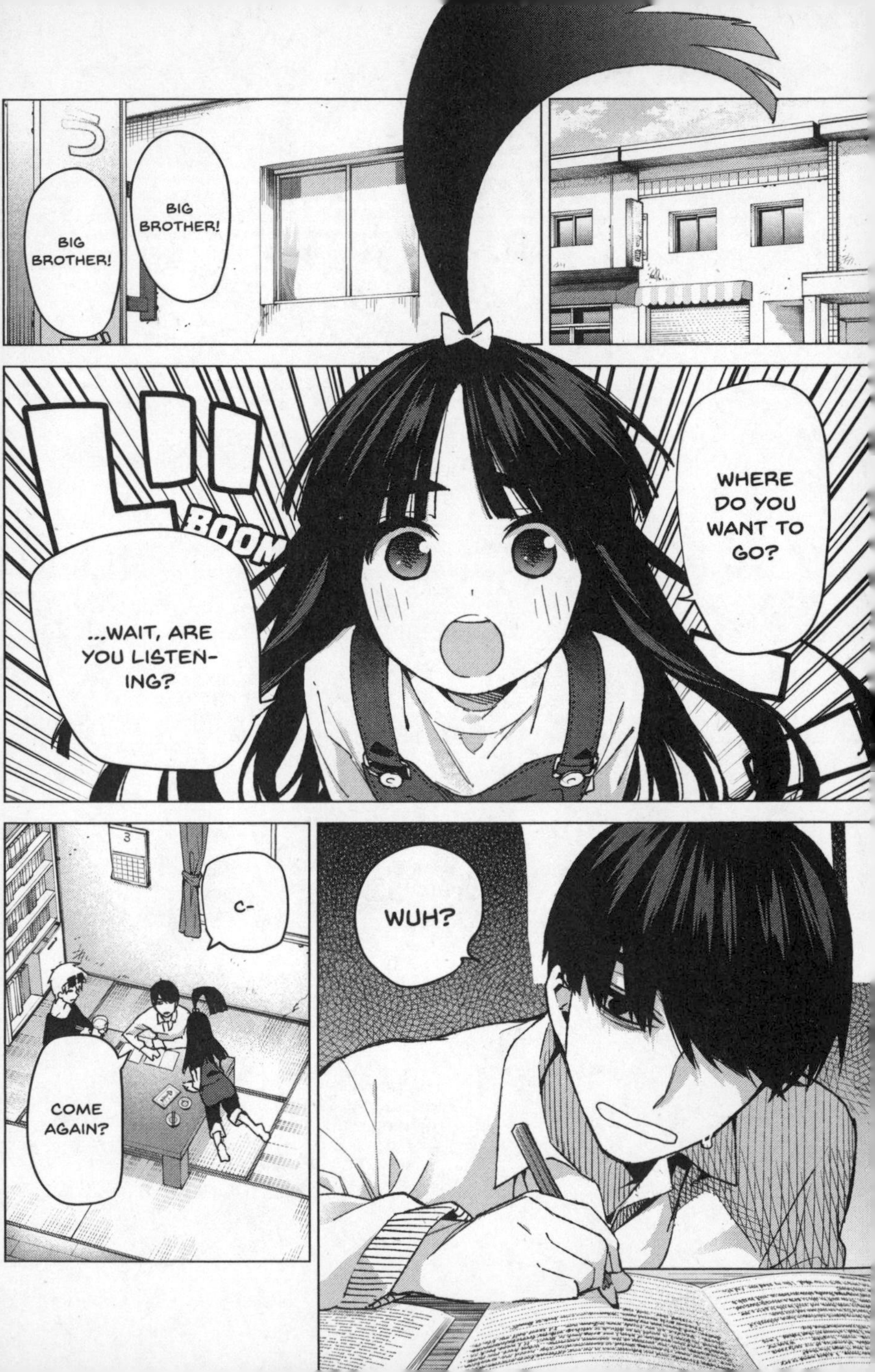
BIG BROTHER!
BIG BROTHER!
WHERE DO YOU WANT TO GO?
BOOM
...WAIT, ARE YOU LISTENING?
WUH?
C-
COME AGAIN?

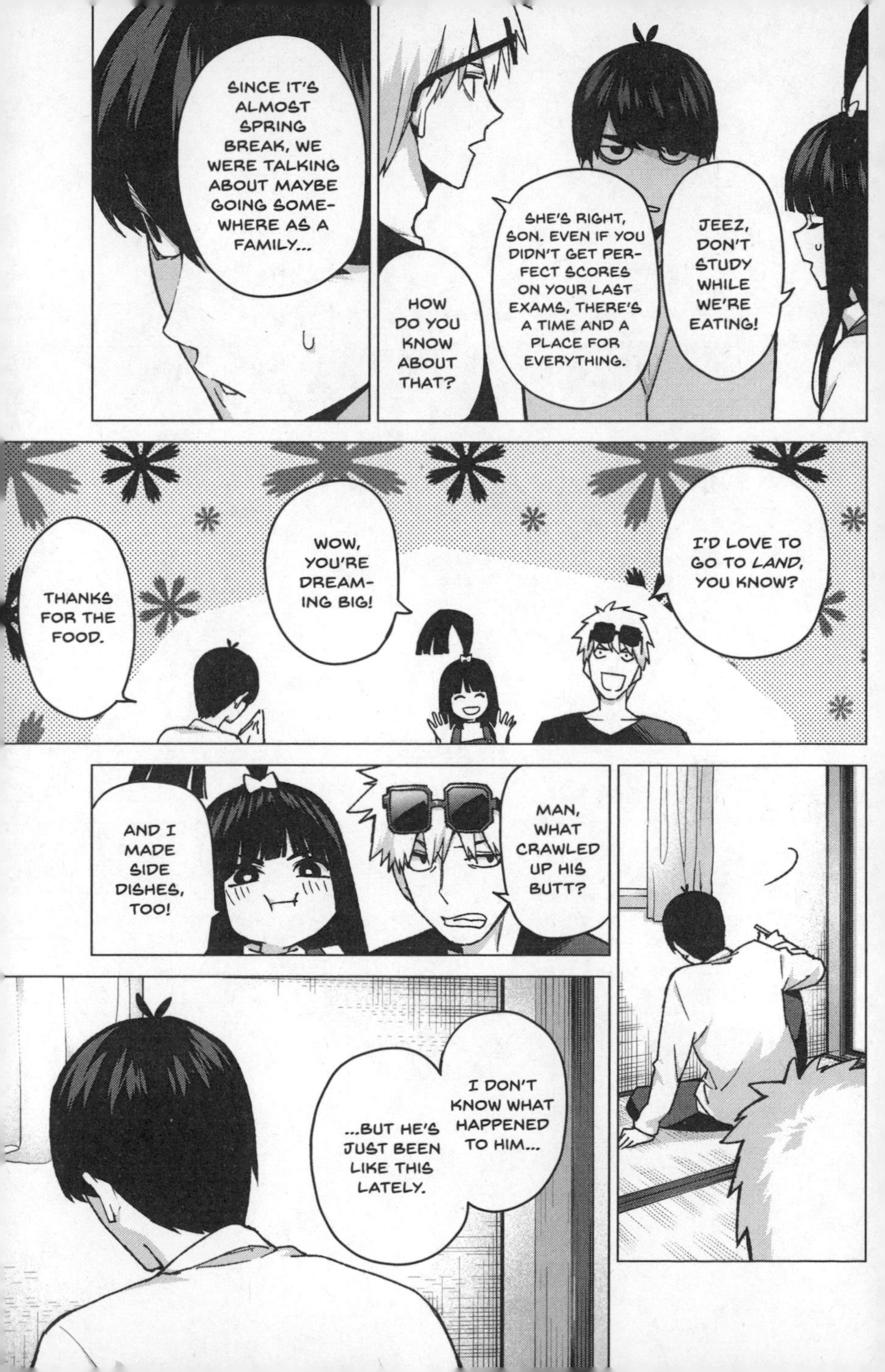
JEEZ, DON'T STUDY WHILE WE'RE EATING!
SHE'S RIGHT, SON. EVEN IF YOU DIDN'T GET PERFECT SCORES ON YOUR LAST EXAMS, THERE'S A TIME AND A PLACE FOR EVERYTHING.
HOW DO YOU KNOW ABOUT THAT?
SINCE IT'S ALMOST SPRING BREAK, WE WERE TALKING ABOUT MAYBE GOING SOMEWHERE AS A FAMILY...
I'D LOVE TO GO TO *LAND*, YOU KNOW?
WOW, YOU'RE DREAMING BIG!
THANKS FOR THE FOOD.
MAN, WHAT CRAWLED UP HIS BUTT?
AND I MADE SIDE DISHES, TOO!
I DON'T KNOW WHAT HAPPENED TO HIM...
...BUT HE'S JUST BEEN LIKE THIS LATELY.

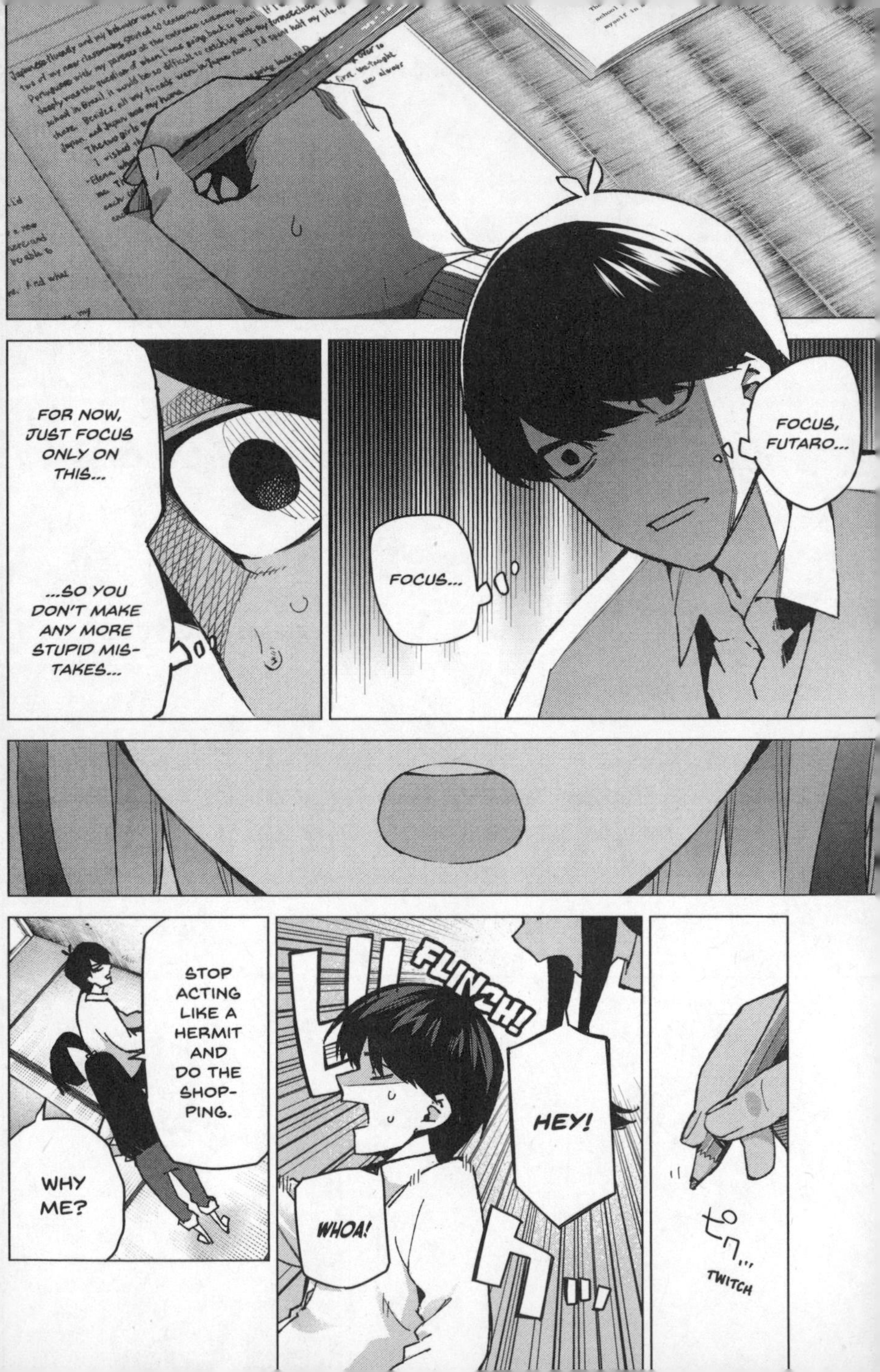
FOCUS, FUTARO...
FOCUS...
FOR NOW, JUST FOCUS ONLY ON THIS...
...SO YOU DON'T MAKE ANY MORE STUPID MISTAKES...
TWITCH
FLINCH!
HEY!
WHOA!
STOP ACTING LIKE A HERMIT AND DO THE SHOPPING.
WHY ME?

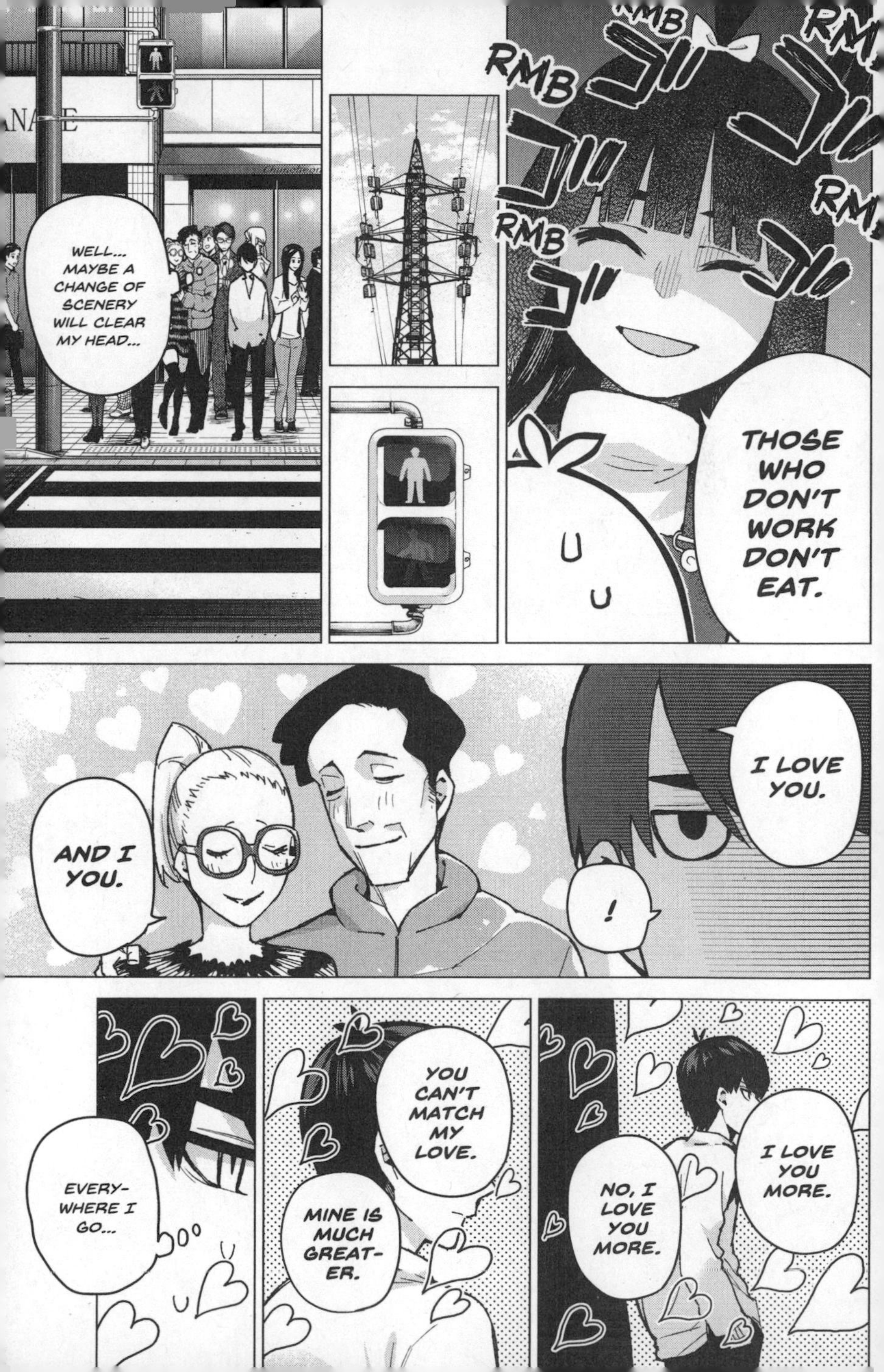
RMB RMB RMB RMB RMB
THOSE WHO DON'T WORK DON'T EAT.
WELL... MAYBE A CHANGE OF SCENERY WILL CLEAR MY HEAD...
I LOVE YOU.
!
AND I YOU.
I LOVE YOU MORE.
NO, I LOVE YOU MORE.
YOU CAN'T MATCH MY LOVE.
MINE IS MUCH GREATER.
EVERYWHERE I GO...

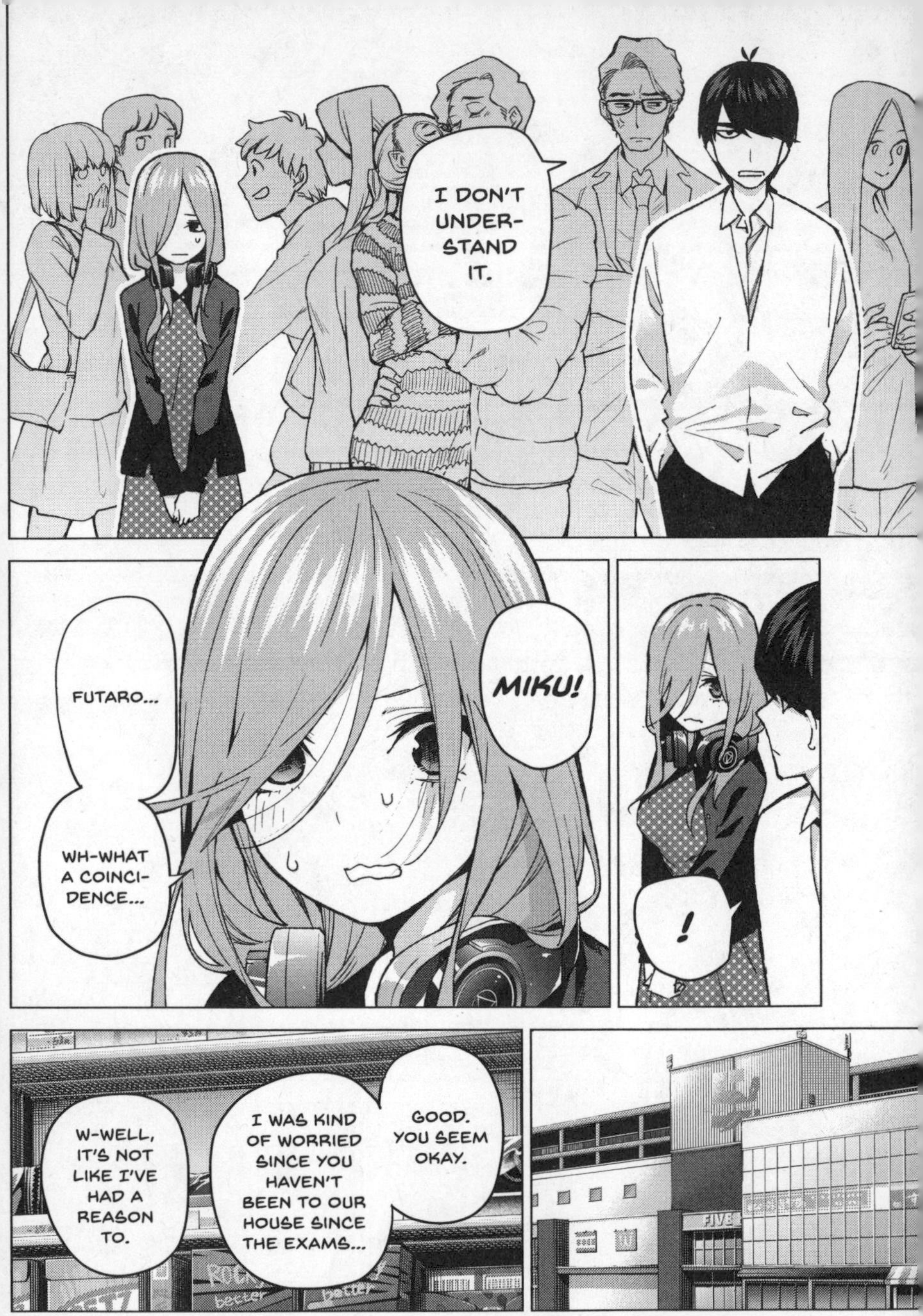
I DON'T UNDERSTAND IT.
!
MIKU!
FUTARO...
WH-WHAT A COINCIDENCE...
GOOD. YOU SEEM OKAY.
I WAS KIND OF WORRIED SINCE YOU HAVEN'T BEEN TO OUR HOUSE SINCE THE EXAMS...
W-WELL, IT'S NOT LIKE I'VE HAD A REASON TO.

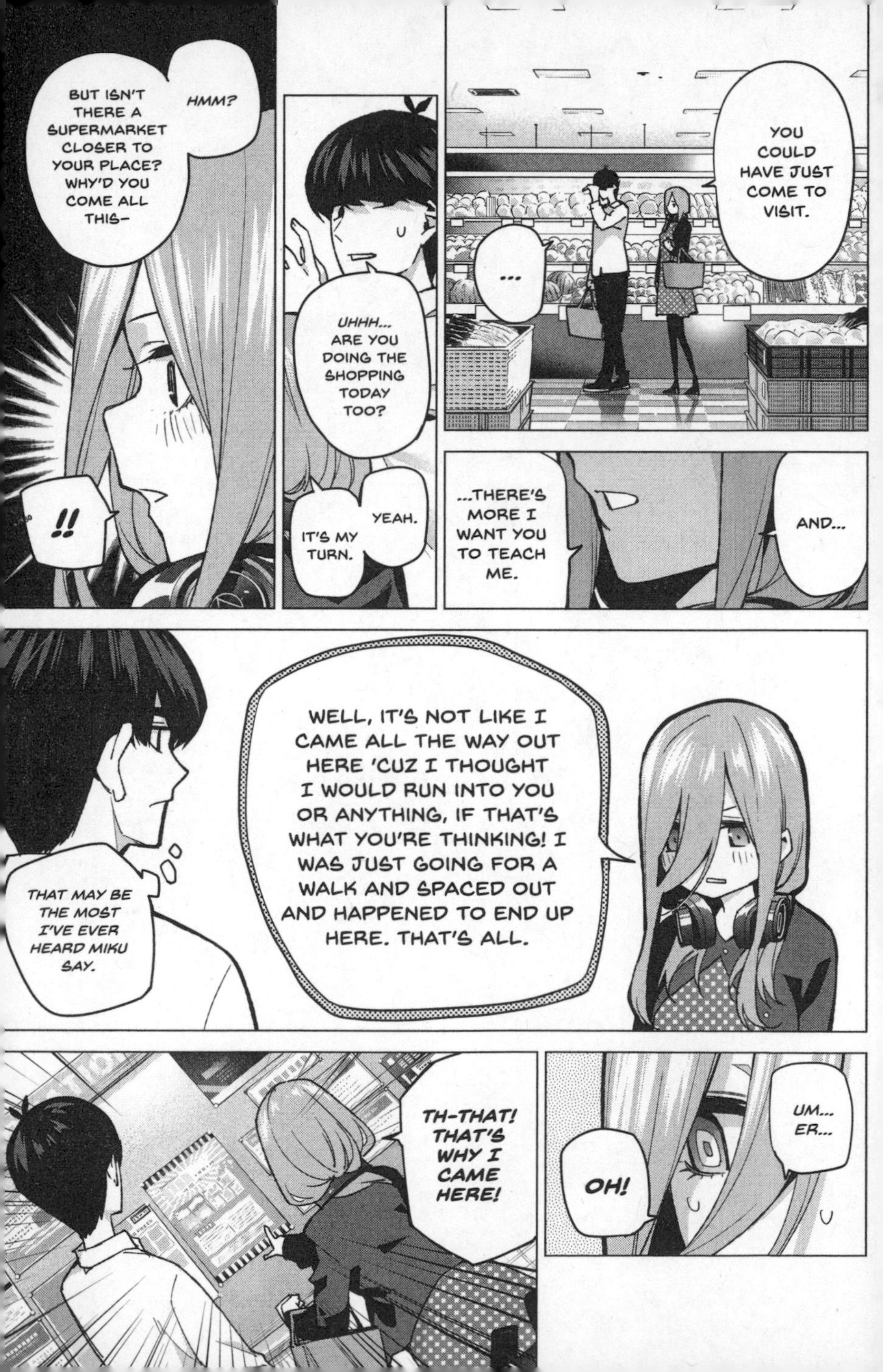
YOU COULD HAVE JUST COME TO VISIT.
...
AND...
...THERE'S MORE I WANT YOU TO TEACH ME.
UHHH... ARE YOU DOING THE SHOPPING TODAY TOO?
YEAH.
IT'S MY TURN.
HMM?
BUT ISN'T THERE A SUPERMARKET CLOSER TO YOUR PLACE? WHY'D YOU COME ALL THIS-
!!
WELL, IT'S NOT LIKE I CAME ALL THE WAY OUT HERE 'CUZ I THOUGHT I WOULD RUN INTO YOU OR ANYTHING, IF THAT'S WHAT YOU'RE THINKING! I WAS JUST GOING FOR A WALK AND SPACED OUT AND HAPPENED TO END UP HERE. THAT'S ALL.
THAT MAY BE THE MOST I'VE EVER HEARD MIKU SAY.
UM... ER...
OH!
TH-THAT! THAT'S WHY I CAME HERE!

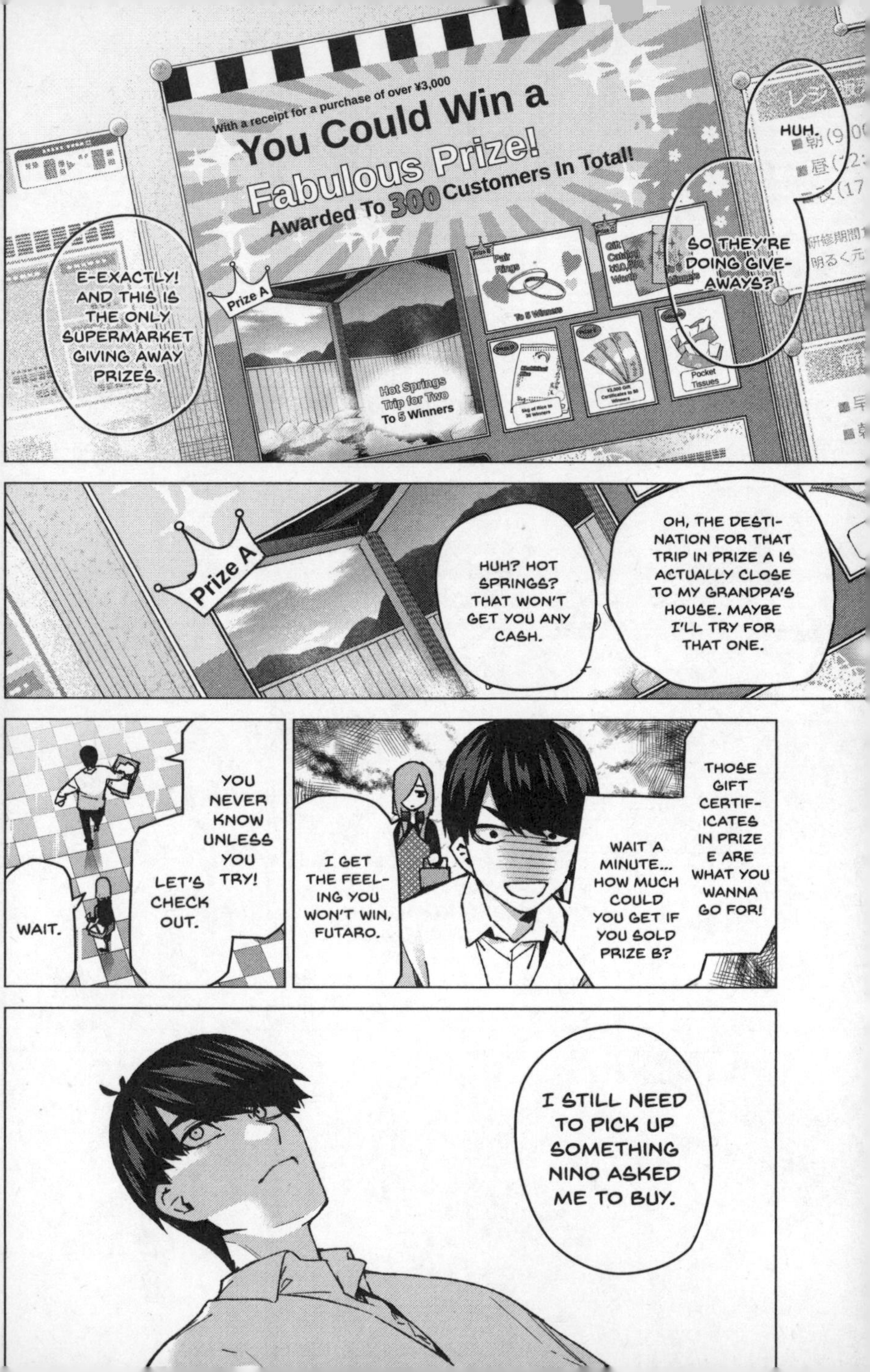
With a receipt for a purchase of over ¥3,000
You Could Win a
Fabulous Prize!
Awarded To 300 Customers In Total!
HUH.
SO THEY'RE DOING GIVE-AWAYS?
Pair Rings
To 5 Winners
Pocket Tissues
Prize A
Hot Springs Trip for Two To 5 Winners
E-EXACTLY! AND THIS IS THE ONLY SUPERMARKET GIVING AWAY PRIZES.
OH, THE DESTINATION FOR THAT TRIP IN PRIZE A IS ACTUALLY CLOSE TO MY GRANDPA'S HOUSE. MAYBE I'LL TRY FOR THAT ONE.
HUH? HOT SPRINGS? THAT WON'T GET YOU ANY CASH.
Prize A
THOSE GIFT CERTIFICATES IN PRIZE E ARE WHAT YOU WANNA GO FOR!
WAIT A MINUTE... HOW MUCH COULD YOU GET IF YOU SOLD PRIZE B?
I GET THE FEELING YOU WON'T WIN, FUTARO.
YOU NEVER KNOW UNLESS YOU TRY!
LET'S CHECK OUT.
WAIT.
I STILL NEED TO PICK UP SOMETHING NINO ASKED ME TO BUY.

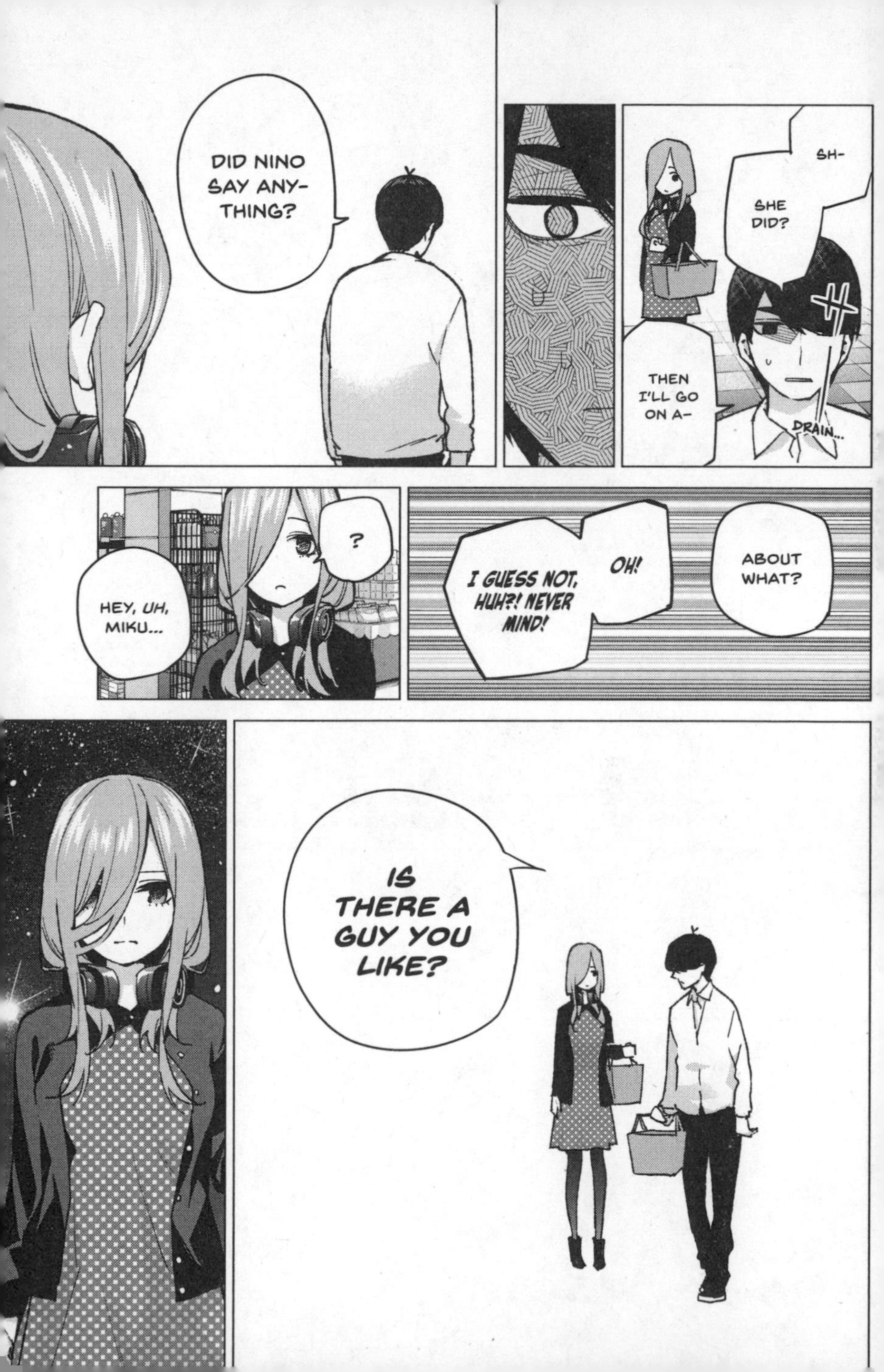
SH-
SHE DID?
THEN I'LL GO ON A-
DRAIN...
DID NINO SAY ANY-THING?
ABOUT WHAT?
OH!
I GUESS NOT. HUH?! NEVER MIND!
?
HEY, UH, MIKU...
IS THERE A GUY YOU LIKE?

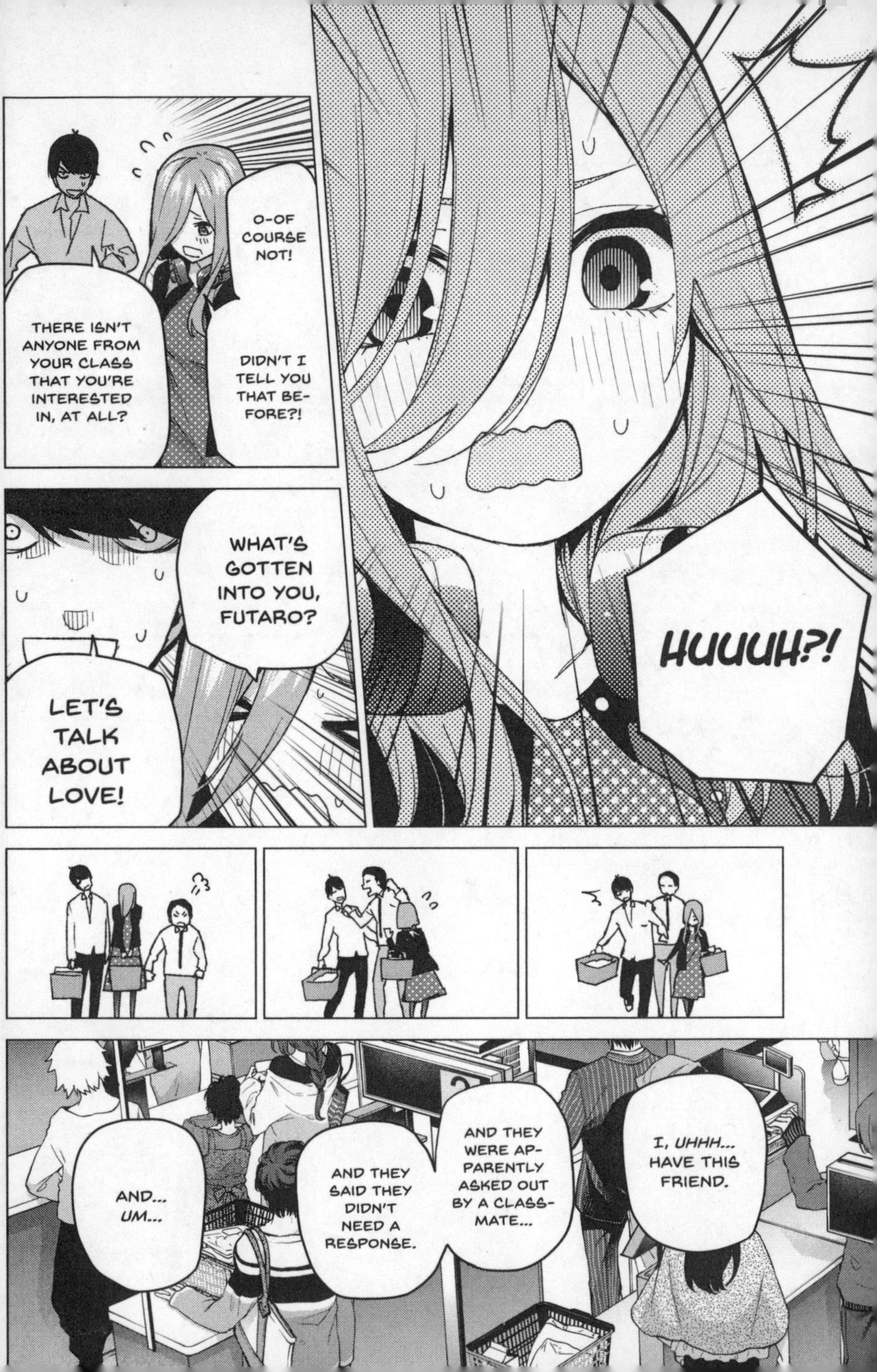
HUUUH?!
O-OF COURSE NOT!
DIDN'T I TELL YOU THAT BE-FORE?!
THERE ISN'T ANYONE FROM YOUR CLASS THAT YOU'RE INTERESTED IN, AT ALL?
WHAT'S GOTTEN INTO YOU, FUTARO?
LET'S TALK ABOUT LOVE!
I, UHHH... HAVE THIS FRIEND.
AND THEY WERE AP-PARENTLY ASKED OUT BY A CLASS-MATE...
AND THEY SAID THEY DIDN'T NEED A RESPONSE.
AND... UM...

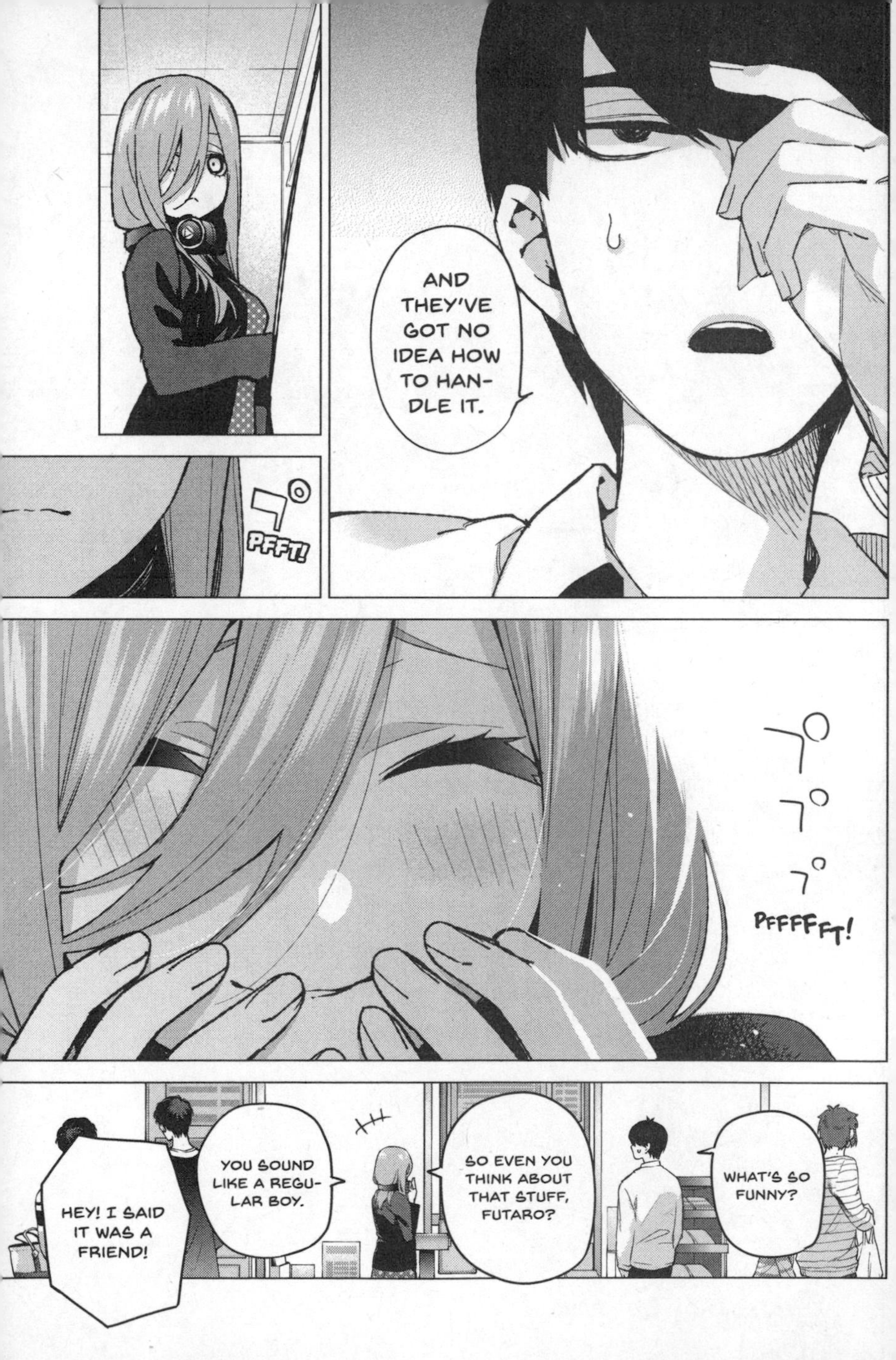
AND THEY'VE GOT NO IDEA HOW TO HAN-DLE IT.
PFFT!
PFFFFFT!
WHAT'S SO FUNNY?
SO EVEN YOU THINK ABOUT THAT STUFF, FUTARO?
YOU SOUND LIKE A REGU-LAR BOY.
HEY! I SAID IT WAS A FRIEND!

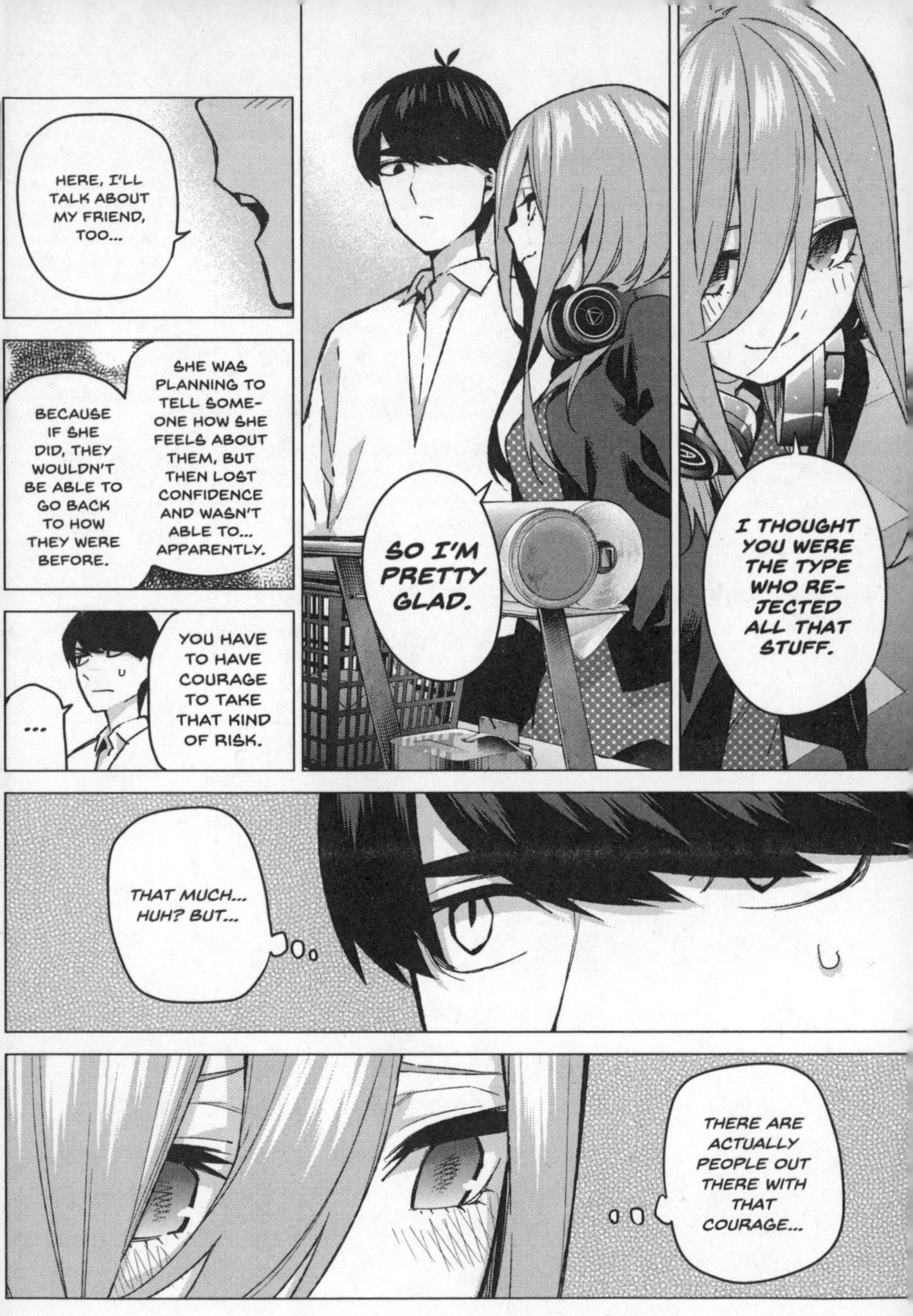
I THOUGHT YOU WERE THE TYPE WHO RE-JECTED ALL THAT STUFF.
SO I'M PRETTY GLAD.
HERE, I'LL TALK ABOUT MY FRIEND, TOO...
SHE WAS PLANNING TO TELL SOME-ONE HOW SHE FEELS ABOUT THEM, BUT THEN LOST CONFIDENCE AND WASN'T ABLE TO... APPARENTLY.
BECAUSE IF SHE DID, THEY WOULDN'T BE ABLE TO GO BACK TO HOW THEY WERE BEFORE.
YOU HAVE TO HAVE COURAGE TO TAKE THAT KIND OF RISK.
...
THAT MUCH... HUH? BUT...
THERE ARE ACTUALLY PEOPLE OUT THERE WITH THAT COURAGE...

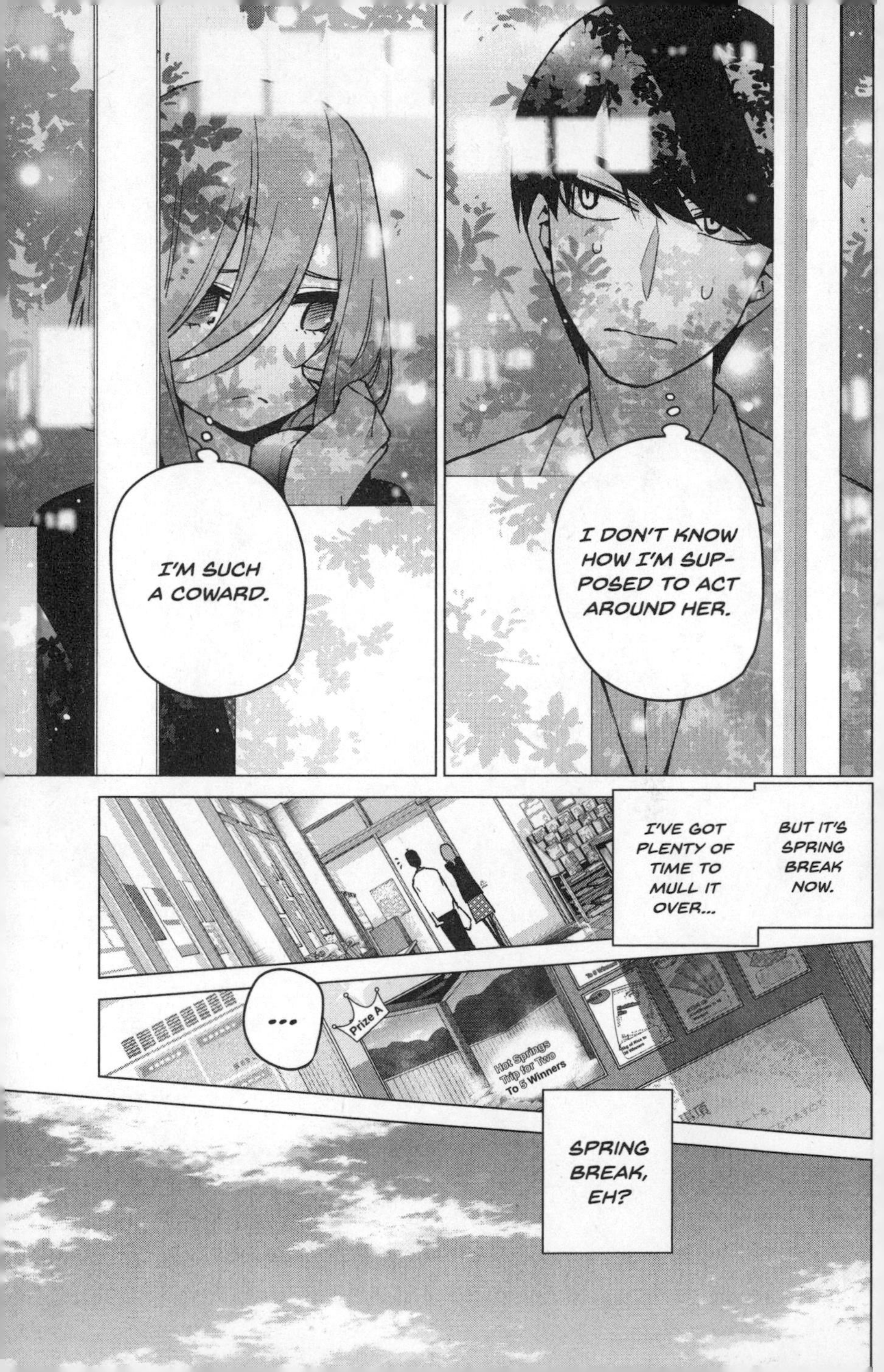
I DON'T KNOW HOW I'M SUP-POSED TO ACT AROUND HER.
I'M SUCH A COWARD.
BUT IT'S SPRING BREAK NOW.
I'VE GOT PLENTY OF TIME TO MULL IT OVER...
Hot Springs Trip for Two To 5 Winners
Prize A
...
SPRING BREAK, EH?

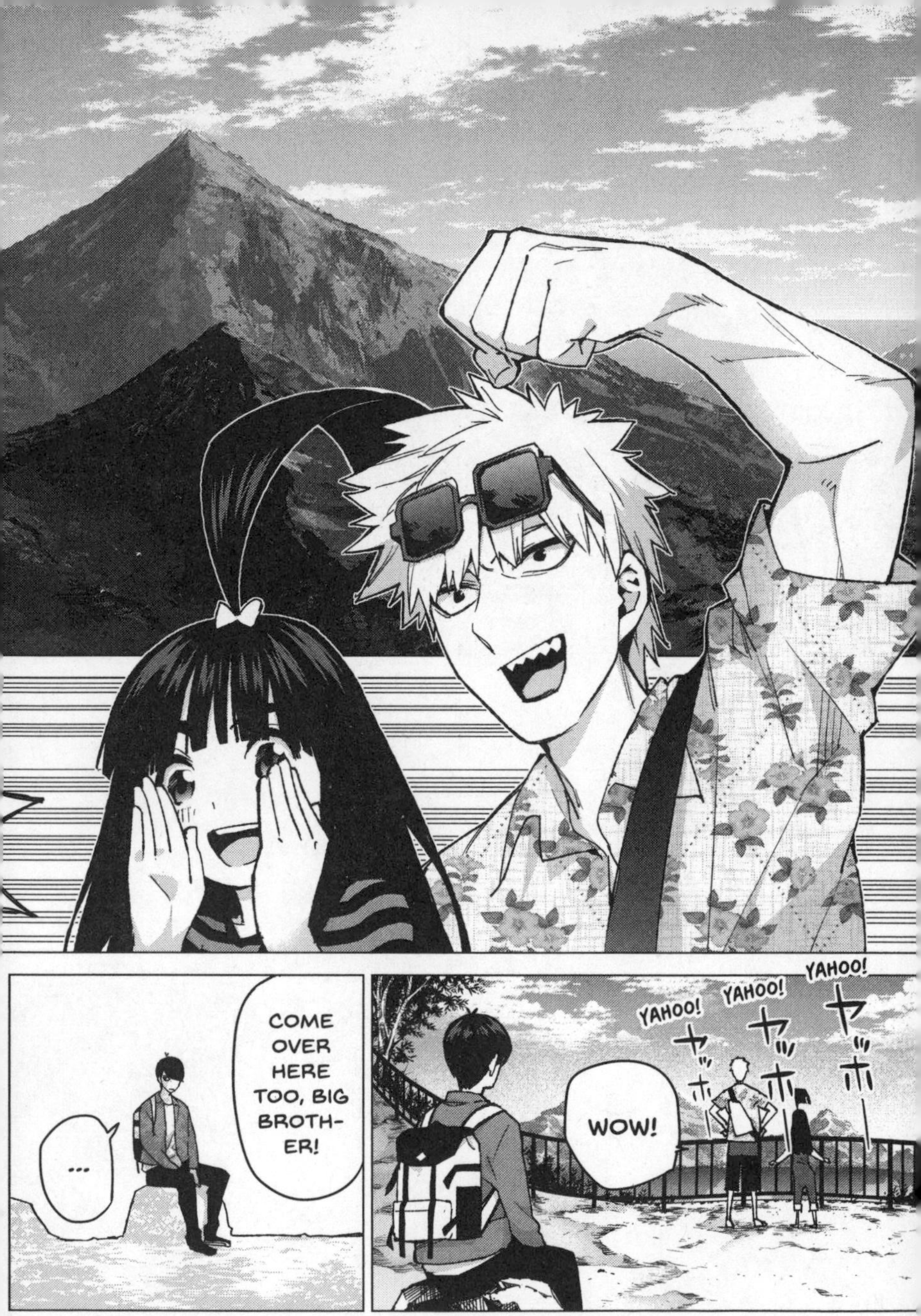
YAHOO!
ヤッホー
YAHOO!
ヤッホ
YAHOO!
ヤッホ
WOW!
COME OVER HERE TOO, BIG BROTHER!
...

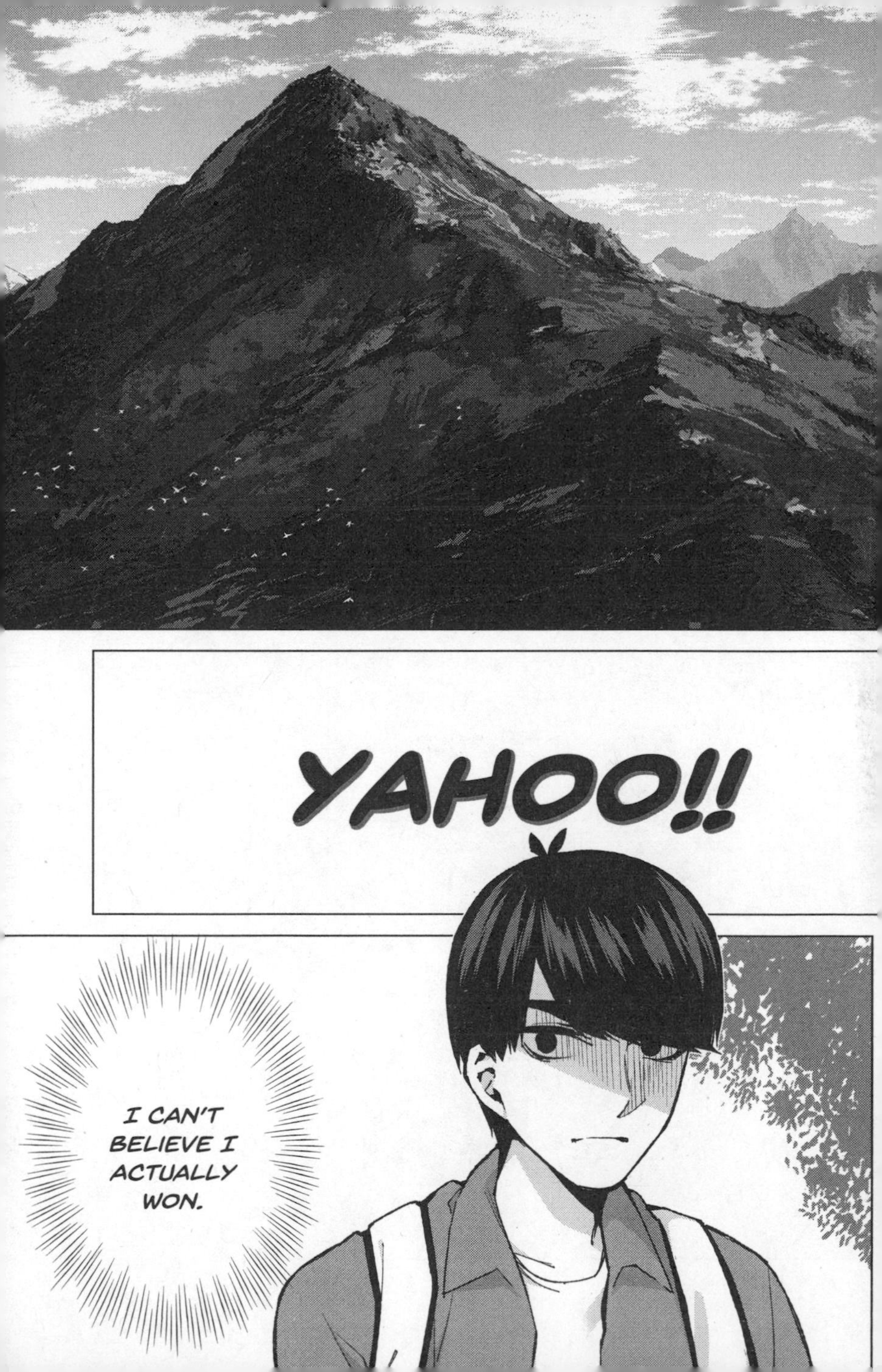
YAHOO!!
I CAN'T BELIEVE I ACTUALLY WON.

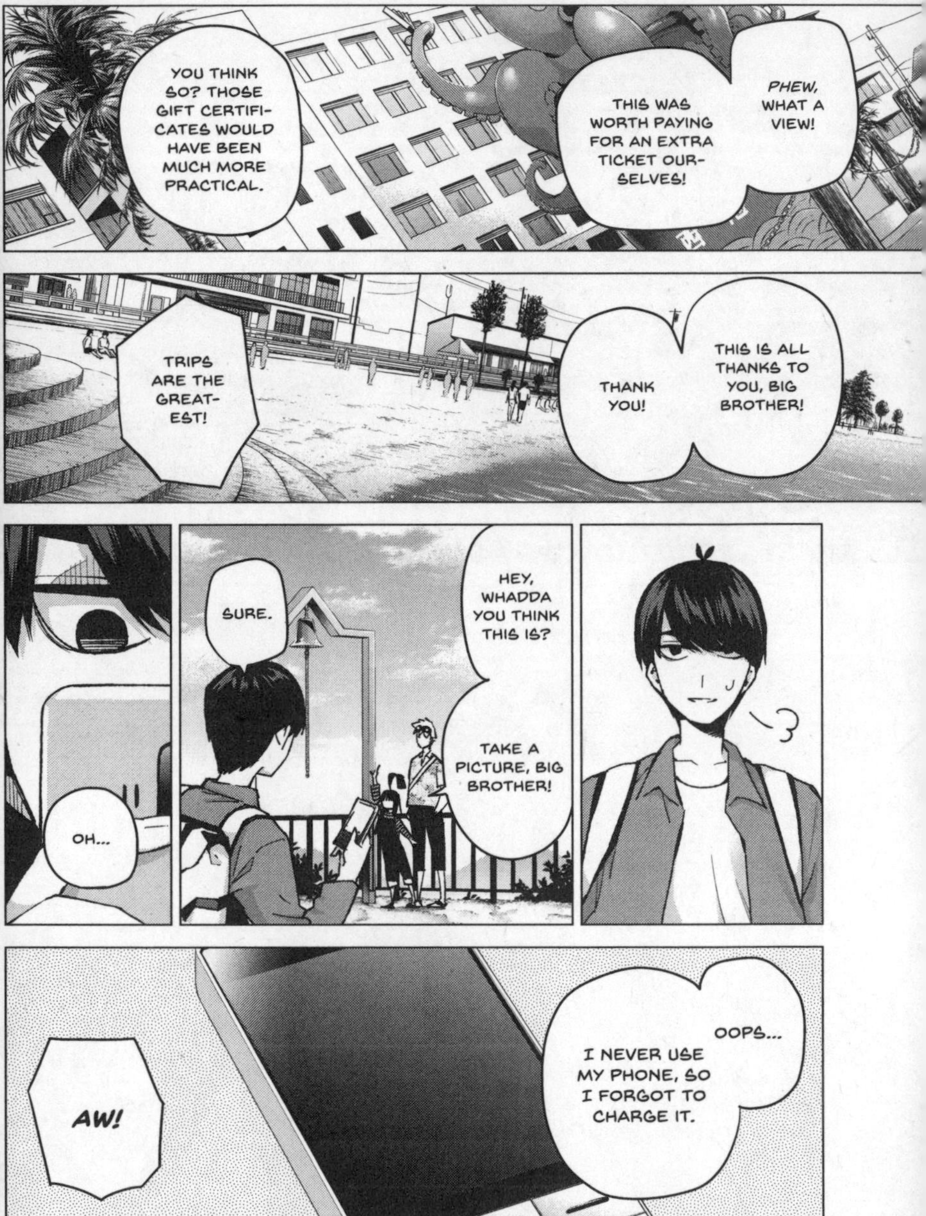
PHEW, WHAT A VIEW!
THIS WAS WORTH PAYING FOR AN EXTRA TICKET OURSELVES!
YOU THINK SO? THOSE GIFT CERTIFICATES WOULD HAVE BEEN MUCH MORE PRACTICAL.
THIS IS ALL THANKS TO YOU, BIG BROTHER!
THANK YOU!
TRIPS ARE THE GREATEST!
HEY, WHADDA YOU THINK THIS IS?
TAKE A PICTURE, BIG BROTHER!
SURE.
OH...
OOPS...
I NEVER USE MY PHONE, SO I FORGOT TO CHARGE IT.
AW!

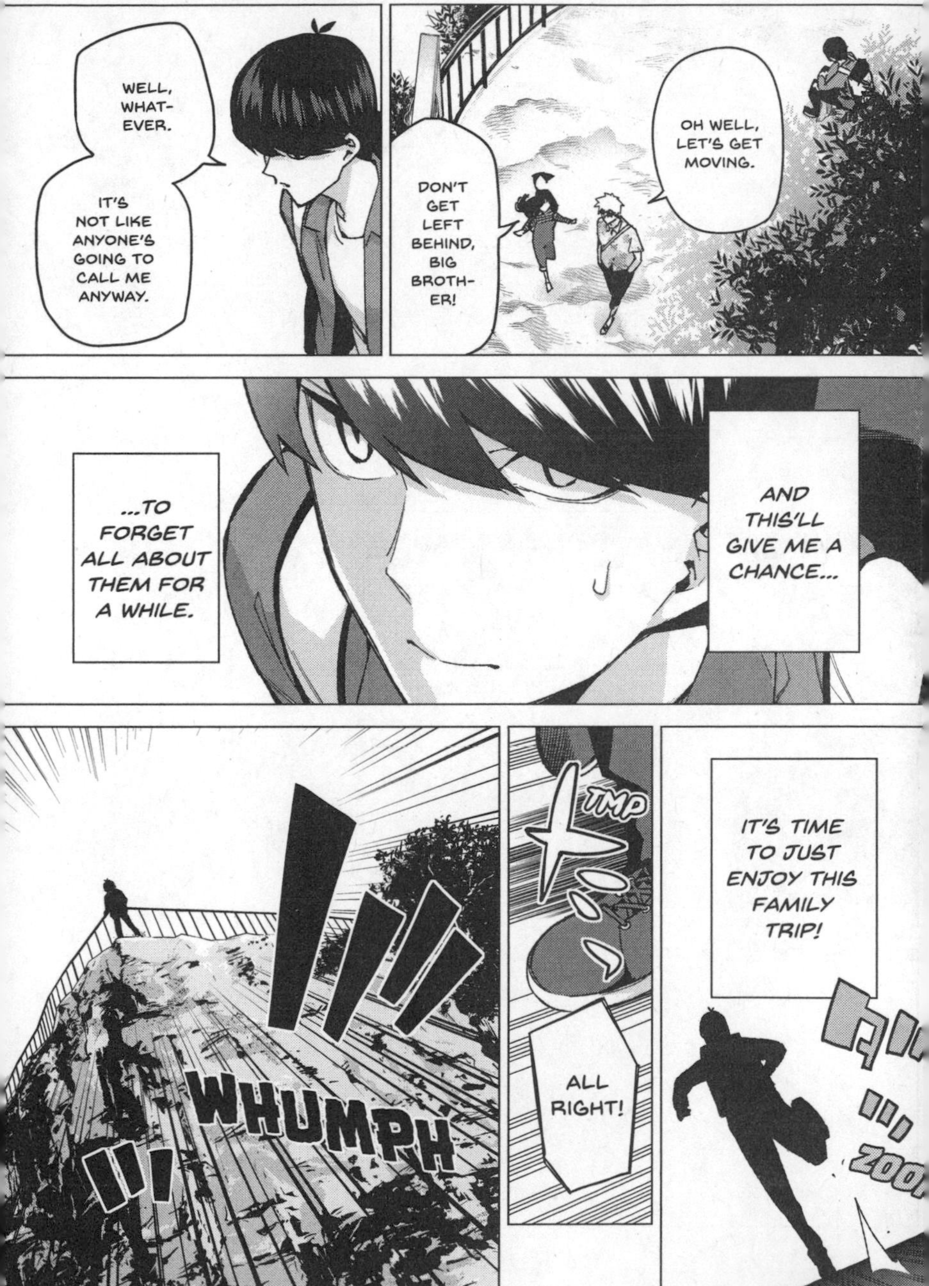
OH WELL, LET'S GET MOVING.
DON'T GET LEFT BEHIND, BIG BROTHER!
WELL, WHATEVER.
IT'S NOT LIKE ANYONE'S GOING TO CALL ME ANYWAY.
AND THIS'LL GIVE ME A CHANCE...
...TO FORGET ALL ABOUT THEM FOR A WHILE.
IT'S TIME TO JUST ENJOY THIS FAMILY TRIP!
TMP
ALL RIGHT!
WHUMPH

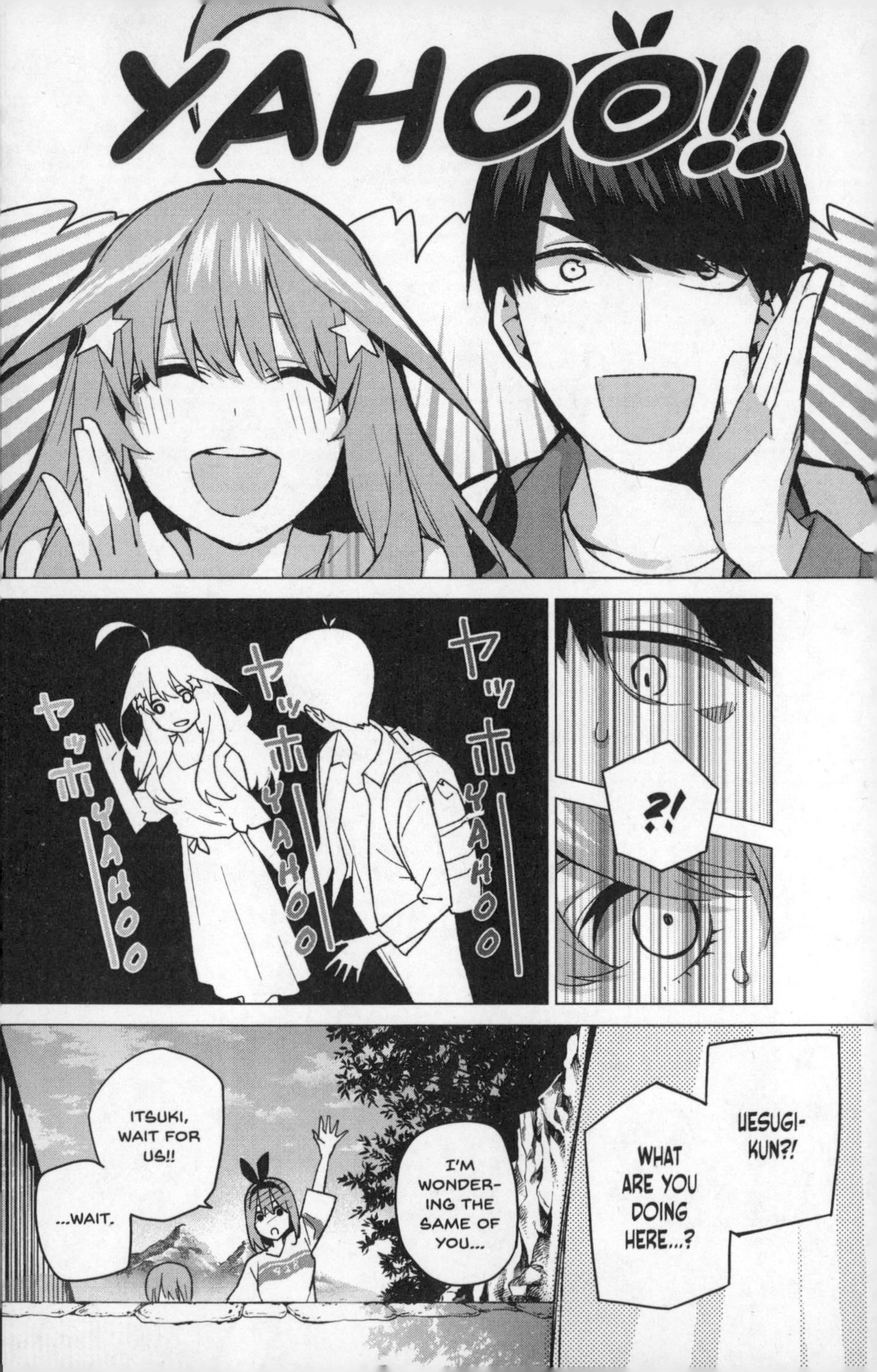
YAHOO!!
?!
ヤッホ YAHOO
ヤッホ YAHOO
ヤッホ YAHOO
UESUGI-KUN?!
WHAT ARE YOU DOING HERE...?
I'M WONDERING THE SAME OF YOU...
ITSUKI, WAIT FOR US!!
...WAIT.

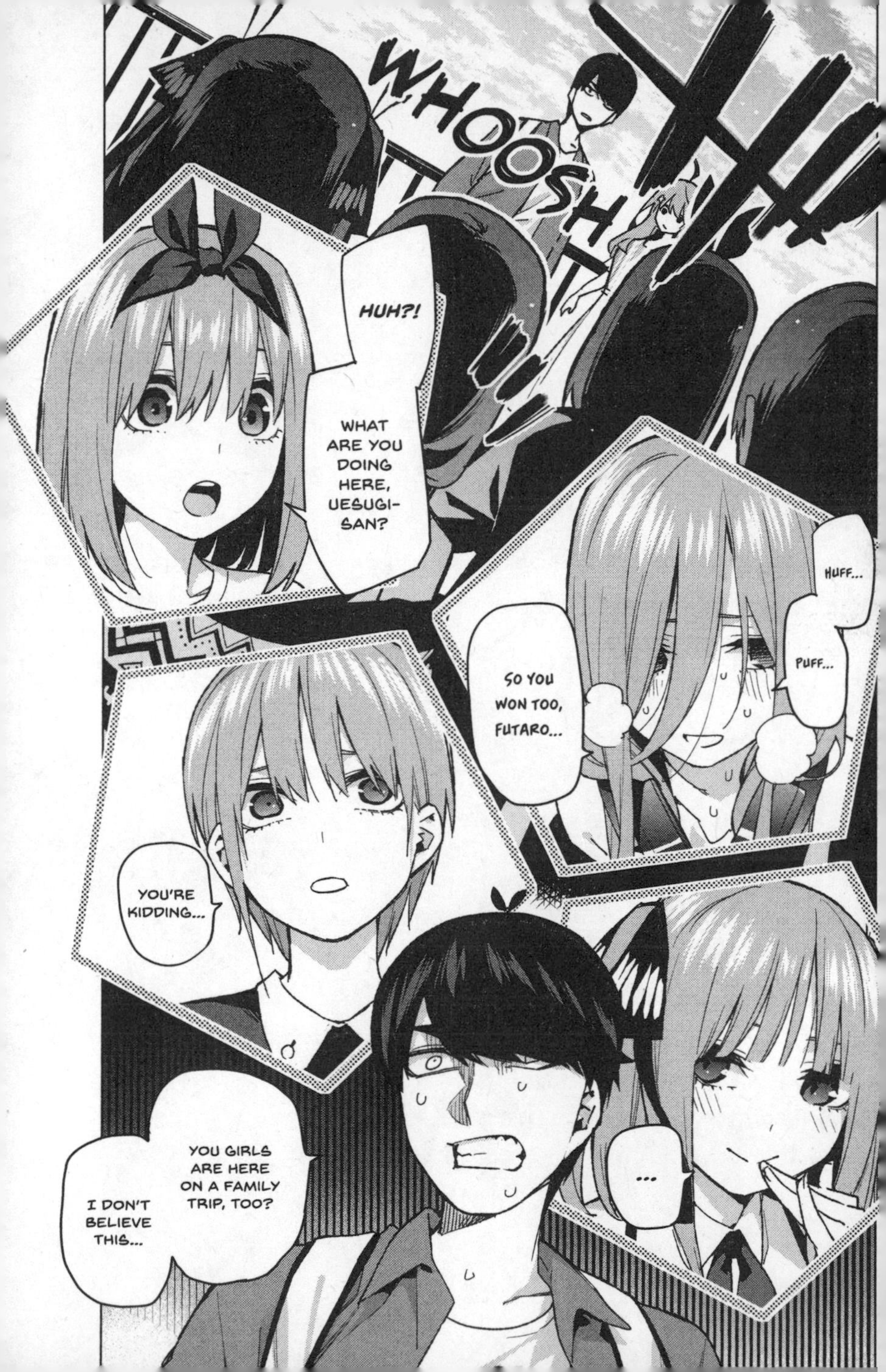
WHOOSH
HUH?!
WHAT ARE YOU DOING HERE, UESUGI-SAN?
HUFF...
PUFF...
SO YOU WON TOO, FUTARO...
YOU'RE KIDDING...
...
YOU GIRLS ARE HERE ON A FAMILY TRIP, TOO?
I DON'T BELIEVE THIS...

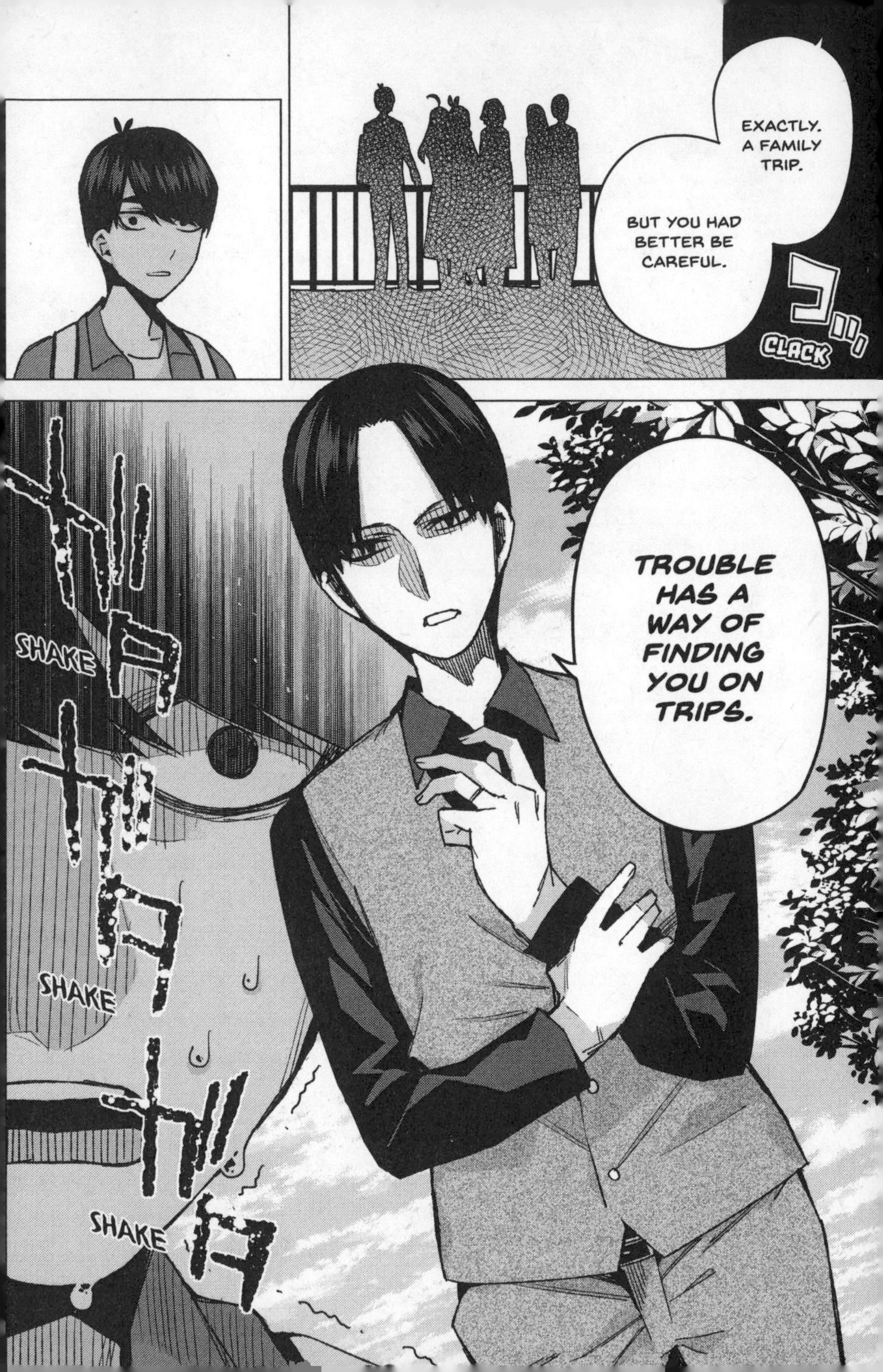
EXACTLY. A FAMILY TRIP.
BUT YOU HAD BETTER BE CAREFUL.
CLACK
TROUBLE HAS A WAY OF FINDING YOU ON TRIPS.
SHAKE
SHAKE
SHAKE

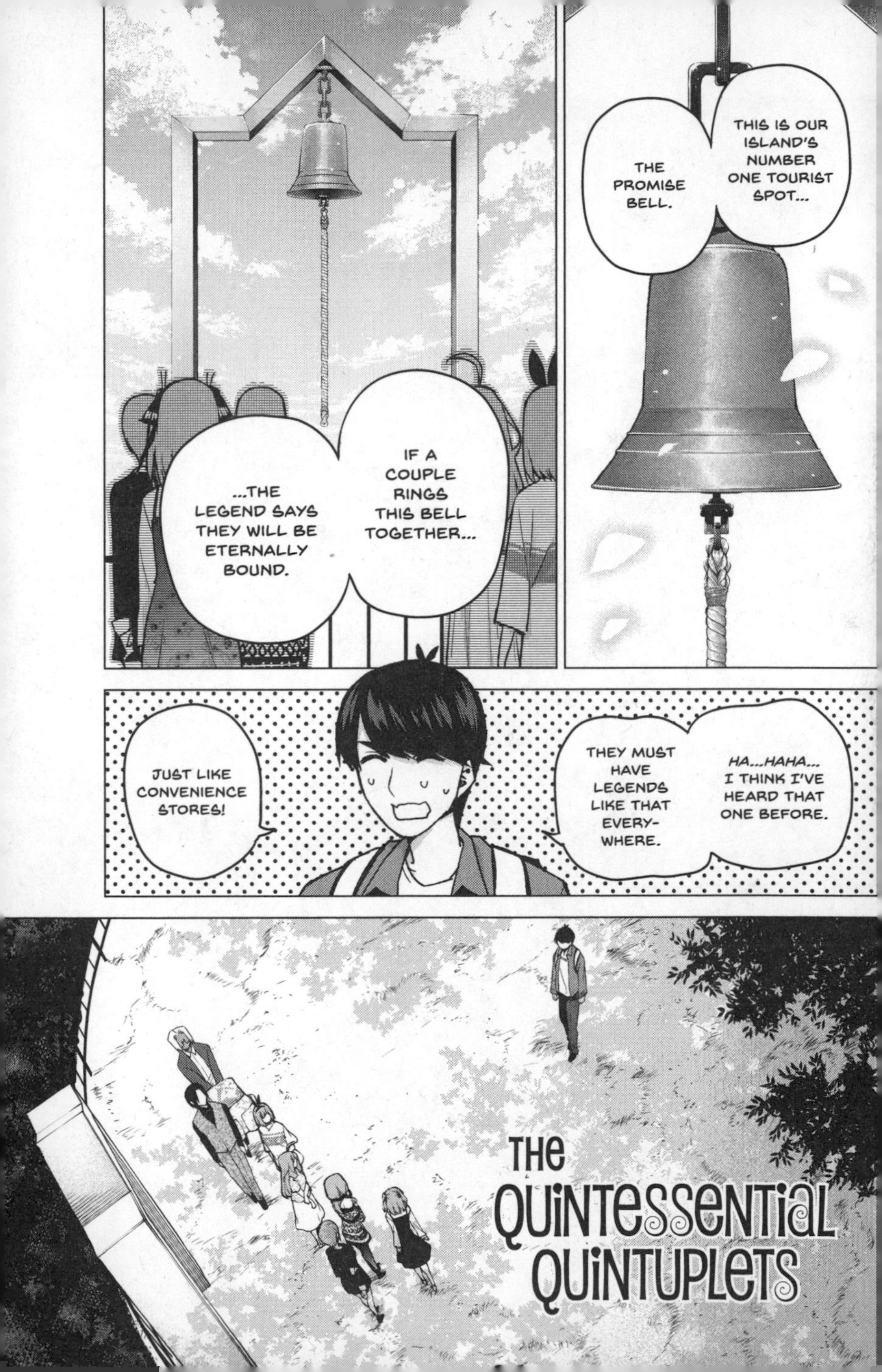
THIS IS OUR ISLAND'S NUMBER ONE TOURIST SPOT...
THE PROMISE BELL.
IF A COUPLE RINGS THIS BELL TOGETHER...
...THE LEGEND SAYS THEY WILL BE ETERNALLY BOUND.
HA...HAHA... I THINK I'VE HEARD THAT ONE BEFORE.
THEY MUST HAVE LEGENDS LIKE THAT EVERY-WHERE.
JUST LIKE CONVENIENCE STORES!
THE QUINTESSENTIAL QUINTUPLETS

CHAPTER 62
SCRAMBLED EGGS ②

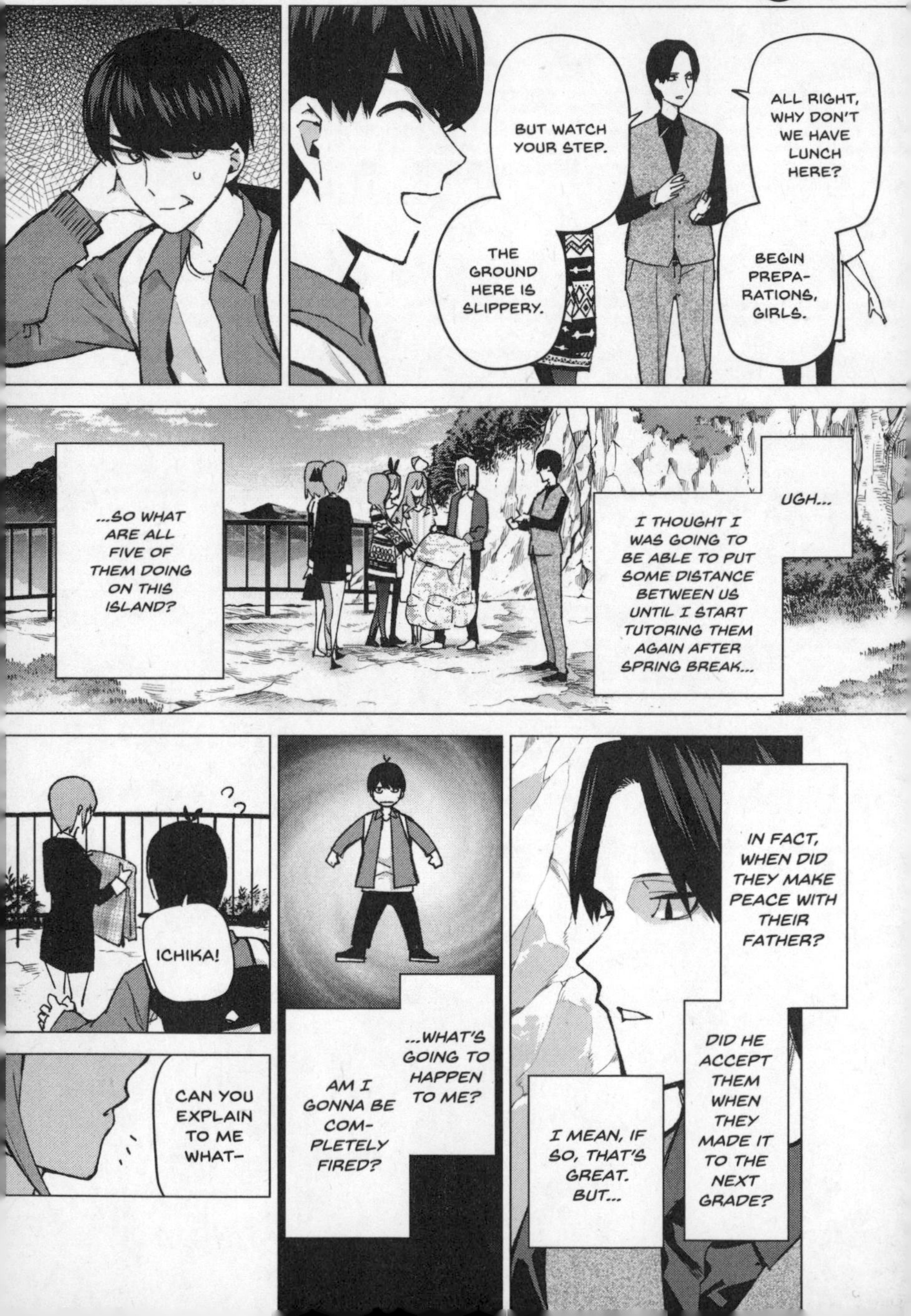

ALL RIGHT, WHY DON'T WE HAVE LUNCH HERE?
BEGIN PREPARATIONS, GIRLS.
BUT WATCH YOUR STEP.
THE GROUND HERE IS SLIPPERY.
UGH...
I THOUGHT I WAS GOING TO BE ABLE TO PUT SOME DISTANCE BETWEEN US UNTIL I START TUTORING THEM AGAIN AFTER SPRING BREAK...
...SO WHAT ARE ALL FIVE OF THEM DOING ON THIS ISLAND?
IN FACT, WHEN DID THEY MAKE PEACE WITH THEIR FATHER?
DID HE ACCEPT THEM WHEN THEY MADE IT TO THE NEXT GRADE?
I MEAN, IF SO, THAT'S GREAT. BUT...
...WHAT'S GOING TO HAPPEN TO ME?
AM I GONNA BE COMPLETELY FIRED?
ICHIKA!
CAN YOU EXPLAIN TO ME WHAT-

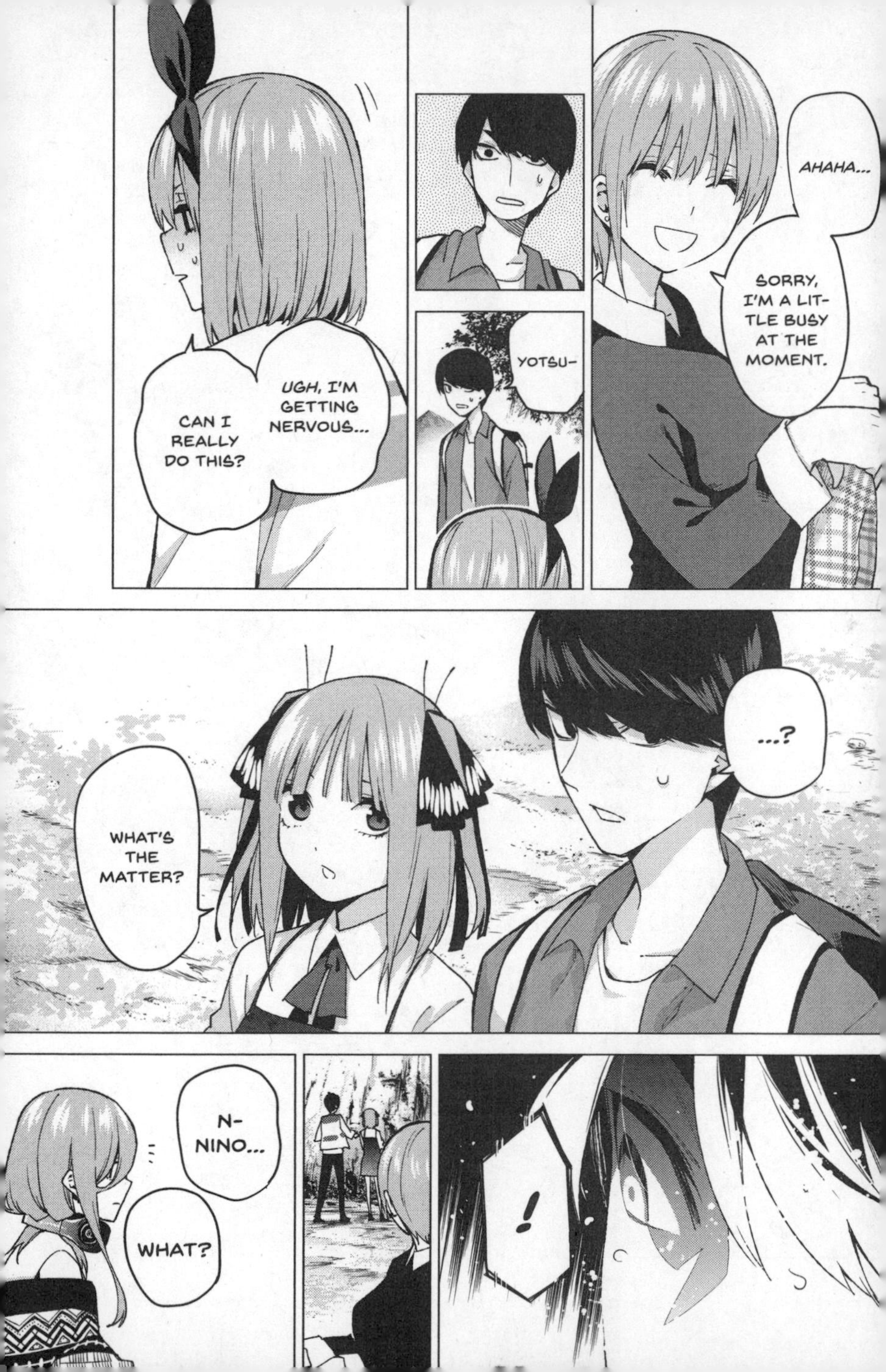
AHAHA...
SORRY, I'M A LITTLE BUSY AT THE MOMENT.
YOTSU-
UGH, I'M GETTING NERVOUS...
CAN I REALLY DO THIS?
...?
WHAT'S THE MATTER?
!
N-NINO...
WHAT?

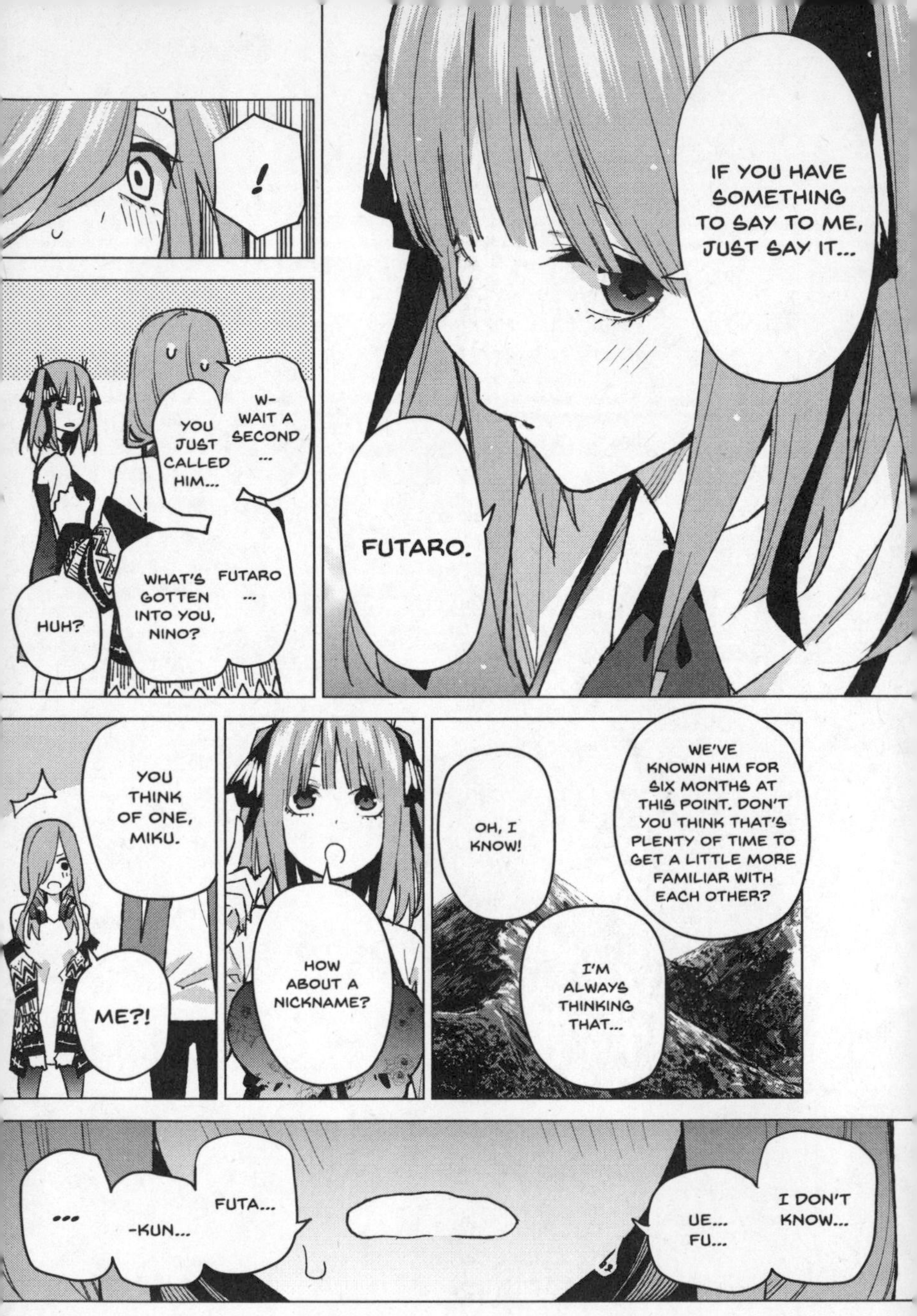
IF YOU HAVE SOMETHING TO SAY TO ME, JUST SAY IT...
FUTARO.
!
W- WAIT A SECOND ...
YOU JUST CALLED HIM...
FUTARO ...
WHAT'S GOTTEN INTO YOU, NINO?
HUH?
WE'VE KNOWN HIM FOR SIX MONTHS AT THIS POINT. DON'T YOU THINK THAT'S PLENTY OF TIME TO GET A LITTLE MORE FAMILIAR WITH EACH OTHER?
OH, I KNOW!
I'M ALWAYS THINKING THAT...
HOW ABOUT A NICKNAME?
YOU THINK OF ONE, MIKU.
ME?!
I DON'T KNOW...
UE... FU...
FUTA...
-KUN...
...

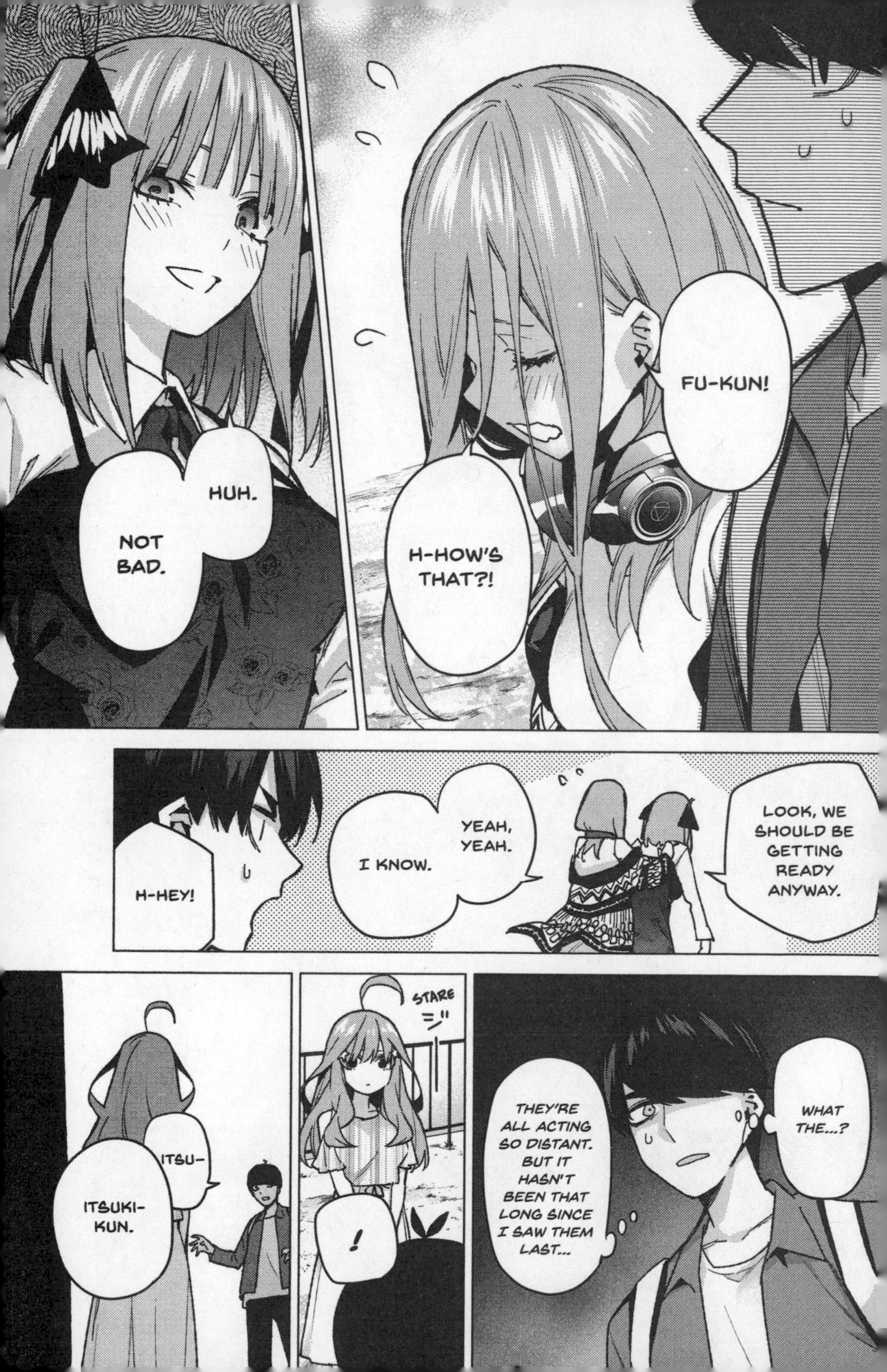
FU-KUN!
H-HOW'S THAT?!
HUH.
NOT BAD.
LOOK, WE SHOULD BE GETTING READY ANYWAY.
YEAH, YEAH.
I KNOW.
H-HEY!
WHAT THE...?
THEY'RE ALL ACTING SO DISTANT. BUT IT HASN'T BEEN THAT LONG SINCE I SAW THEM LAST...
STARE
!
ITSU-
ITSUKI-KUN.

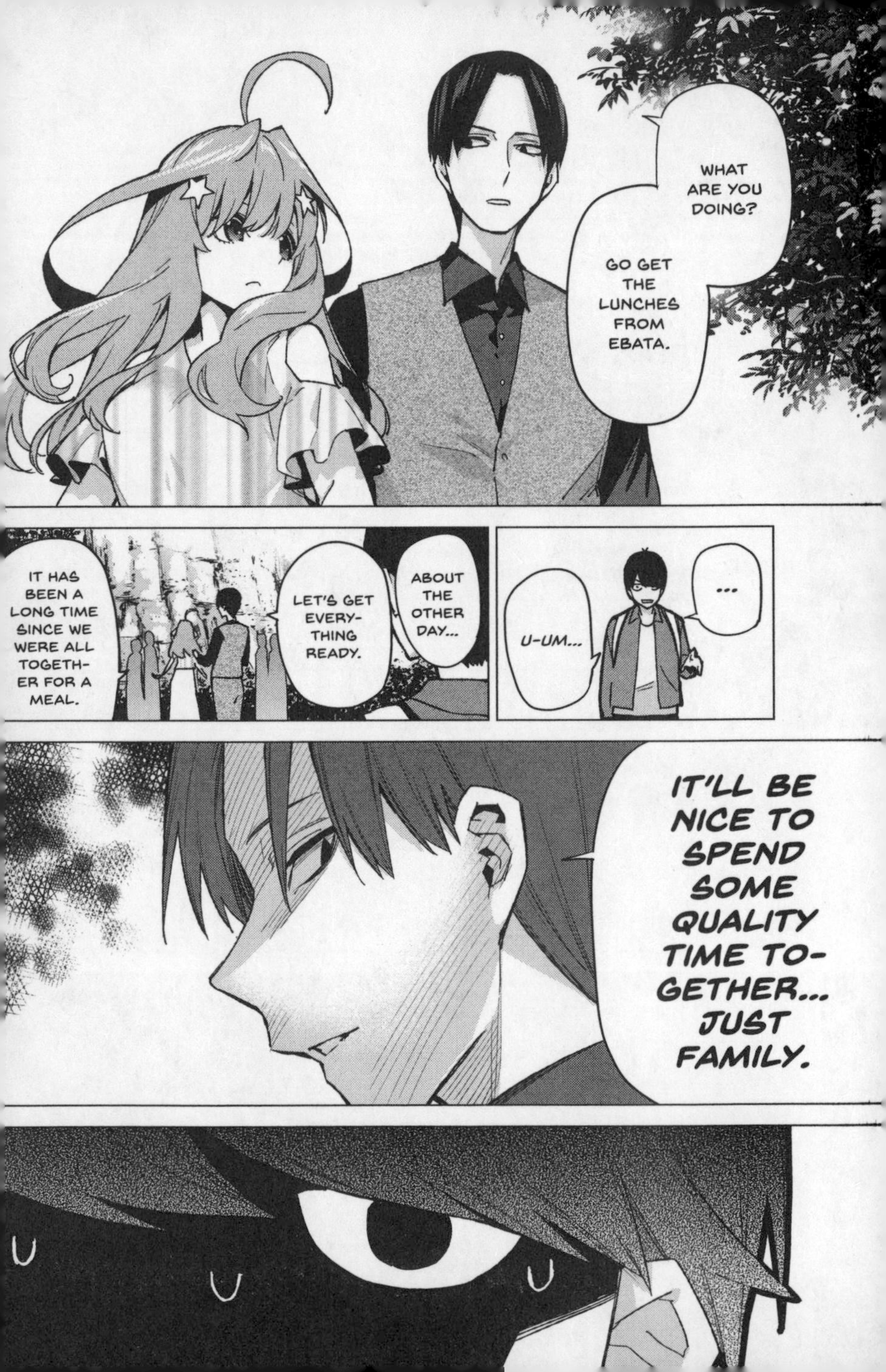
WHAT ARE YOU DOING?
GO GET THE LUNCHES FROM EBATA.
...
U-UM...
ABOUT THE OTHER DAY...
LET'S GET EVERY-THING READY.
IT HAS BEEN A LONG TIME SINCE WE WERE ALL TOGETH-ER FOR A MEAL.
IT'LL BE NICE TO SPEND SOME QUALITY TIME TO-GETHER... JUST FAMILY.

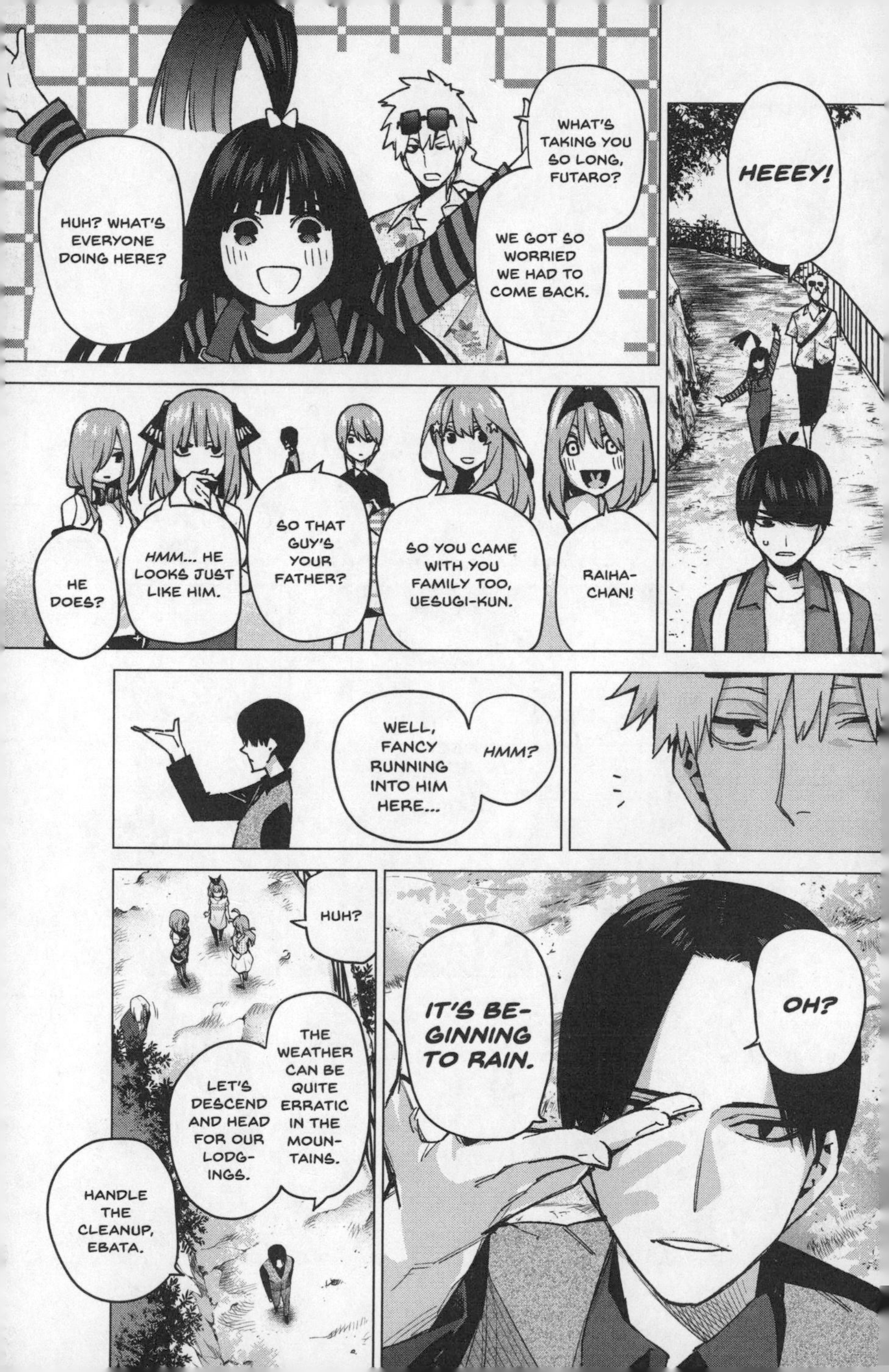
HEEEY!
WHAT'S TAKING YOU SO LONG, FUTARO?
WE GOT SO WORRIED WE HAD TO COME BACK.
HUH? WHAT'S EVERYONE DOING HERE?
RAIHA-CHAN!
SO YOU CAME WITH YOU FAMILY TOO, UESUGI-KUN.
SO THAT GUY'S YOUR FATHER?
HMM... HE LOOKS JUST LIKE HIM.
HE DOES?
HMM?
WELL, FANCY RUNNING INTO HIM HERE...
OH?
IT'S BE-GINNING TO RAIN.
HUH?
THE WEATHER CAN BE QUITE ERRATIC IN THE MOUN-TAINS.
LET'S DESCEND AND HEAD FOR OUR LODG-INGS.
HANDLE THE CLEANUP, EBATA.

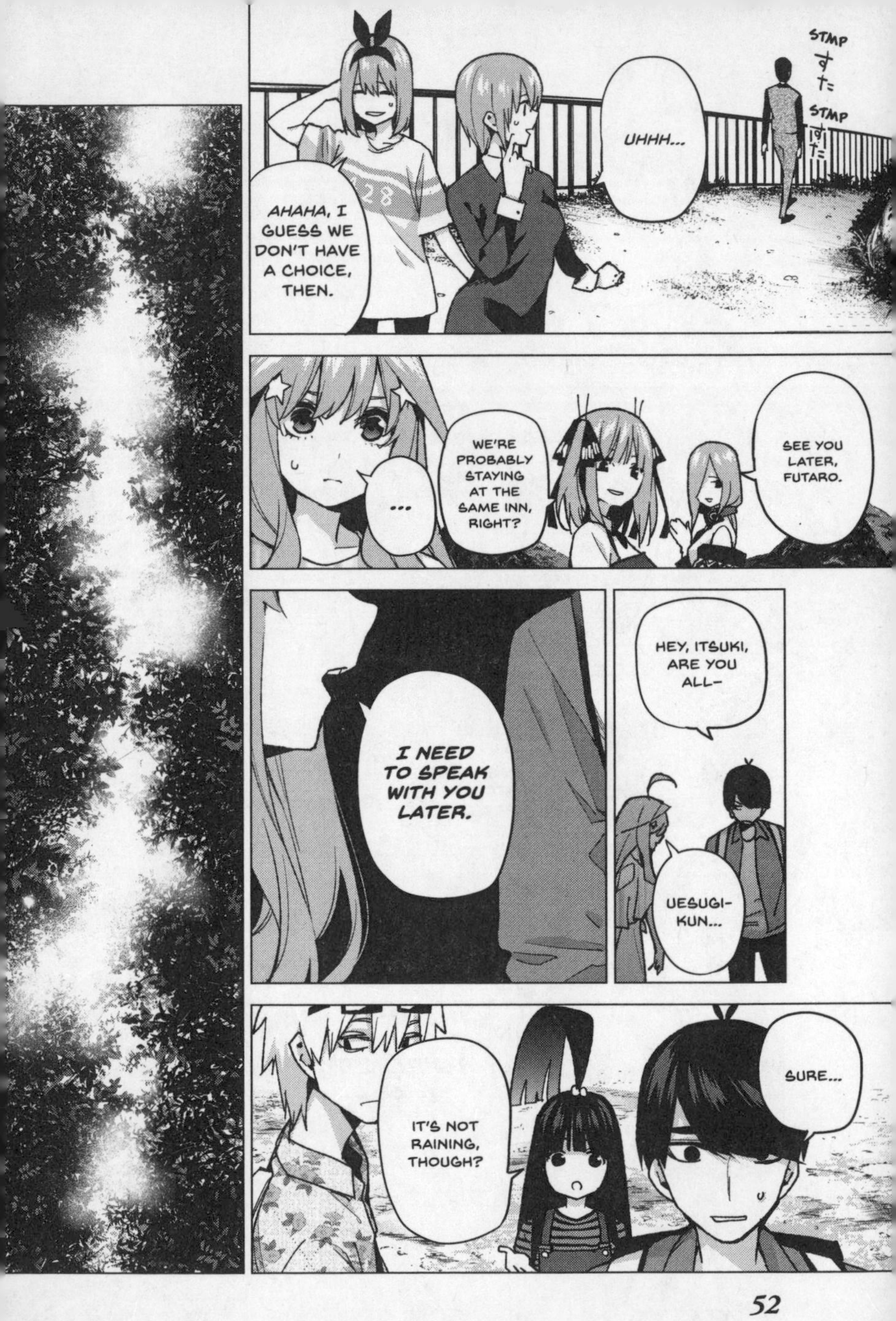
STMP すた
STMP すた
UHHH...
AHAHA, I GUESS WE DON'T HAVE A CHOICE, THEN.
SEE YOU LATER, FUTARO.
WE'RE PROBABLY STAYING AT THE SAME INN, RIGHT?
...
HEY, ITSUKI, ARE YOU ALL—
UESUGI-KUN...
I NEED TO SPEAK WITH YOU LATER.
SURE...
IT'S NOT RAINING, THOUGH?

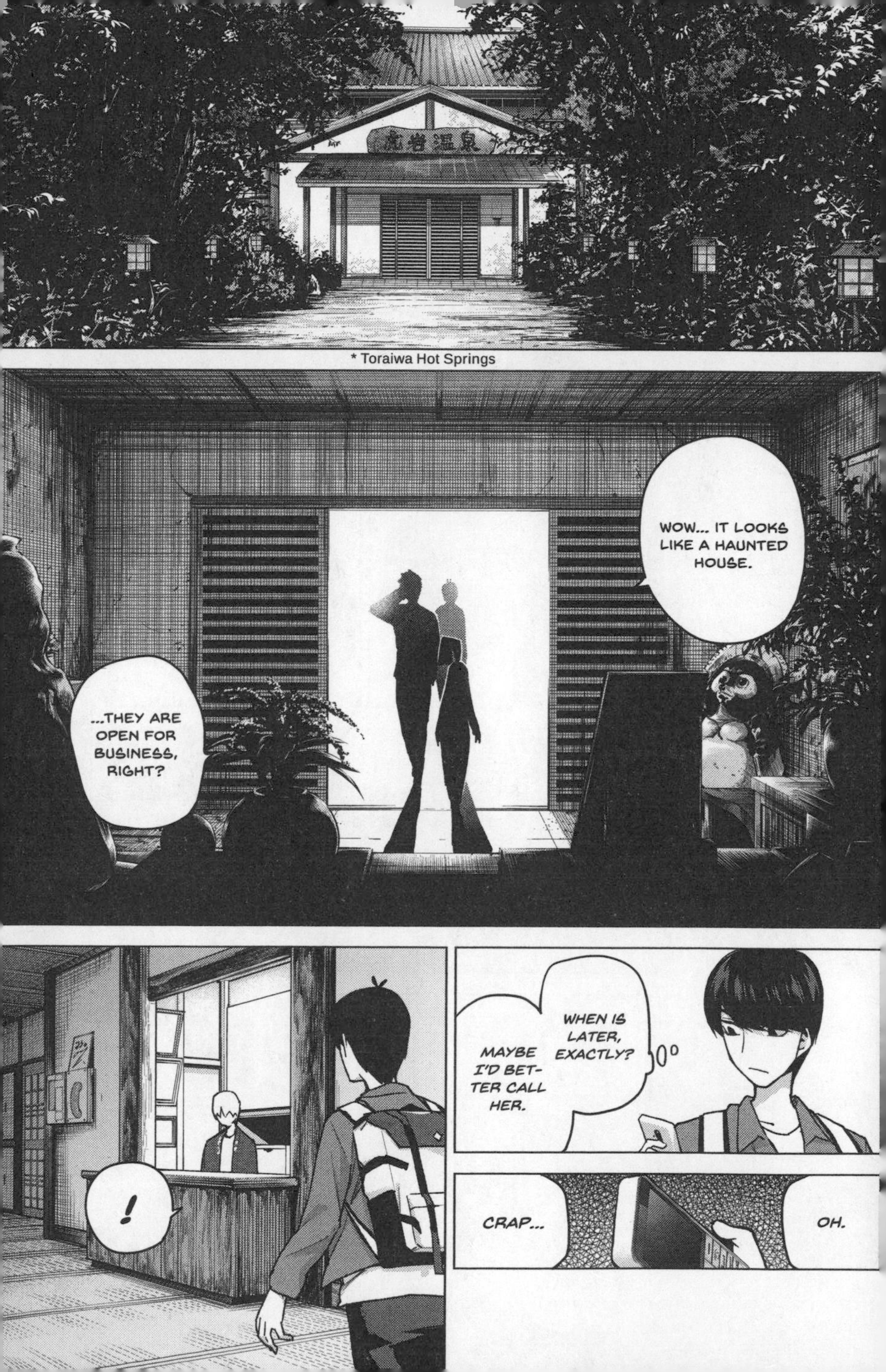
虎岩温泉
* Toraiwa Hot Springs
WOW... IT LOOKS LIKE A HAUNTED HOUSE.
...THEY ARE OPEN FOR BUSINESS, RIGHT?
WHEN IS LATER, EXACTLY?
MAYBE I'D BETTER CALL HER.
OH.
CRAP...
!

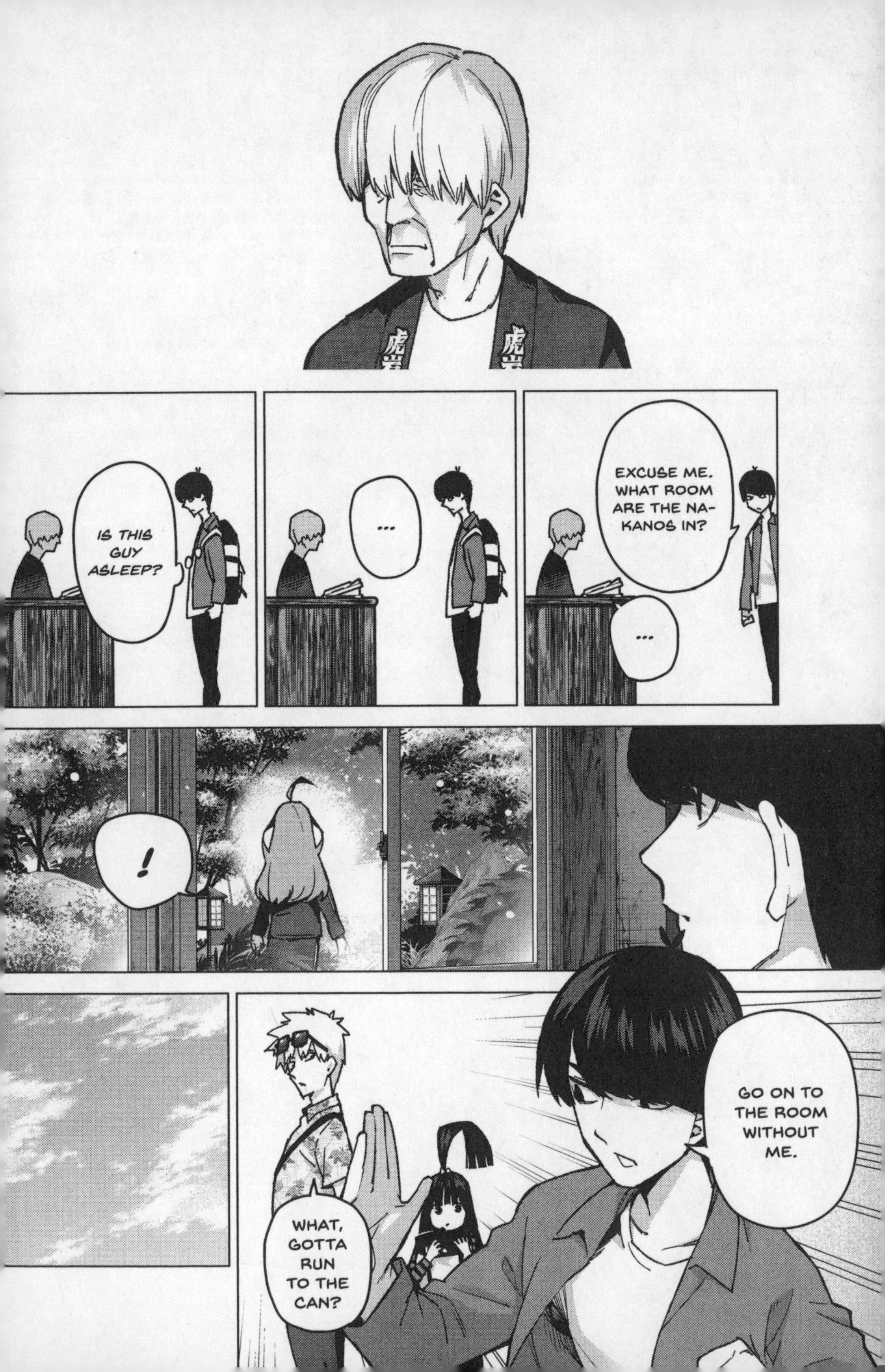
EXCUSE ME. WHAT ROOM ARE THE NA-KANOS IN?
...
...
IS THIS GUY ASLEEP?
!
GO ON TO THE ROOM WITHOUT ME.
WHAT, GOTTA RUN TO THE CAN?

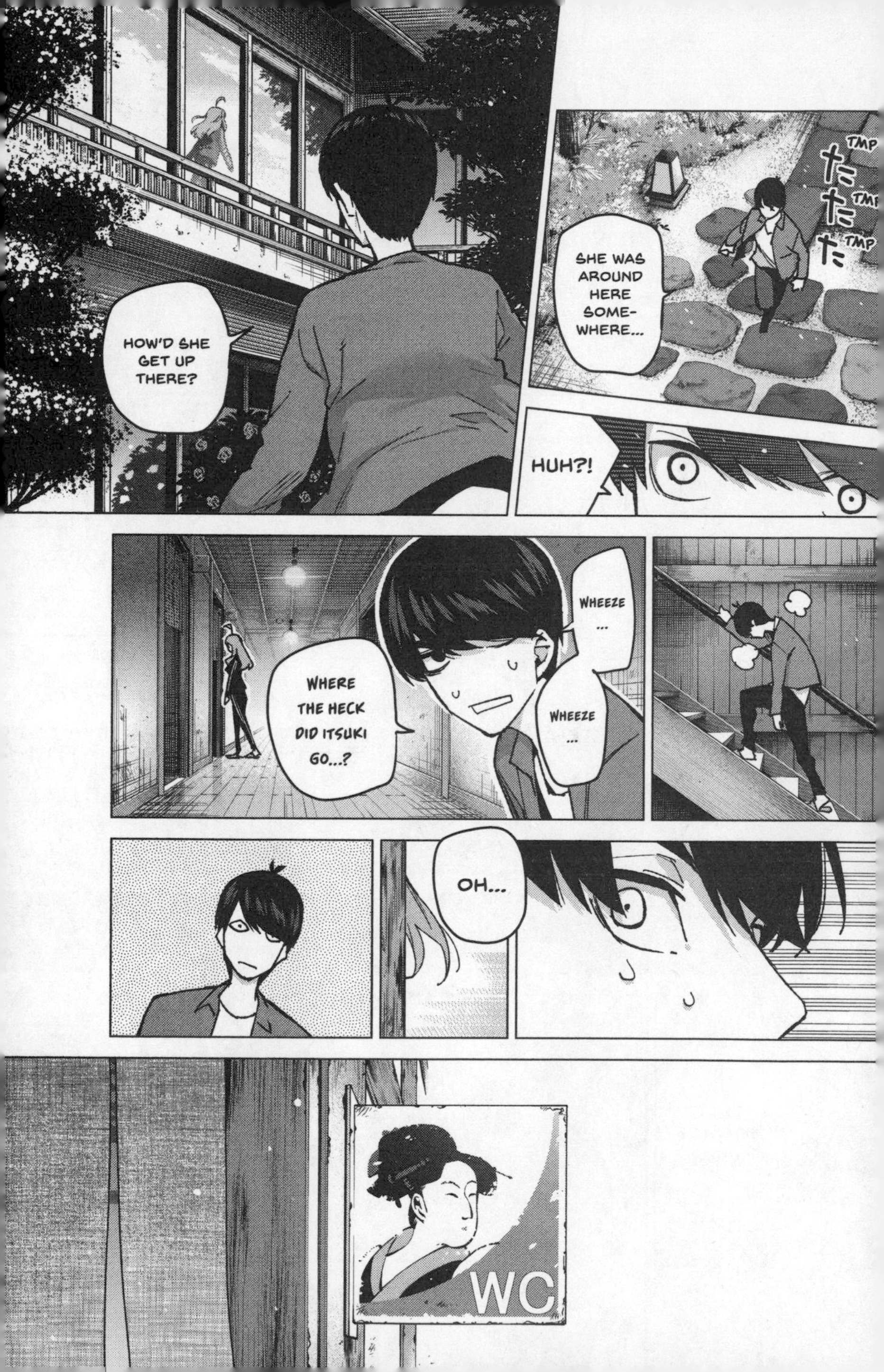

TMP
TMP
TMP
たたた
SHE WAS AROUND HERE SOME-WHERE...
HUH?!
HOW'D SHE GET UP THERE?
WHEEZE ...
WHEEZE ...
WHERE THE HECK DID ITSUKI GO...?
OH...
WC

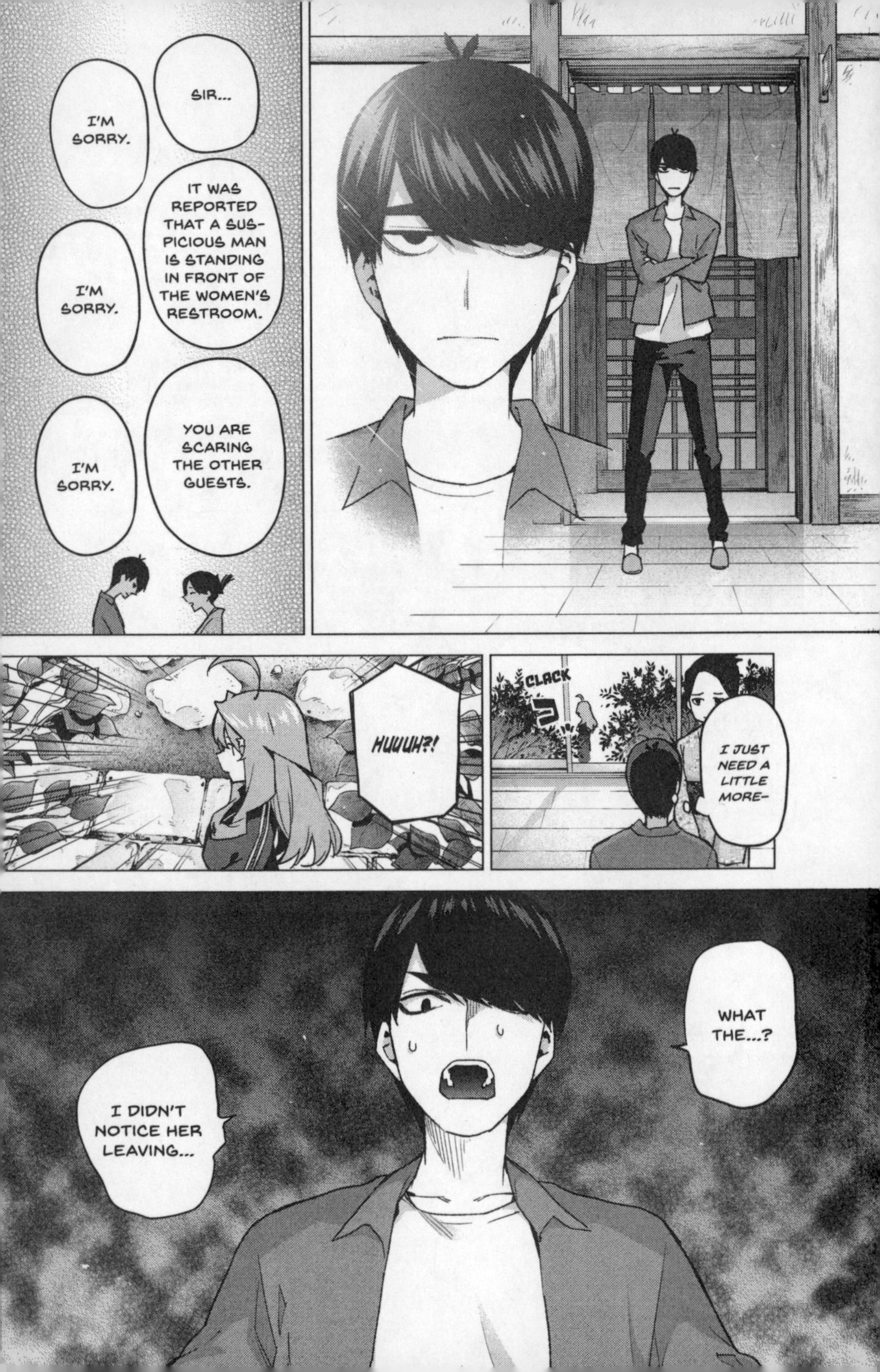
SIR...
I'M SORRY.
IT WAS REPORTED THAT A SUSPICIOUS MAN IS STANDING IN FRONT OF THE WOMEN'S RESTROOM.
I'M SORRY.
YOU ARE SCARING THE OTHER GUESTS.
I'M SORRY.
I JUST NEED A LITTLE MORE-
CLACK
HUUUH?!
WHAT THE...?
I DIDN'T NOTICE HER LEAVING...

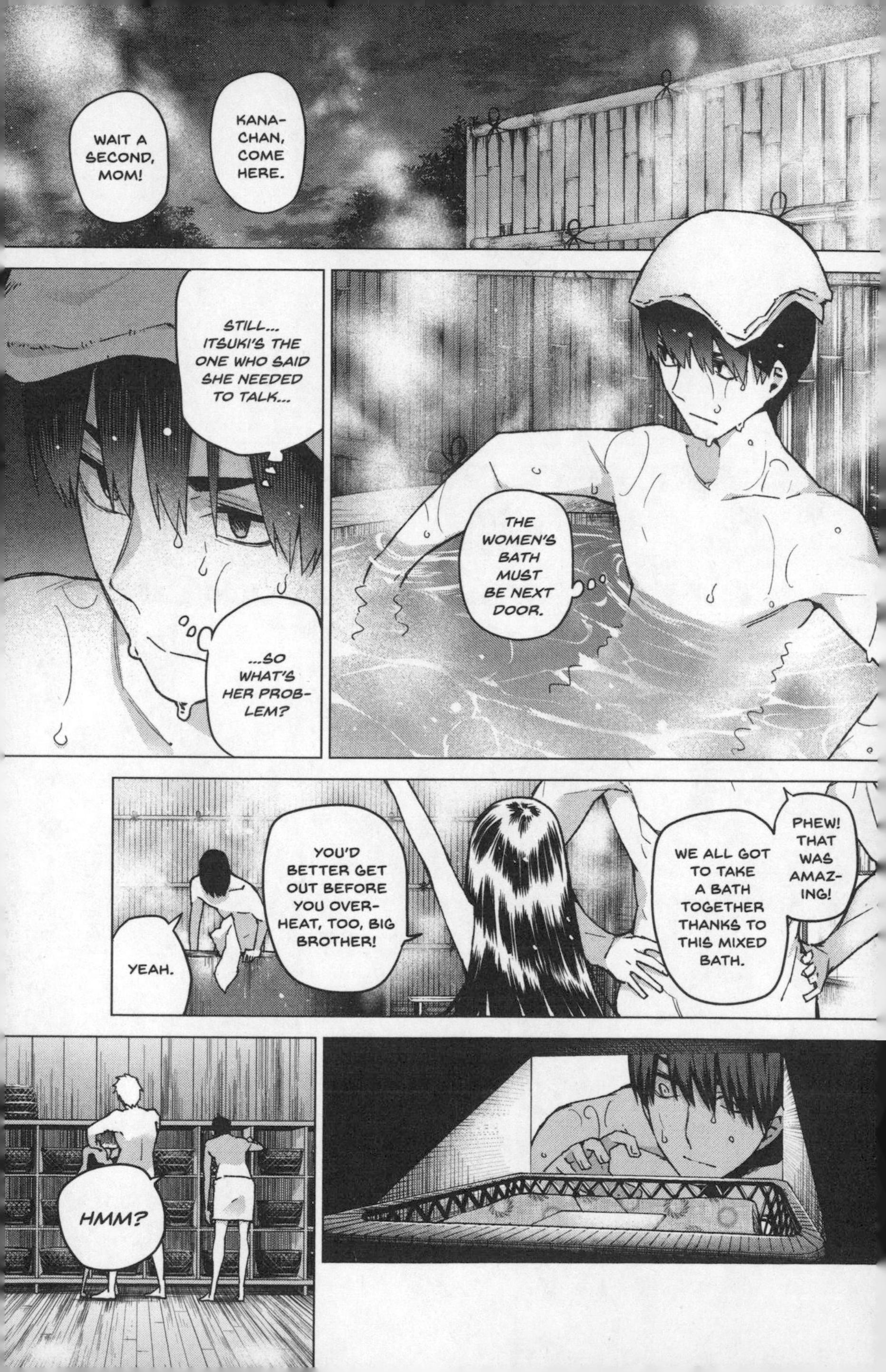
KANA-CHAN, COME HERE.
WAIT A SECOND, MOM!
THE WOMEN'S BATH MUST BE NEXT DOOR.
STILL... ITSUKI'S THE ONE WHO SAID SHE NEEDED TO TALK...
...SO WHAT'S HER PROBLEM?
PHEW! THAT WAS AMAZING!
WE ALL GOT TO TAKE A BATH TOGETHER THANKS TO THIS MIXED BATH.
YOU'D BETTER GET OUT BEFORE YOU OVERHEAT, TOO, BIG BROTHER!
YEAH.
HMM?

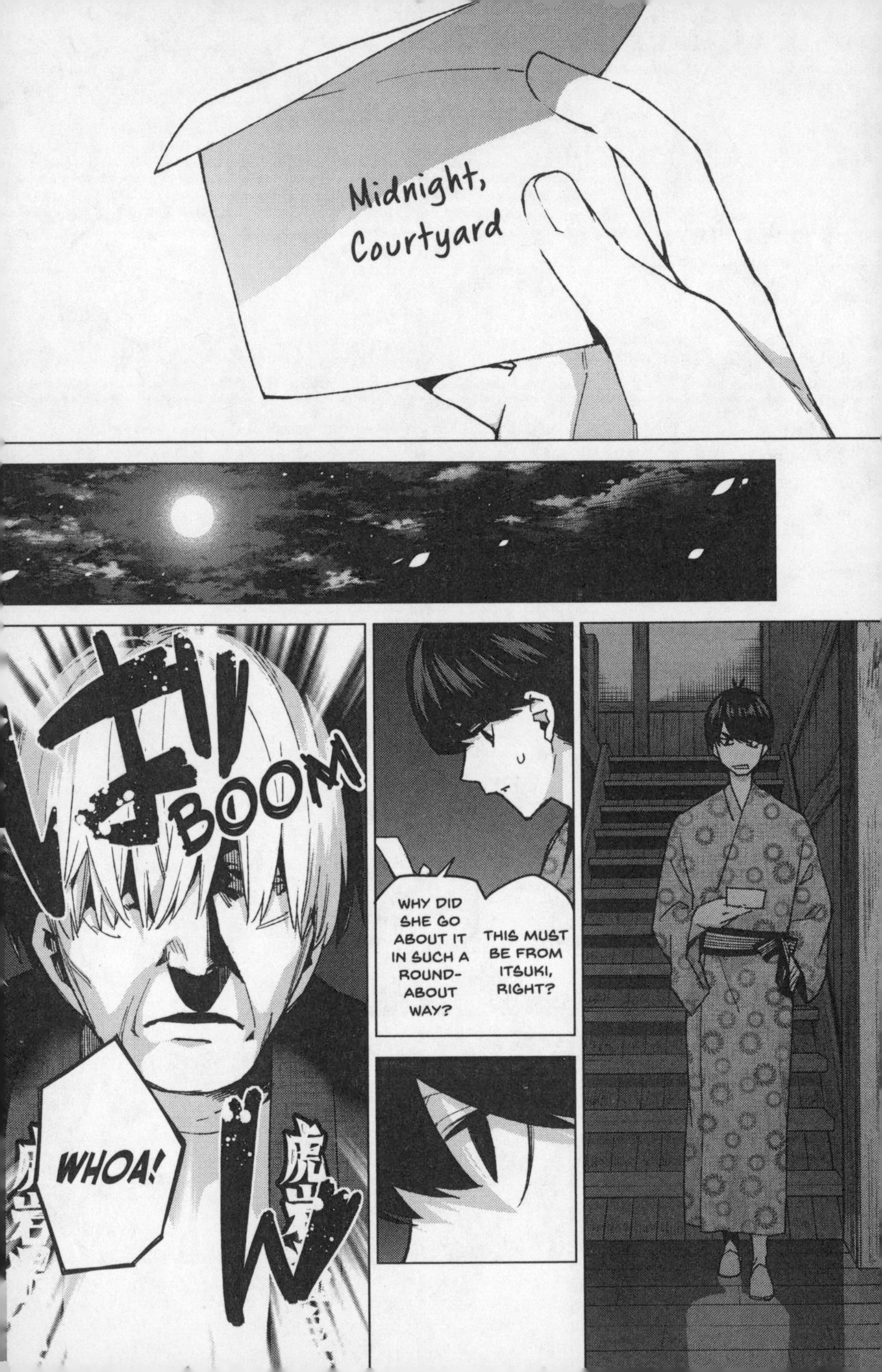
Midnight, Courtyard
THIS MUST BE FROM ITSUKI, RIGHT?
WHY DID SHE GO ABOUT IT IN SUCH A ROUND-ABOUT WAY?
BOOM
WHOA!

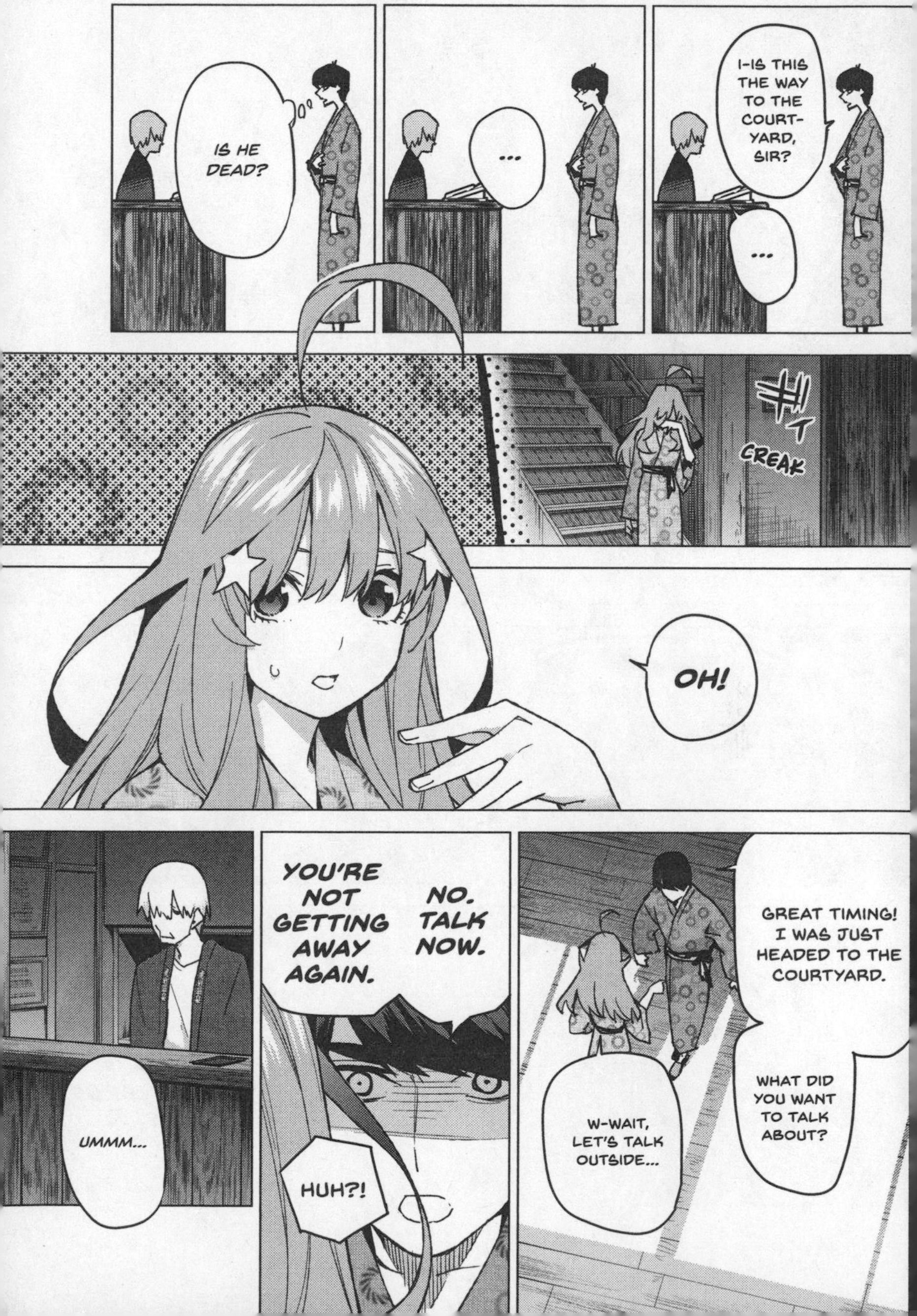
I-IS THIS THE WAY TO THE COURT-YARD, SIR?
...
...
IS HE DEAD?
CREAK
OH!
GREAT TIMING! I WAS JUST HEADED TO THE COURTYARD.
WHAT DID YOU WANT TO TALK ABOUT?
W-WAIT, LET'S TALK OUTSIDE...
NO. TALK NOW.
YOU'RE NOT GETTING AWAY AGAIN.
HUH?!
UMMM...

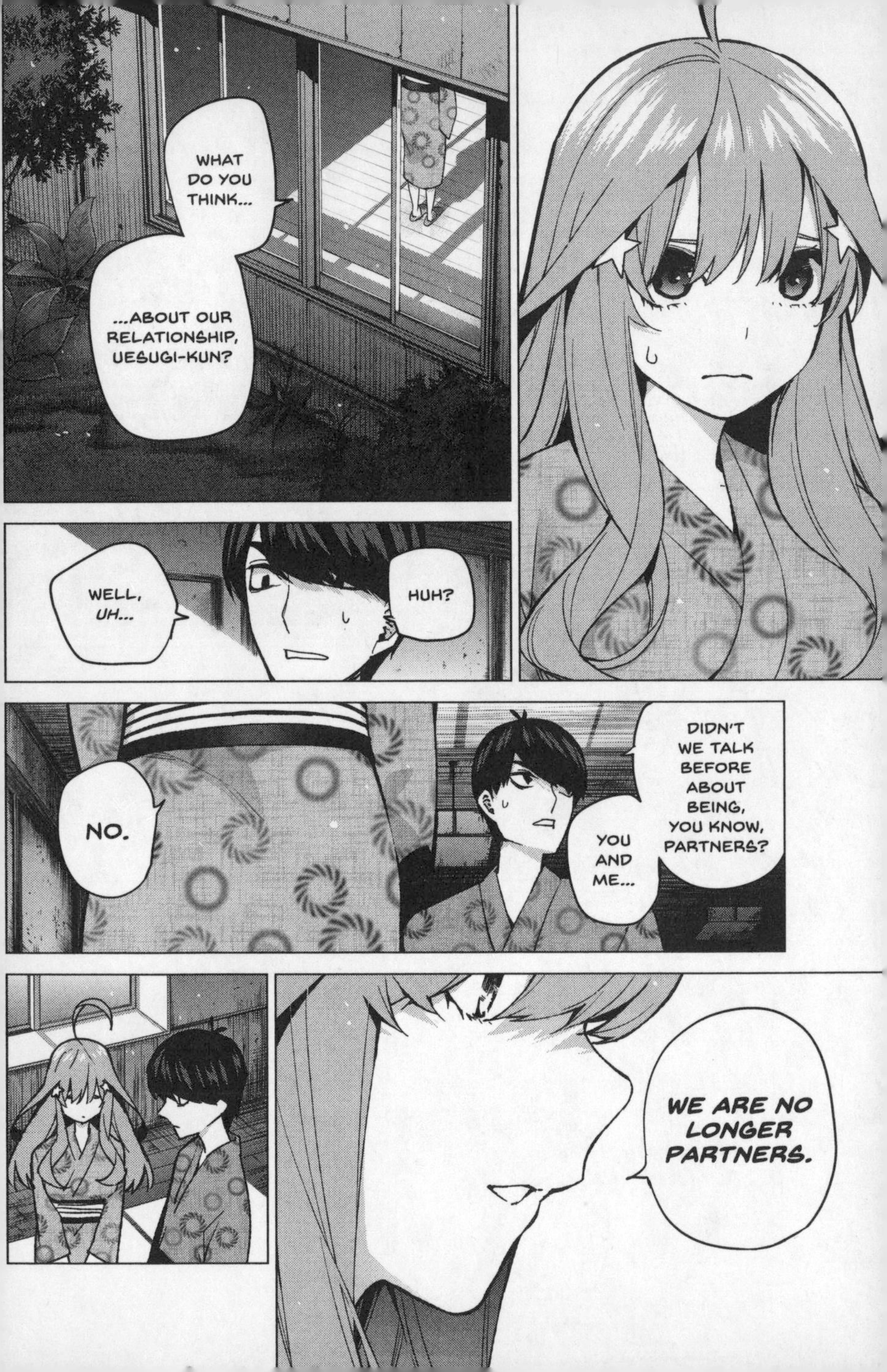
WHAT DO YOU THINK...
...ABOUT OUR RELATIONSHIP, UESUGI-KUN?
HUH?
WELL, UH...
DIDN'T WE TALK BEFORE ABOUT BEING, YOU KNOW, PARTNERS?
YOU AND ME...
NO.
WE ARE NO LONGER PARTNERS.

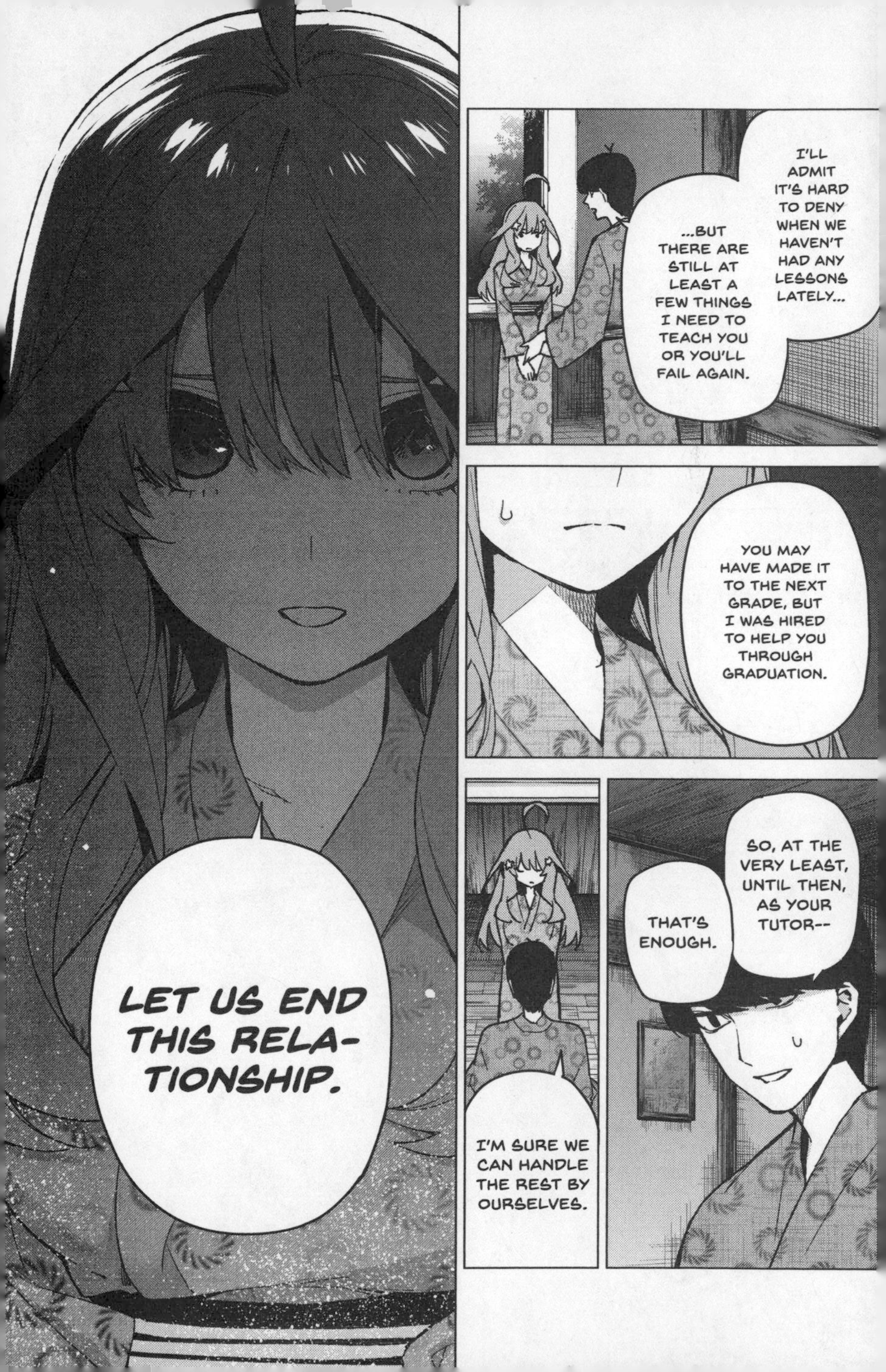
I'LL ADMIT IT'S HARD TO DENY WHEN WE HAVEN'T HAD ANY LESSONS LATELY...
...BUT THERE ARE STILL AT LEAST A FEW THINGS I NEED TO TEACH YOU OR YOU'LL FAIL AGAIN.
YOU MAY HAVE MADE IT TO THE NEXT GRADE, BUT I WAS HIRED TO HELP YOU THROUGH GRADUATION.
SO, AT THE VERY LEAST, UNTIL THEN, AS YOUR TUTOR--
THAT'S ENOUGH.
I'M SURE WE CAN HANDLE THE REST BY OURSELVES.
LET US END THIS RELA-TIONSHIP.

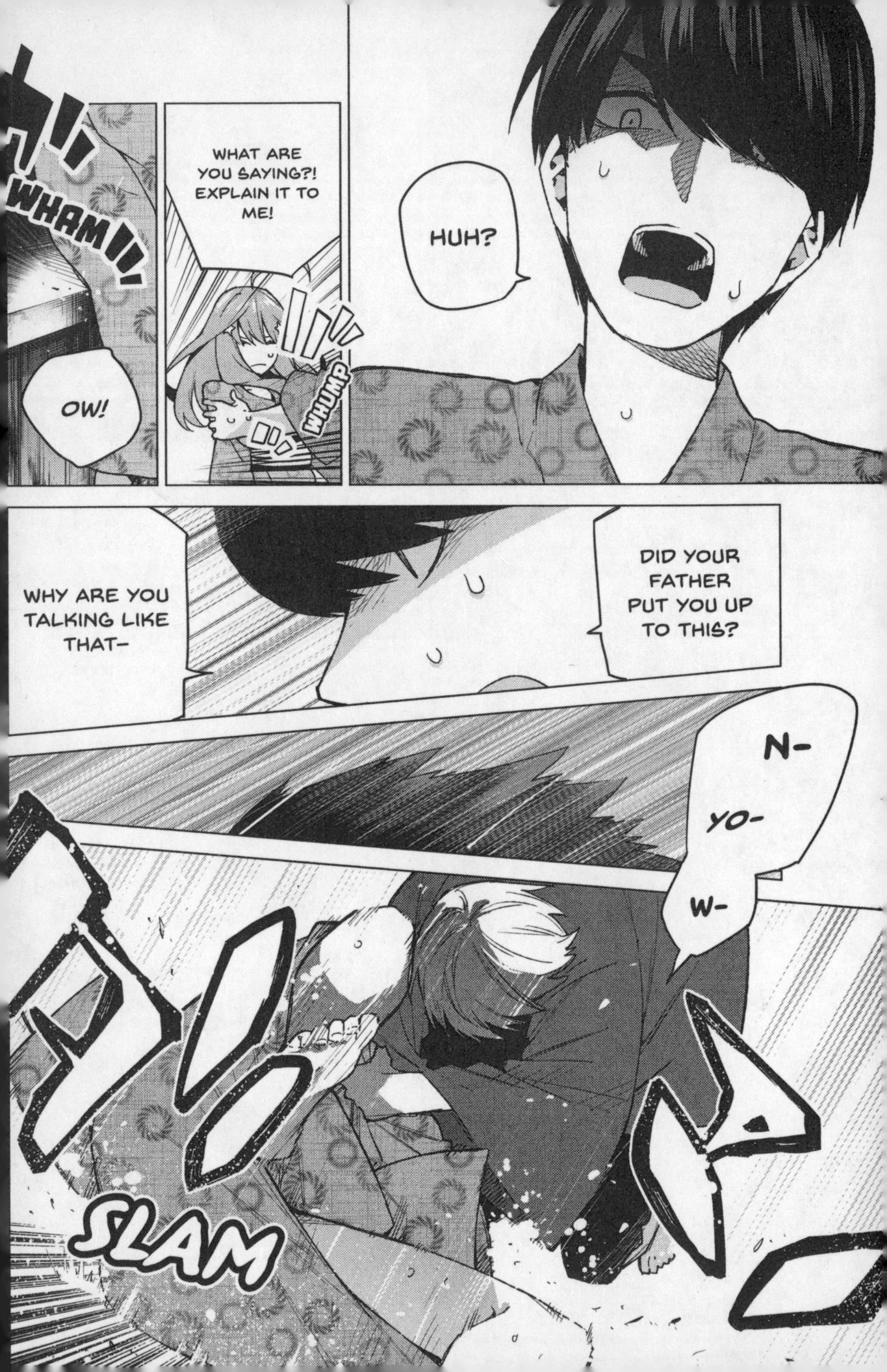
HUH?
WHAT ARE YOU SAYING?! EXPLAIN IT TO ME!
WHUMP
WHAM!!
OW!
DID YOUR FATHER PUT YOU UP TO THIS?
WHY ARE YOU TALKING LIKE THAT-
N- YO- W-
SLAM

...?

...?

...MISTER.

I THOUGHT YOU WERE DEAD...

=

HE'S SAYING SOMETHING!!

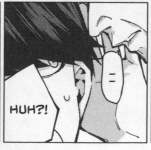

HUH?!

=

HUH?!

WHAT WAS THAT?!

=

KEEP YOUR HANDS OFF MY GRAND-DAUGHTERS.

OR YOU'RE A DEAD MAN.

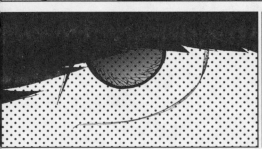

I'VE GOT NO IDEA WHAT'S EVEN GOING ON ANYMORE.

I WANNA GO HOME.

CHAPTER 63
SCRAMBLED EGGS ③

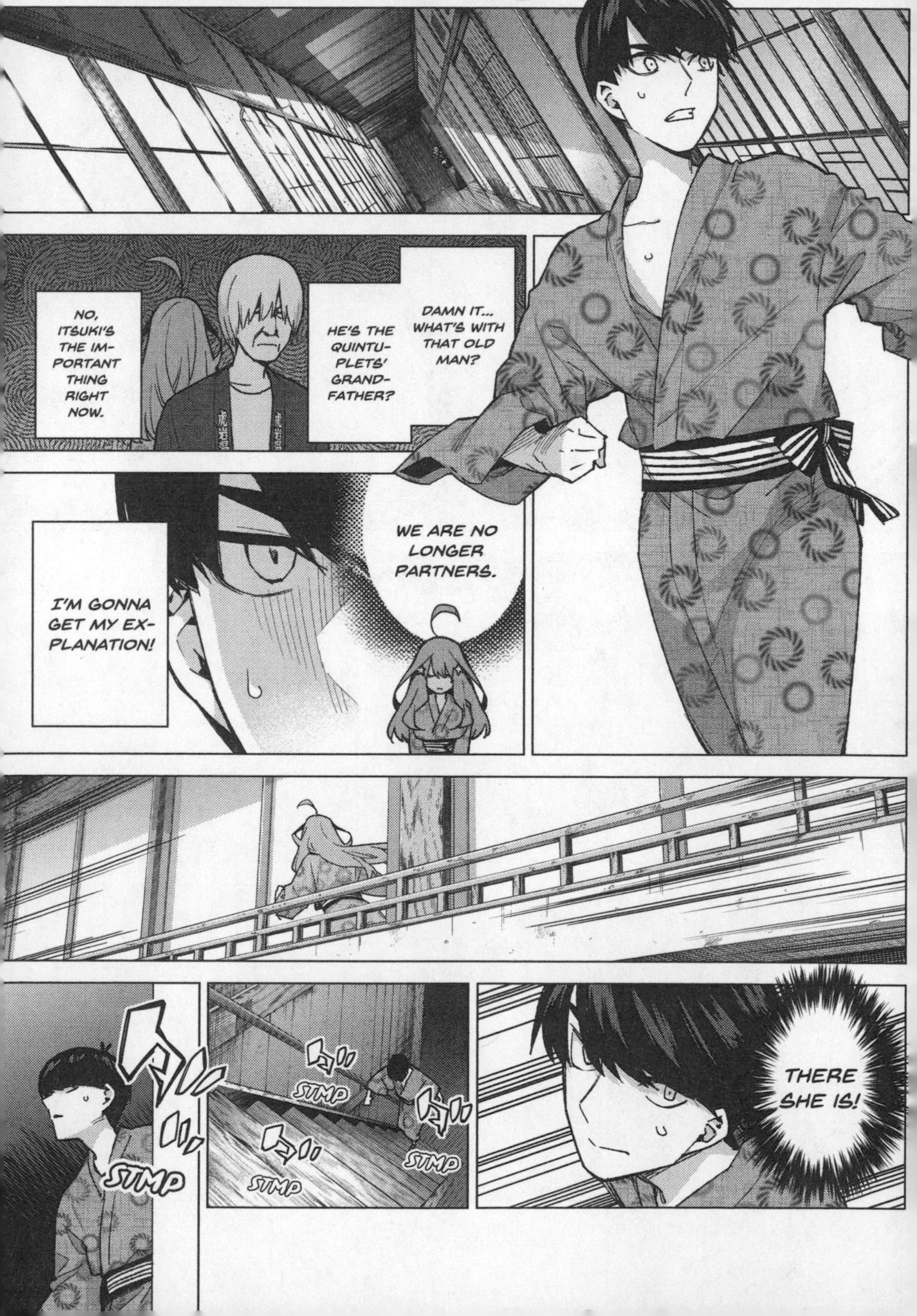
DAMN IT... WHAT'S WITH THAT OLD MAN?
HE'S THE QUINTU-PLETS' GRAND-FATHER?
NO, ITSUKI'S THE IM-PORTANT THING RIGHT NOW.
WE ARE NO LONGER PARTNERS.
I'M GONNA GET MY EX-PLANATION!
THERE SHE IS!
STMP
STMP
STMP
STMP

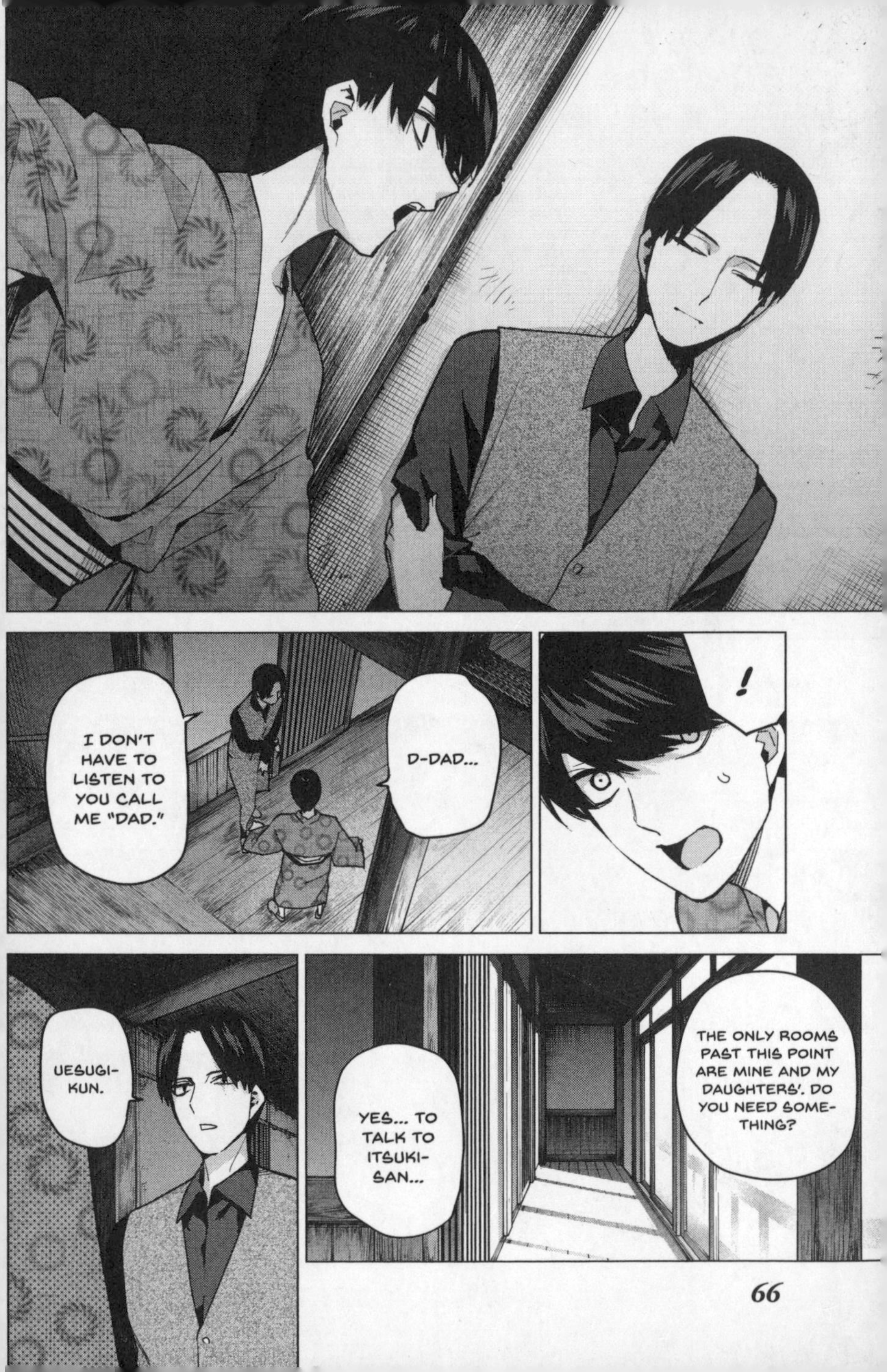
!
D-DAD...
I DON'T HAVE TO LISTEN TO YOU CALL ME "DAD."
THE ONLY ROOMS PAST THIS POINT ARE MINE AND MY DAUGHTERS'. DO YOU NEED SOMETHING?
YES... TO TALK TO ITSUKI-SAN...
UESUGI-KUN.

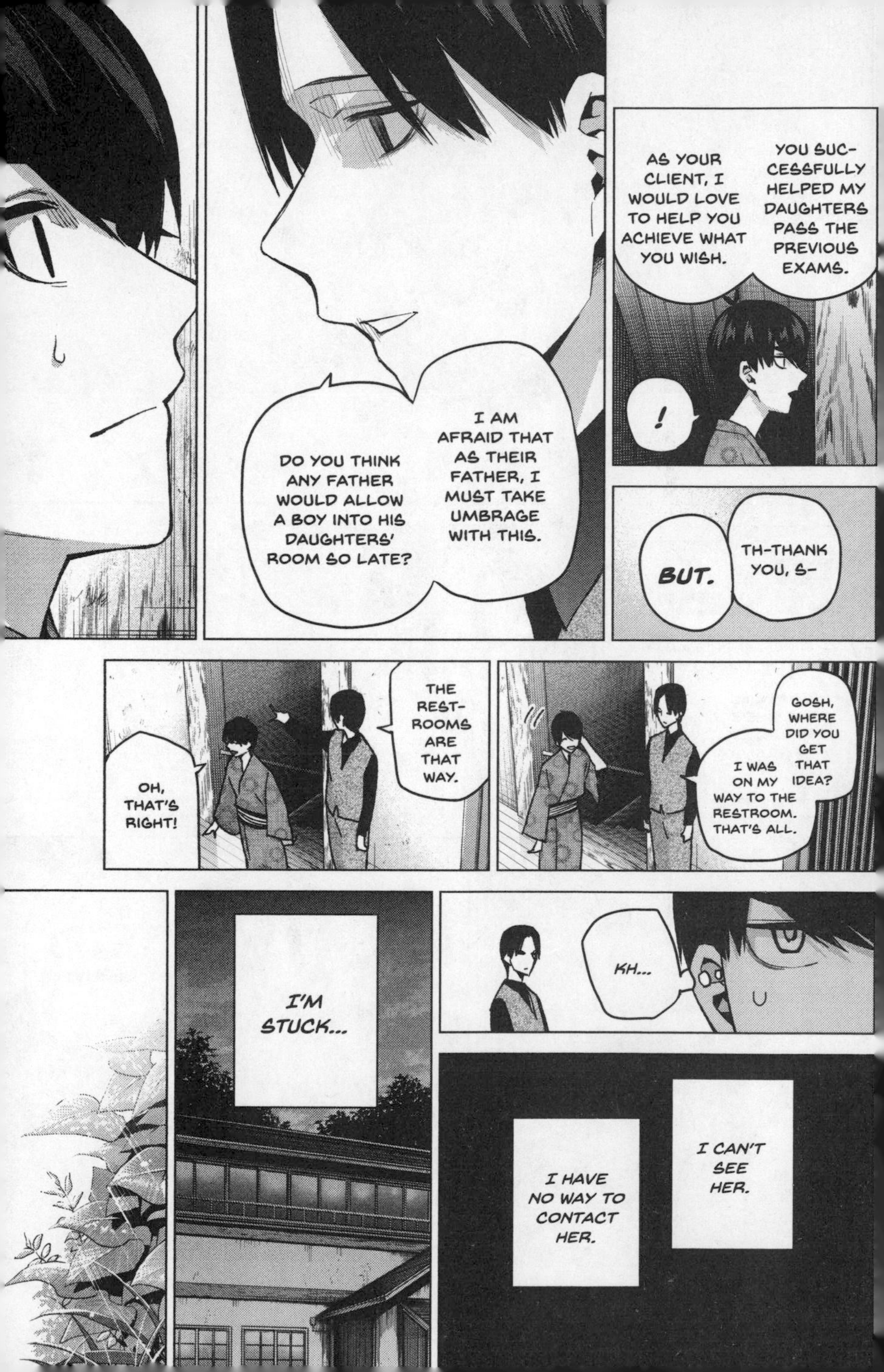
YOU SUCCESSFULLY HELPED MY DAUGHTERS PASS THE PREVIOUS EXAMS.
AS YOUR CLIENT, I WOULD LOVE TO HELP YOU ACHIEVE WHAT YOU WISH.
!
TH-THANK YOU, S-
BUT.
I AM AFRAID THAT AS THEIR FATHER, I MUST TAKE UMBRAGE WITH THIS.
DO YOU THINK ANY FATHER WOULD ALLOW A BOY INTO HIS DAUGHTERS' ROOM SO LATE?
GOSH, WHERE DID YOU GET THAT IDEA?
I WAS ON MY WAY TO THE RESTROOM. THAT'S ALL.
THE RESTROOMS ARE THAT WAY.
OH, THAT'S RIGHT!
KH...
I CAN'T SEE HER.
I HAVE NO WAY TO CONTACT HER.
I'M STUCK...

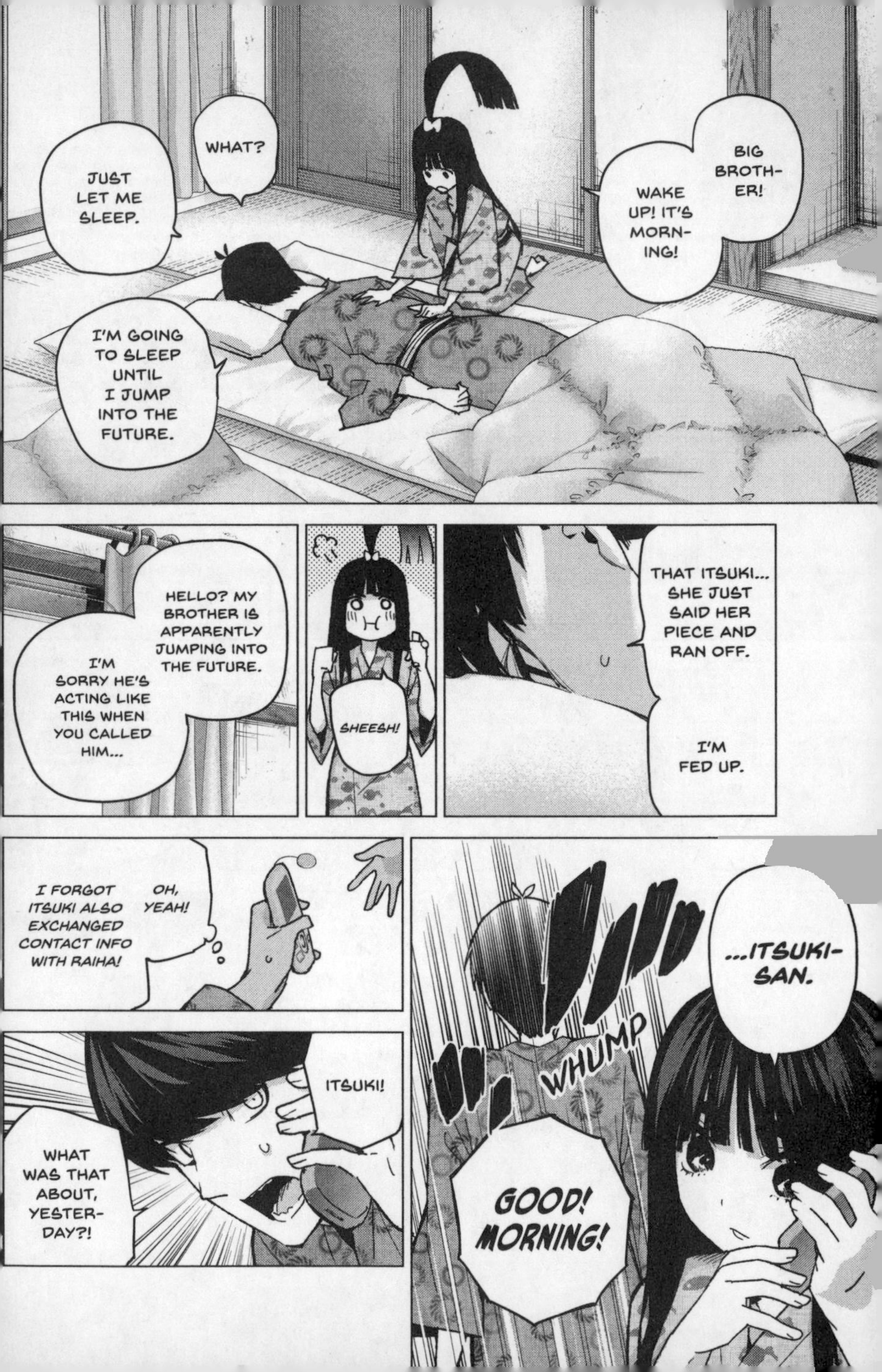
BIG BROTHER-! WAKE UP! IT'S MORNING!
WHAT?
JUST LET ME SLEEP.
I'M GOING TO SLEEP UNTIL I JUMP INTO THE FUTURE.
THAT ITSUKI... SHE JUST SAID HER PIECE AND RAN OFF.
I'M FED UP.
SHEESH!
HELLO? MY BROTHER IS APPARENTLY JUMPING INTO THE FUTURE.
I'M SORRY HE'S ACTING LIKE THIS WHEN YOU CALLED HIM...
...ITSUKI-SAN.
WHUMP
GOOD! MORNING!
OH, YEAH!
I FORGOT ITSUKI ALSO EXCHANGED CONTACT INFO WITH RAIHA!
ITSUKI!
WHAT WAS THAT ABOUT, YESTERDAY?!

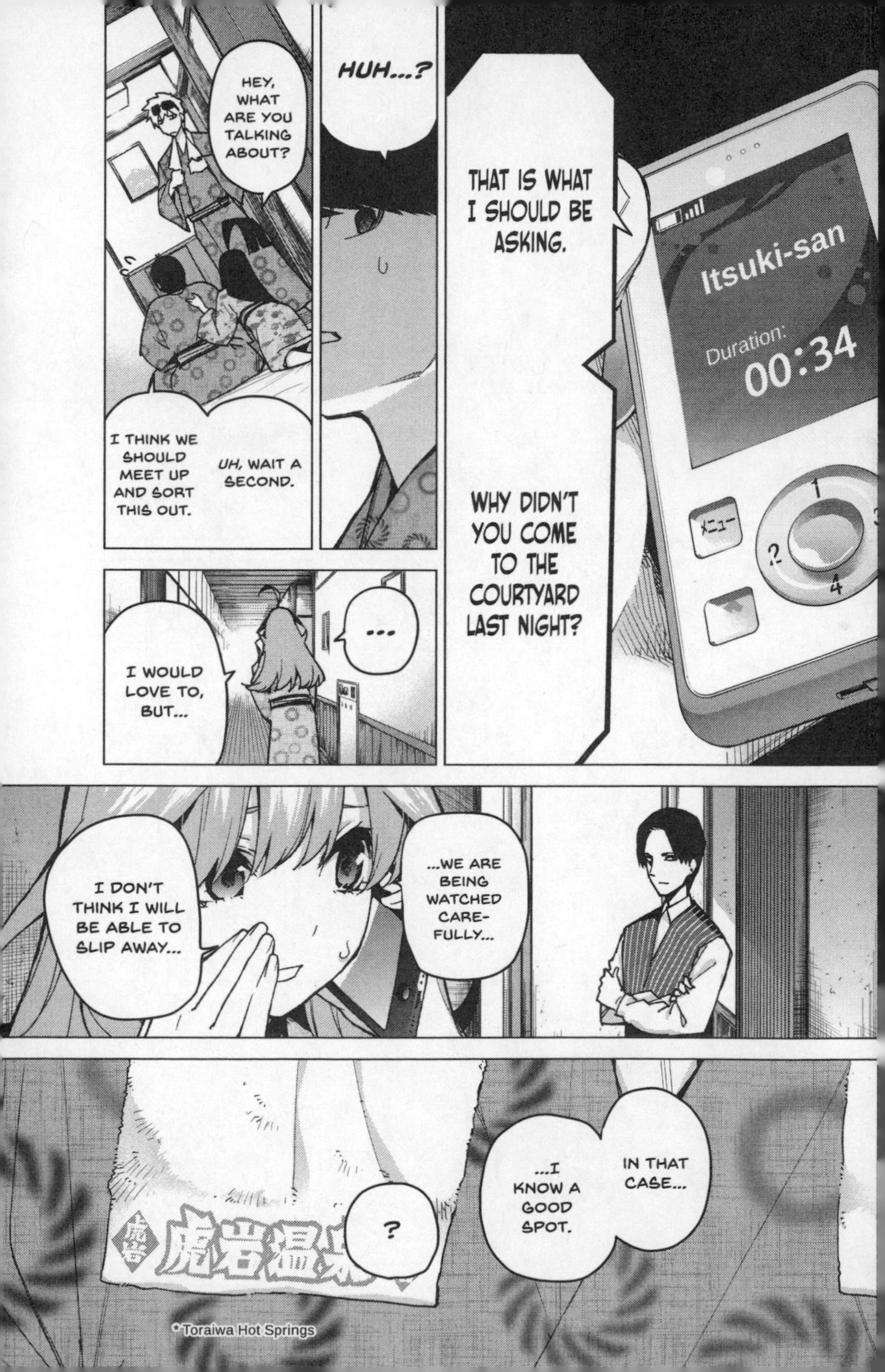
THAT IS WHAT I SHOULD BE ASKING.
Itsuki-san
Duration:
00:34
WHY DIDN'T YOU COME TO THE COURTYARD LAST NIGHT?
HUH...?
UH, WAIT A SECOND.
HEY, WHAT ARE YOU TALKING ABOUT?
I THINK WE SHOULD MEET UP AND SORT THIS OUT.
...
I WOULD LOVE TO, BUT...
...WE ARE BEING WATCHED CAREFULLY...
I DON'T THINK I WILL BE ABLE TO SLIP AWAY...
IN THAT CASE...
...I KNOW A GOOD SPOT.
?
虎岩温
*Toraiwa Hot Springs

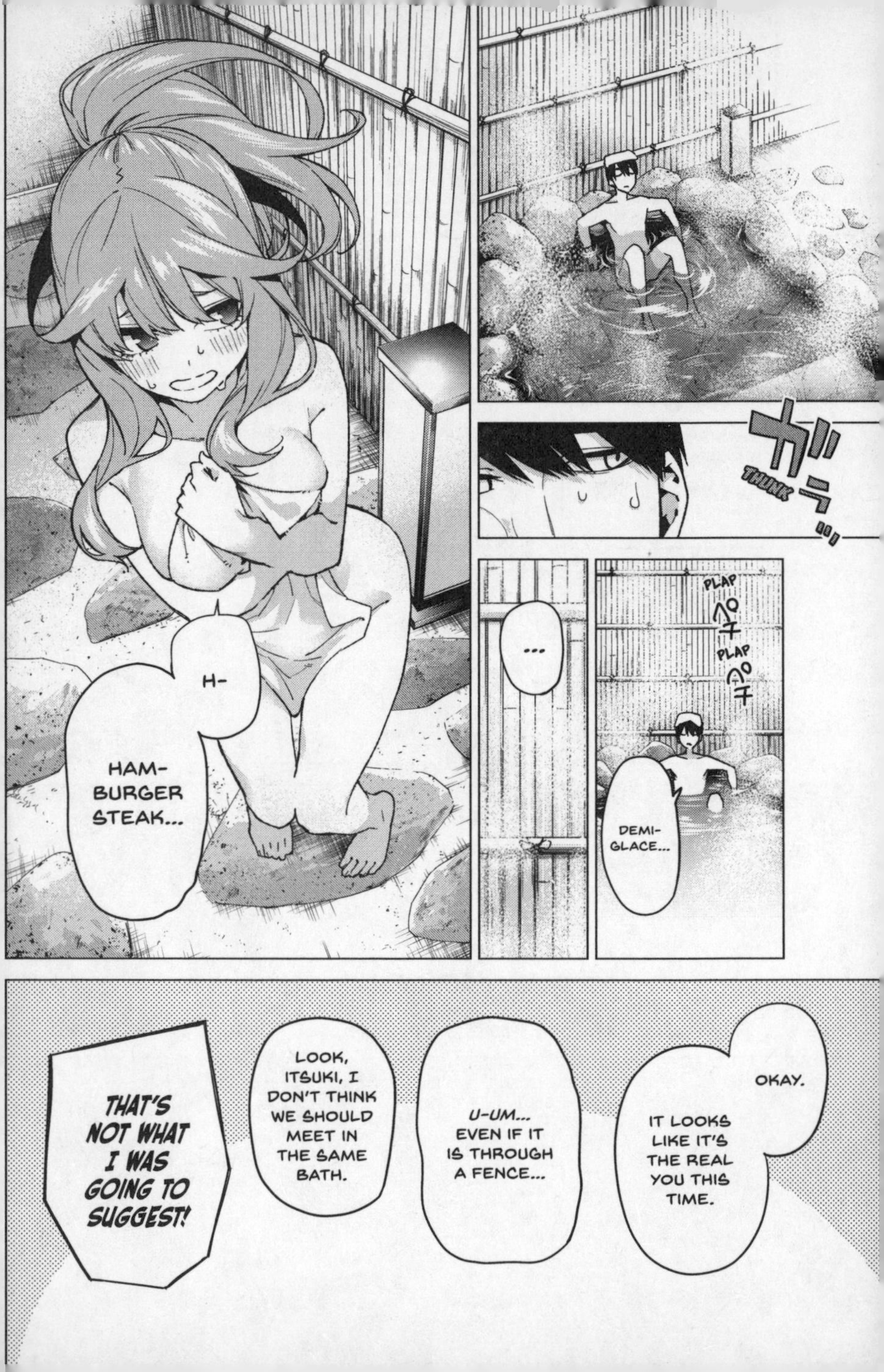
THUNK
PLAP
PLAP
DEMI-GLACE...
...
H-
HAM-BURGER STEAK...
OKAY.
IT LOOKS LIKE IT'S THE REAL YOU THIS TIME.
U-UM... EVEN IF IT IS THROUGH A FENCE...
LOOK, ITSUKI, I DON'T THINK WE SHOULD MEET IN THE SAME BATH.
THAT'S NOT WHAT I WAS GOING TO SUGGEST!

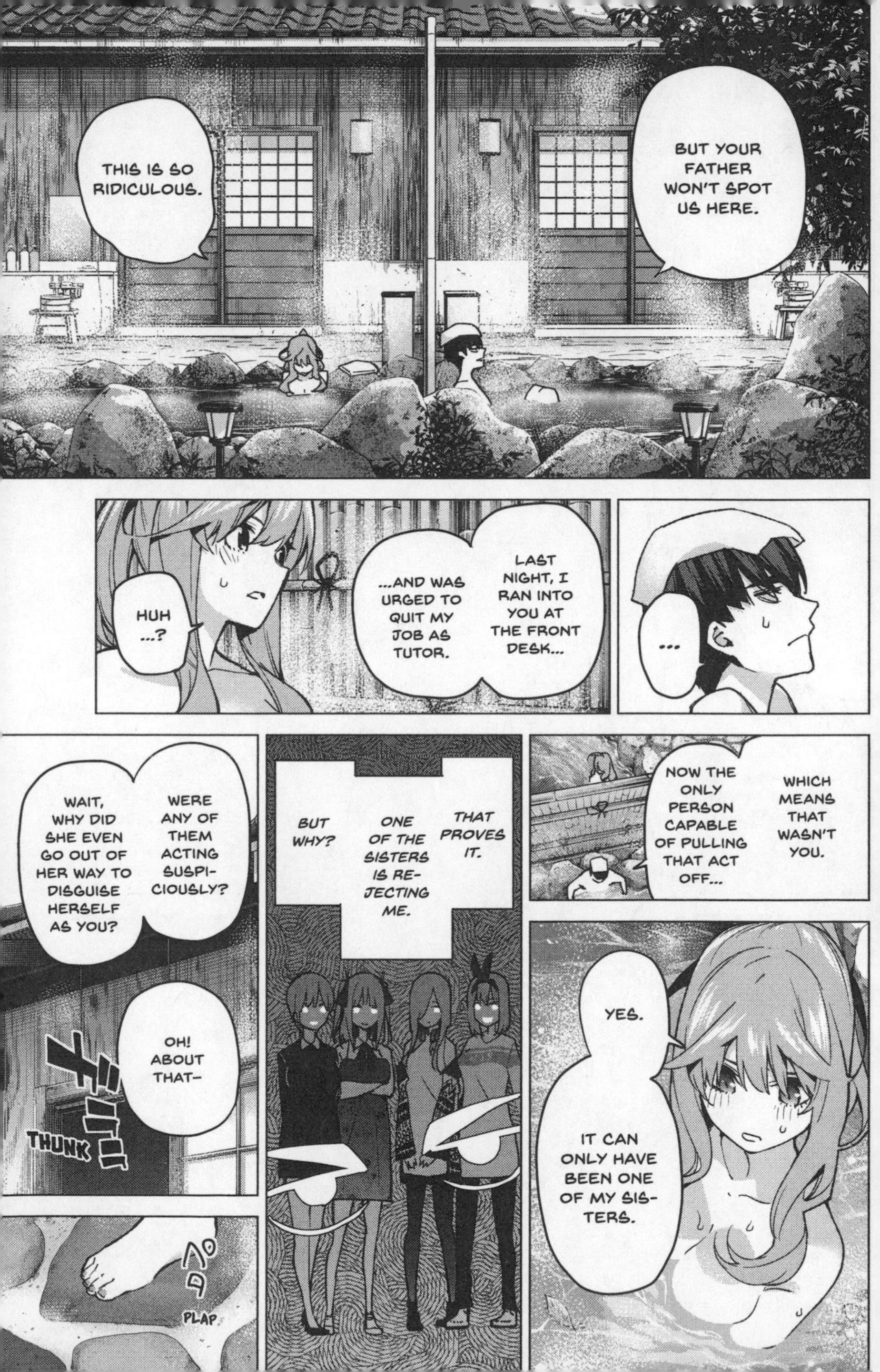
BUT YOUR FATHER WON'T SPOT US HERE.
THIS IS SO RIDICULOUS.
...
LAST NIGHT, I RAN INTO YOU AT THE FRONT DESK...
...AND WAS URGED TO QUIT MY JOB AS TUTOR.
HUH ...?
WHICH MEANS THAT WASN'T YOU.
NOW THE ONLY PERSON CAPABLE OF PULLING THAT ACT OFF...
YES.
IT CAN ONLY HAVE BEEN ONE OF MY SISTERS.
THAT PROVES IT.
ONE OF THE SISTERS IS REJECTING ME.
BUT WHY?
WERE ANY OF THEM ACTING SUSPICIOUSLY?
WAIT, WHY DID SHE EVEN GO OUT OF HER WAY TO DISGUISE HERSELF AS YOU?
OH! ABOUT THAT–
THUNK
PLAP

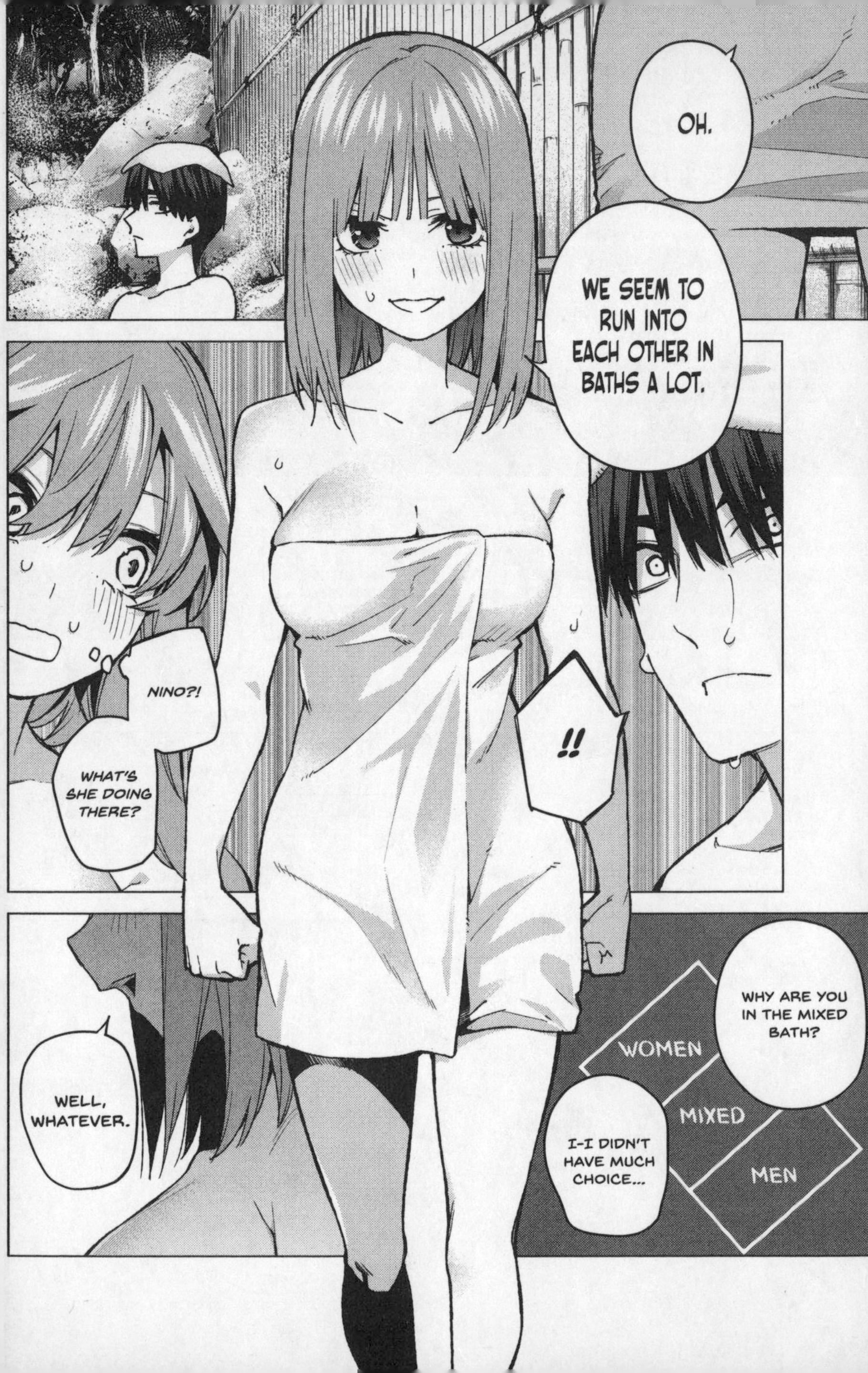
OH.
WE SEEM TO RUN INTO EACH OTHER IN BATHS A LOT.
!!
NINO?!
WHAT'S SHE DOING THERE?
WHY ARE YOU IN THE MIXED BATH?
WOMEN
MIXED
MEN
I-I DIDN'T HAVE MUCH CHOICE...
WELL, WHATEVER.

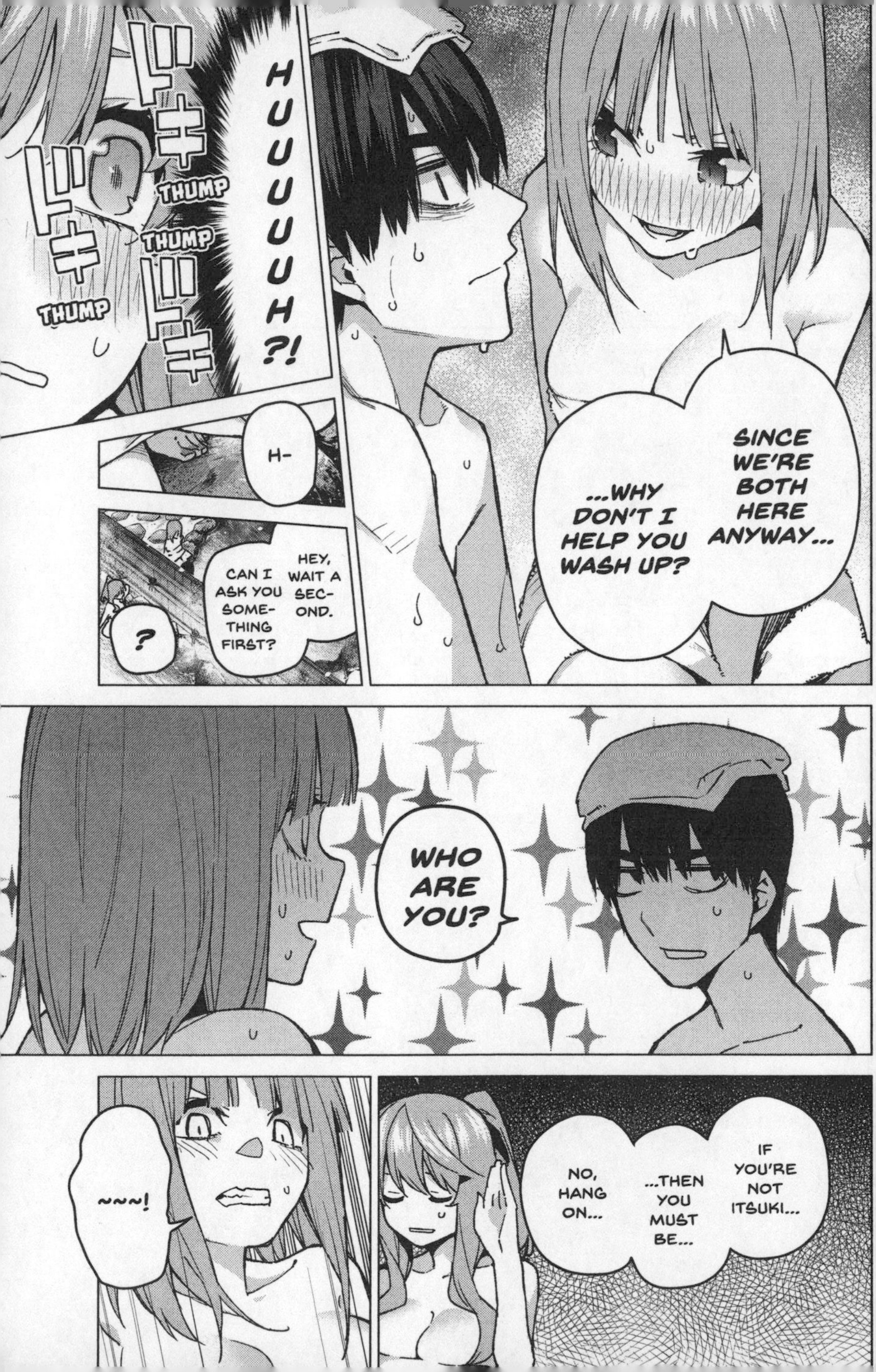
SINCE WE'RE BOTH HERE ANYWAY...
...WHY DON'T I HELP YOU WASH UP?
HUUUUUUUH?!
THUMP
THUMP
THUMP
H-
HEY, WAIT A SEC-OND.
CAN I ASK YOU SOME-THING FIRST?
?
WHO ARE YOU?
IF YOU'RE NOT ITSUKI...
...THEN YOU MUST BE...
NO, HANG ON...
~~~!
~~~

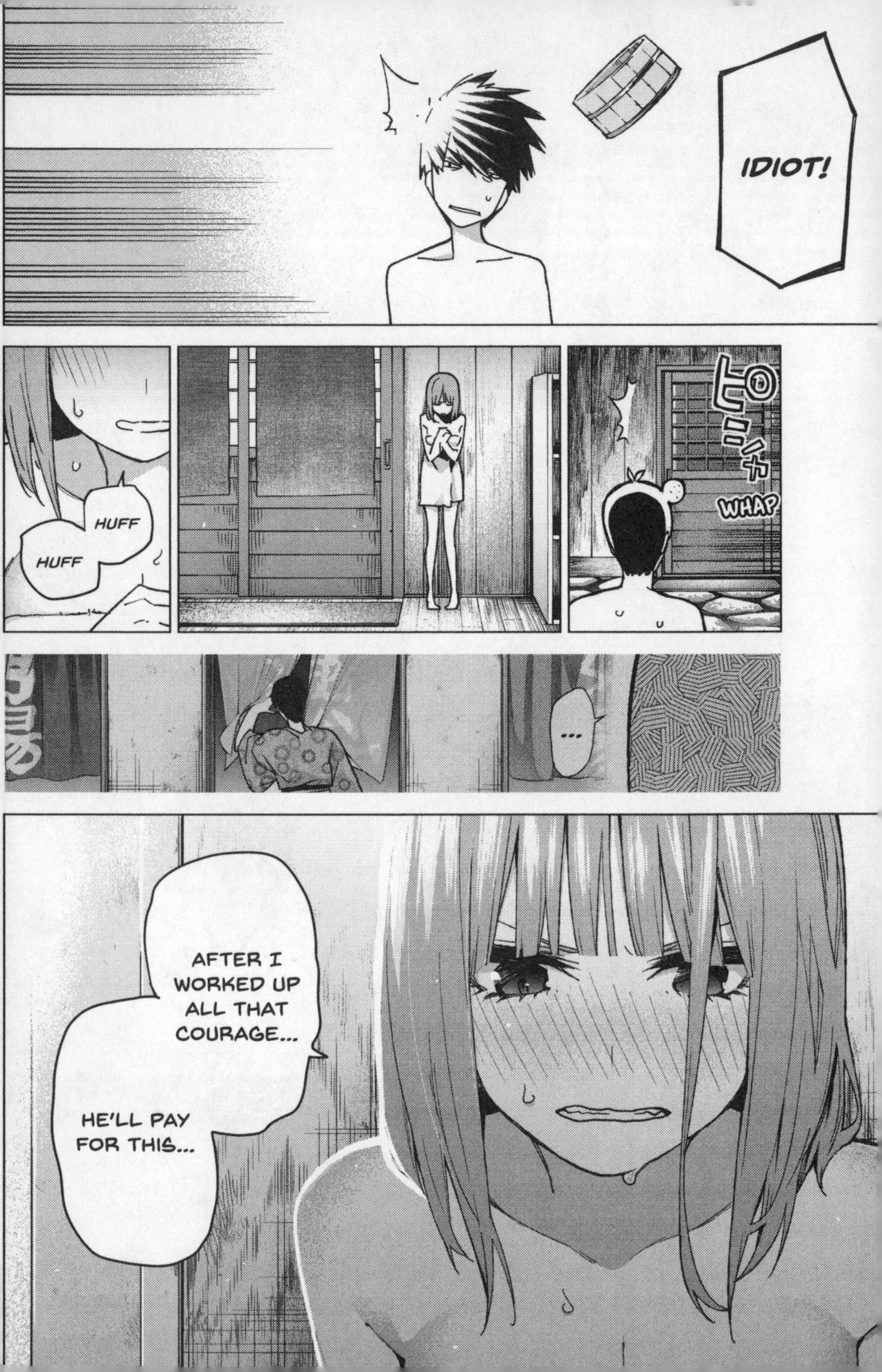
IDIOT!
ピシャ
WHAP
HUFF
HUFF
...
AFTER I WORKED UP ALL THAT COURAGE...
HE'LL PAY FOR THIS...

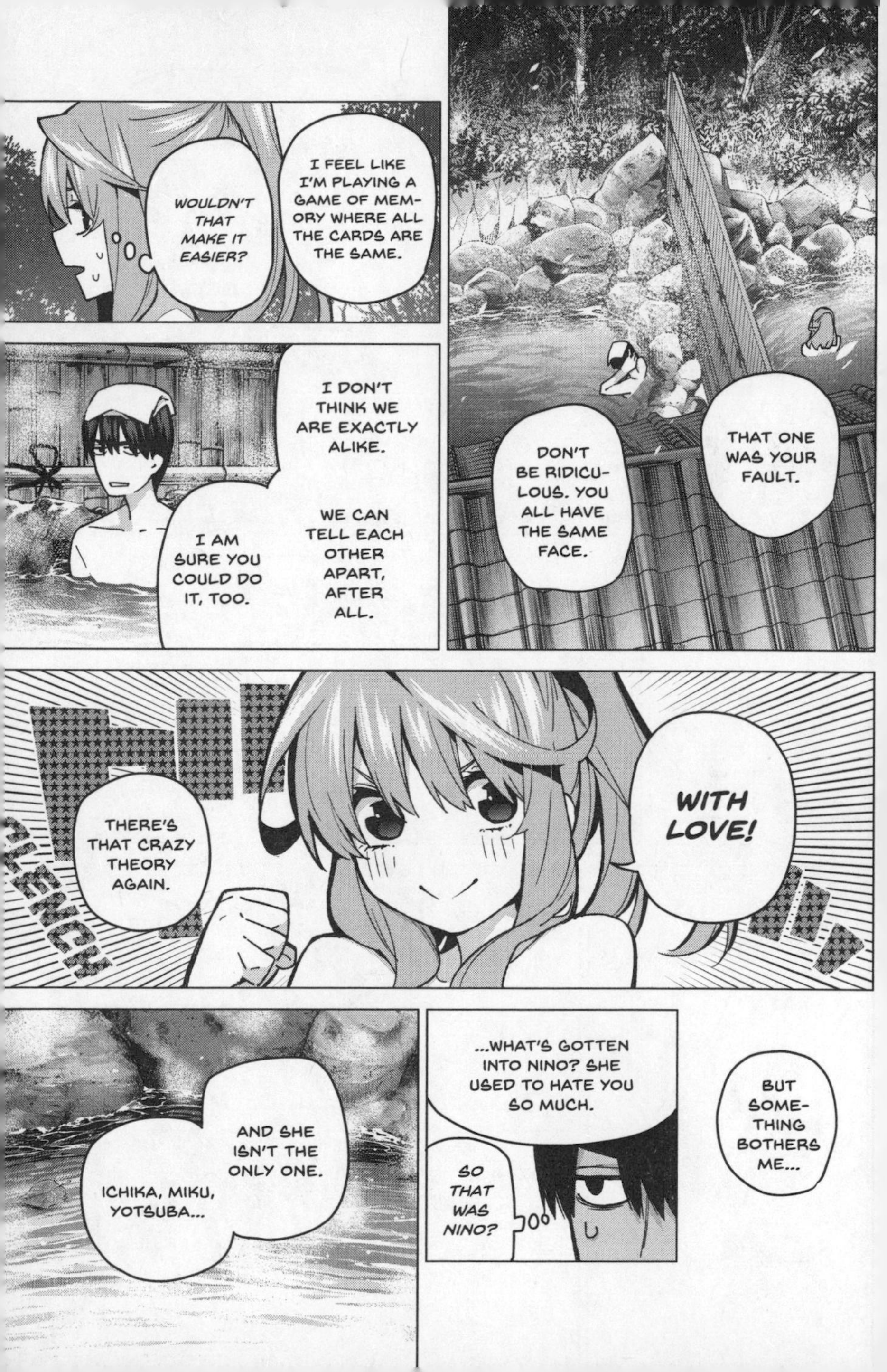
THAT ONE WAS YOUR FAULT.
DON'T BE RIDICULOUS. YOU ALL HAVE THE SAME FACE.
I FEEL LIKE I'M PLAYING A GAME OF MEMORY WHERE ALL THE CARDS ARE THE SAME.
WOULDN'T THAT MAKE IT EASIER?
I DON'T THINK WE ARE EXACTLY ALIKE.
WE CAN TELL EACH OTHER APART, AFTER ALL.
I AM SURE YOU COULD DO IT, TOO.
WITH LOVE!
THERE'S THAT CRAZY THEORY AGAIN.
BUT SOMETHING BOTHERS ME...
...WHAT'S GOTTEN INTO NINO? SHE USED TO HATE YOU SO MUCH.
SO THAT WAS NINO?
AND SHE ISN'T THE ONLY ONE.
ICHIKA, MIKU, YOTSUBA...

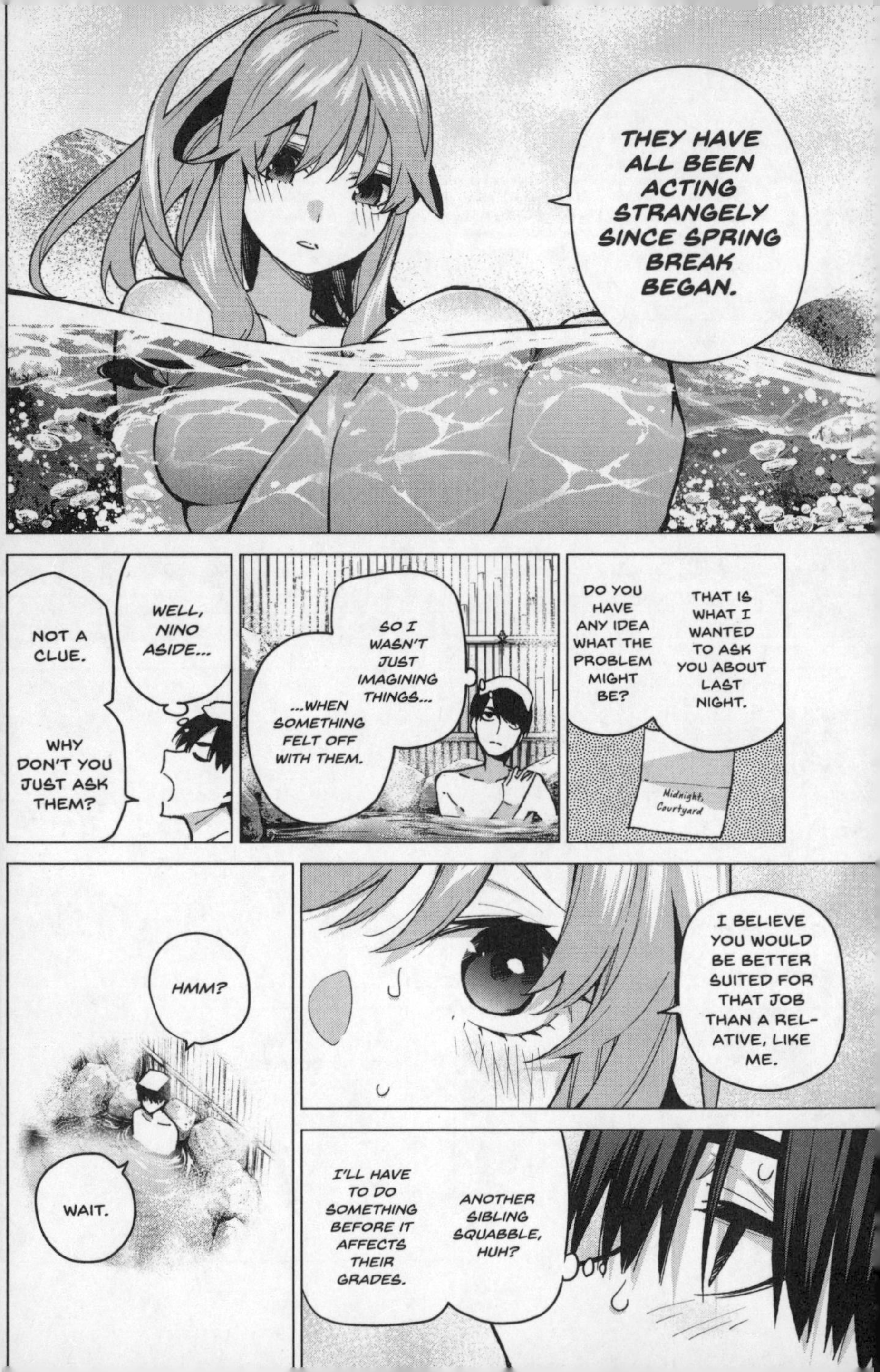
THEY HAVE ALL BEEN ACTING STRANGELY SINCE SPRING BREAK BEGAN.
THAT IS WHAT I WANTED TO ASK YOU ABOUT LAST NIGHT.
DO YOU HAVE ANY IDEA WHAT THE PROBLEM MIGHT BE?
Midnight, Courtyard
SO I WASN'T JUST IMAGINING THINGS...
...WHEN SOMETHING FELT OFF WITH THEM.
WELL, NINO ASIDE...
NOT A CLUE.
WHY DON'T YOU JUST ASK THEM?
I BELIEVE YOU WOULD BE BETTER SUITED FOR THAT JOB THAN A REL-ATIVE, LIKE ME.
ANOTHER SIBLING SQUABBLE, HUH?
I'LL HAVE TO DO SOMETHING BEFORE IT AFFECTS THEIR GRADES.
HMM?
WAIT.

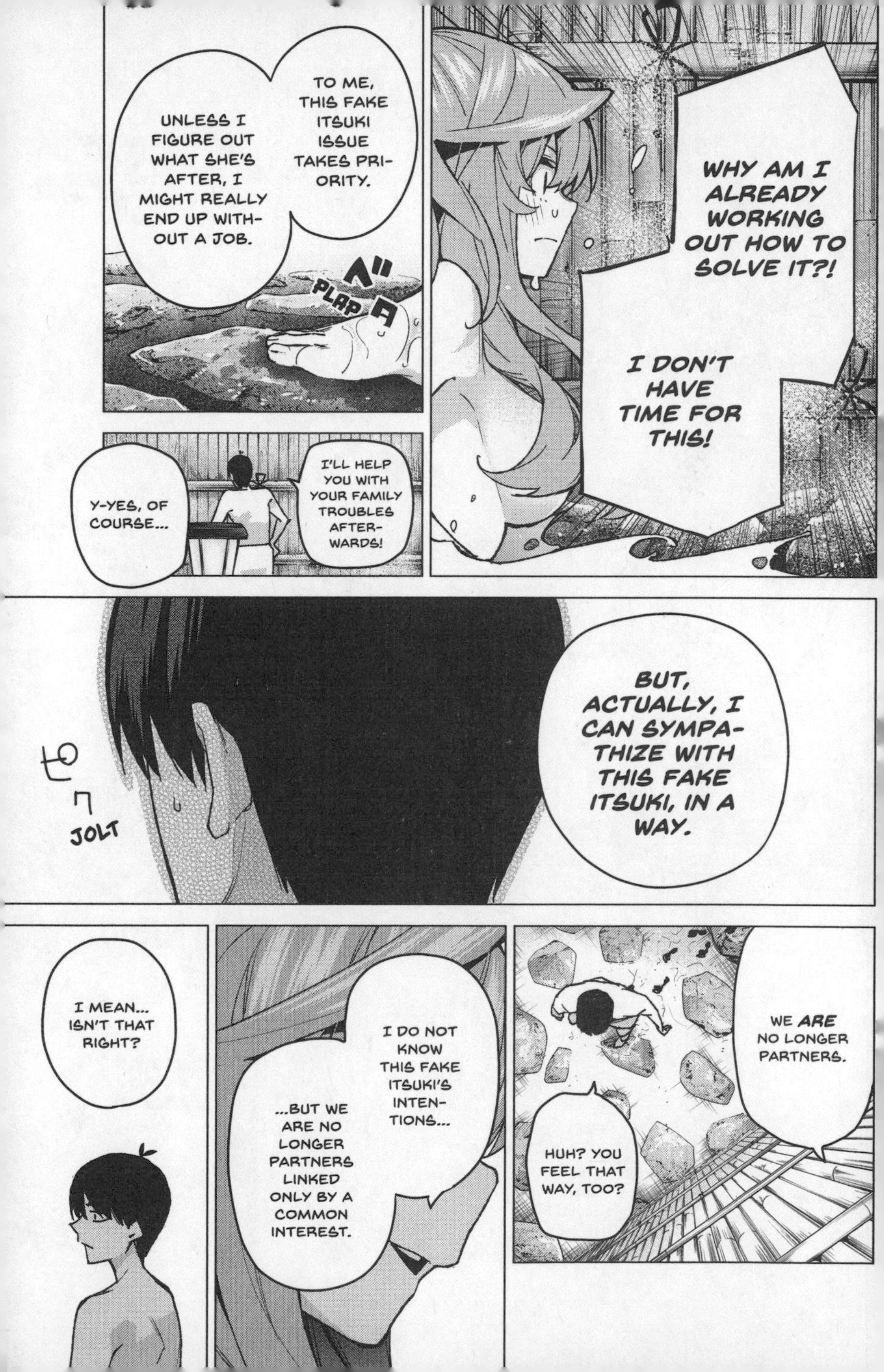
WHY AM I ALREADY WORKING OUT HOW TO SOLVE IT?!
I DON'T HAVE TIME FOR THIS!
TO ME, THIS FAKE ITSUKI ISSUE TAKES PRIORITY.
UNLESS I FIGURE OUT WHAT SHE'S AFTER, I MIGHT REALLY END UP WITHOUT A JOB.
PLAP
I'LL HELP YOU WITH YOUR FAMILY TROUBLES AFTERWARDS!
Y-YES, OF COURSE...
BUT, ACTUALLY, I CAN SYMPATHIZE WITH THIS FAKE ITSUKI, IN A WAY.
JOLT
WE ARE NO LONGER PARTNERS.
HUH? YOU FEEL THAT WAY, TOO?
I DO NOT KNOW THIS FAKE ITSUKI'S INTENTIONS...
...BUT WE ARE NO LONGER PARTNERS LINKED ONLY BY A COMMON INTEREST.
I MEAN... ISN'T THAT RIGHT?

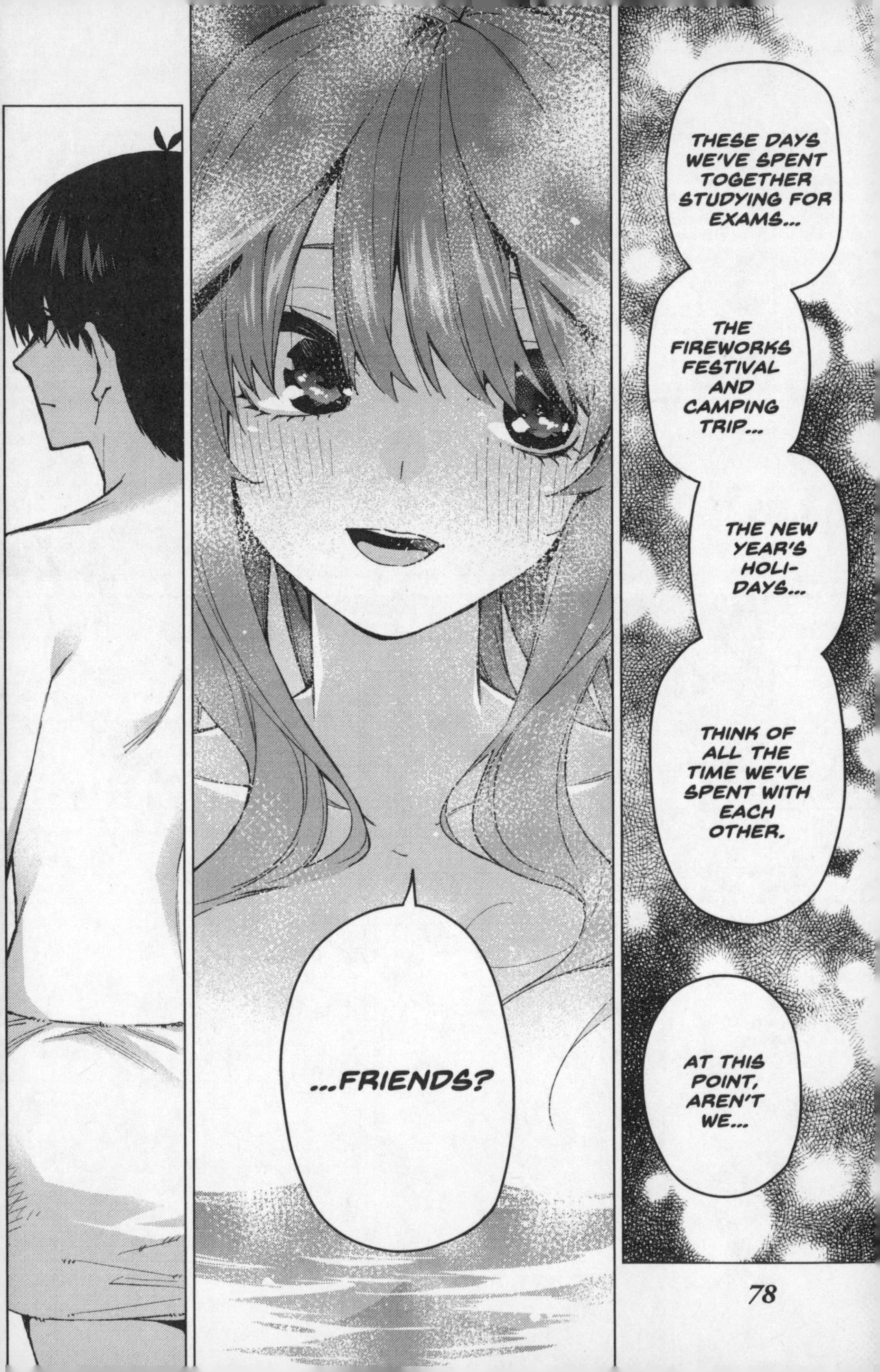

THESE DAYS WE'VE SPENT TOGETHER STUDYING FOR EXAMS...
THE FIREWORKS FESTIVAL AND CAMPING TRIP...
THE NEW YEAR'S HOLI-DAYS...
THINK OF ALL THE TIME WE'VE SPENT WITH EACH OTHER.
AT THIS POINT, AREN'T WE...
...FRIENDS?

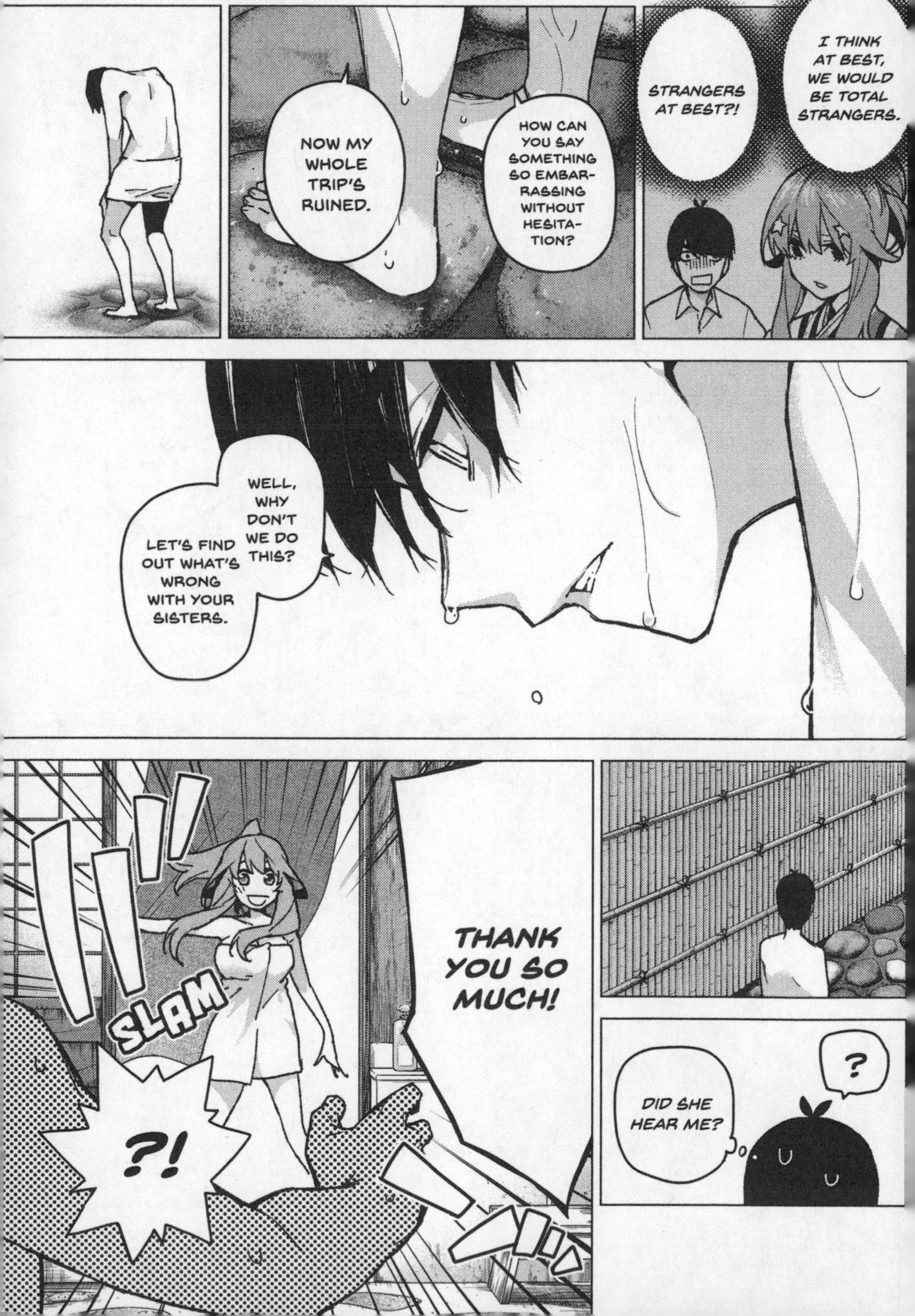
I THINK AT BEST, WE WOULD BE TOTAL STRANGERS.
STRANGERS AT BEST?!
HOW CAN YOU SAY SOMETHING SO EMBARRASSING WITHOUT HESITATION?
NOW MY WHOLE TRIP'S RUINED.
WELL, WHY DON'T WE DO THIS?
LET'S FIND OUT WHAT'S WRONG WITH YOUR SISTERS.
?
DID SHE HEAR ME?
THANK YOU SO MUCH!
SLAM
?!

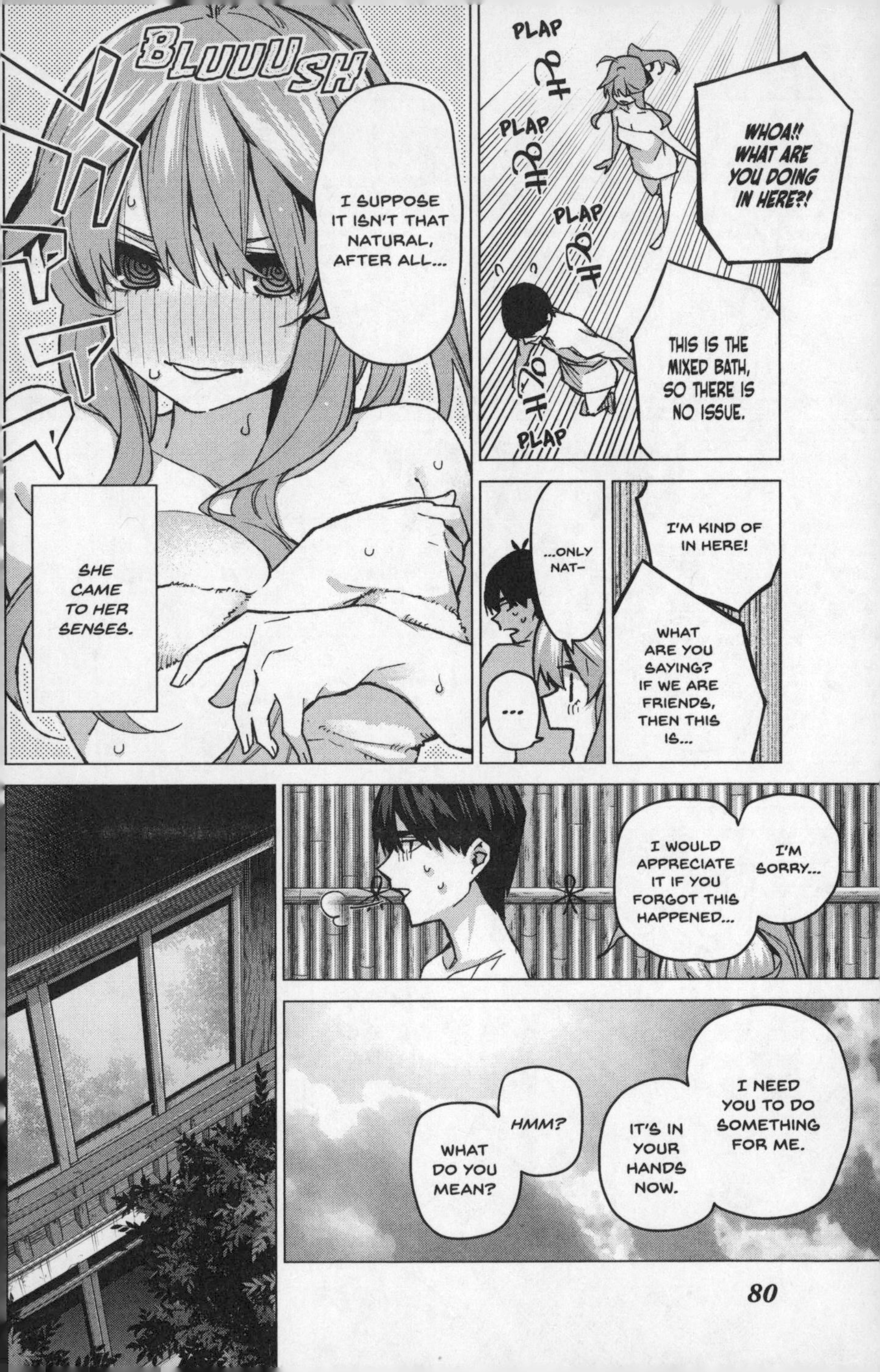
PLAP
PLAP
PLAP
PLAP
WHOA!! WHAT ARE YOU DOING IN HERE?!
THIS IS THE MIXED BATH, SO THERE IS NO ISSUE.
I'M KIND OF IN HERE!
WHAT ARE YOU SAYING? IF WE ARE FRIENDS, THEN THIS IS...
...ONLY NAT-
...
BLUUUSH
I SUPPOSE IT ISN'T THAT NATURAL, AFTER ALL...
SHE CAME TO HER SENSES.
I'M SORRY...
I WOULD APPRECIATE IT IF YOU FORGOT THIS HAPPENED...
I NEED YOU TO DO SOMETHING FOR ME.
IT'S IN YOUR HANDS NOW.
HMM?
WHAT DO YOU MEAN?

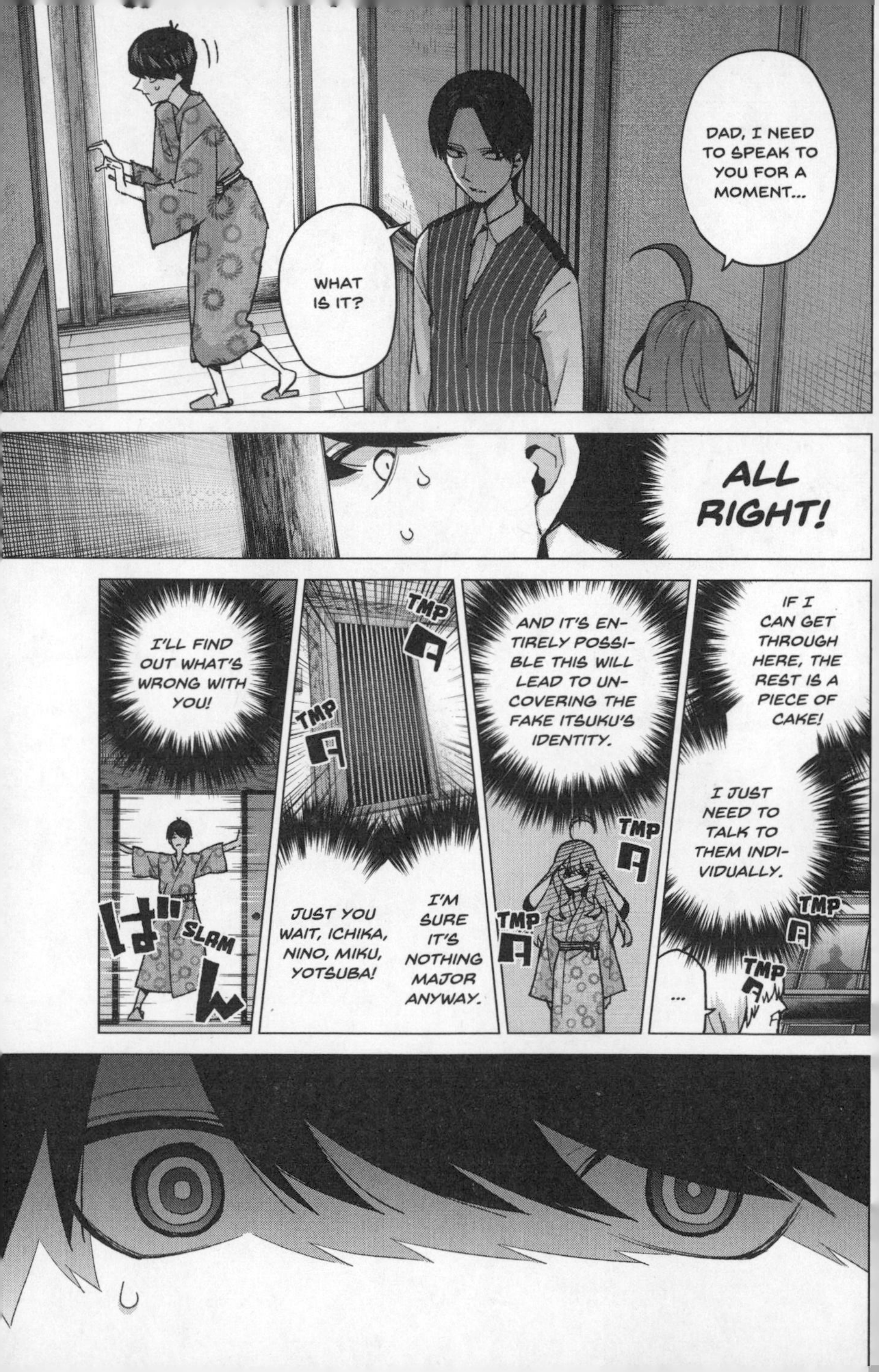
DAD, I NEED TO SPEAK TO YOU FOR A MOMENT...
WHAT IS IT?
ALL RIGHT!
IF I CAN GET THROUGH HERE, THE REST IS A PIECE OF CAKE!
I JUST NEED TO TALK TO THEM INDIVIDUALLY.
TMP
TMP
...
AND IT'S ENTIRELY POSSIBLE THIS WILL LEAD TO UNCOVERING THE FAKE ITSUKU'S IDENTITY.
TMP
TMP
TMP
TMP
I'M SURE IT'S NOTHING MAJOR ANYWAY.
JUST YOU WAIT, ICHIKA, NINO, MIKU, YOTSUBA!
I'LL FIND OUT WHAT'S WRONG WITH YOU!
SLAM

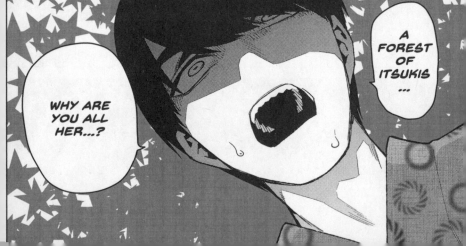

A FOREST OF ITSUKIS ...

WHY ARE YOU ALL HER...?

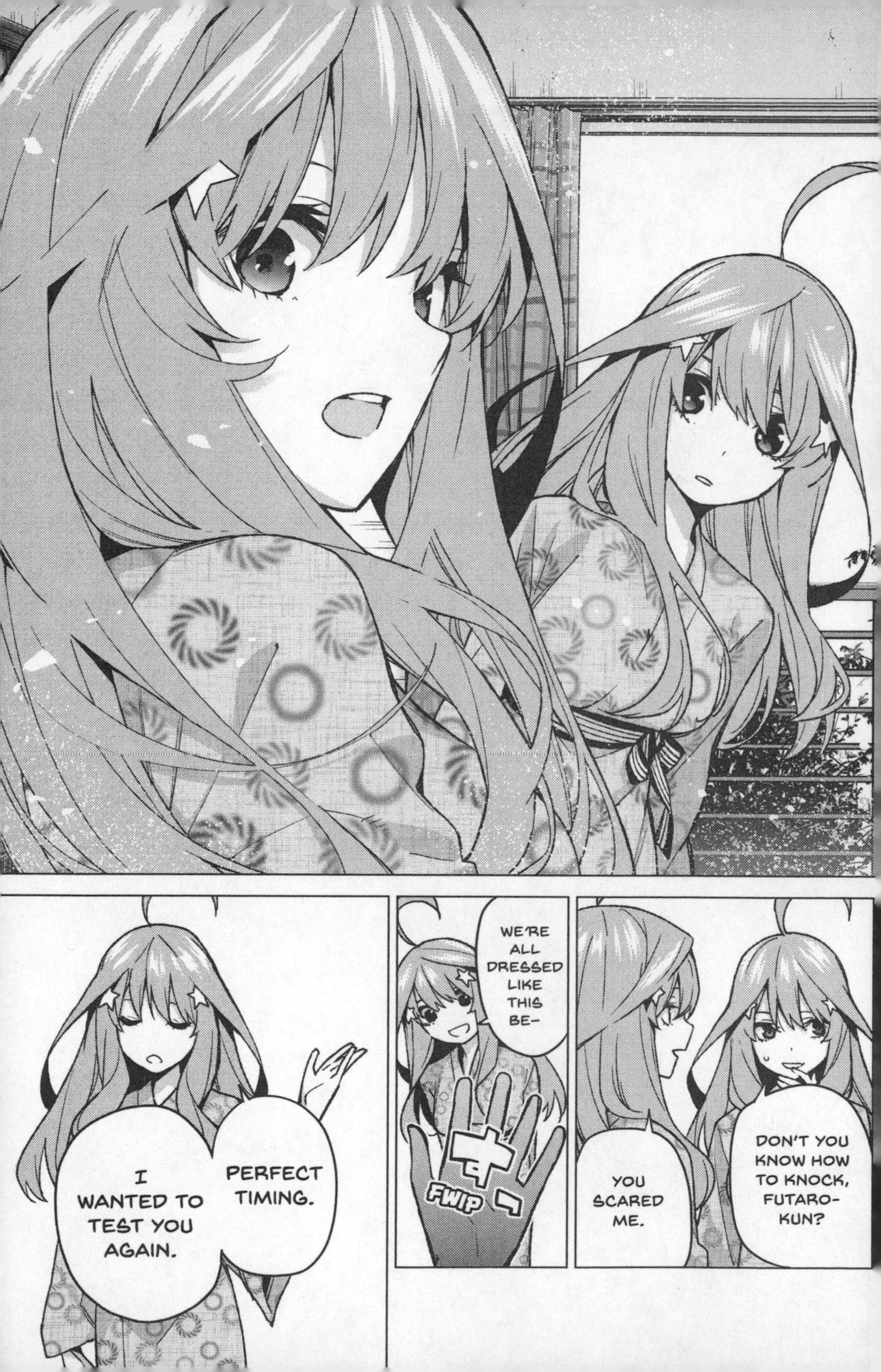
DON'T YOU KNOW HOW TO KNOCK, FUTARO-KUN?
YOU SCARED ME.
WE'RE ALL DRESSED LIKE THIS BE-
FWIP
PERFECT TIMING.
I WANTED TO TEST YOU AGAIN.

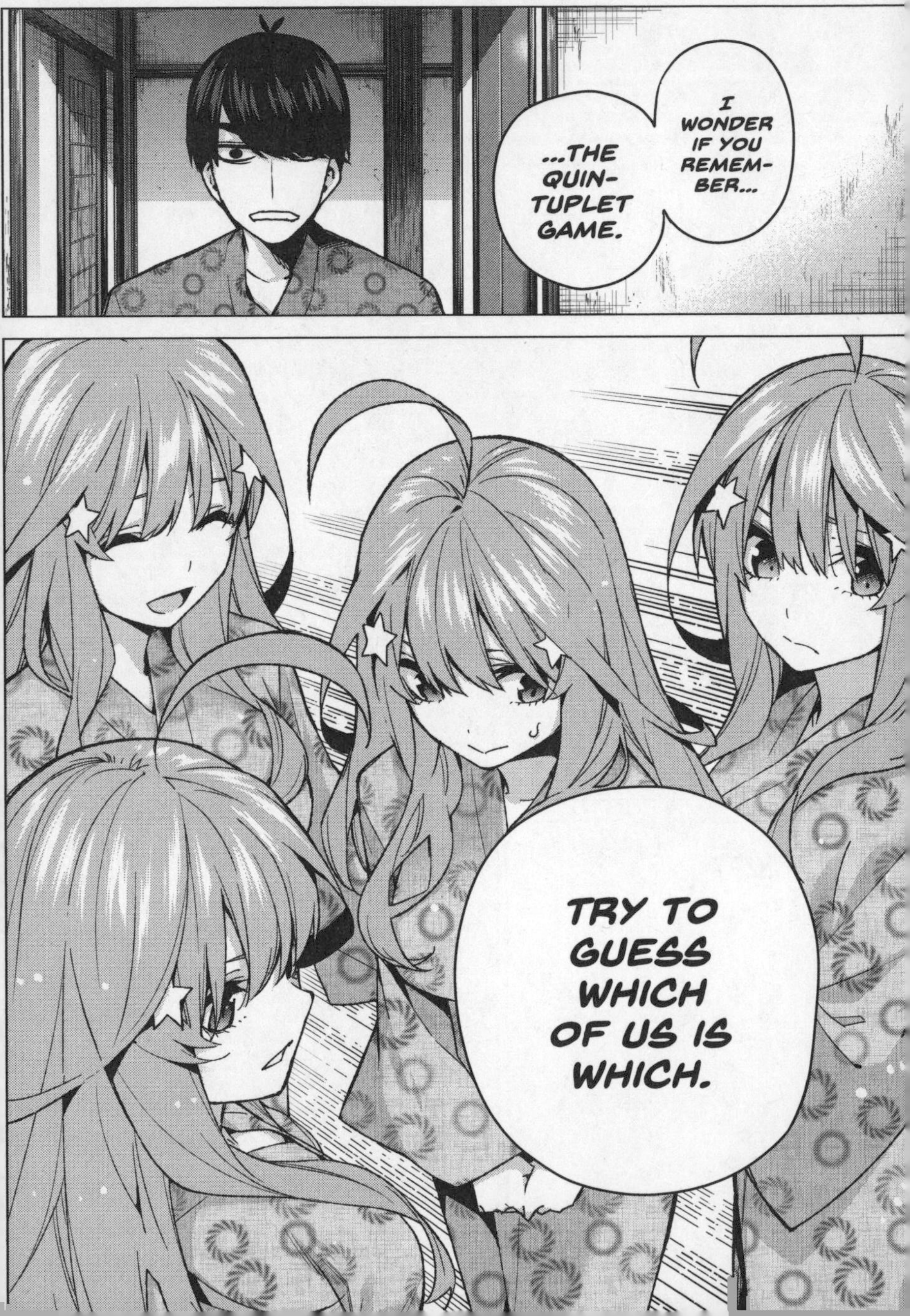
I WONDER IF YOU REMEMBER...
...THE QUINTUPLET GAME.
TRY TO GUESS WHICH OF US IS WHICH.

CHAPTER 64
SCRAMBLED EGGS ④

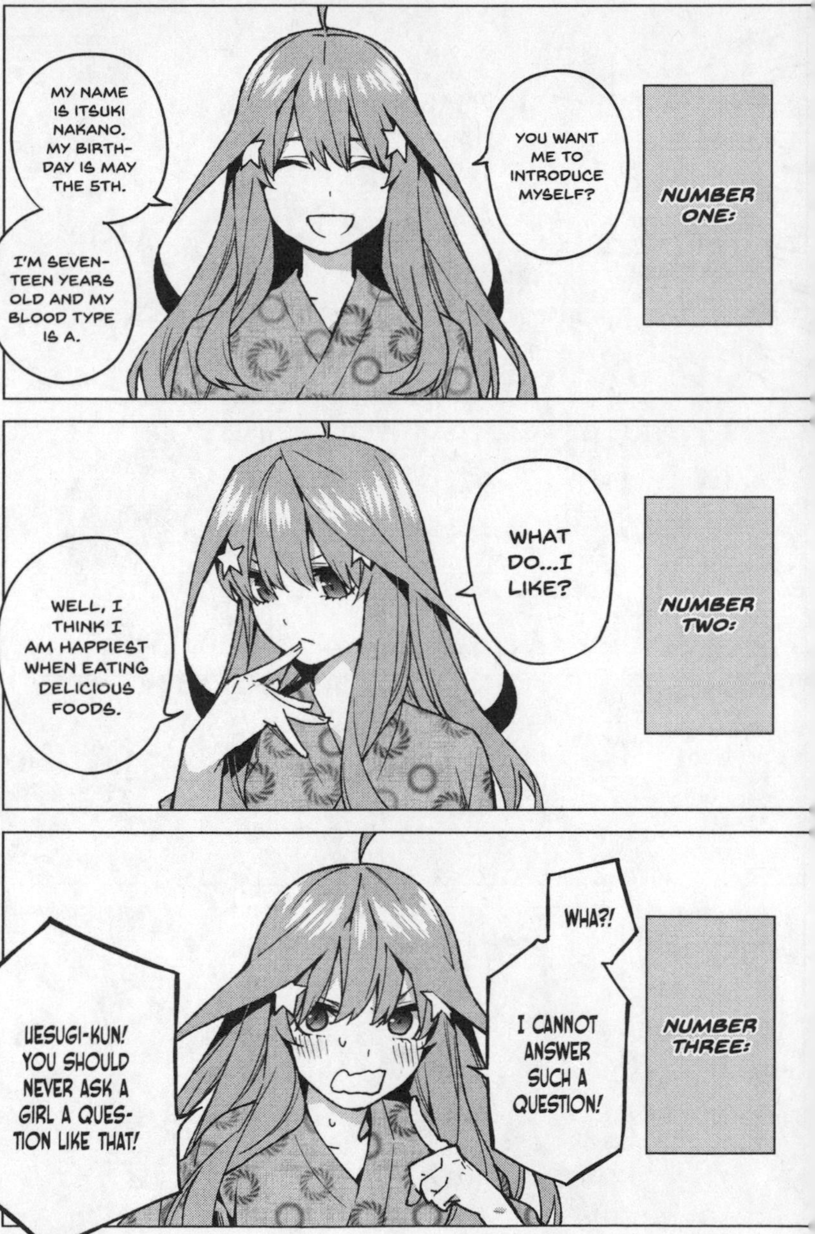

NUMBER ONE:
YOU WANT ME TO INTRODUCE MYSELF?
MY NAME IS ITSUKI NAKANO. MY BIRTH-DAY IS MAY THE 5TH.
I'M SEVEN-TEEN YEARS OLD AND MY BLOOD TYPE IS A.
NUMBER TWO:
WHAT DO...I LIKE?
WELL, I THINK I AM HAPPIEST WHEN EATING DELICIOUS FOODS.
NUMBER THREE:
WHA?!
I CANNOT ANSWER SUCH A QUESTION!
UESUGI-KUN! YOU SHOULD NEVER ASK A GIRL A QUES-TION LIKE THAT!

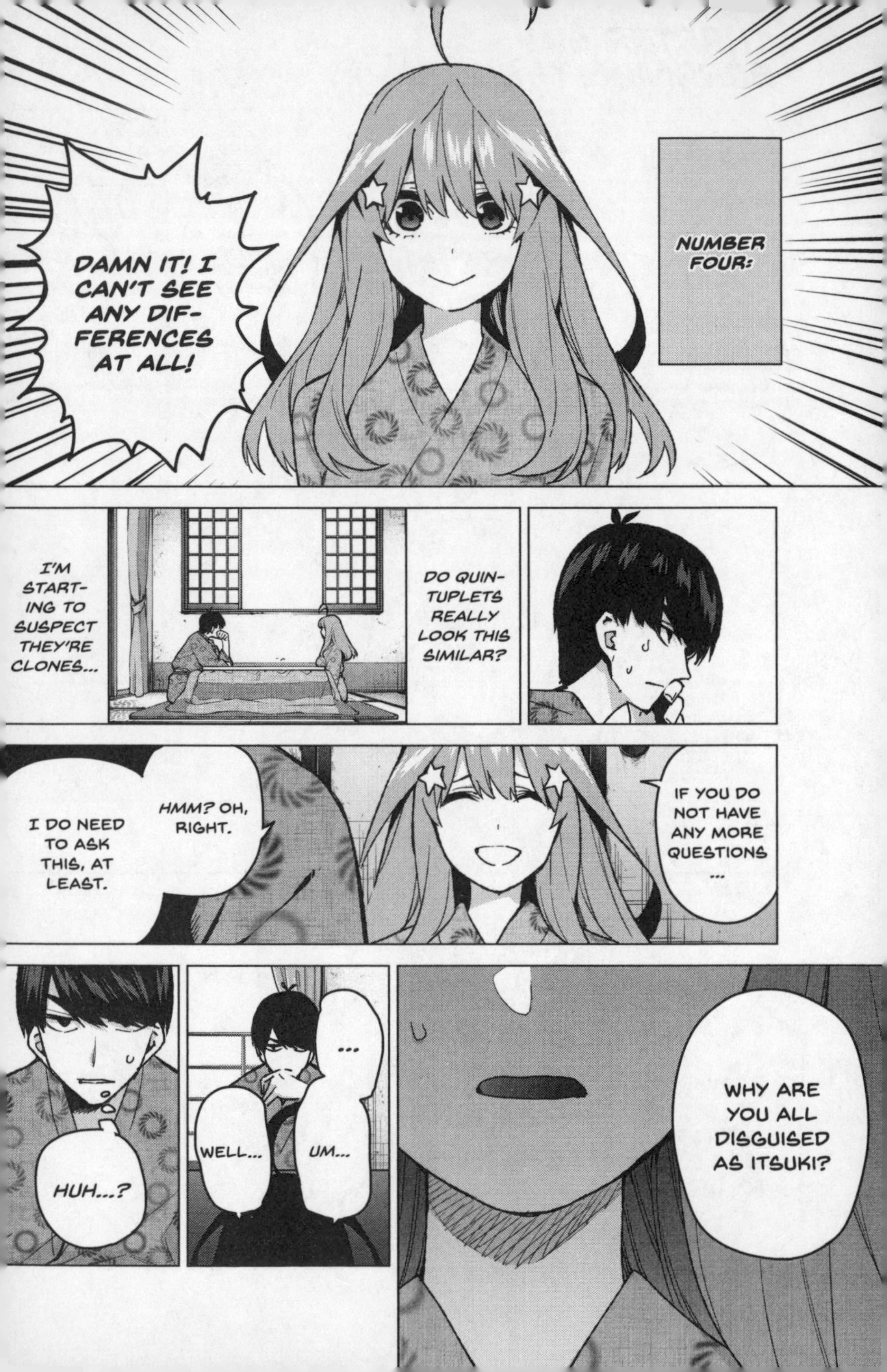
NUMBER FOUR:
DAMN IT! I CAN'T SEE ANY DIF-FERENCES AT ALL!
DO QUIN-TUPLETS REALLY LOOK THIS SIMILAR?
I'M START-ING TO SUSPECT THEY'RE CLONES...
IF YOU DO NOT HAVE ANY MORE QUESTIONS ...
HMM? OH, RIGHT.
I DO NEED TO ASK THIS, AT LEAST.
WHY ARE YOU ALL DISGUISED AS ITSUKI?
...
UM...
WELL...
HUH...?

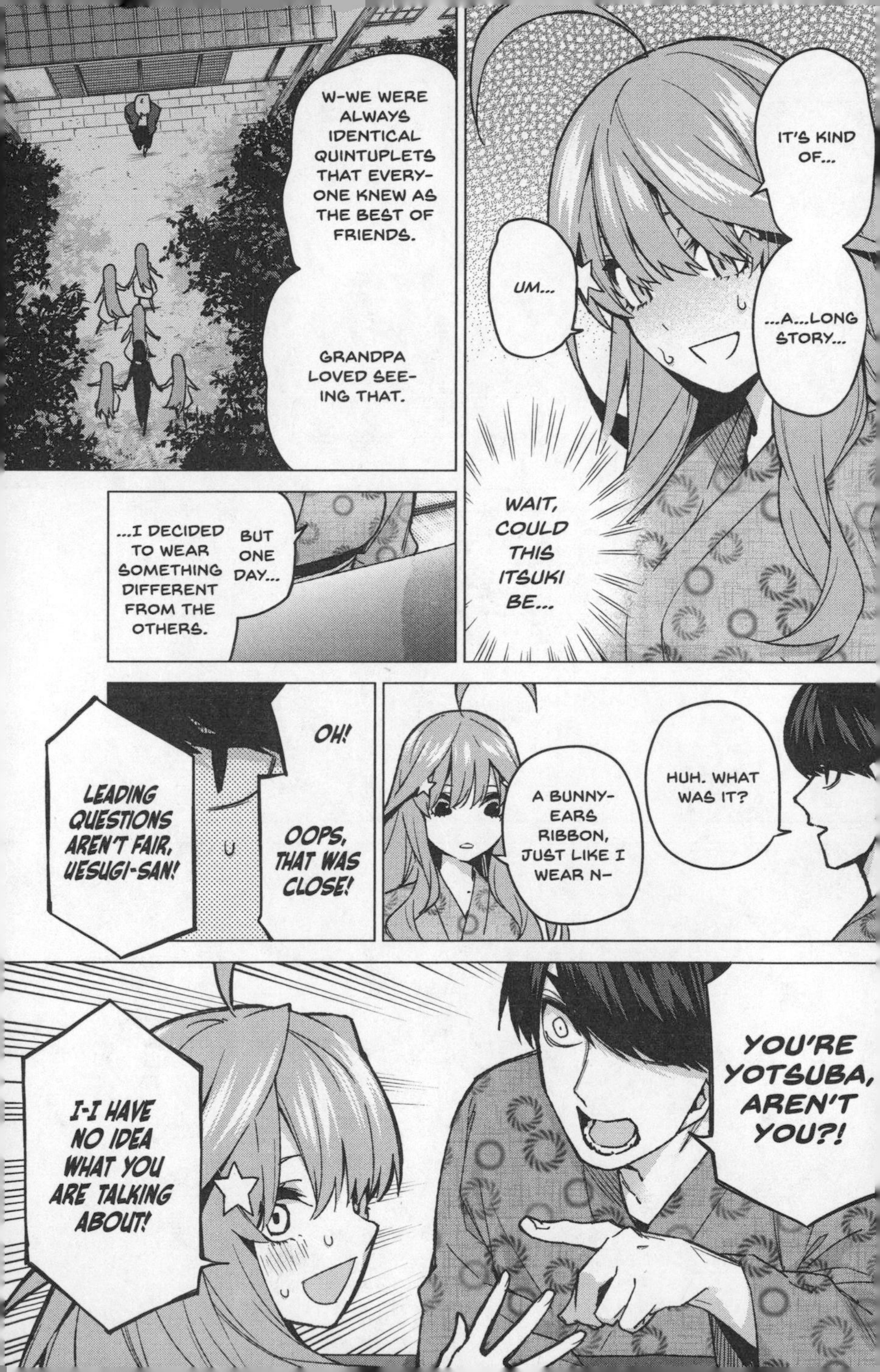
UM...
IT'S KIND OF...
...A...LONG STORY...
WAIT, COULD THIS ITSUKI BE...
W-WE WERE ALWAYS IDENTICAL QUINTUPLETS THAT EVERY-ONE KNEW AS THE BEST OF FRIENDS.
GRANDPA LOVED SEE-ING THAT.
BUT ONE DAY...
...I DECIDED TO WEAR SOMETHING DIFFERENT FROM THE OTHERS.
HUH. WHAT WAS IT?
A BUNNY-EARS RIBBON, JUST LIKE I WEAR N-
OH!
OOPS, THAT WAS CLOSE!
LEADING QUESTIONS AREN'T FAIR, UESUGI-SAN!
YOU'RE YOTSUBA, AREN'T YOU?!
I-I HAVE NO IDEA WHAT YOU ARE TALKING ABOUT!

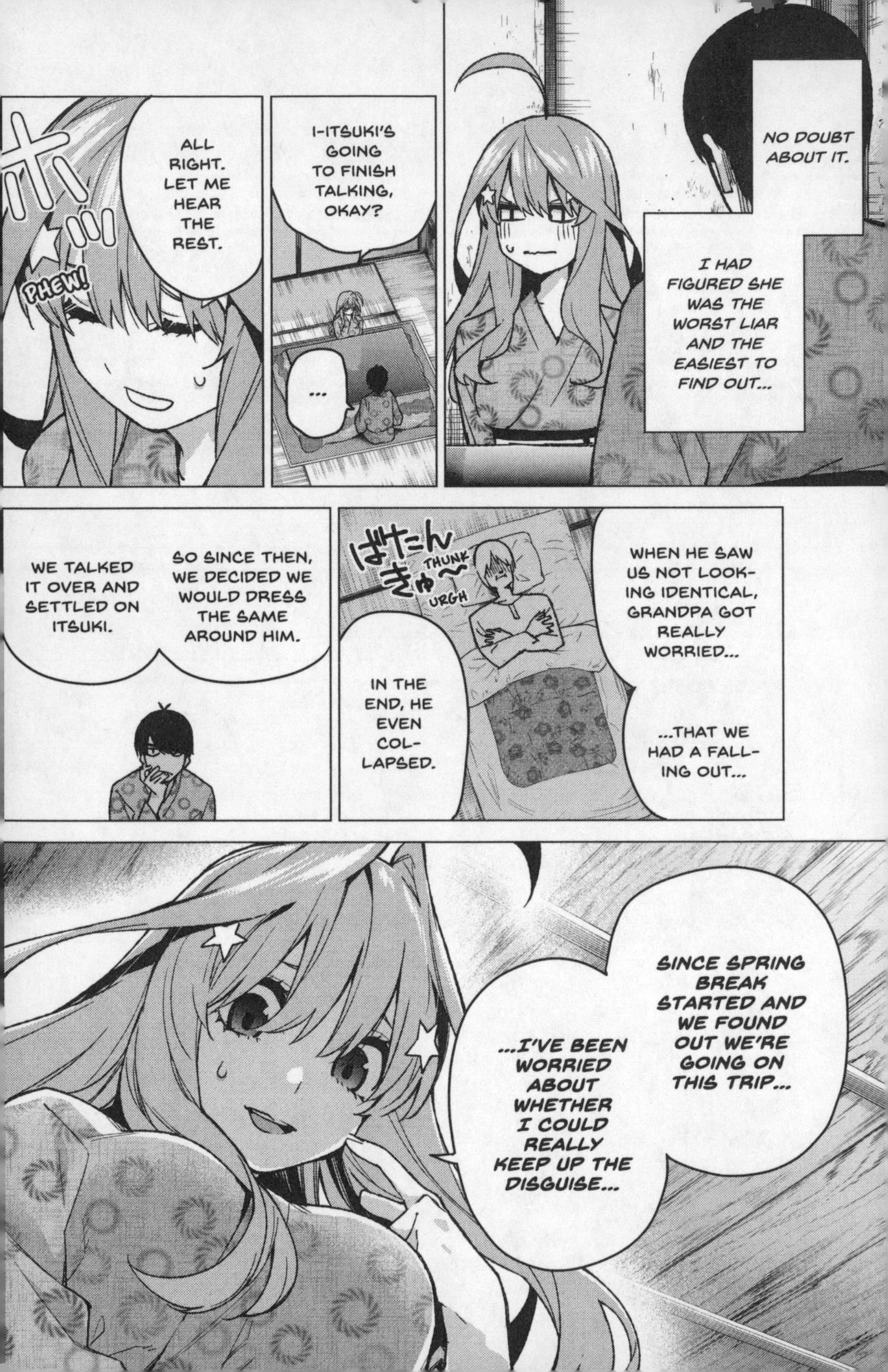
NO DOUBT ABOUT IT.
I HAD FIGURED SHE WAS THE WORST LIAR AND THE EASIEST TO FIND OUT...
I-ITSUKI'S GOING TO FINISH TALKING, OKAY?
...
ホッ
PHEW!
ALL RIGHT. LET ME HEAR THE REST.
WHEN HE SAW US NOT LOOKING IDENTICAL, GRANDPA GOT REALLY WORRIED...
...THAT WE HAD A FALLING OUT...
ばたん
THUNK
きゅ～
URGH
IN THE END, HE EVEN COLLAPSED.
SO SINCE THEN, WE DECIDED WE WOULD DRESS THE SAME AROUND HIM.
WE TALKED IT OVER AND SETTLED ON ITSUKI.
SINCE SPRING BREAK STARTED AND WE FOUND OUT WE'RE GOING ON THIS TRIP...
...I'VE BEEN WORRIED ABOUT WHETHER I COULD REALLY KEEP UP THE DISGUISE...

	1	2	3	4
Problem	?	?	?	DISGUISE
Fake Itsuki	?	?	?	X

I WAS RIGHT. IT WASN'T A BIG DEAL IN THE SLIGHTEST.

THIS MUST'VE BEEN THE REASON YOTSUBA SEEMED SO DISTANT.

THAT DROPS THE CHANCES OF YOTSUBA BEING THE FAKE ITSUKI PRETTY LOW.

!

SO YOU WERE WORRIED ABOUT THIS THE WHOLE TIME?

AH HA HA ...

EVERYONE SEEMED TO BE HAVING FUN, SO I COULDN'T BRING IT UP...

YOU'RE SOME GRANDKIDS IF YOU'RE WILLING TO DO ALL THAT FOR THAT SCARY OLD GUY.

NOT AT ALL!

HE'S A VERY KIND MAN.

I LOVE HIM.

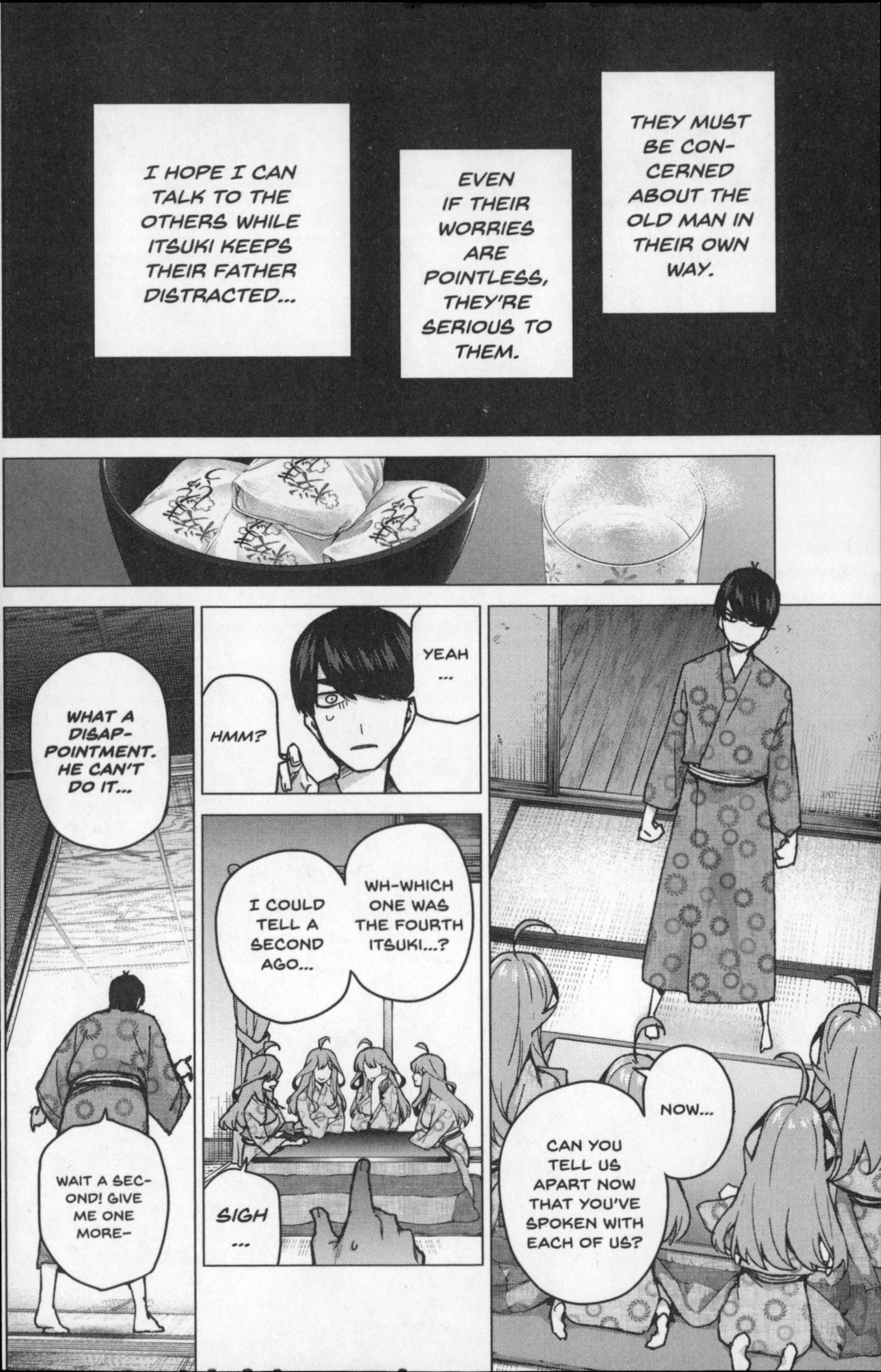
THEY MUST BE CON-CERNED ABOUT THE OLD MAN IN THEIR OWN WAY.
EVEN IF THEIR WORRIES ARE POINTLESS, THEY'RE SERIOUS TO THEM.
I HOPE I CAN TALK TO THE OTHERS WHILE ITSUKI KEEPS THEIR FATHER DISTRACTED...
NOW...
CAN YOU TELL US APART NOW THAT YOU'VE SPOKEN WITH EACH OF US?
YEAH...
HMM?
WH-WHICH ONE WAS THE FOURTH ITSUKI...?
I COULD TELL A SECOND AGO...
SIGH...
WHAT A DISAP-POINTMENT. HE CAN'T DO IT...
WAIT A SEC-OND! GIVE ME ONE MORE-

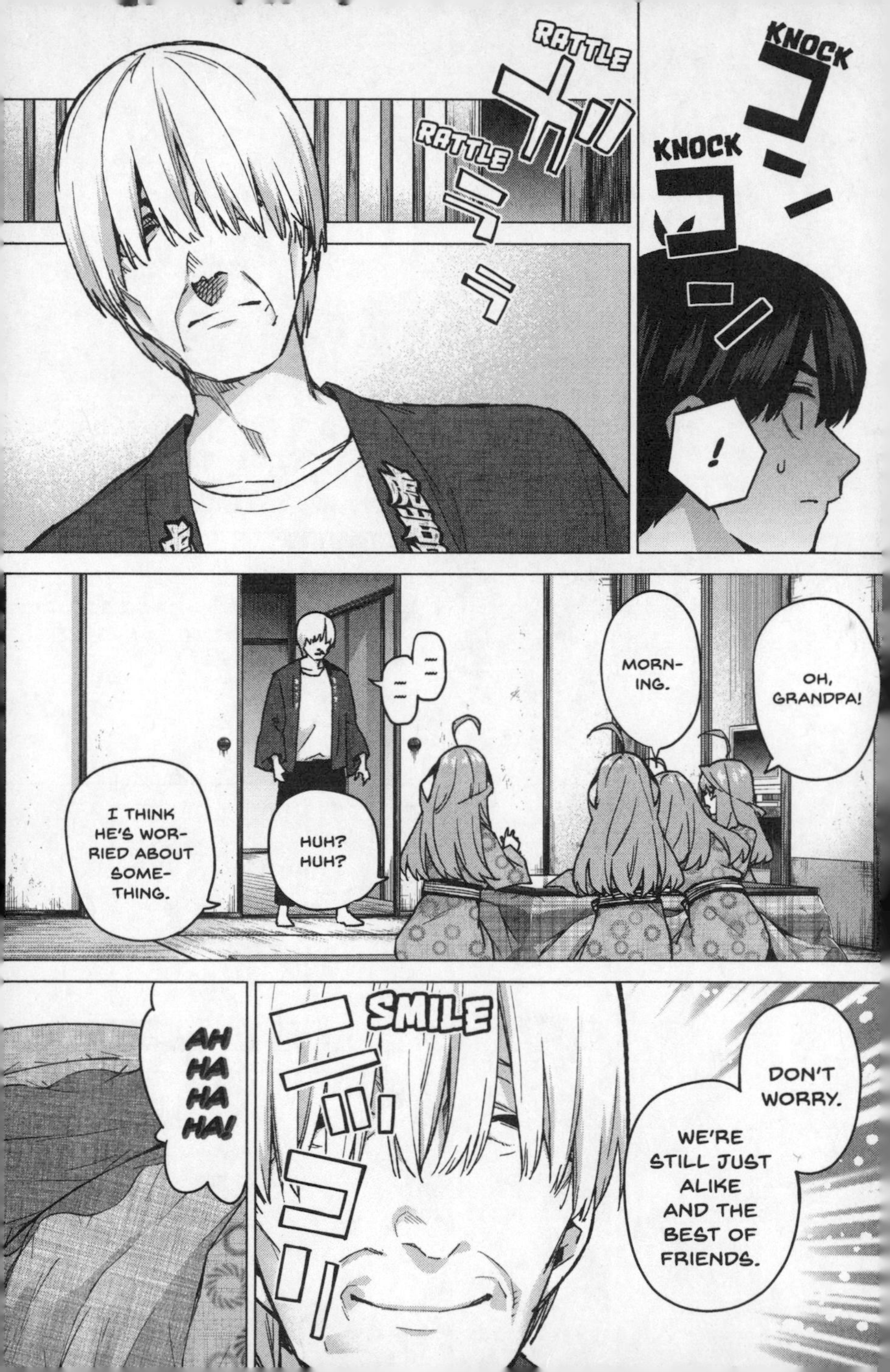
KNOCK
KNOCK
RATTLE
RATTLE
OH, GRANDPA!
MORN-ING.
HUH? HUH?
I THINK HE'S WOR-RIED ABOUT SOME-THING.
DON'T WORRY.
WE'RE STILL JUST ALIKE AND THE BEST OF FRIENDS.
SMILE
AH HA HA HA!

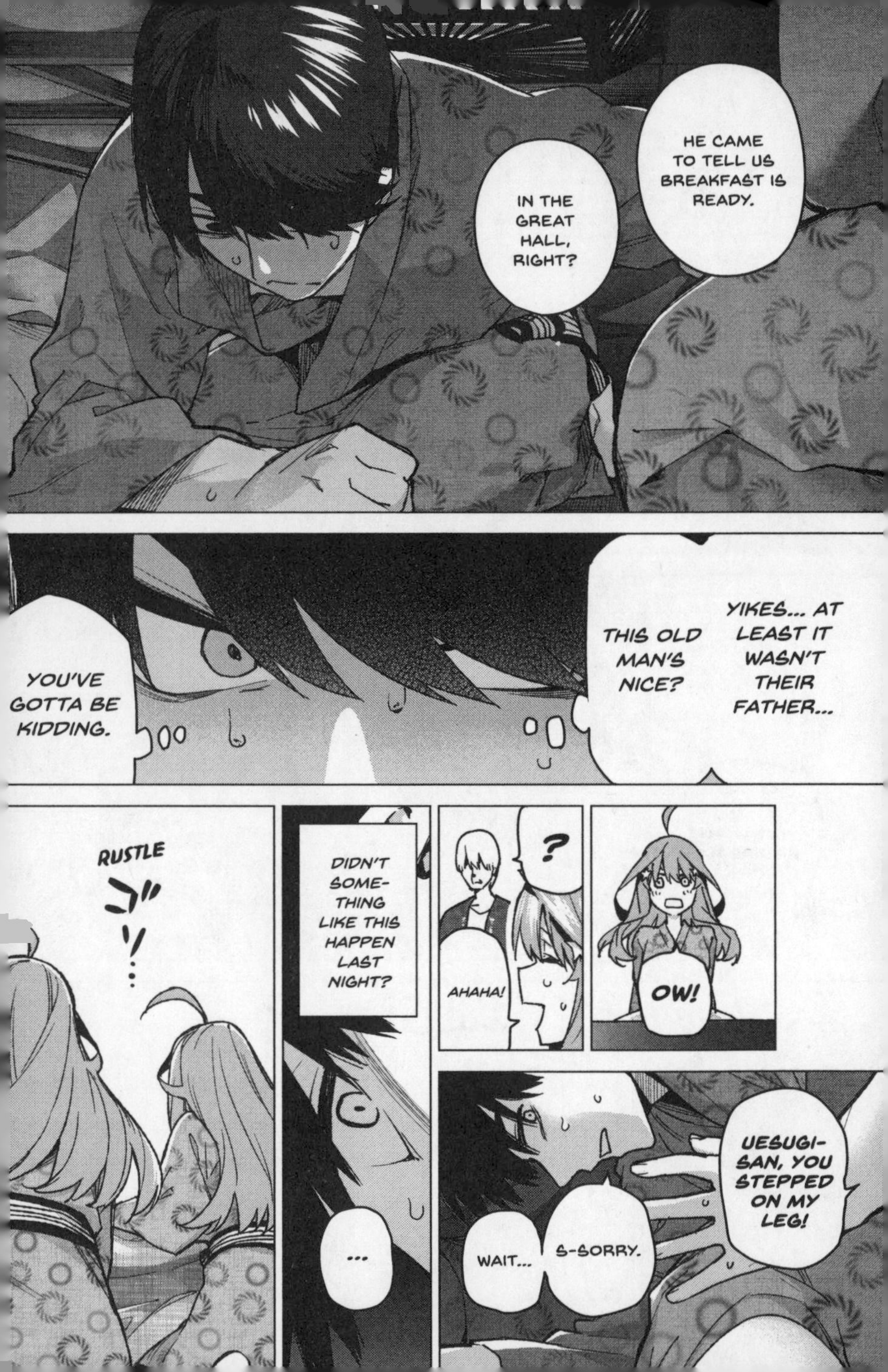

HE CAME TO TELL US BREAKFAST IS READY.
IN THE GREAT HALL, RIGHT?
YIKES... AT LEAST IT WASN'T THEIR FATHER...
THIS OLD MAN'S NICE?
YOU'VE GOTTA BE KIDDING.
OW!
?
AHAHA!
UESUGI-SAN, YOU STEPPED ON MY LEG!
S-SORRY.
WAIT...
DIDN'T SOMETHING LIKE THIS HAPPEN LAST NIGHT?
...
RUSTLE
ゴソ...

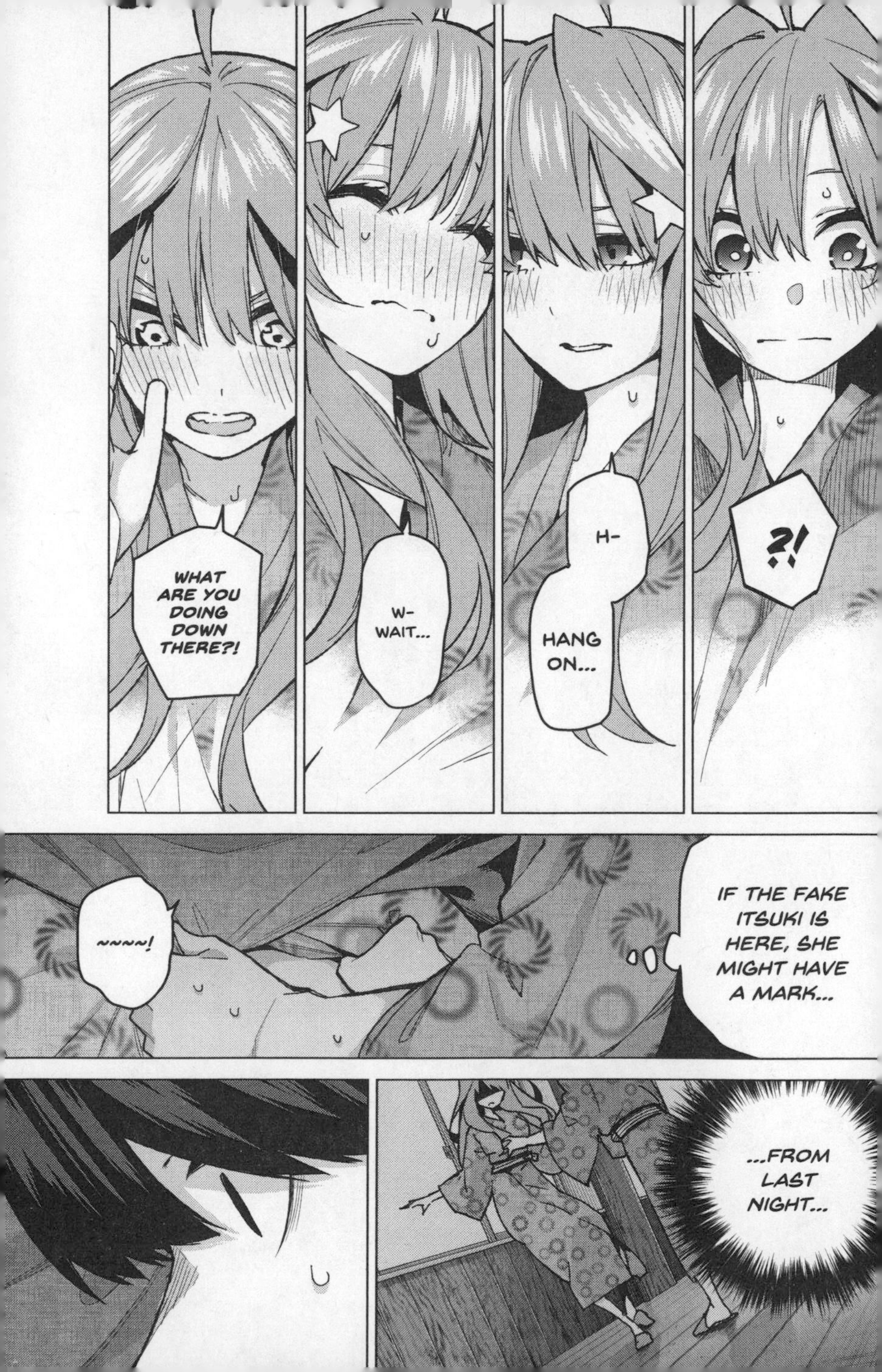
?!
H- HANG ON...
W- WAIT...
WHAT ARE YOU DOING DOWN THERE?!
IF THE FAKE ITSUKI IS HERE, SHE MIGHT HAVE A MARK...
~~~~!
...FROM LAST NIGHT...
~~~~

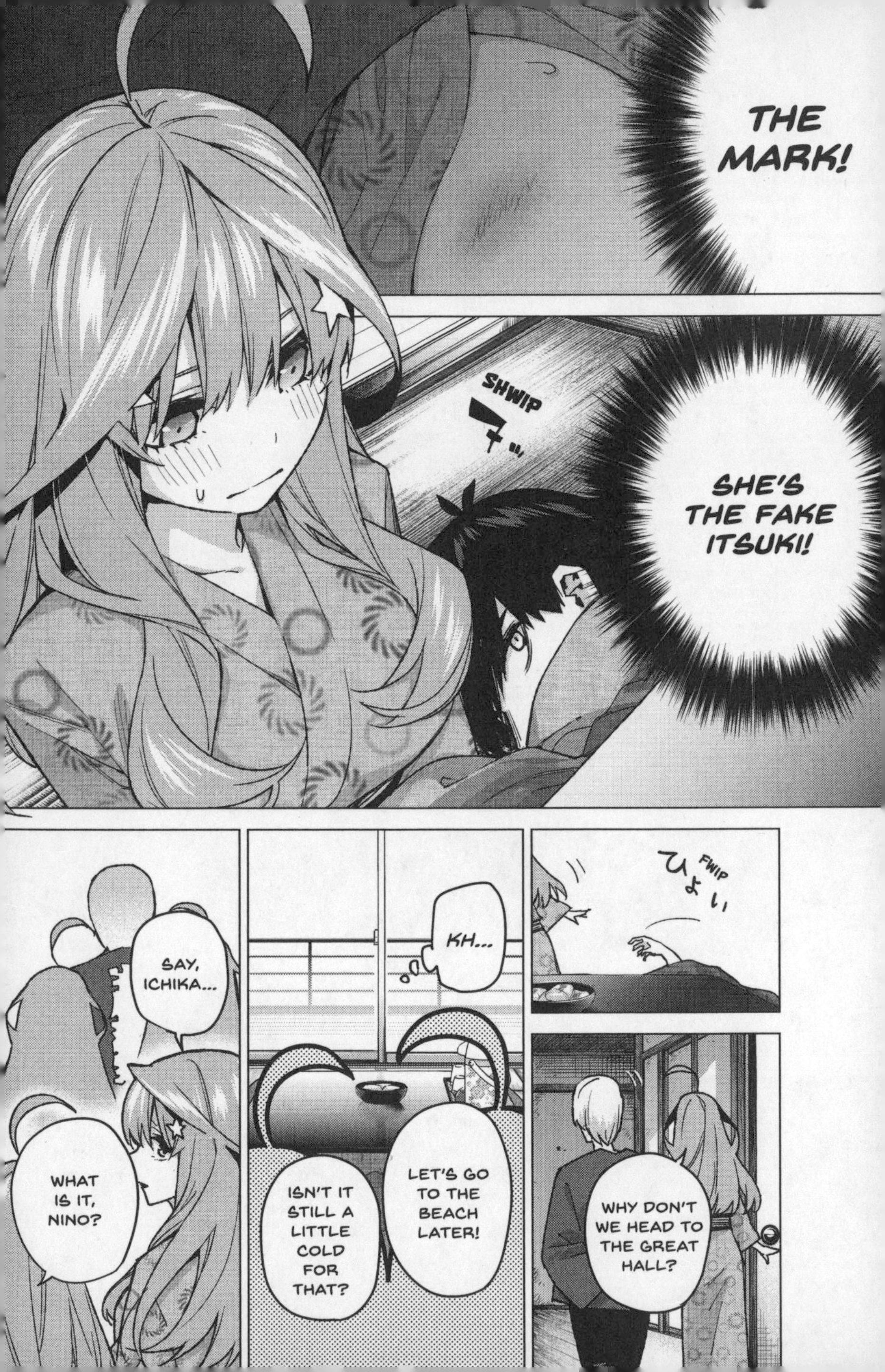
THE MARK!
SHWIP
SHE'S THE FAKE ITSUKI!
FWIP ひょい
WHY DON'T WE HEAD TO THE GREAT HALL?
KH...
LET'S GO TO THE BEACH LATER!
ISN'T IT STILL A LITTLE COLD FOR THAT?
SAY, ICHIKA...
WHAT IS IT, NINO?

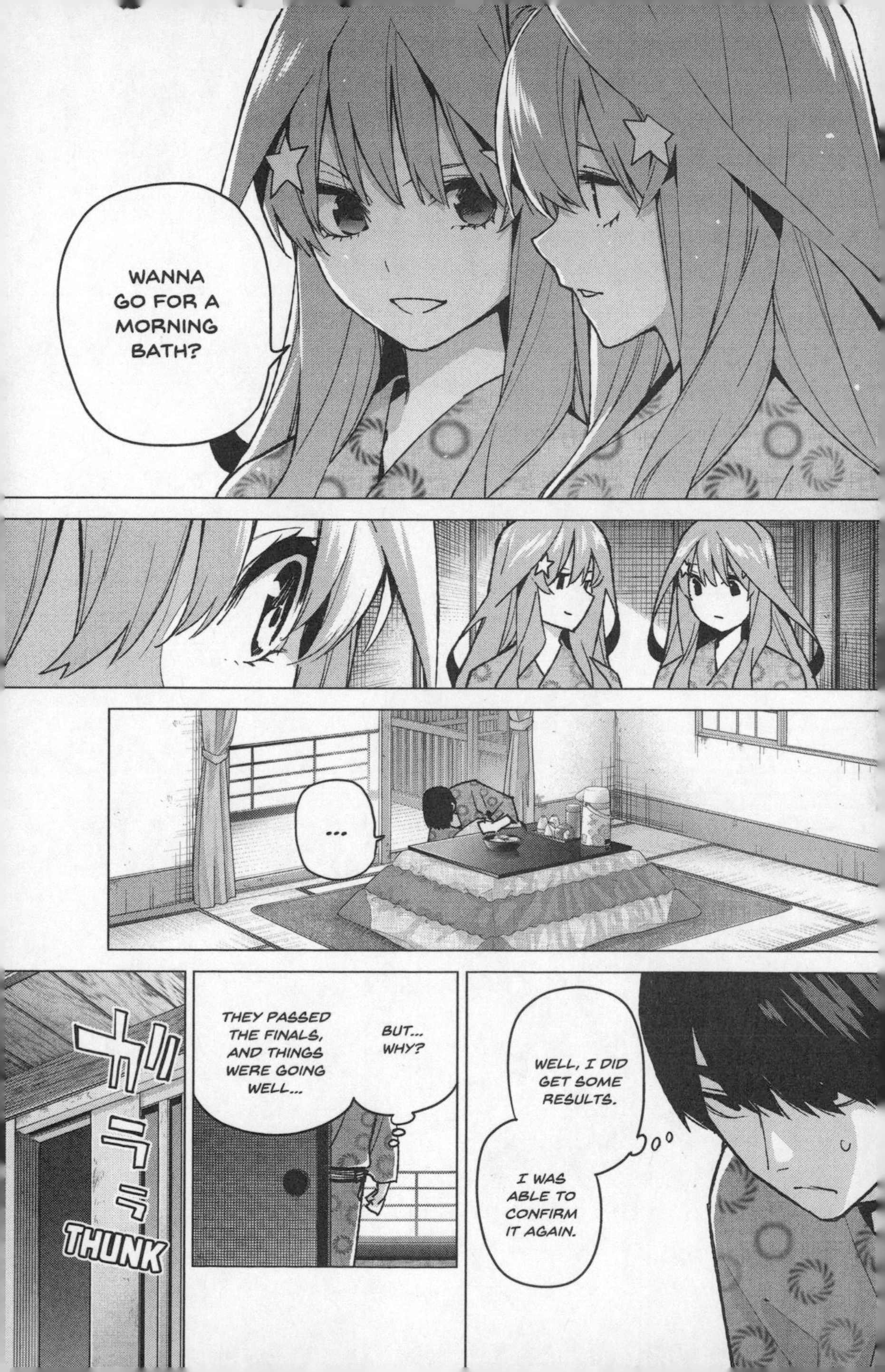
WANNA GO FOR A MORNING BATH?
...
WELL, I DID GET SOME RESULTS.
I WAS ABLE TO CONFIRM IT AGAIN.
BUT... WHY?
THEY PASSED THE FINALS, AND THINGS WERE GOING WELL...
THUNK

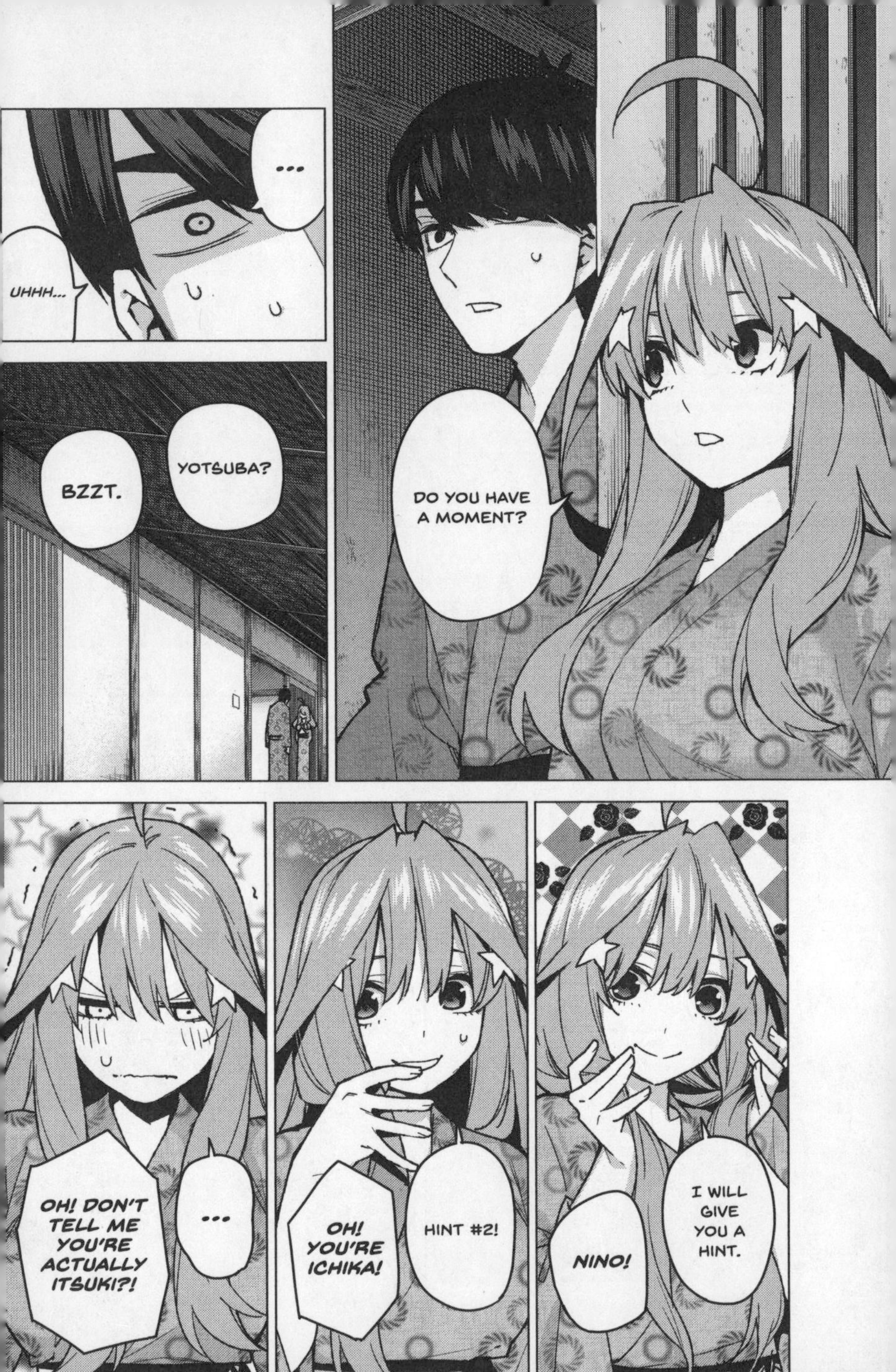
DO YOU HAVE A MOMENT?
...
UHHH...
YOTSUBA?
BZZT.
I WILL GIVE YOU A HINT.
NINO!
HINT #2!
OH! YOU'RE ICHIKA!
...
OH! DON'T TELL ME YOU'RE ACTUALLY ITSUKI?!

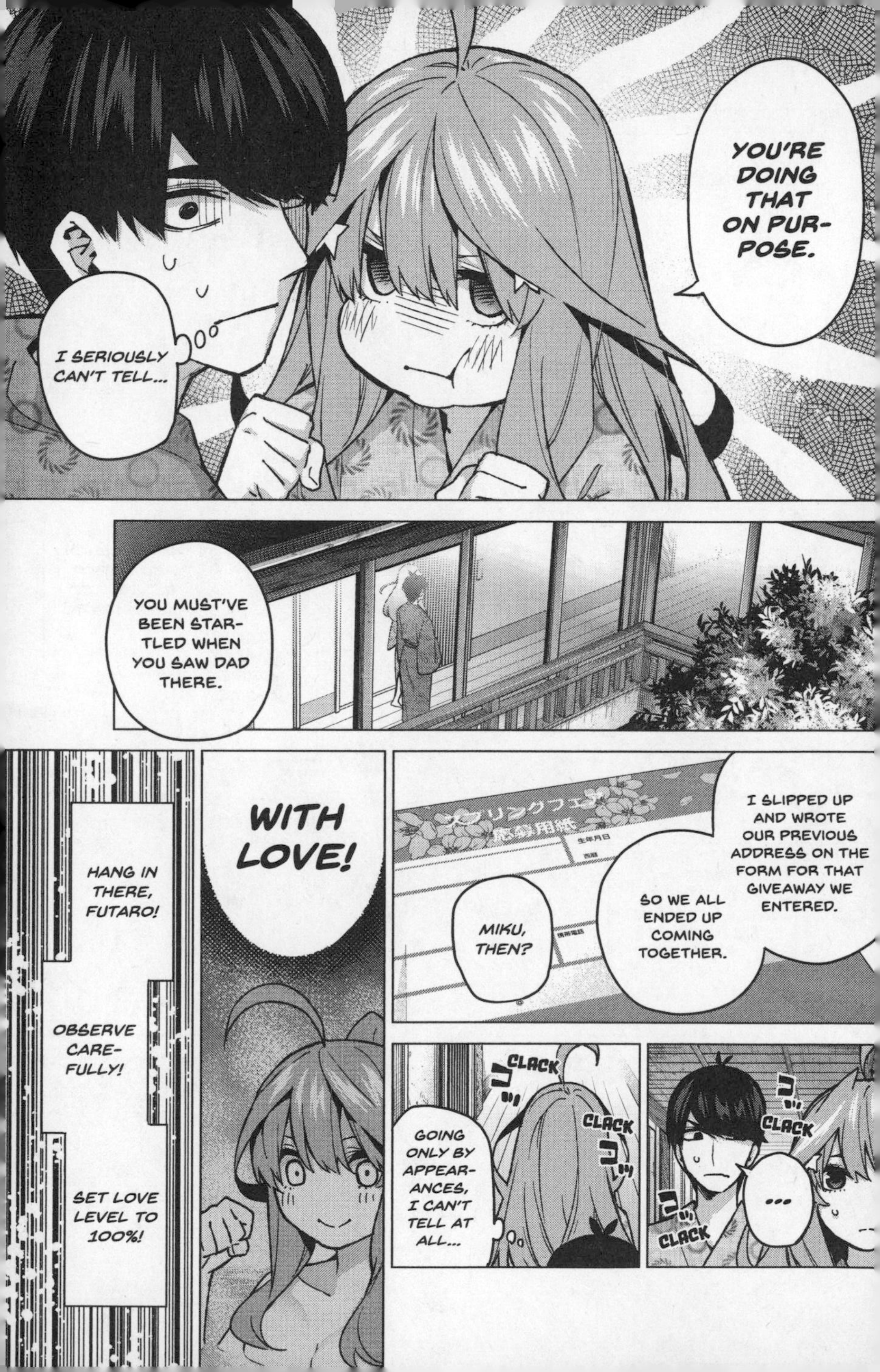
YOU'RE DOING THAT ON PURPOSE.
I SERIOUSLY CAN'T TELL...
YOU MUST'VE BEEN STARTLED WHEN YOU SAW DAD THERE.
I SLIPPED UP AND WROTE OUR PREVIOUS ADDRESS ON THE FORM FOR THAT GIVEAWAY WE ENTERED.
SO WE ALL ENDED UP COMING TOGETHER.
MIKU, THEN?
CLACK
CLACK
...
CLACK
CLACK
CLACK
GOING ONLY BY APPEARANCES, I CAN'T TELL AT ALL...
WITH LOVE!
HANG IN THERE, FUTARO!
OBSERVE CAREFULLY!
SET LOVE LEVEL TO 100%!

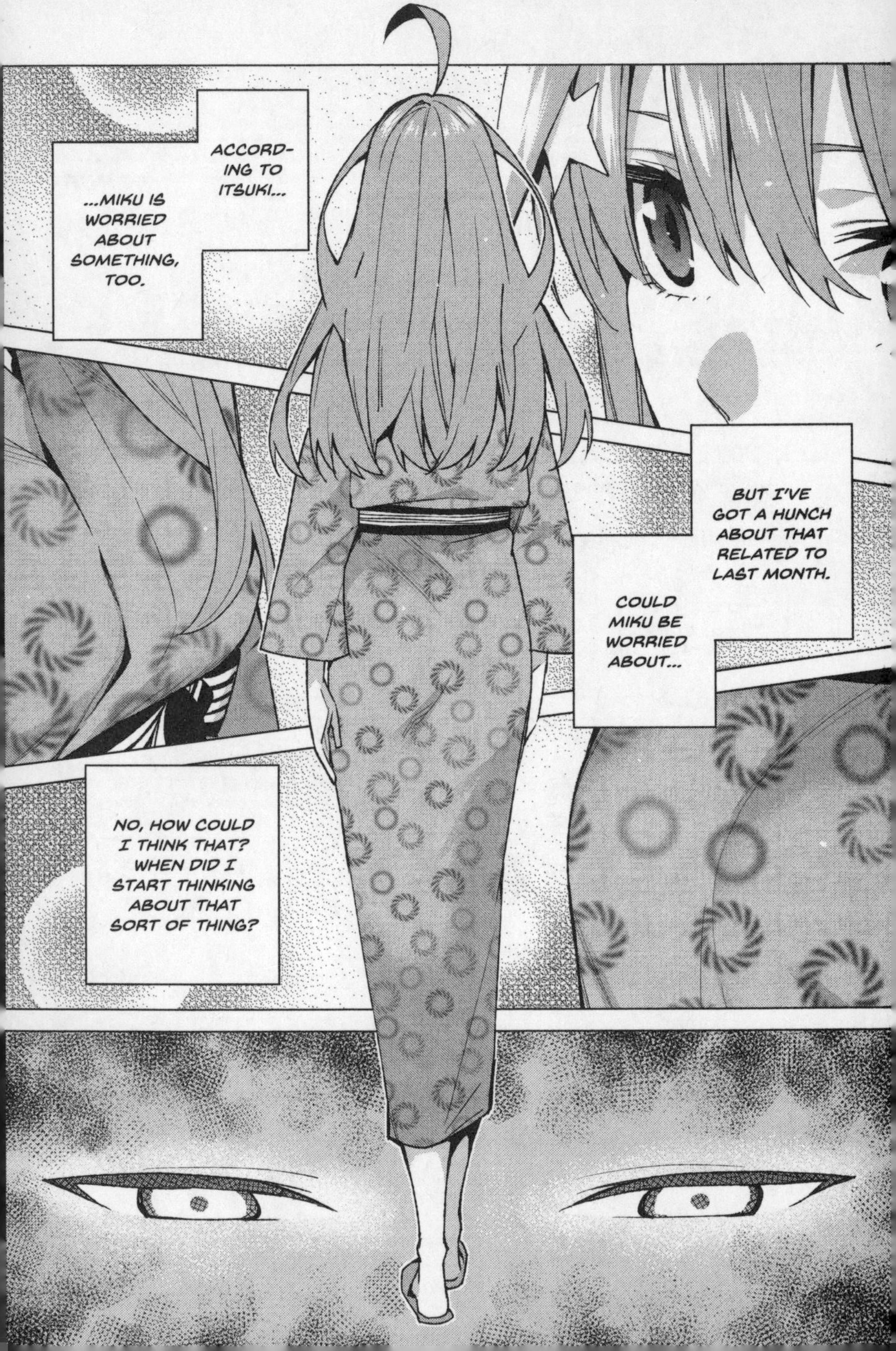
ACCORDING TO ITSUKI...
...MIKU IS WORRIED ABOUT SOMETHING, TOO.
BUT I'VE GOT A HUNCH ABOUT THAT RELATED TO LAST MONTH.
COULD MIKU BE WORRIED ABOUT...
NO, HOW COULD I THINK THAT? WHEN DID I START THINKING ABOUT THAT SORT OF THING?

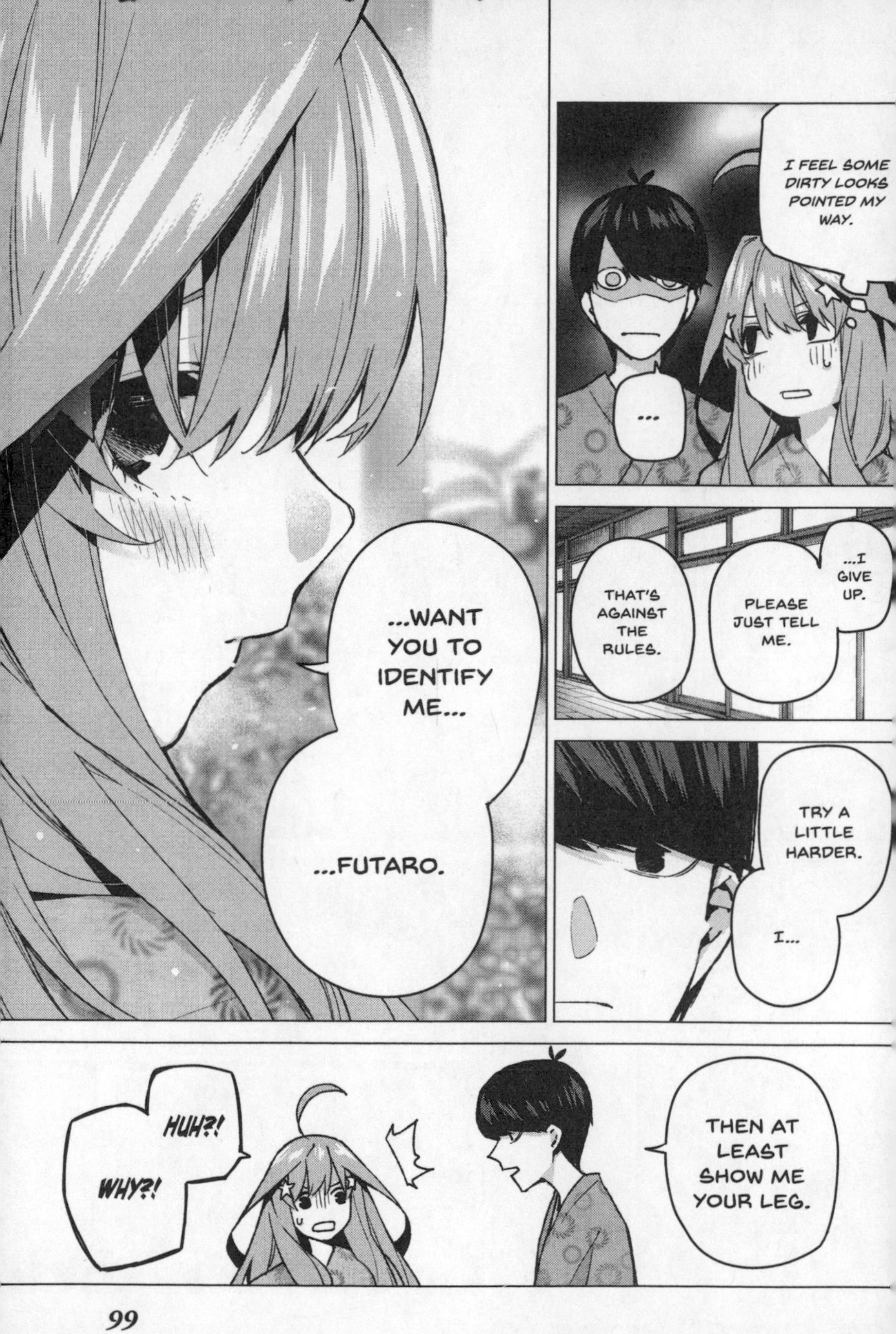
I FEEL SOME DIRTY LOOKS POINTED MY WAY.
...
...I GIVE UP.
PLEASE JUST TELL ME.
THAT'S AGAINST THE RULES.
TRY A LITTLE HARDER.
I...
...WANT YOU TO IDENTIFY ME...
...FUTARO.
THEN AT LEAST SHOW ME YOUR LEG.
HUH?!
WHY?!

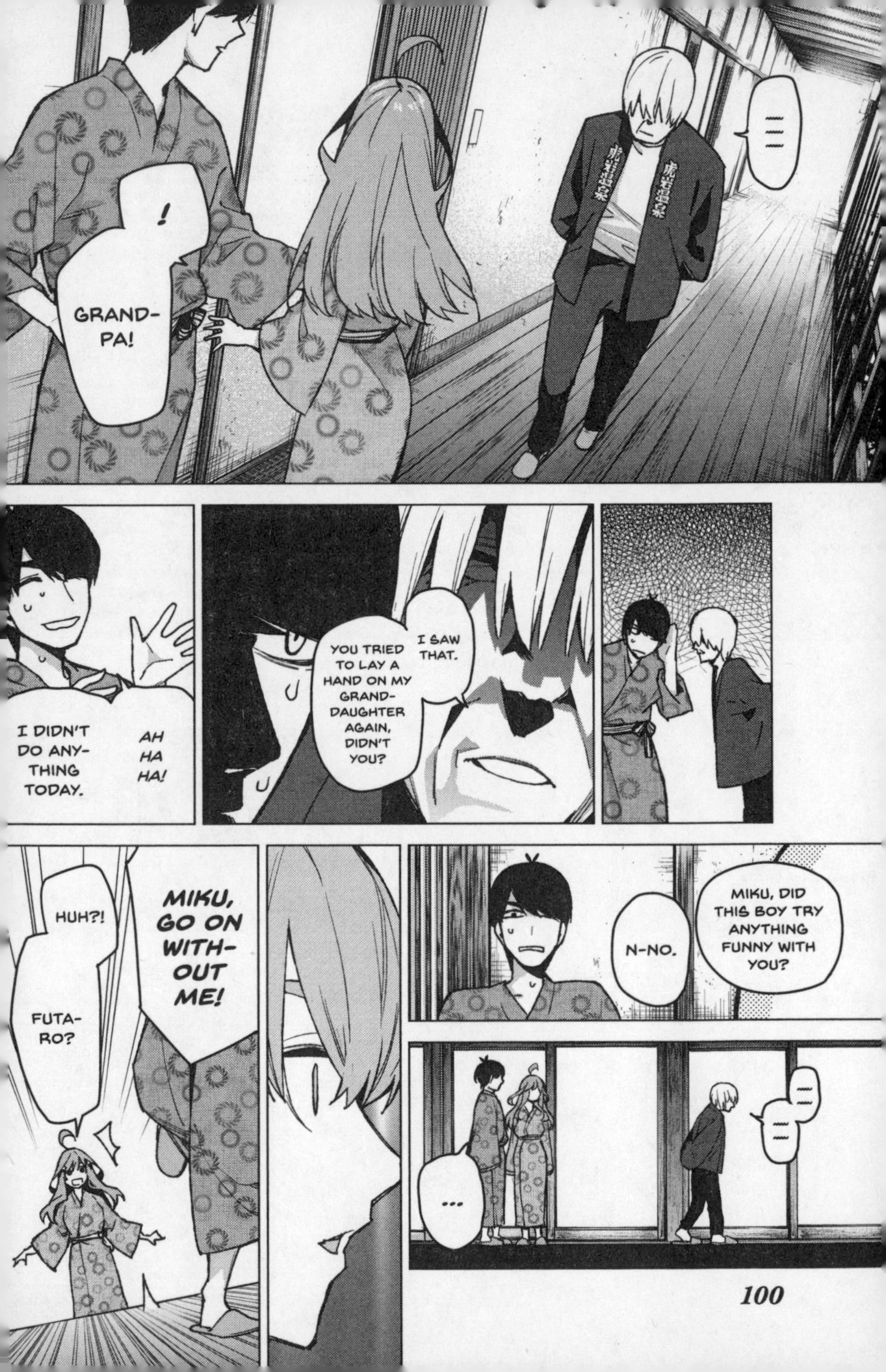

— —
!
GRAND-PA!
I SAW THAT.
YOU TRIED TO LAY A HAND ON MY GRAND-DAUGHTER AGAIN, DIDN'T YOU?
AH HA HA!
I DIDN'T DO ANY-THING TODAY.
MIKU, DID THIS BOY TRY ANYTHING FUNNY WITH YOU?
N-NO.
— —
— —
...
MIKU, GO ON WITH-OUT ME!
HUH?!
FUTA-RO?

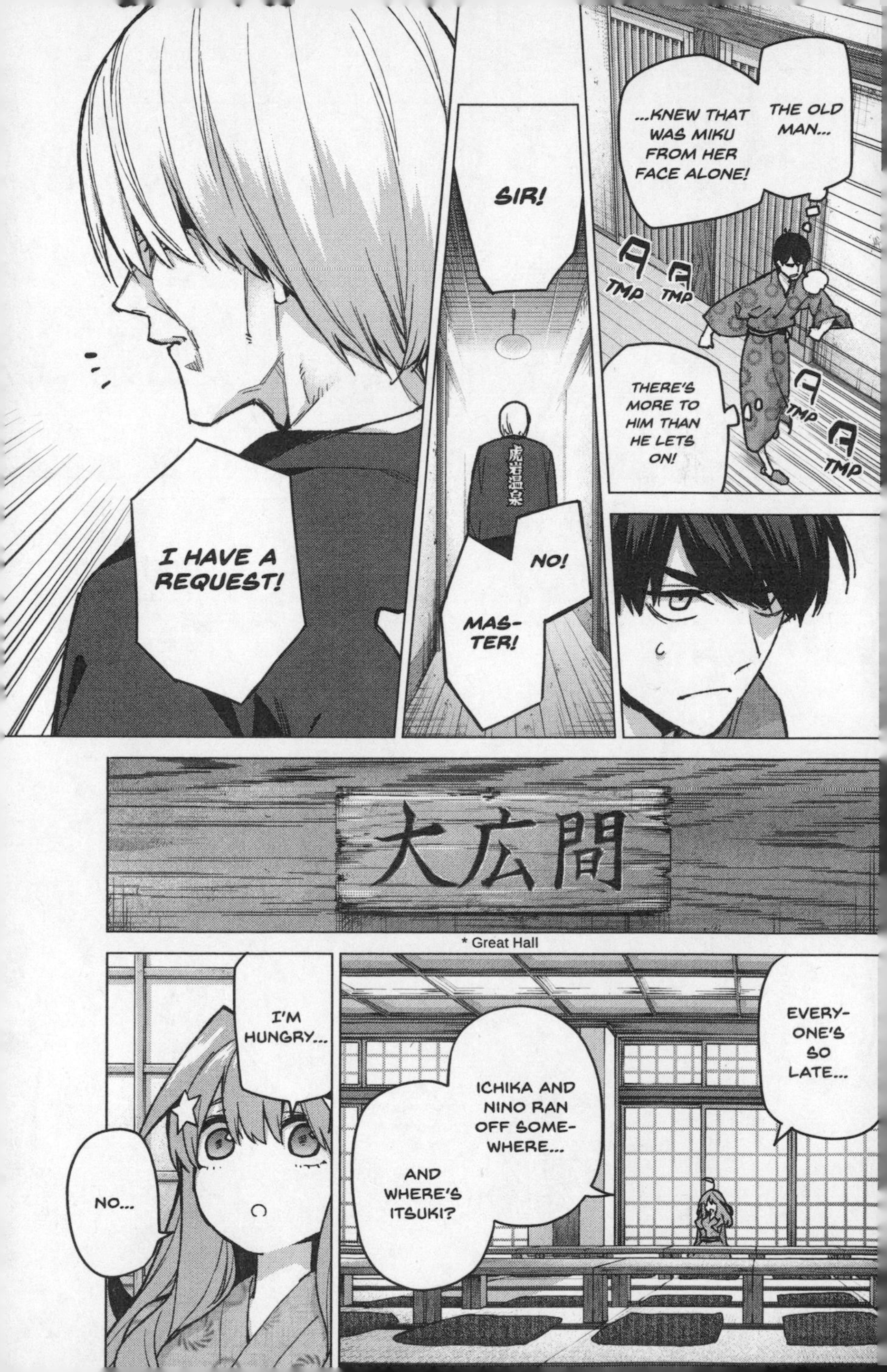
THE OLD MAN...
...KNEW THAT WAS MIKU FROM HER FACE ALONE!
TMP TMP
TMP TMP
THERE'S MORE TO HIM THAN HE LETS ON!
SIR!
NO!
MAS-TER!
I HAVE A REQUEST!
大広間
* Great Hall
EVERY-ONE'S SO LATE...
ICHIKA AND NINO RAN OFF SOME-WHERE...
AND WHERE'S ITSUKI?
I'M HUNGRY...
NO...

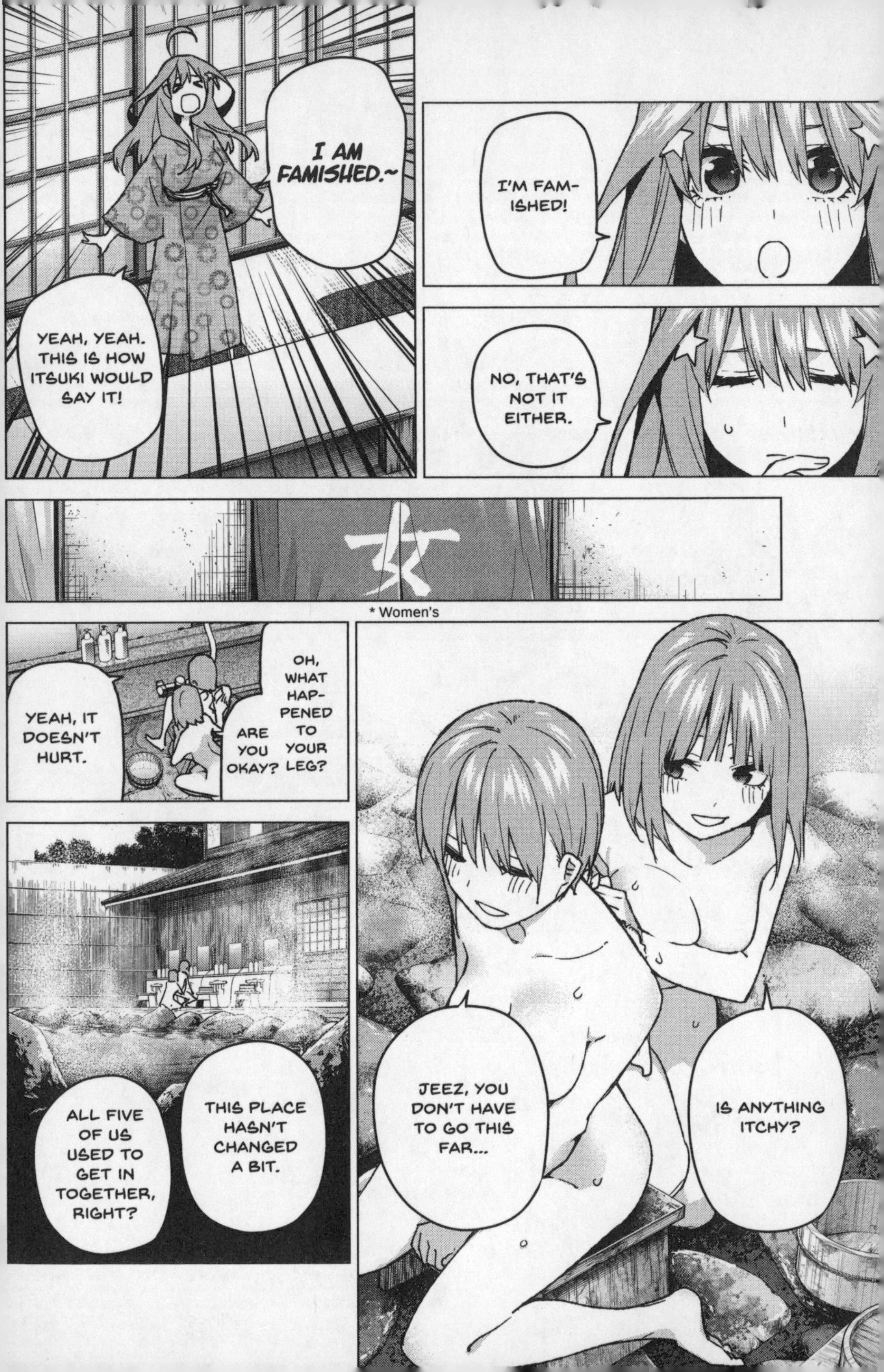
I'M FAM-ISHED!
NO, THAT'S NOT IT EITHER.
I AM FAMISHED.~
YEAH, YEAH. THIS IS HOW ITSUKI WOULD SAY IT!
女
* Women's
IS ANYTHING ITCHY?
JEEZ, YOU DON'T HAVE TO GO THIS FAR...
OH, WHAT HAP-PENED TO YOUR LEG?
ARE YOU OKAY?
YEAH, IT DOESN'T HURT.
THIS PLACE HASN'T CHANGED A BIT.
ALL FIVE OF US USED TO GET IN TOGETHER, RIGHT?

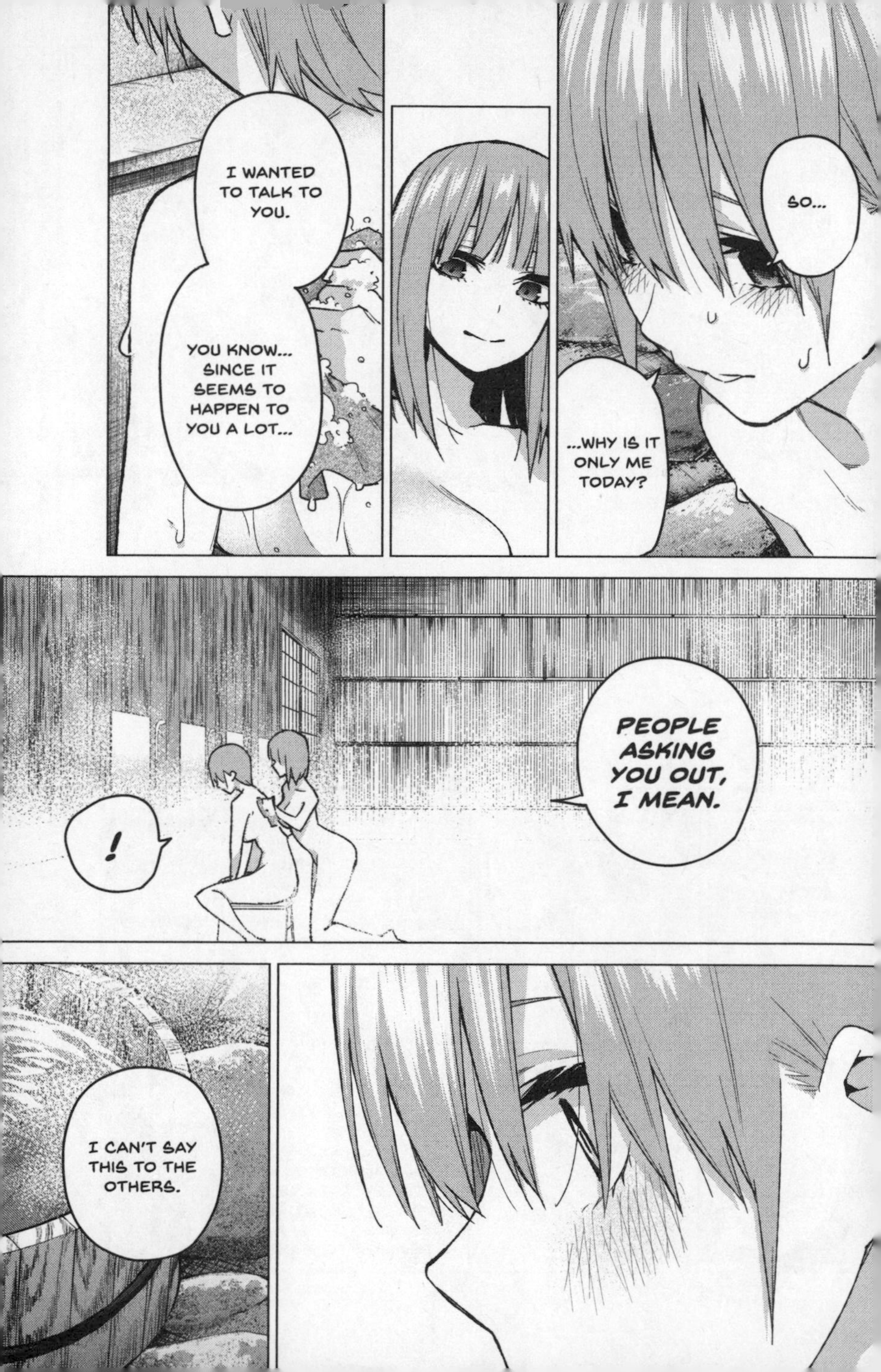
SO...
...WHY IS IT ONLY ME TODAY?
I WANTED TO TALK TO YOU.
YOU KNOW... SINCE IT SEEMS TO HAPPEN TO YOU A LOT...
PEOPLE ASKING YOU OUT, I MEAN.
!
I CAN'T SAY THIS TO THE OTHERS.

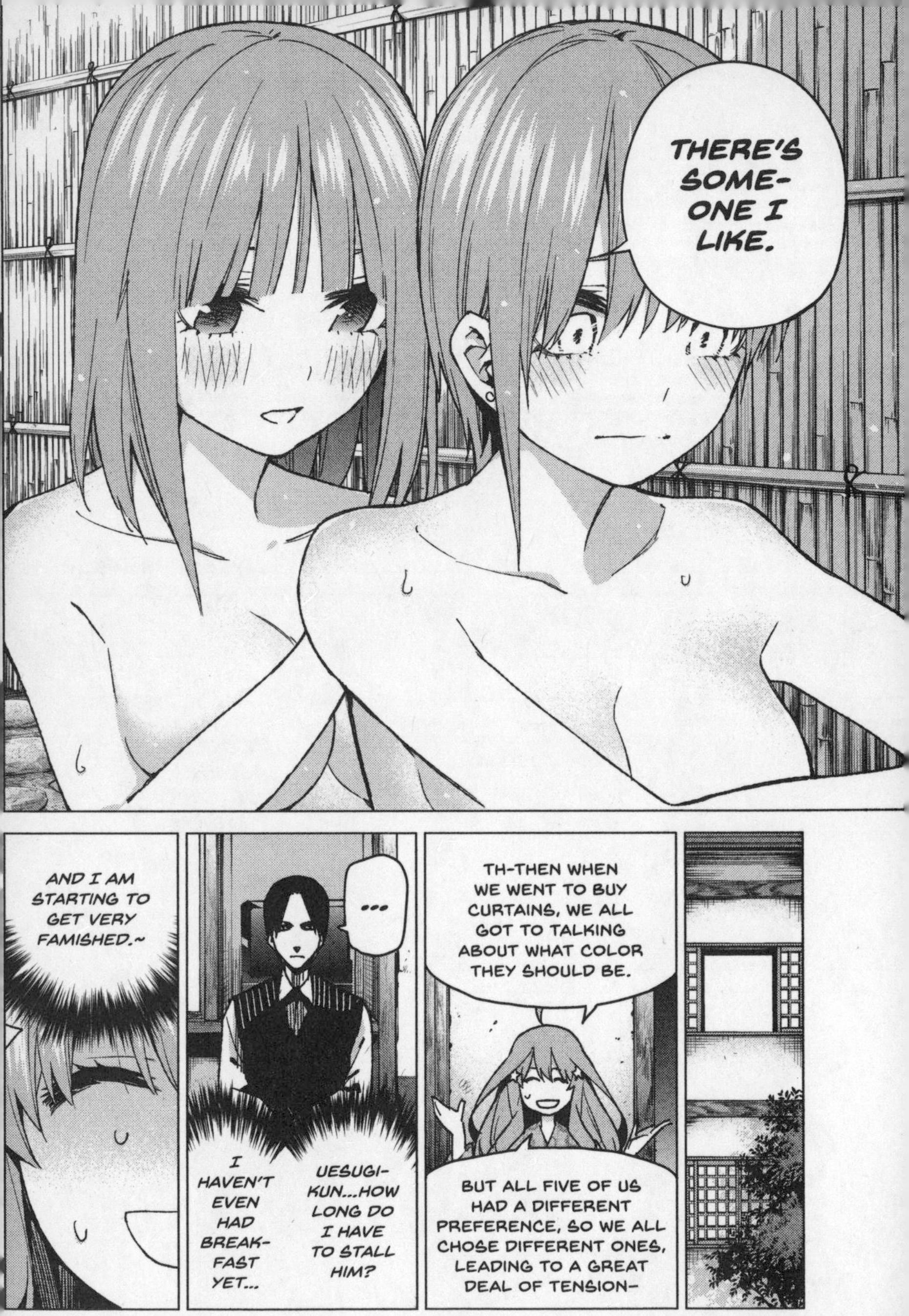
THERE'S SOME-ONE I LIKE.
TH-THEN WHEN WE WENT TO BUY CURTAINS, WE ALL GOT TO TALKING ABOUT WHAT COLOR THEY SHOULD BE.
BUT ALL FIVE OF US HAD A DIFFERENT PREFERENCE, SO WE ALL CHOSE DIFFERENT ONES, LEADING TO A GREAT DEAL OF TENSION–
...
UESUGI-KUN...HOW LONG DO I HAVE TO STALL HIM?
I HAVEN'T EVEN HAD BREAK-FAST YET...
AND I AM STARTING TO GET VERY FAMISHED.~

CHAPTER 65 SCRAMBLED EGGS ⑤

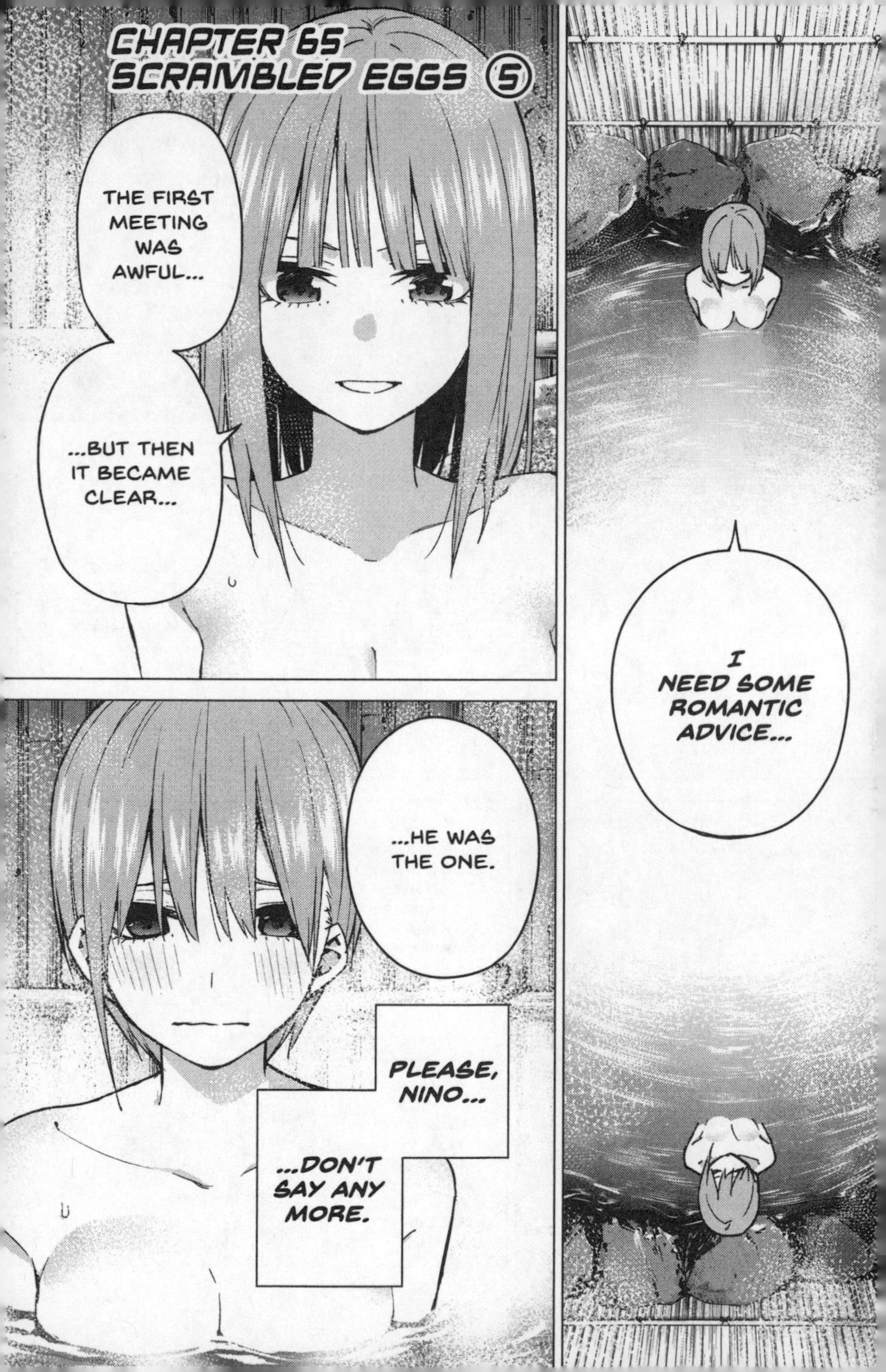
I NEED SOME ROMANTIC ADVICE...
THE FIRST MEETING WAS AWFUL...
...BUT THEN IT BECAME CLEAR...
...HE WAS THE ONE.
PLEASE, NINO...
...DON'T SAY ANY MORE.

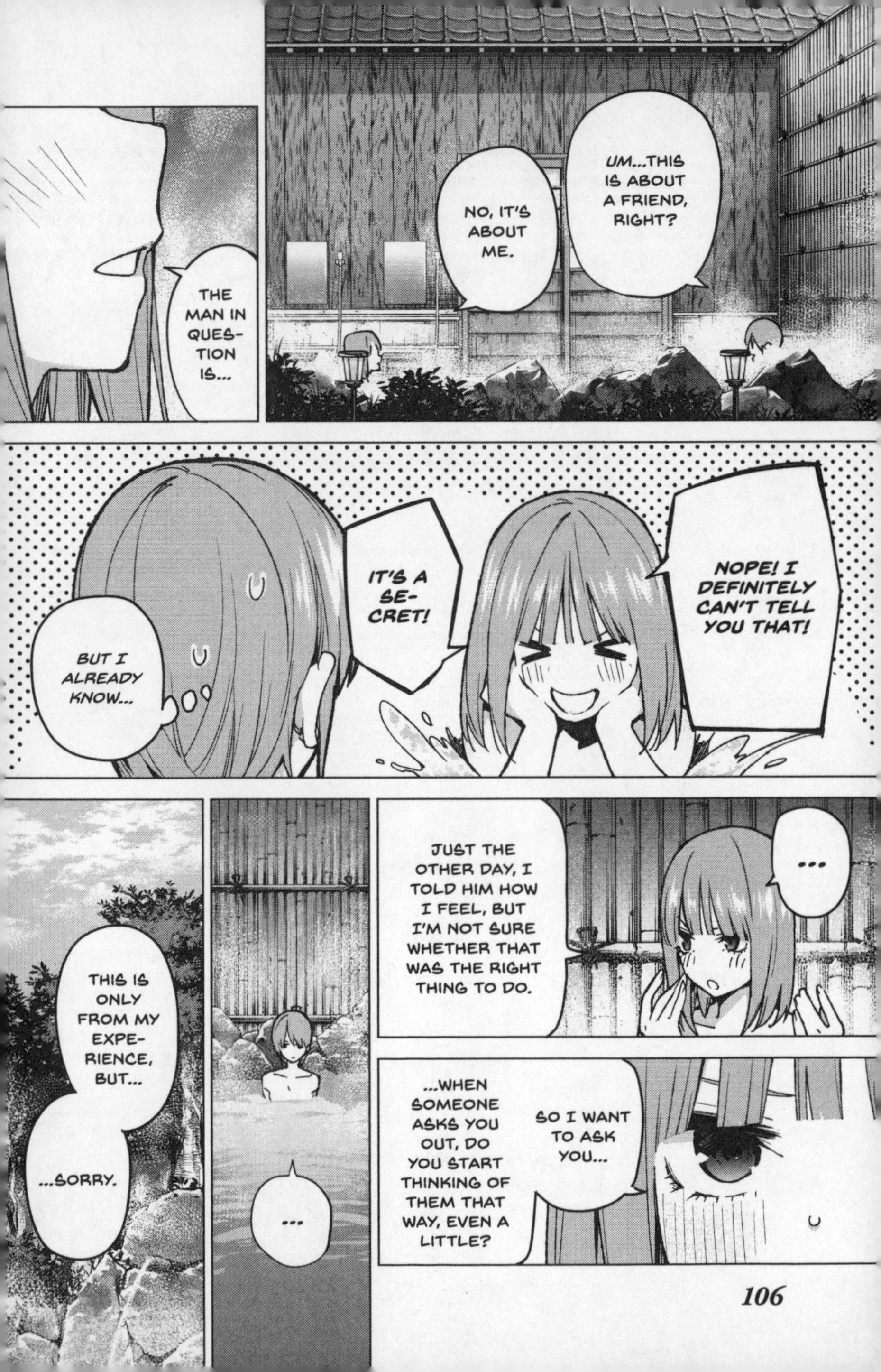
UM...THIS IS ABOUT A FRIEND, RIGHT?
NO, IT'S ABOUT ME.
THE MAN IN QUES-TION IS...
NOPE! I DEFINITELY CAN'T TELL YOU THAT!
IT'S A SE-CRET!
BUT I ALREADY KNOW...
...
JUST THE OTHER DAY, I TOLD HIM HOW I FEEL, BUT I'M NOT SURE WHETHER THAT WAS THE RIGHT THING TO DO.
SO I WANT TO ASK YOU...
...WHEN SOMEONE ASKS YOU OUT, DO YOU START THINKING OF THEM THAT WAY, EVEN A LITTLE?
...
THIS IS ONLY FROM MY EXPE-RIENCE, BUT...
...SORRY.

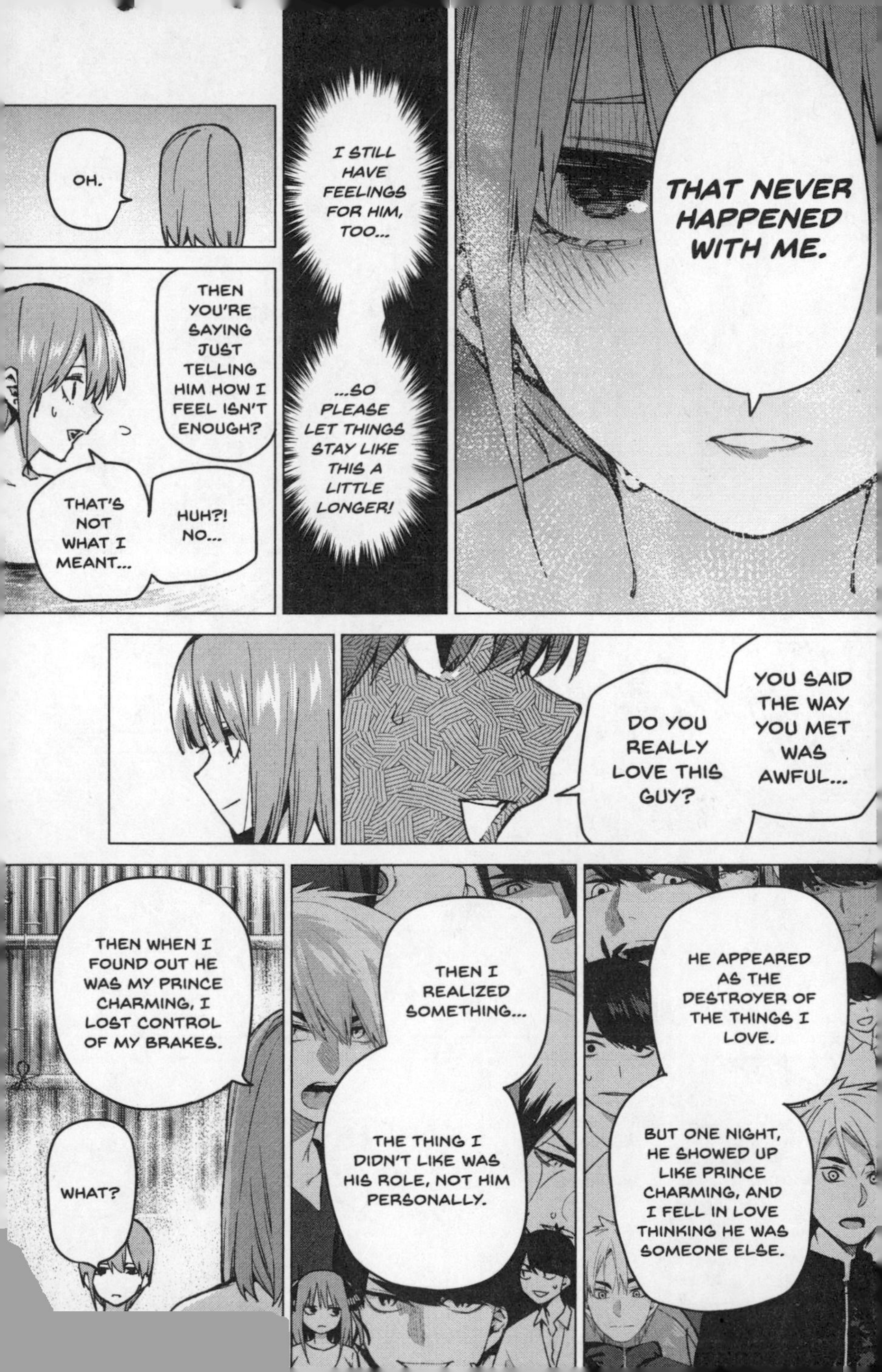
THAT NEVER HAPPENED WITH ME.
I STILL HAVE FEELINGS FOR HIM, TOO...
...SO PLEASE LET THINGS STAY LIKE THIS A LITTLE LONGER!
OH.
THEN YOU'RE SAYING JUST TELLING HIM HOW I FEEL ISN'T ENOUGH?
HUH?! NO...
THAT'S NOT WHAT I MEANT...
YOU SAID THE WAY YOU MET WAS AWFUL...
DO YOU REALLY LOVE THIS GUY?
HE APPEARED AS THE DESTROYER OF THE THINGS I LOVE.
BUT ONE NIGHT, HE SHOWED UP LIKE PRINCE CHARMING, AND I FELL IN LOVE THINKING HE WAS SOMEONE ELSE.
THEN I REALIZED SOMETHING...
THE THING I DIDN'T LIKE WAS HIS ROLE, NOT HIM PERSONALLY.
THEN WHEN I FOUND OUT HE WAS MY PRINCE CHARMING, I LOST CONTROL OF MY BRAKES.
WHAT?

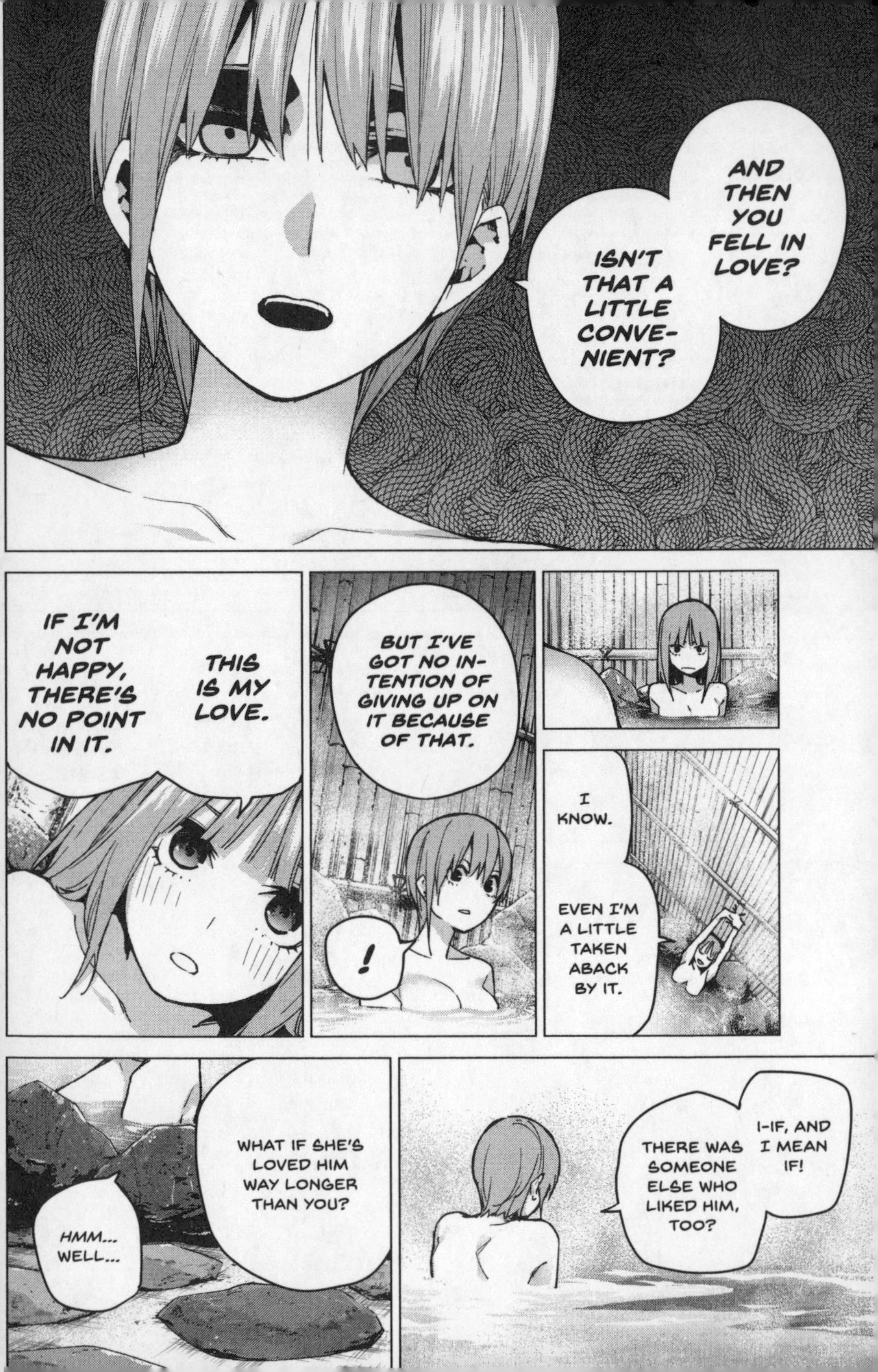
AND THEN YOU FELL IN LOVE?
ISN'T THAT A LITTLE CONVENIENT?
I KNOW.
EVEN I'M A LITTLE TAKEN ABACK BY IT.
BUT I'VE GOT NO INTENTION OF GIVING UP ON IT BECAUSE OF THAT.
!
THIS IS MY LOVE.
IF I'M NOT HAPPY, THERE'S NO POINT IN IT.
I-IF, AND I MEAN IF!
THERE WAS SOMEONE ELSE WHO LIKED HIM, TOO?
WHAT IF SHE'S LOVED HIM WAY LONGER THAN YOU?
HMM... WELL...

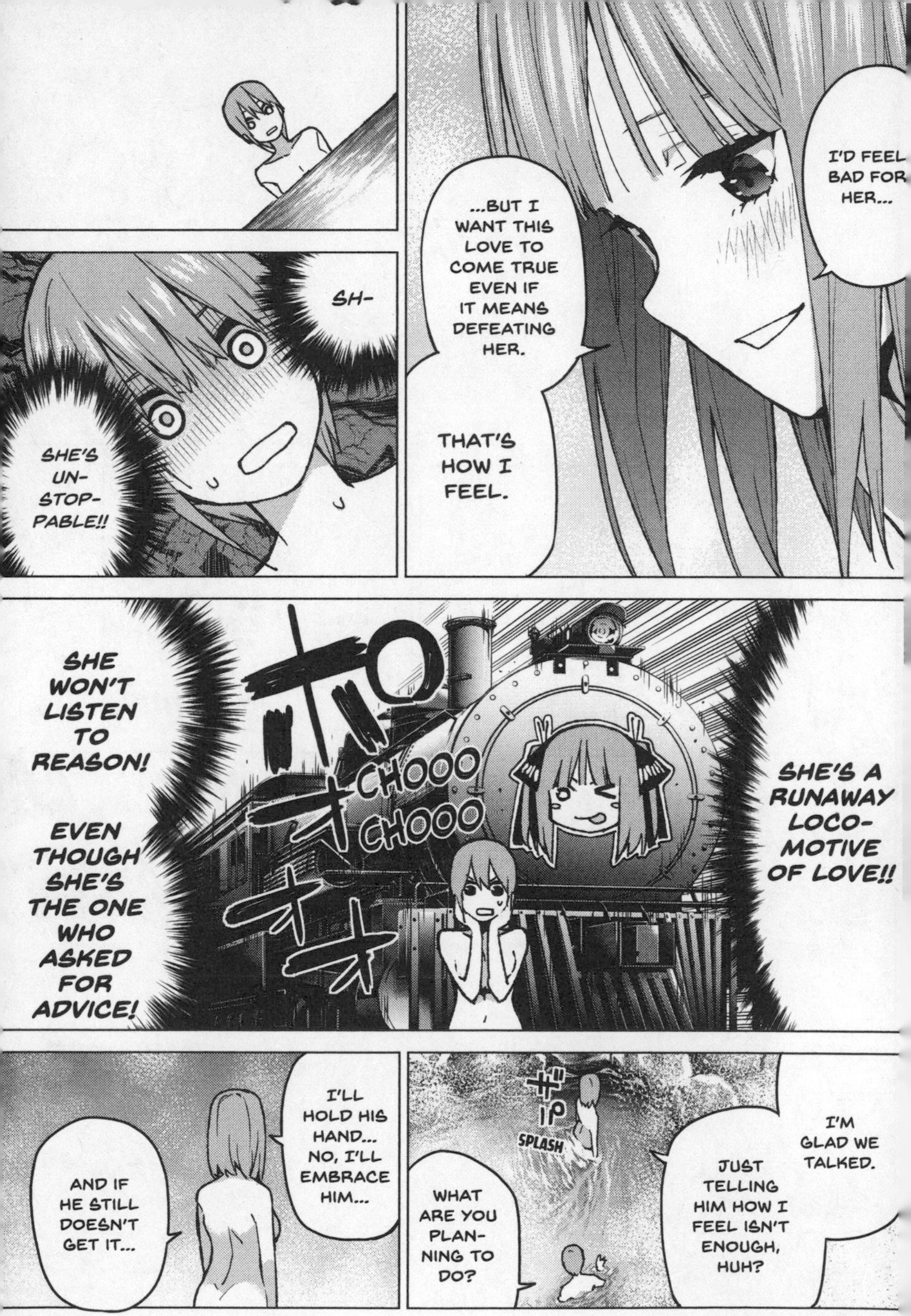
I'D FEEL BAD FOR HER...
...BUT I WANT THIS LOVE TO COME TRUE EVEN IF IT MEANS DEFEATING HER.
THAT'S HOW I FEEL.
SH-
SHE'S UN-STOP-PABLE!!
SHE'S A RUNAWAY LOCO-MOTIVE OF LOVE!!
CHOOO CHOOO
SHE WON'T LISTEN TO REASON!
EVEN THOUGH SHE'S THE ONE WHO ASKED FOR ADVICE!
I'M GLAD WE TALKED.
JUST TELLING HIM HOW I FEEL ISN'T ENOUGH, HUH?
SPLASH
WHAT ARE YOU PLAN-NING TO DO?
I'LL HOLD HIS HAND... NO, I'LL EMBRACE HIM...
AND IF HE STILL DOESN'T GET IT...

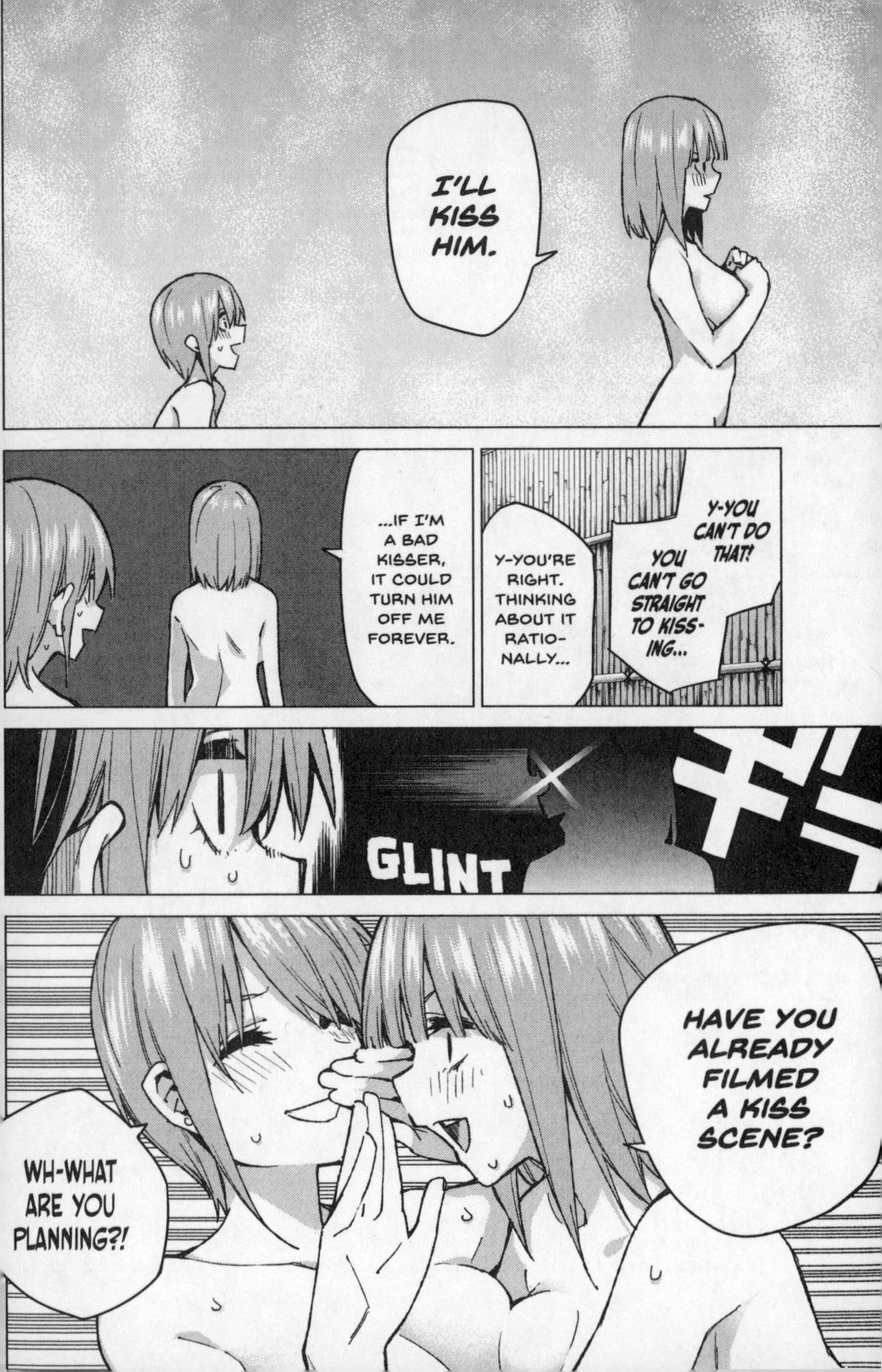
I'LL KISS HIM.
Y-YOU CAN'T DO THAT!
YOU CAN'T GO STRAIGHT TO KISS-ING...
Y-YOU'RE RIGHT. THINKING ABOUT IT RATIO-NALLY...
...IF I'M A BAD KISSER, IT COULD TURN HIM OFF ME FOREVER.
GLINT
HAVE YOU ALREADY FILMED A KISS SCENE?
WH-WHAT ARE YOU PLANNING?!

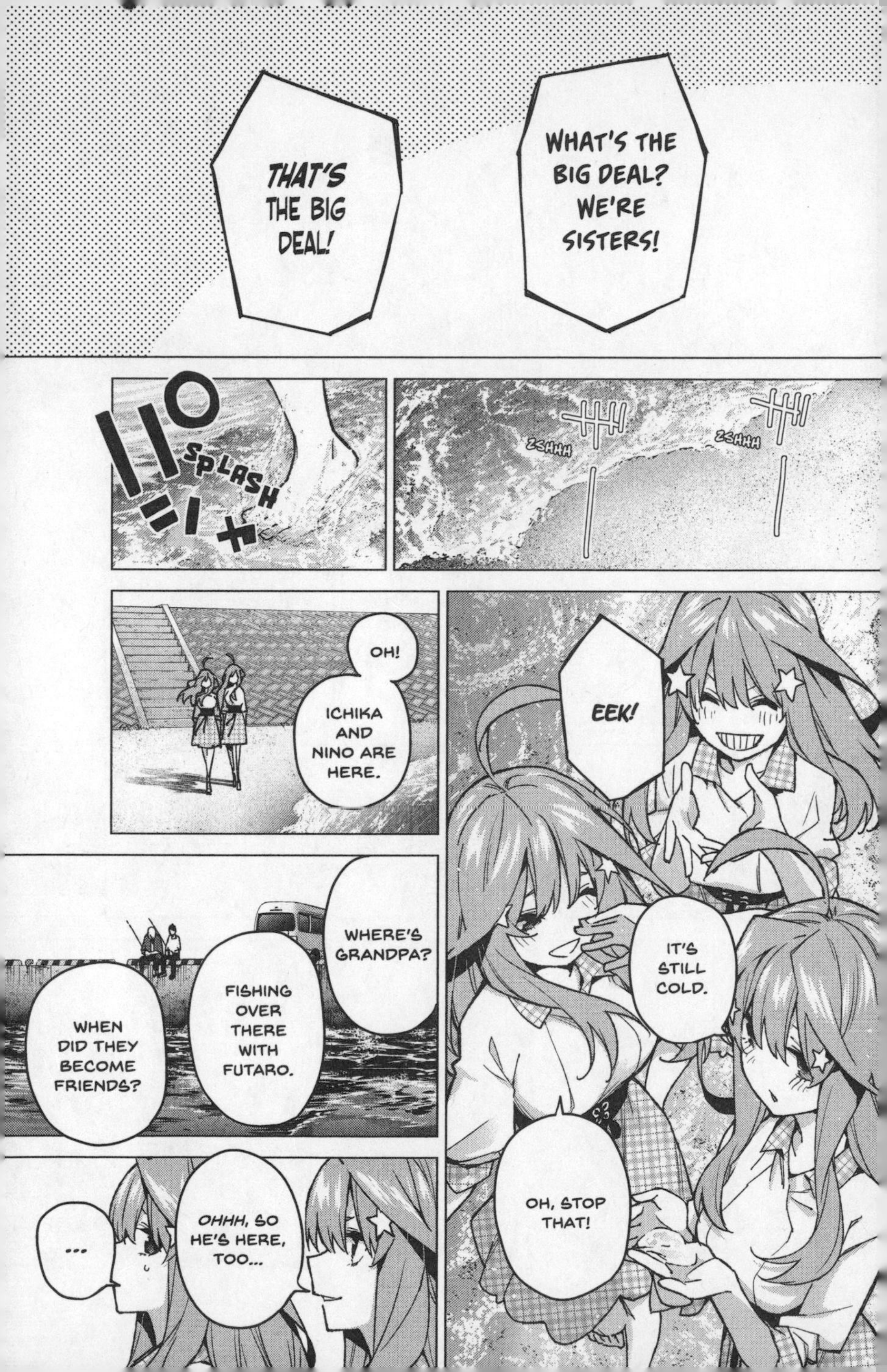
WHAT'S THE BIG DEAL? WE'RE SISTERS!
THAT'S THE BIG DEAL!
ZSHHH
ZSHHH
SPLASH
EEK!
IT'S STILL COLD.
OH, STOP THAT!
OH!
ICHIKA AND NINO ARE HERE.
WHERE'S GRANDPA?
FISHING OVER THERE WITH FUTARO.
WHEN DID THEY BECOME FRIENDS?
OHHH, SO HE'S HERE, TOO...
...

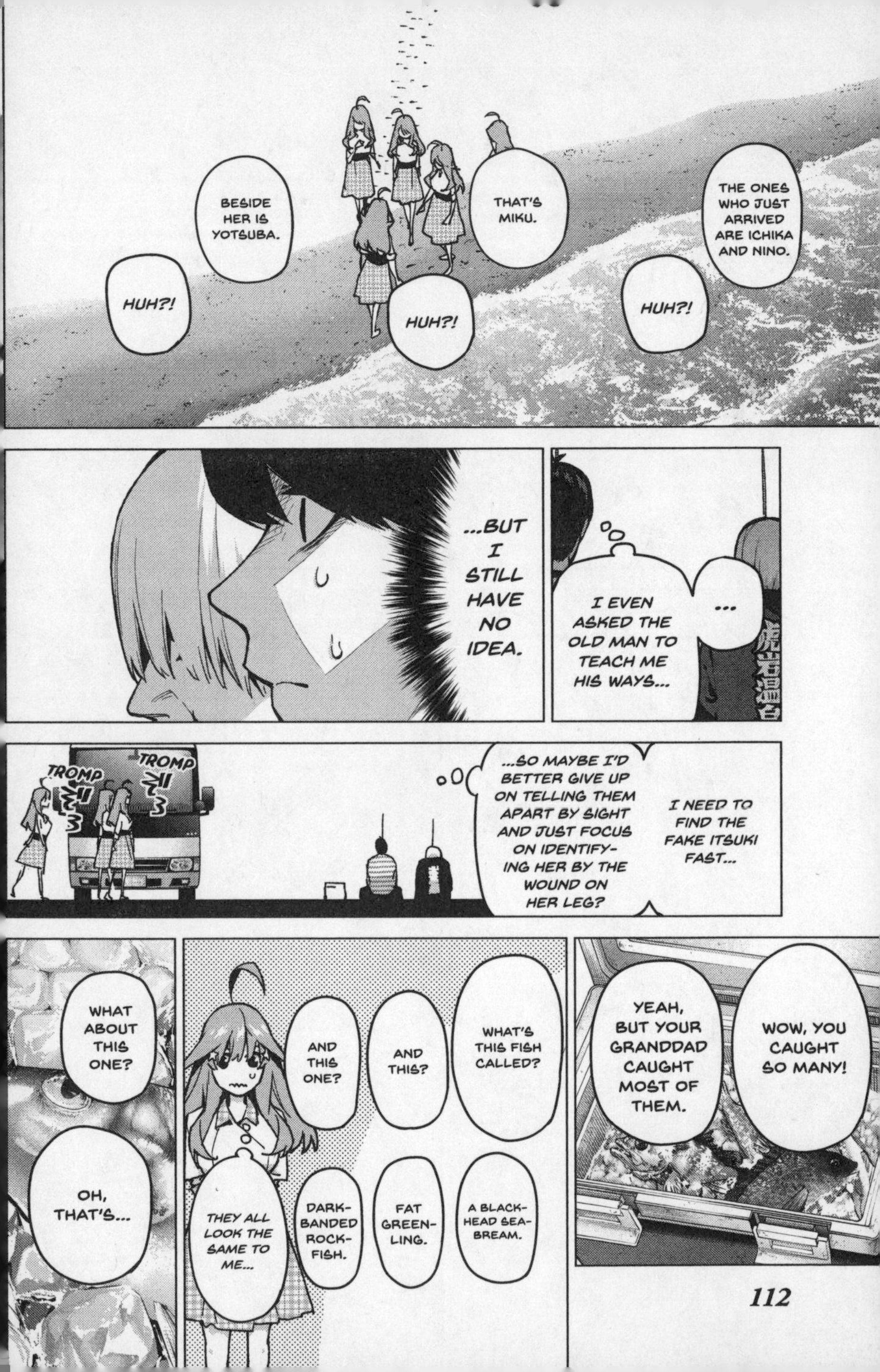
THE ONES WHO JUST ARRIVED ARE ICHIKA AND NINO.
HUH?!
THAT'S MIKU.
HUH?!
BESIDE HER IS YOTSUBA.
HUH?!
I EVEN ASKED THE OLD MAN TO TEACH ME HIS WAYS...
...
...BUT I STILL HAVE NO IDEA.
I NEED TO FIND THE FAKE ITSUKI FAST...
...SO MAYBE I'D BETTER GIVE UP ON TELLING THEM APART BY SIGHT AND JUST FOCUS ON IDENTIFY-ING HER BY THE WOUND ON HER LEG?
TROMP
TROMP
WOW, YOU CAUGHT SO MANY!
YEAH, BUT YOUR GRANDDAD CAUGHT MOST OF THEM.
WHAT'S THIS FISH CALLED?
A BLACK-HEAD SEA-BREAM.
AND THIS?
FAT GREEN-LING.
AND THIS ONE?
DARK-BANDED ROCK-FISH.
THEY ALL LOOK THE SAME TO ME...
WHAT ABOUT THIS ONE?
OH, THAT'S...

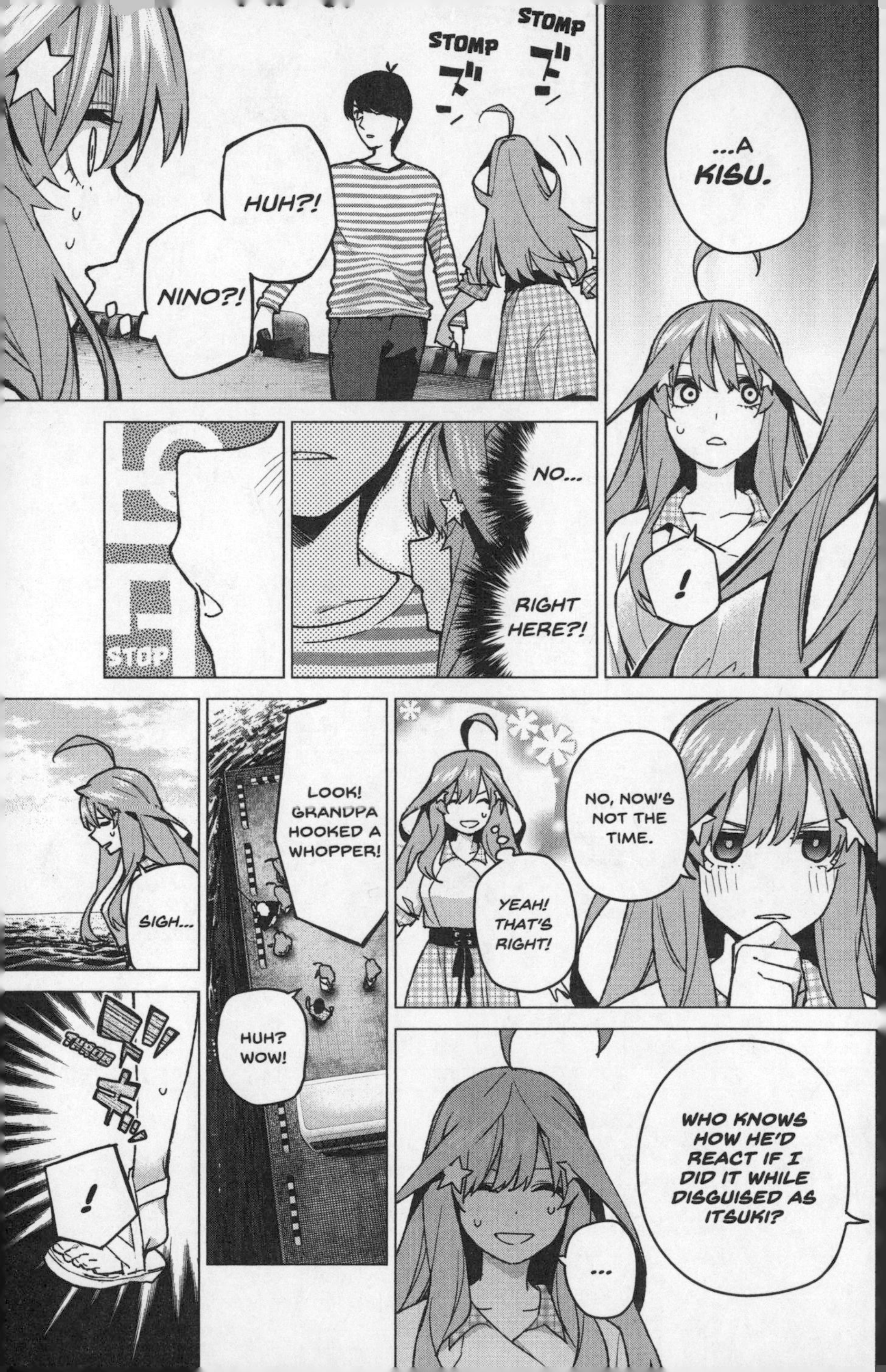
...A KISU.
!
STOMP
STOMP
HUH?!
NINO?!
NO...
RIGHT HERE?!
STOP
NO, NOW'S NOT THE TIME.
YEAH! THAT'S RIGHT!
WHO KNOWS HOW HE'D REACT IF I DID IT WHILE DISGUISED AS ITSUKI?
...
LOOK! GRANDPA HOOKED A WHOPPER!
HUH? WOW!
SIGH...
THROB
!

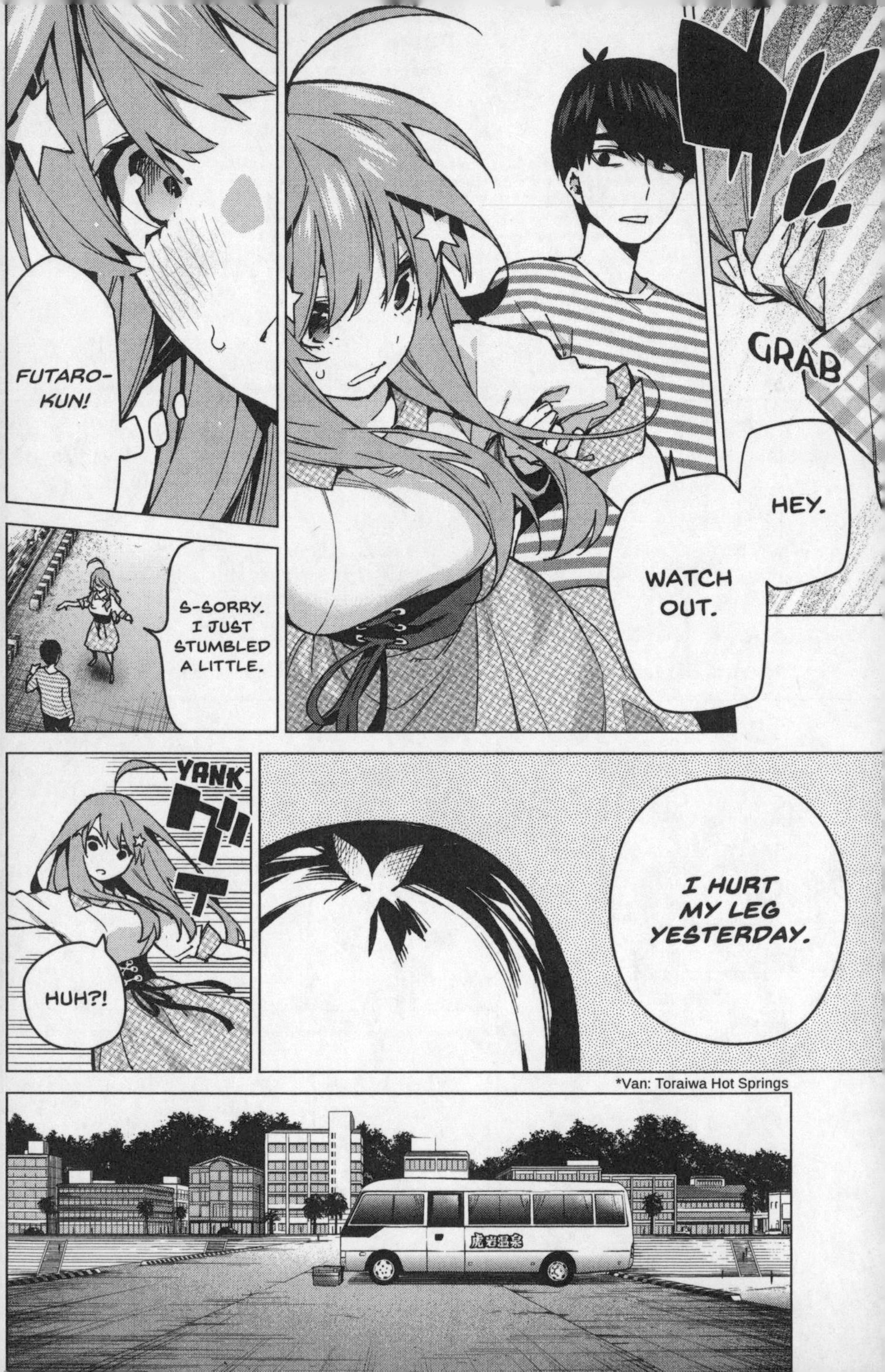
GRAB
HEY.
WATCH OUT.
FUTARO-KUN!
S-SORRY. I JUST STUMBLED A LITTLE.
I HURT MY LEG YESTERDAY.
YANK
HUH?!
虎岩温泉
*Van: Toraiwa Hot Springs

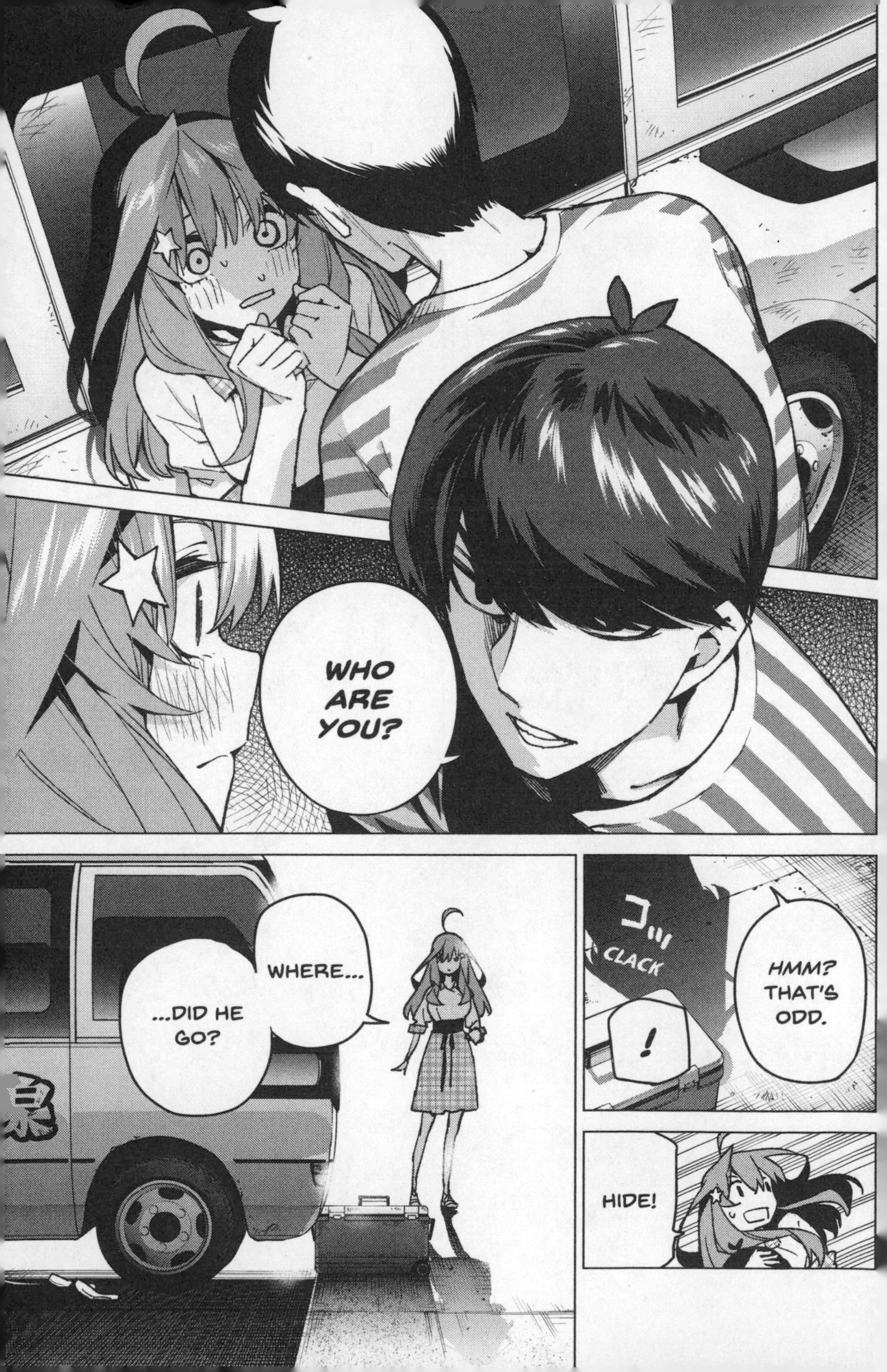
WHO ARE YOU?
HMM? THAT'S ODD.
コッ
CLACK
!
HIDE!
WHERE...
...DID HE GO?

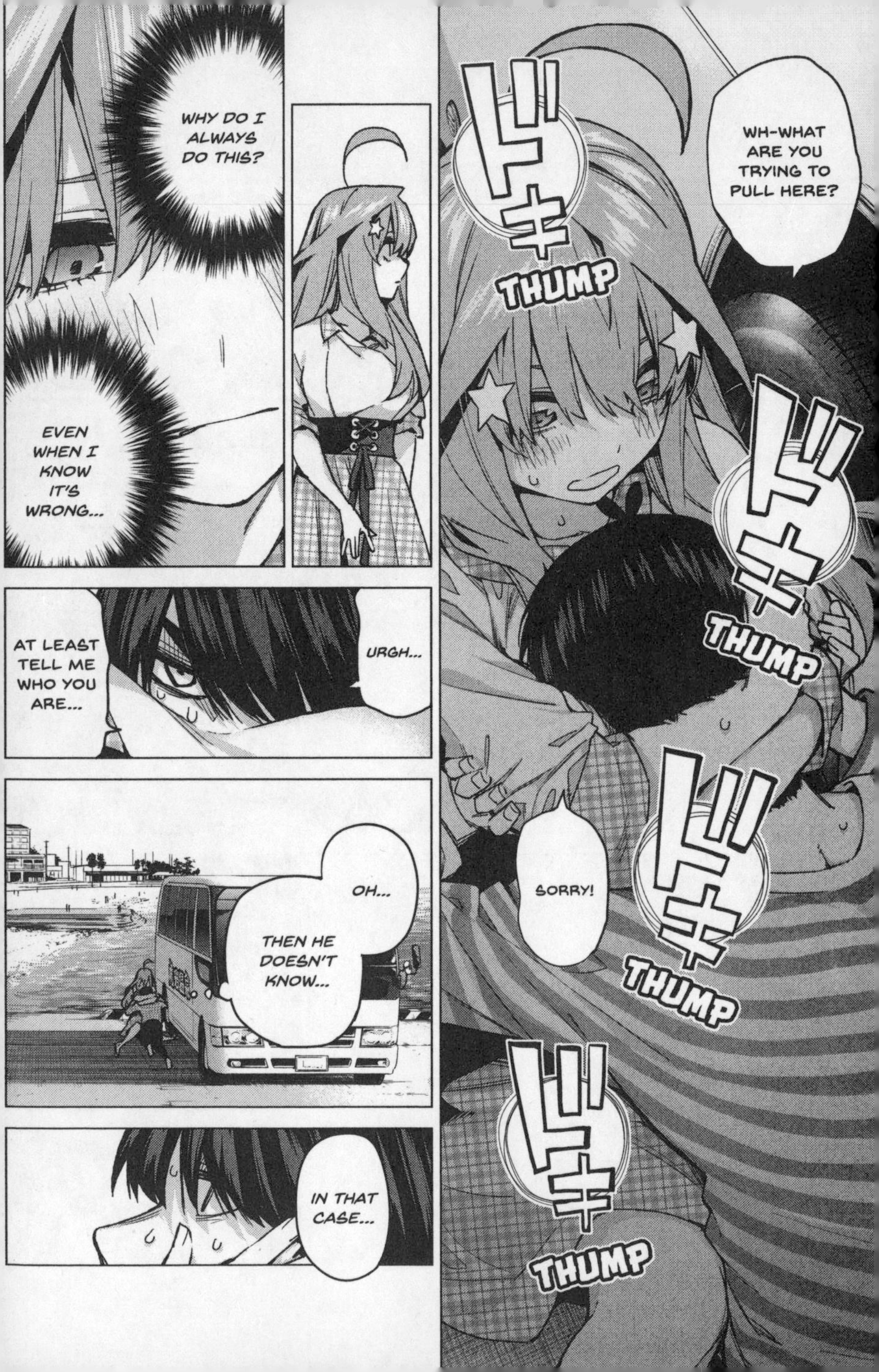
WH-WHAT ARE YOU TRYING TO PULL HERE?
ドキ
THUMP
ドキ
THUMP
SORRY!
ドキ
THUMP
ドキ
THUMP
WHY DO I ALWAYS DO THIS?
EVEN WHEN I KNOW IT'S WRONG...
URGH...
AT LEAST TELL ME WHO YOU ARE...
OH...
THEN HE DOESN'T KNOW...
IN THAT CASE...

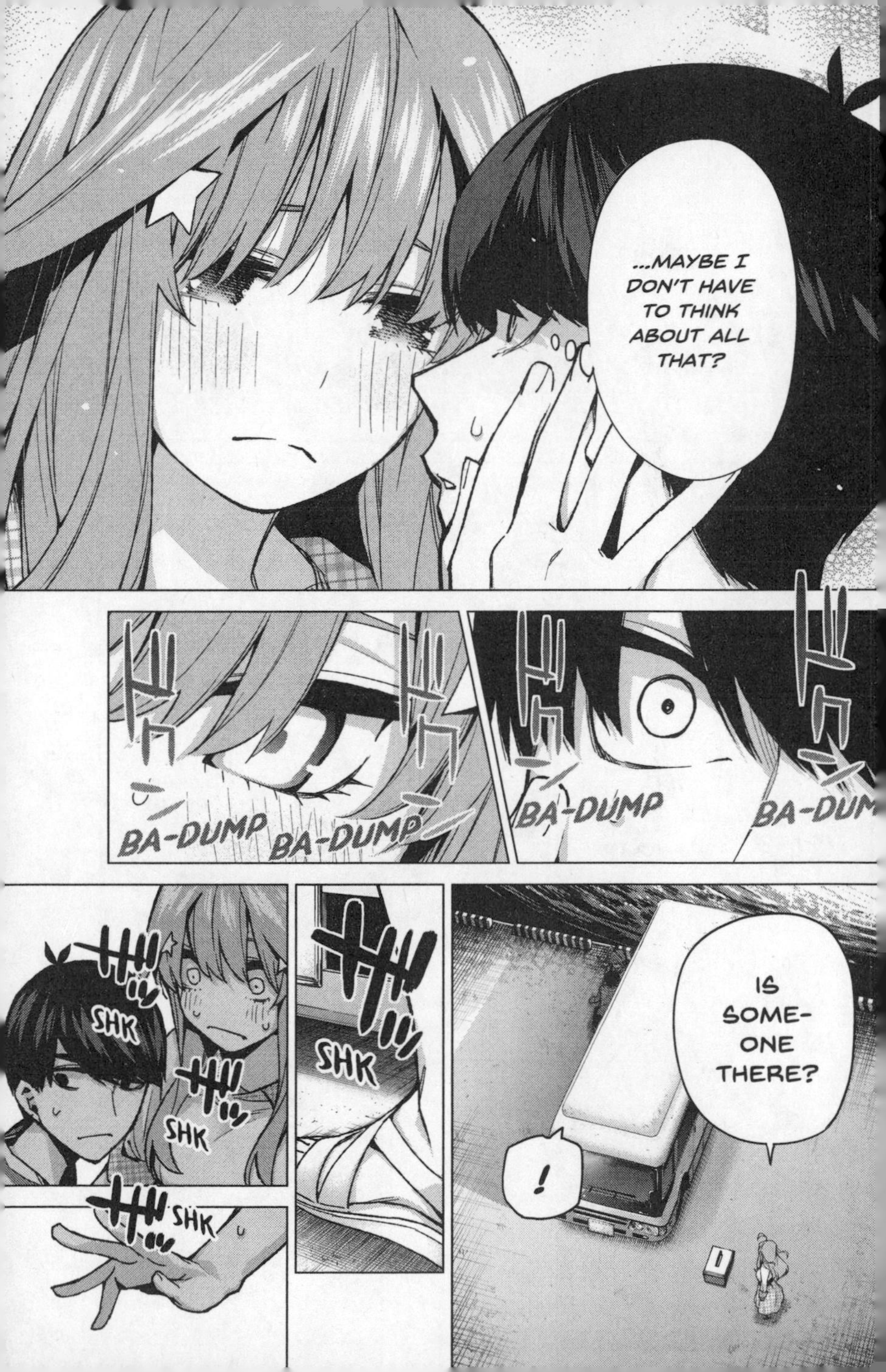
...MAYBE I DON'T HAVE TO THINK ABOUT ALL THAT?
BA-DUM
BA-DUMP
BA-DUMP
BA-DUMP
IS SOME-ONE THERE?
!
SHK
SHK
SHK
SHK

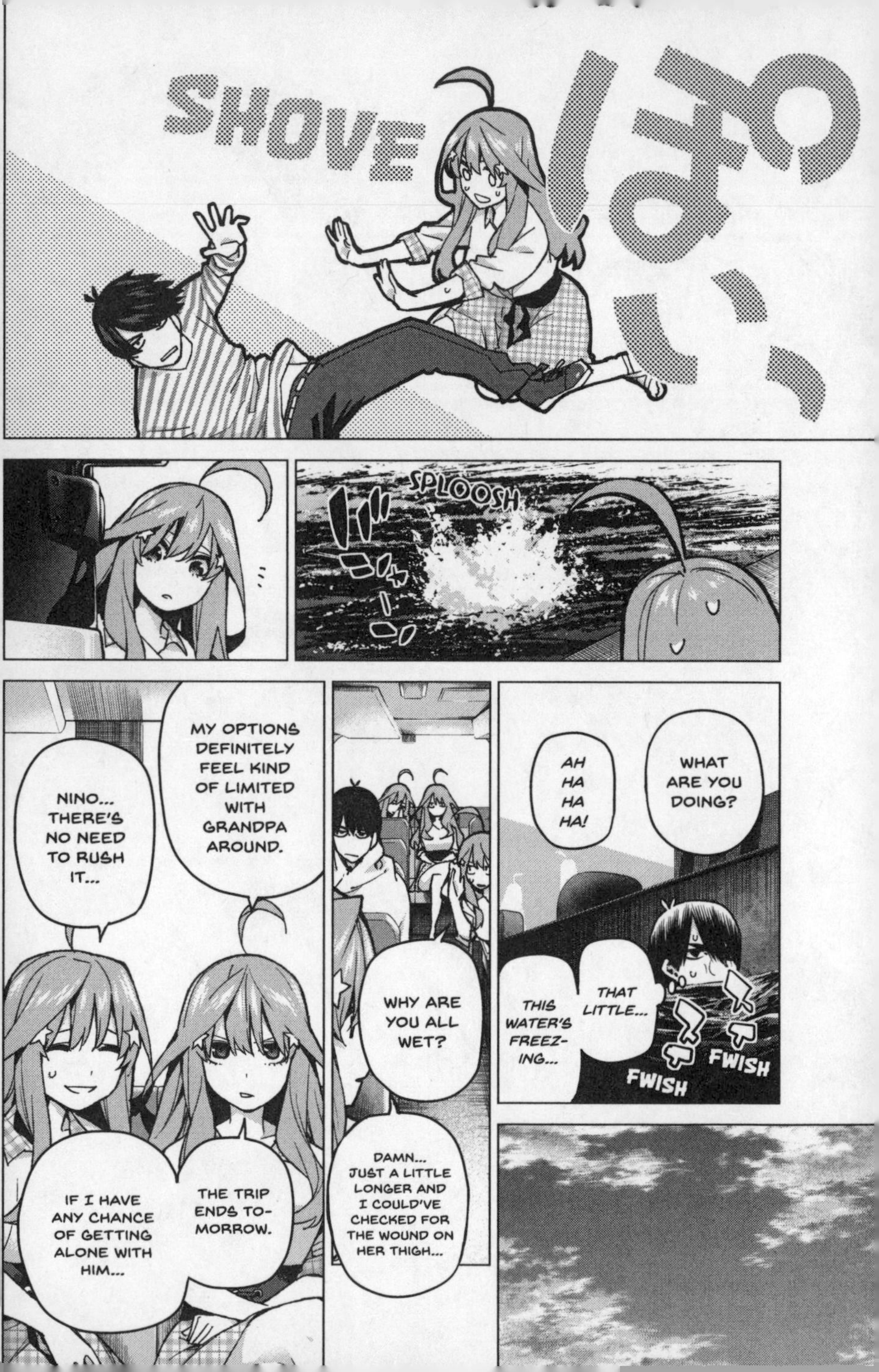
SHOVE
SPLOOSH
WHAT ARE YOU DOING?
AH HA HA HA!
THAT LITTLE...
THIS WATER'S FREEZ- ING...
FWISH
FWISH
WHY ARE YOU ALL WET?
DAMN... JUST A LITTLE LONGER AND I COULD'VE CHECKED FOR THE WOUND ON HER THIGH...
MY OPTIONS DEFINITELY FEEL KIND OF LIMITED WITH GRANDPA AROUND.
NINO... THERE'S NO NEED TO RUSH IT...
THE TRIP ENDS TO- MORROW.
IF I HAVE ANY CHANCE OF GETTING ALONE WITH HIM...

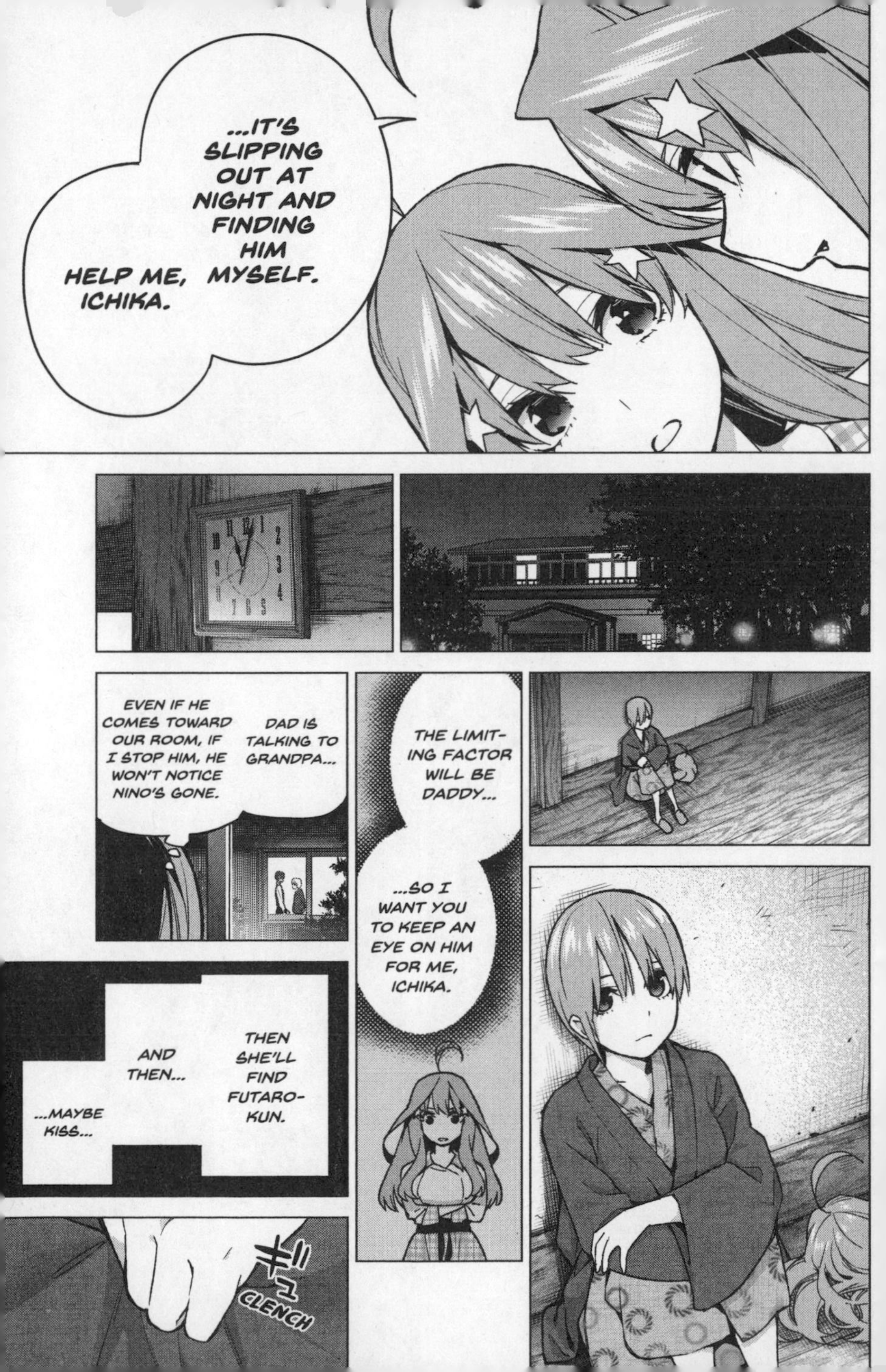
...IT'S SLIPPING OUT AT NIGHT AND FINDING HIM MYSELF.
HELP ME, ICHIKA.
THE LIMIT-ING FACTOR WILL BE DADDY...
...SO I WANT YOU TO KEEP AN EYE ON HIM FOR ME, ICHIKA.
DAD IS TALKING TO GRANDPA...
EVEN IF HE COMES TOWARD OUR ROOM, IF I STOP HIM, HE WON'T NOTICE NINO'S GONE.
THEN SHE'LL FIND FUTARO-KUN.
AND THEN...
...MAYBE KISS...
ギュ
CLENCH

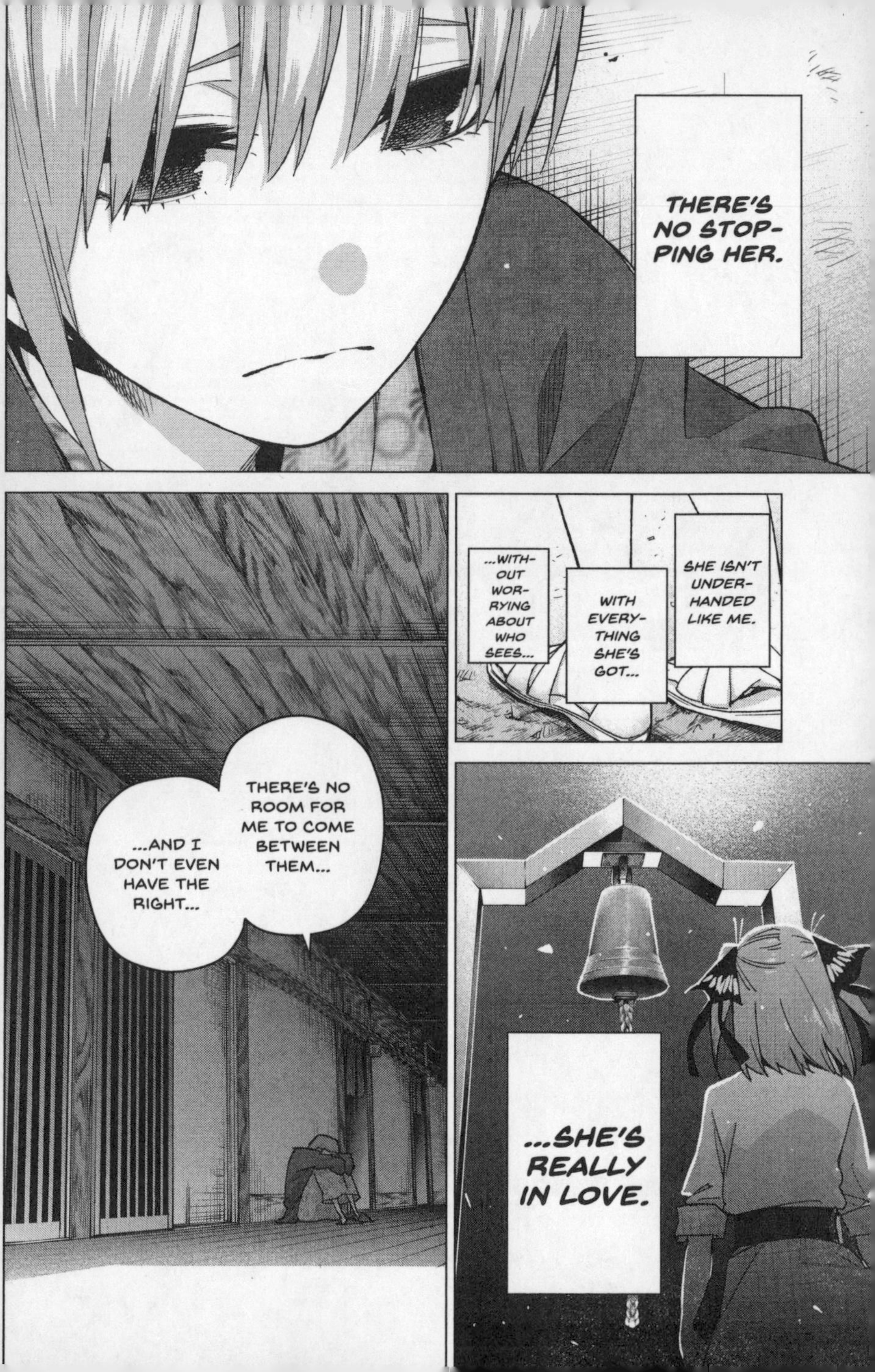
THERE'S NO STOPPING HER.
SHE ISN'T UNDERHANDED LIKE ME.
WITH EVERYTHING SHE'S GOT...
...WITHOUT WORRYING ABOUT WHO SEES...
...SHE'S REALLY IN LOVE.
THERE'S NO ROOM FOR ME TO COME BETWEEN THEM...
...AND I DON'T EVEN HAVE THE RIGHT...

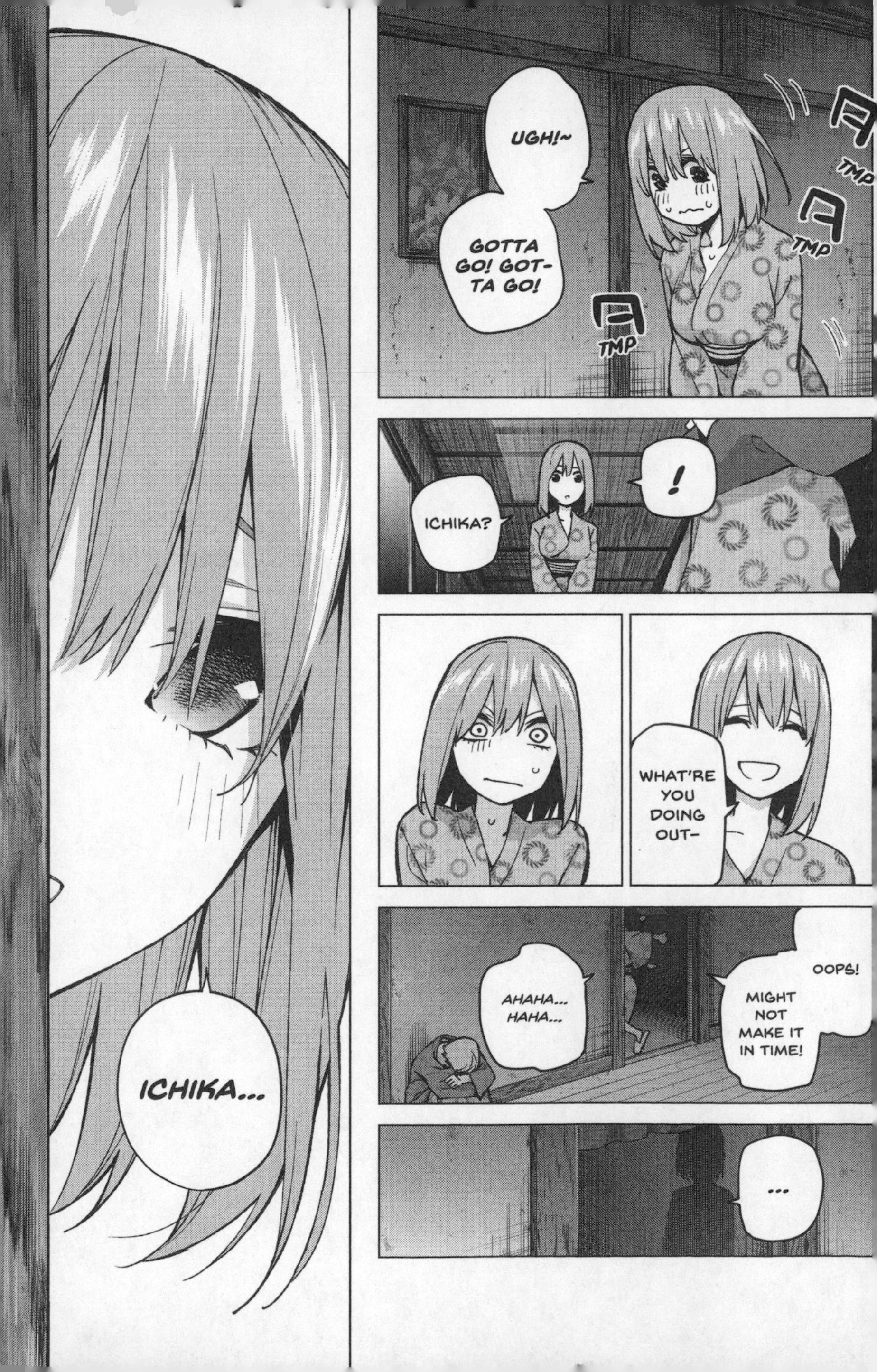
UGH!~
GOTTA GO! GOT-TA GO!
TMP
TMP
TMP
!
ICHIKA?
WHAT'RE YOU DOING OUT-
OOPS!
MIGHT NOT MAKE IT IN TIME!
AHAHA... HAHA...
...
ICHIKA...

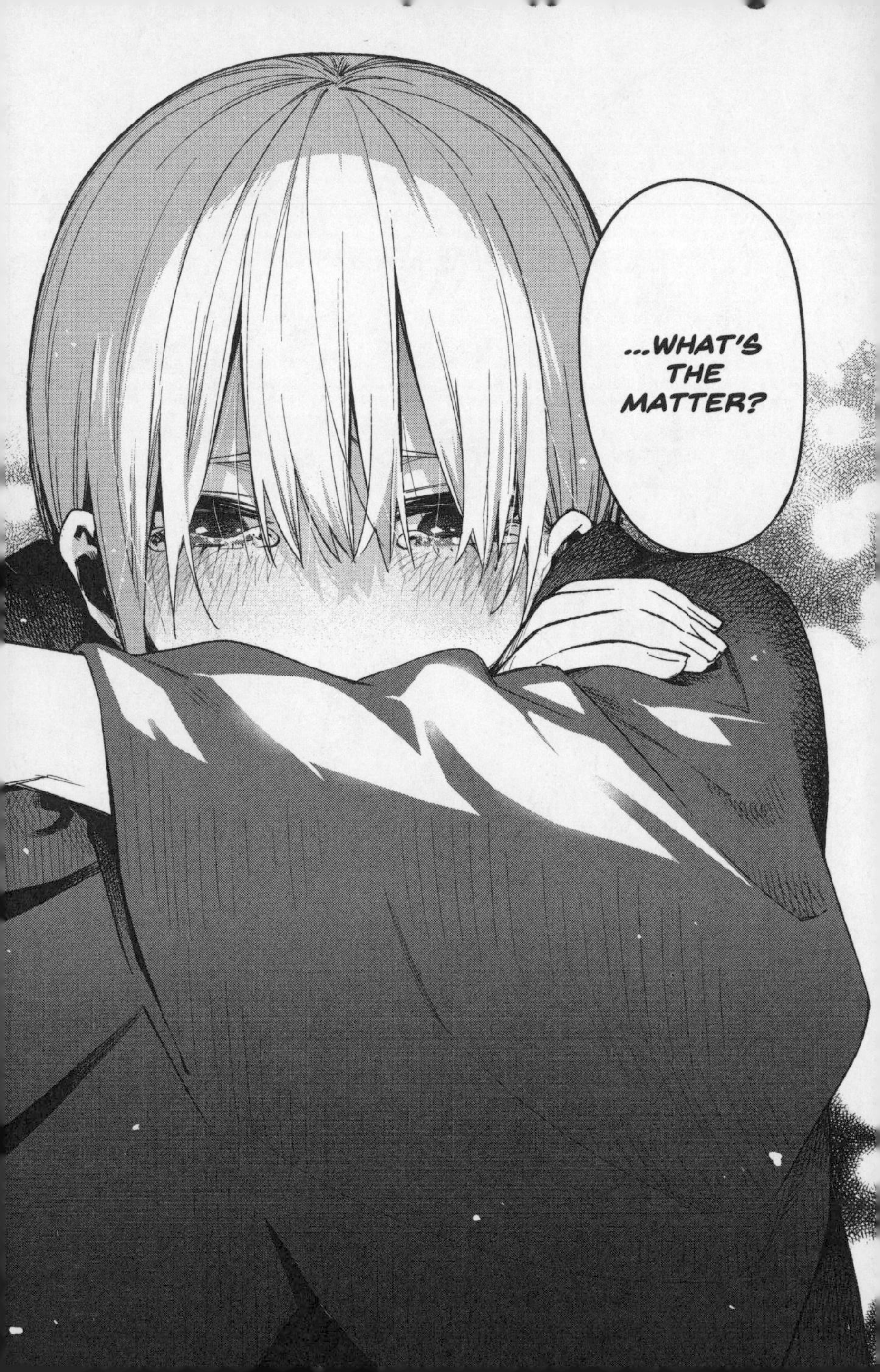
...WHAT'S THE MATTER?

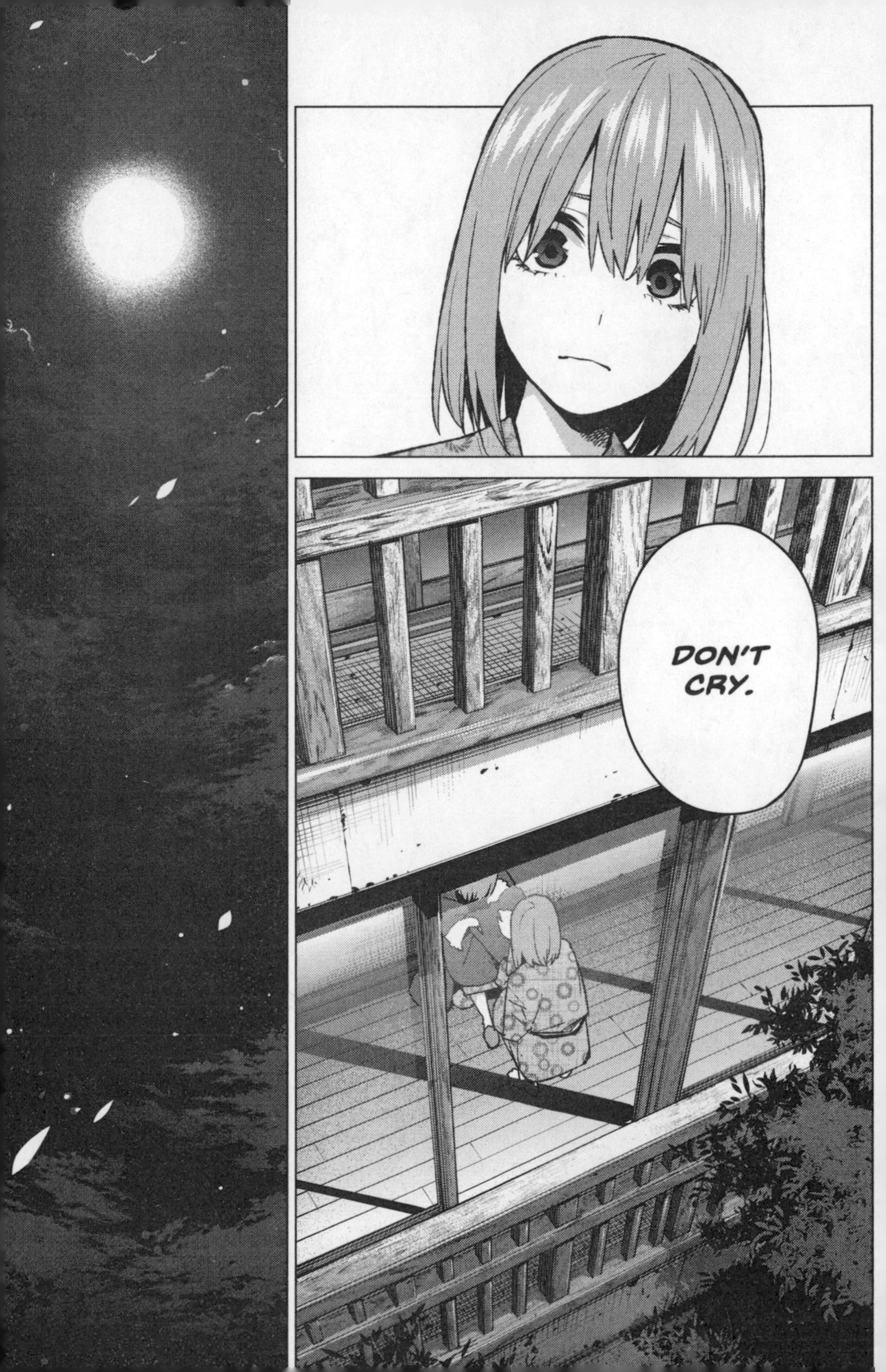
DON'T CRY.

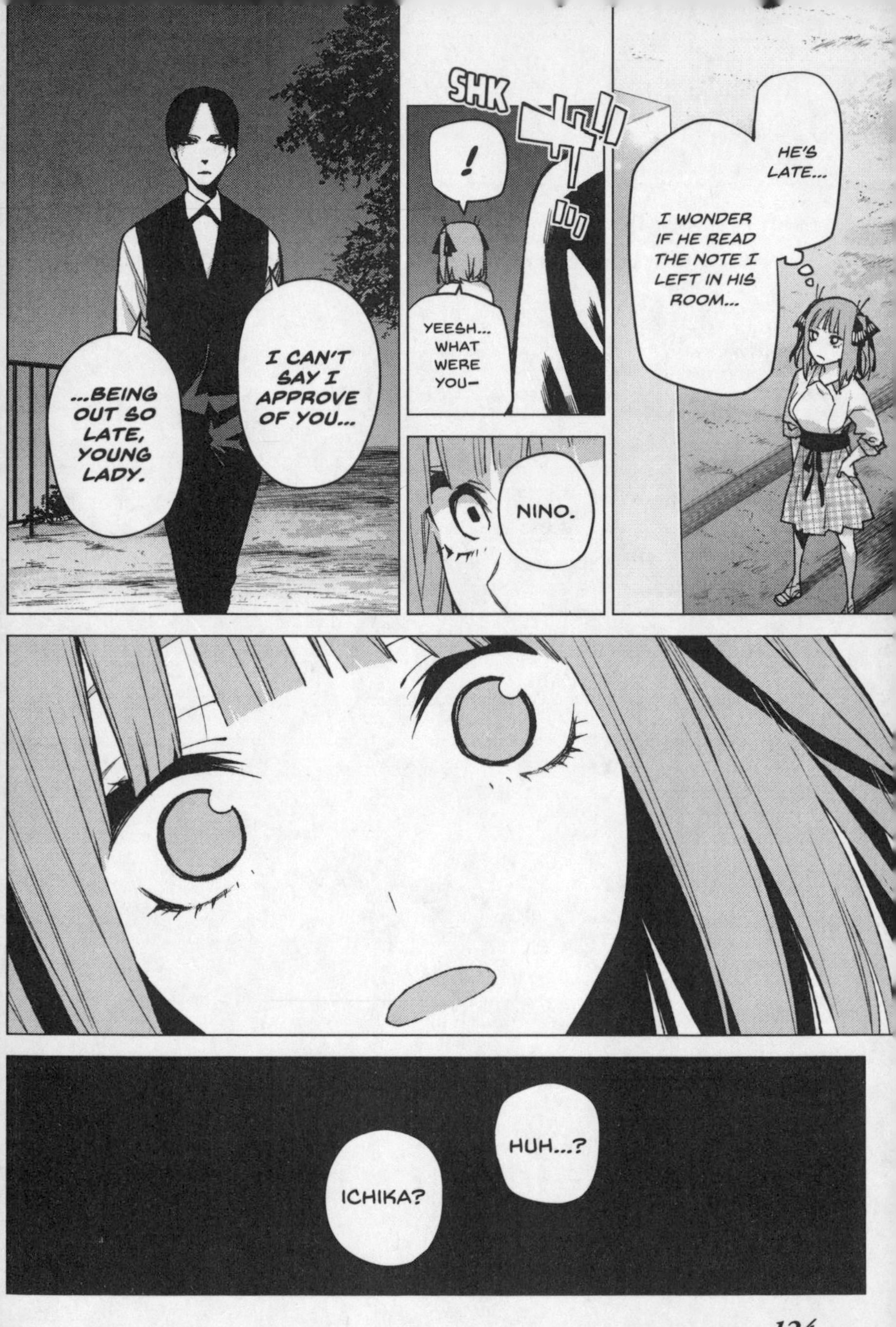
HE'S LATE...
I WONDER IF HE READ THE NOTE I LEFT IN HIS ROOM...
SHK
!
YEESH... WHAT WERE YOU—
NINO.
I CAN'T SAY I APPROVE OF YOU...
...BEING OUT SO LATE, YOUNG LADY.
HUH...?
ICHIKA?

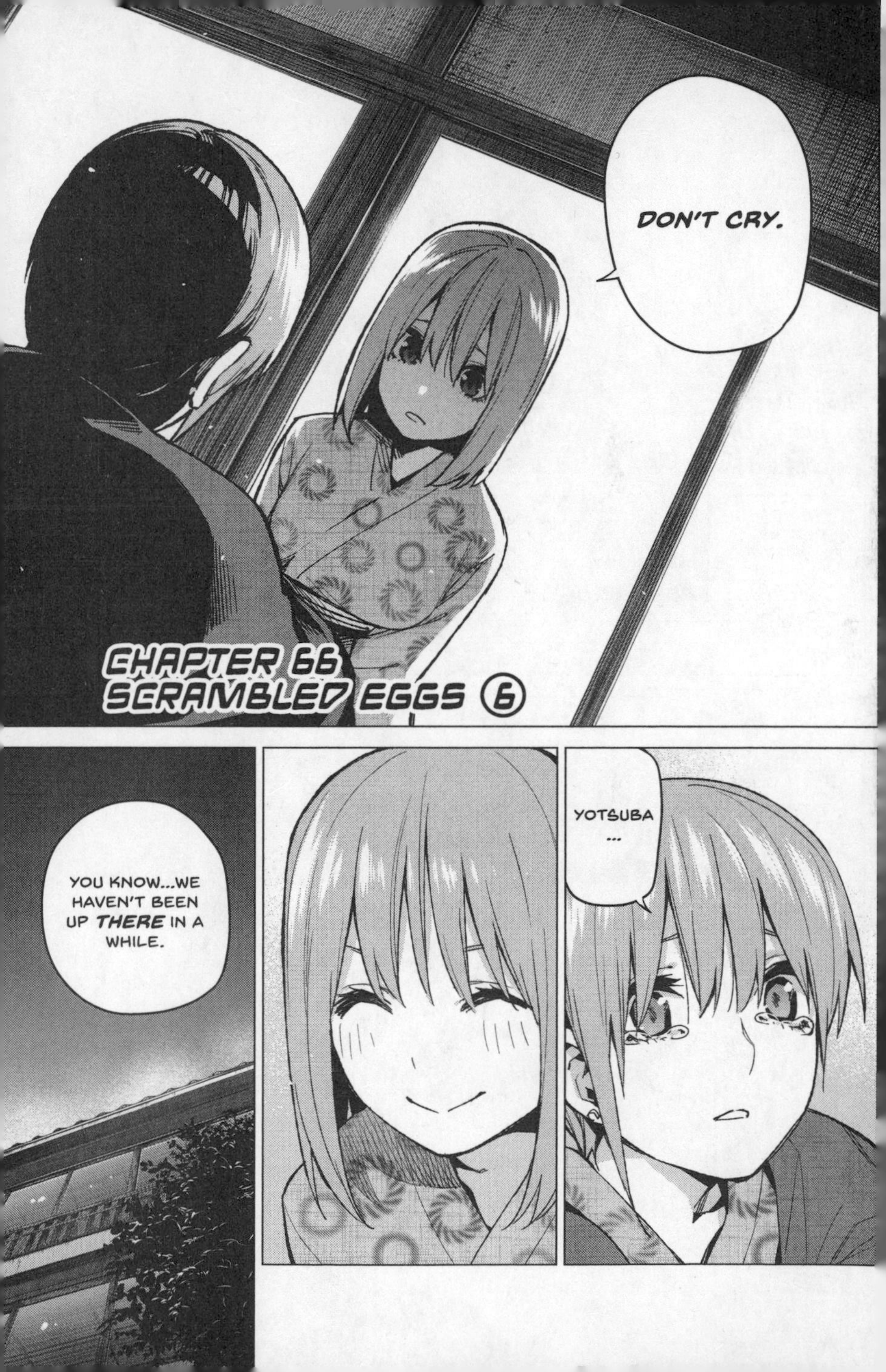
DON'T CRY.
CHAPTER 66
SCRAMBLED EGGS ⑥
YOTSUBA ...
YOU KNOW...WE HAVEN'T BEEN UP THERE IN A WHILE.

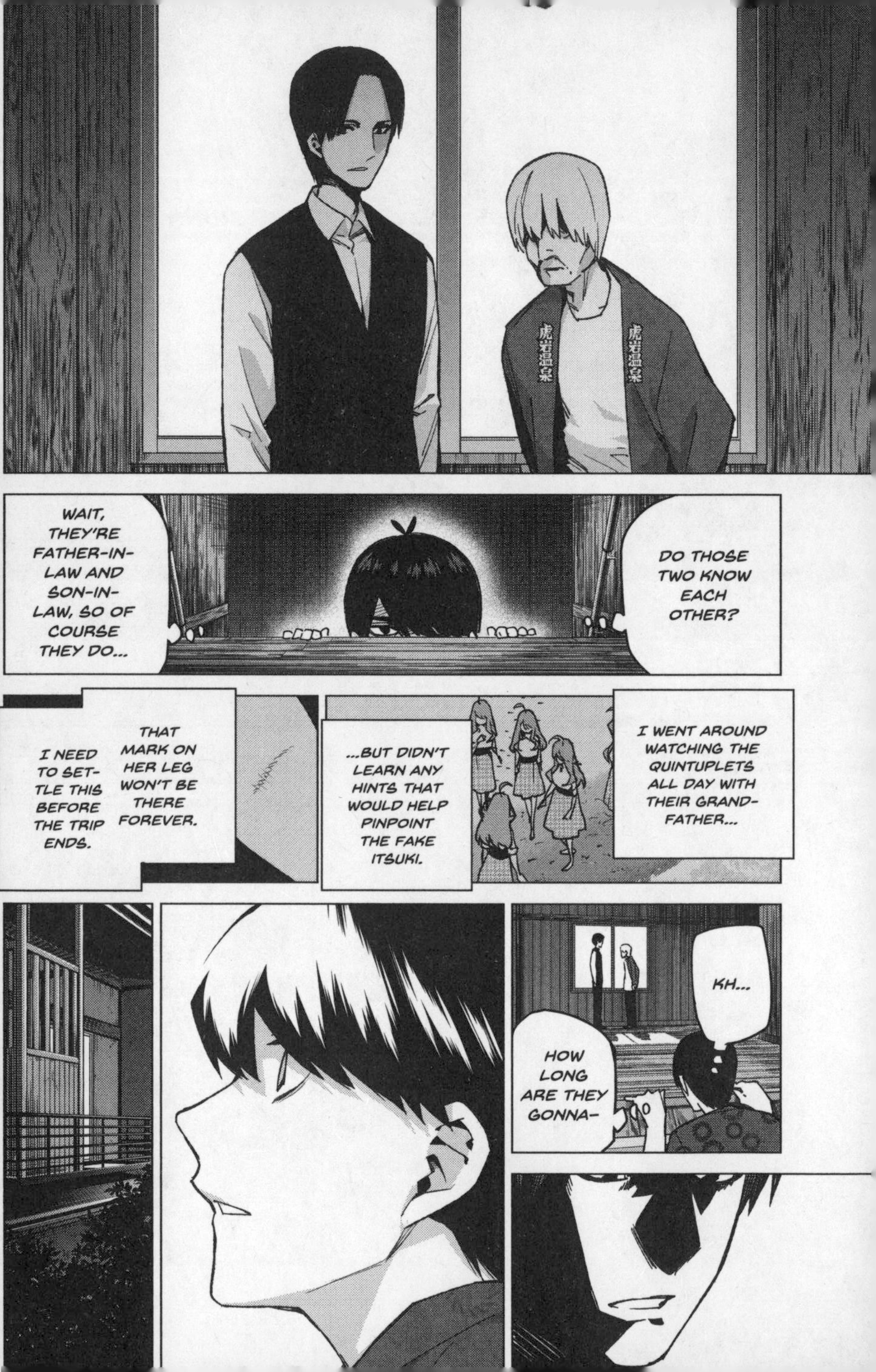
虎岩温泉
DO THOSE TWO KNOW EACH OTHER?
WAIT, THEY'RE FATHER-IN-LAW AND SON-IN-LAW, SO OF COURSE THEY DO...
I WENT AROUND WATCHING THE QUINTUPLETS ALL DAY WITH THEIR GRAND-FATHER...
...BUT DIDN'T LEARN ANY HINTS THAT WOULD HELP PINPOINT THE FAKE ITSUKI.
THAT MARK ON HER LEG WON'T BE THERE FOREVER.
I NEED TO SETTLE THIS BEFORE THE TRIP ENDS.
KH...
HOW LONG ARE THEY GONNA-

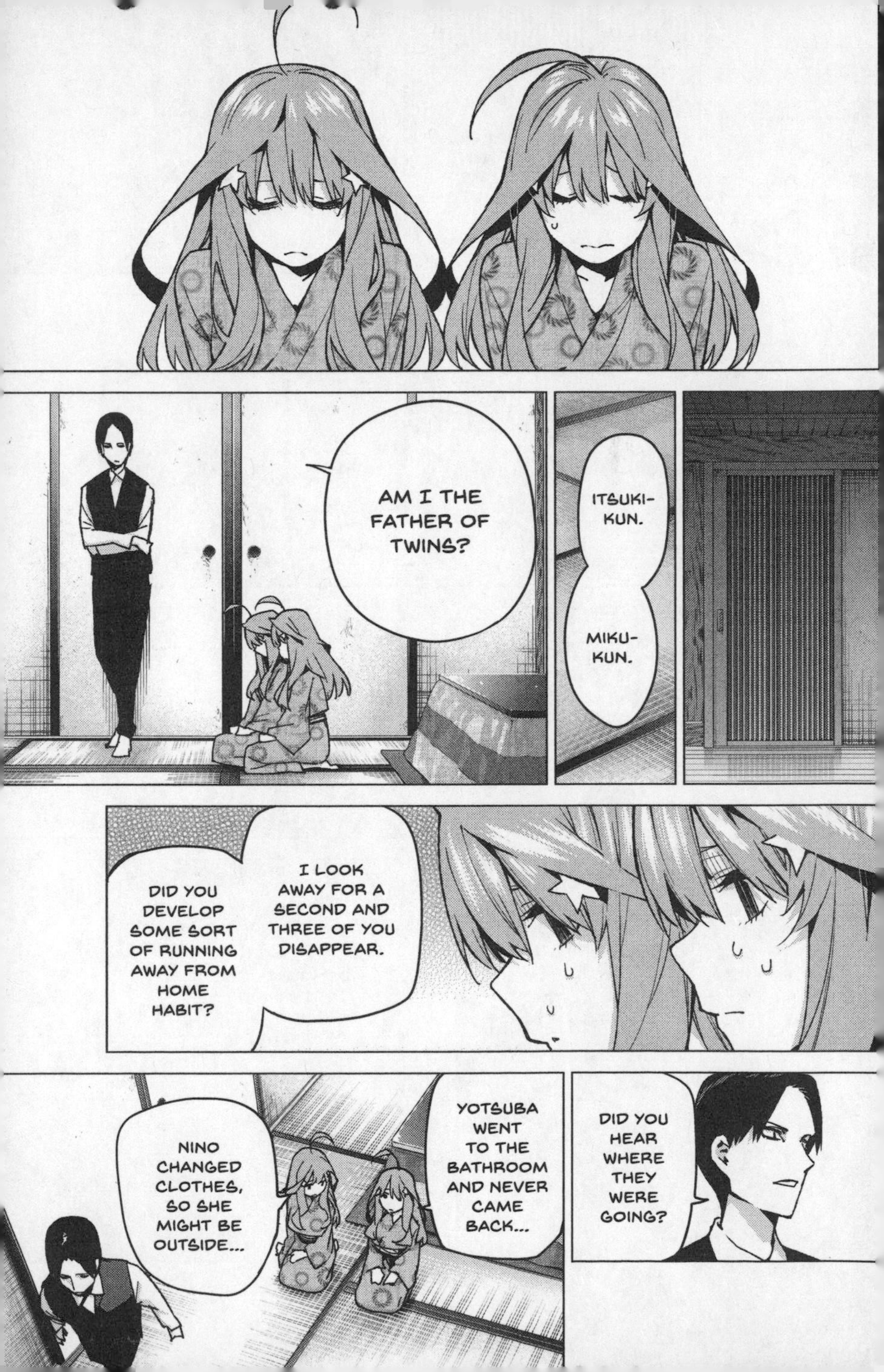
ITSUKI-KUN.
MIKU-KUN.
AM I THE FATHER OF TWINS?
I LOOK AWAY FOR A SECOND AND THREE OF YOU DISAPPEAR.
DID YOU DEVELOP SOME SORT OF RUNNING AWAY FROM HOME HABIT?
DID YOU HEAR WHERE THEY WERE GOING?
YOTSUBA WENT TO THE BATHROOM AND NEVER CAME BACK...
NINO CHANGED CLOTHES, SO SHE MIGHT BE OUTSIDE...

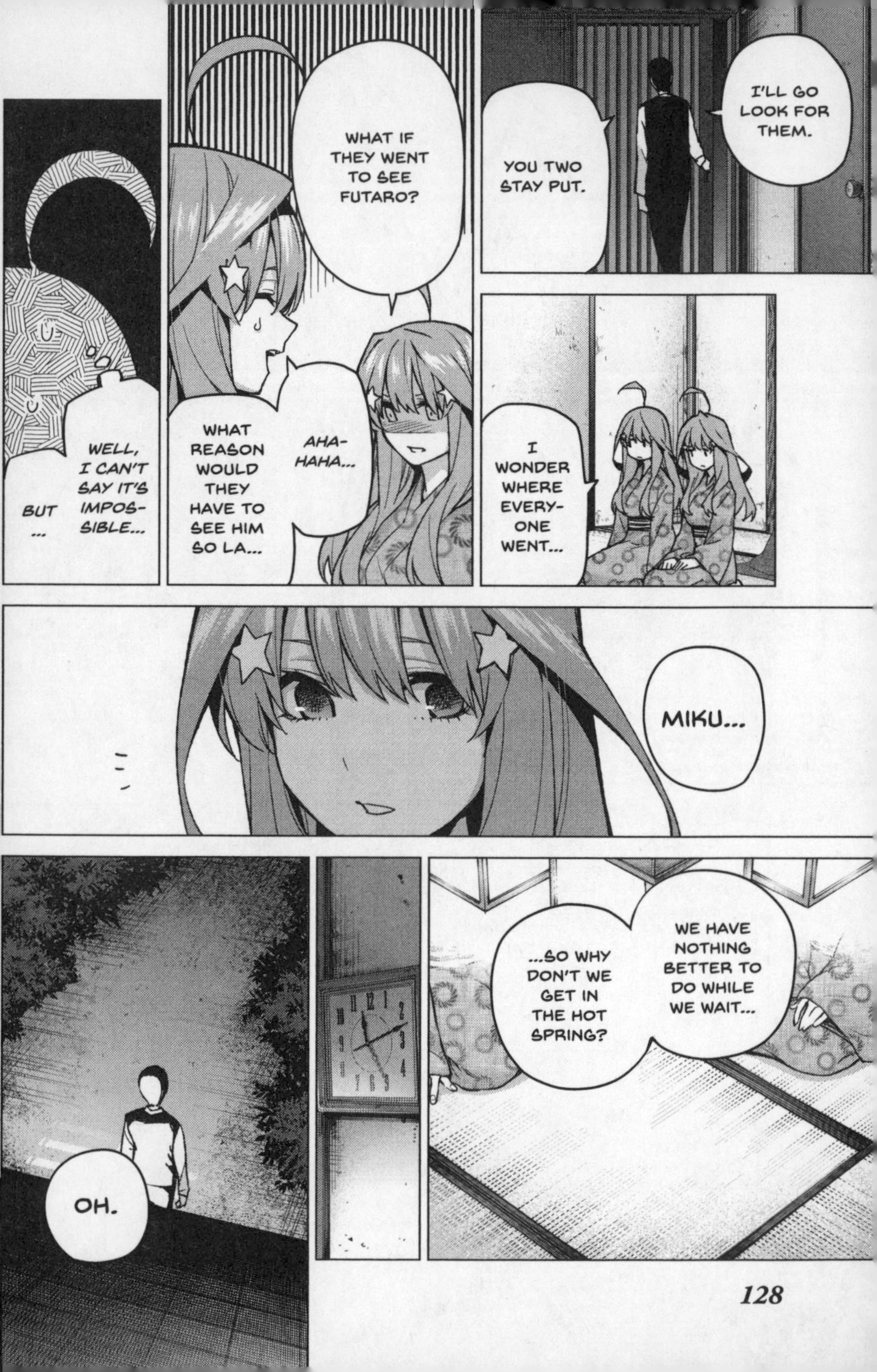
I'LL GO LOOK FOR THEM.
YOU TWO STAY PUT.
I WONDER WHERE EVERY-ONE WENT...
WHAT IF THEY WENT TO SEE FUTARO?
AHA-HAHA...
WHAT REASON WOULD THEY HAVE TO SEE HIM SO LA...
WELL, I CAN'T SAY IT'S IMPOS-SIBLE...
BUT ...
MIKU...
WE HAVE NOTHING BETTER TO DO WHILE WE WAIT...
...SO WHY DON'T WE GET IN THE HOT SPRING?
OH.

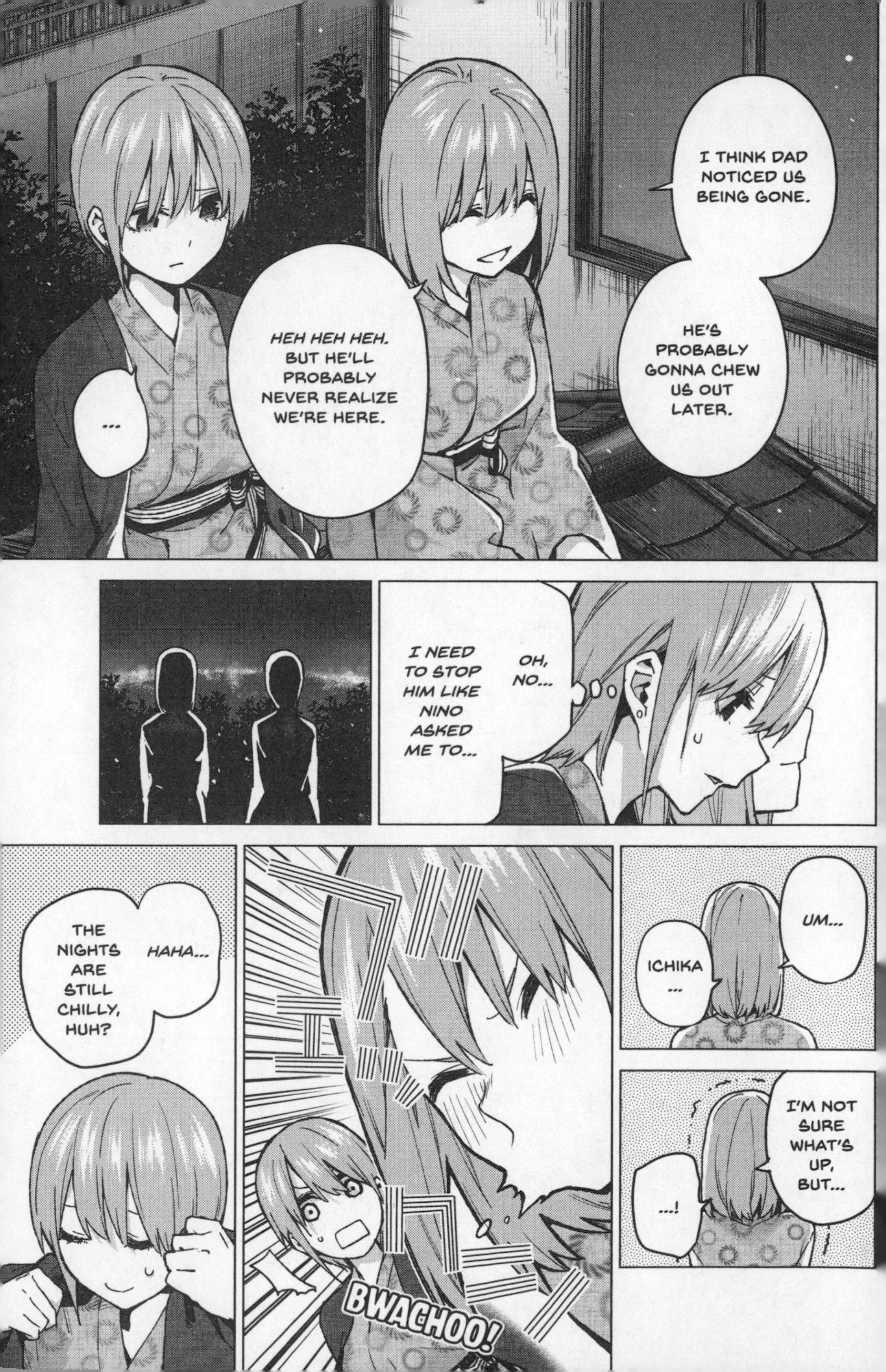
I THINK DAD NOTICED US BEING GONE.
HE'S PROBABLY GONNA CHEW US OUT LATER.
HEH HEH HEH. BUT HE'LL PROBABLY NEVER REALIZE WE'RE HERE.
...
OH, NO...
I NEED TO STOP HIM LIKE NINO ASKED ME TO...
UM...
ICHIKA...
I'M NOT SURE WHAT'S UP, BUT...
...!
BWACHOO!
HAHA...
THE NIGHTS ARE STILL CHILLY, HUH?

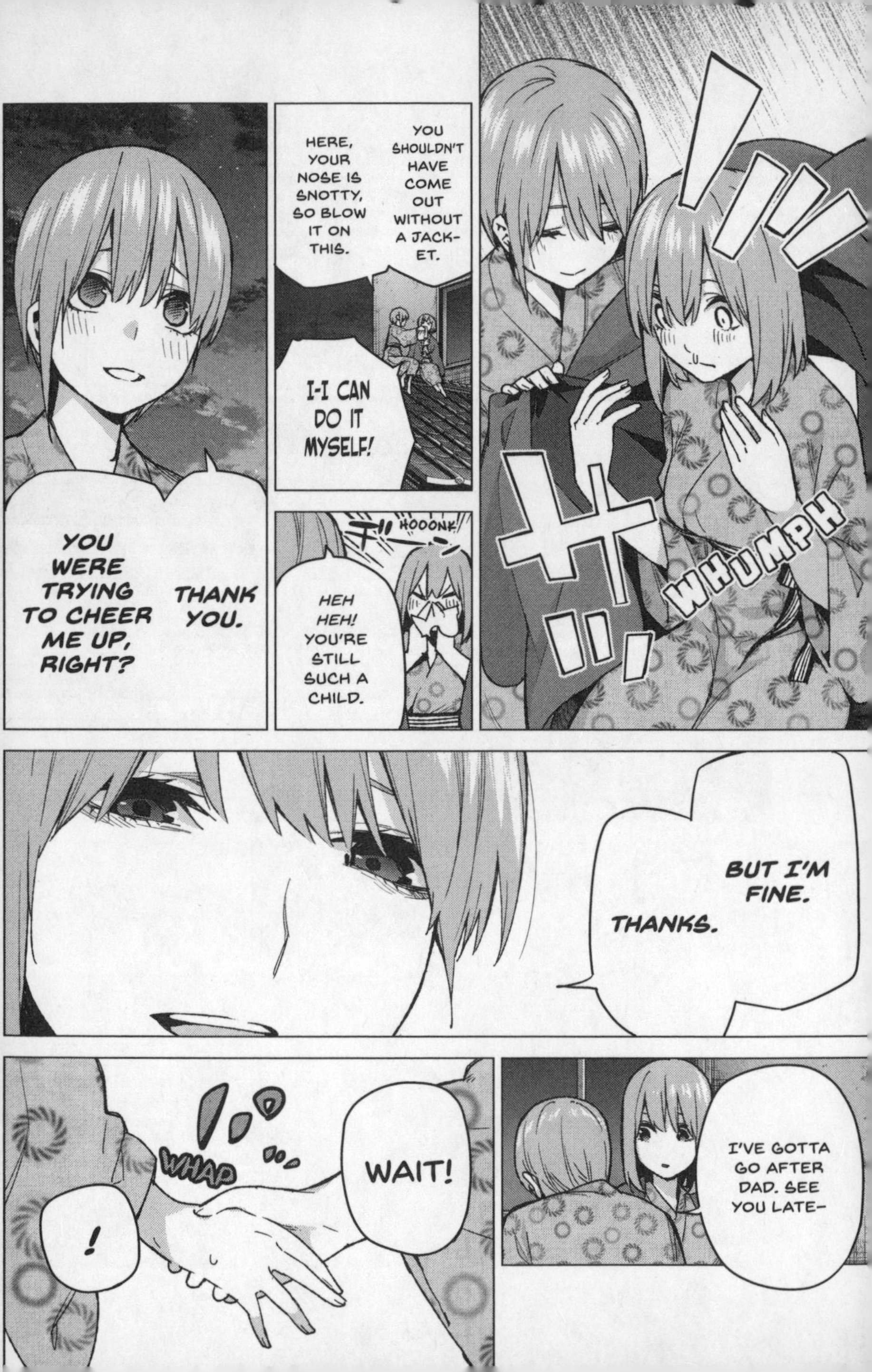
WHUMPH
YOU SHOULDN'T HAVE COME OUT WITHOUT A JACKET.
HERE, YOUR NOSE IS SNOTTY, SO BLOW IT ON THIS.
I-I CAN DO IT MYSELF!
HOOONK
HEH HEH! YOU'RE STILL SUCH A CHILD.
YOU WERE TRYING TO CHEER ME UP, RIGHT?
THANK YOU.
BUT I'M FINE.
THANKS.
I'VE GOTTA GO AFTER DAD. SEE YOU LATE-
WAIT!
WHAP
!

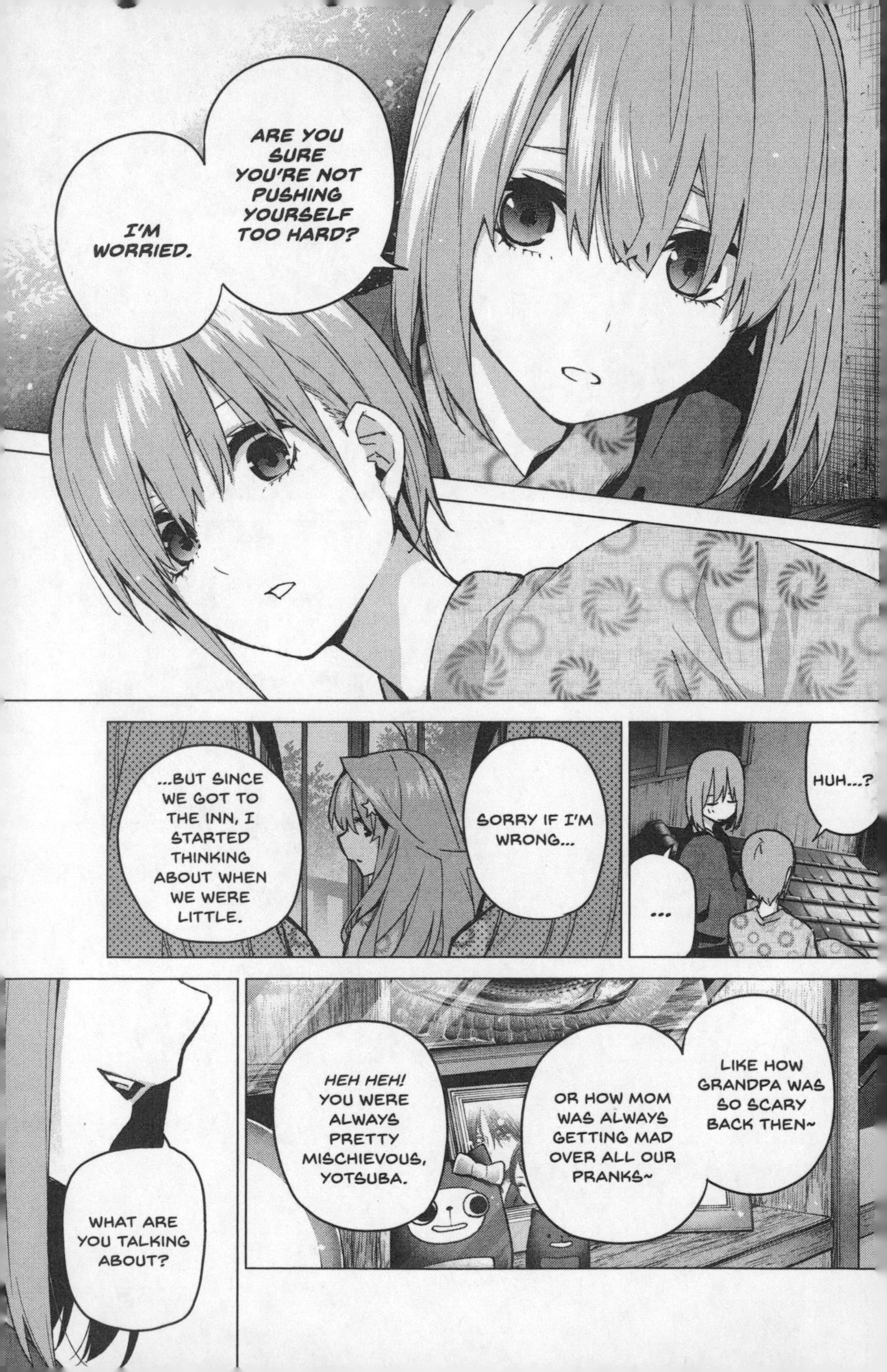
ARE YOU SURE YOU'RE NOT PUSHING YOURSELF TOO HARD?
I'M WORRIED.
HUH...?
...
SORRY IF I'M WRONG...
...BUT SINCE WE GOT TO THE INN, I STARTED THINKING ABOUT WHEN WE WERE LITTLE.
LIKE HOW GRANDPA WAS SO SCARY BACK THEN~
OR HOW MOM WAS ALWAYS GETTING MAD OVER ALL OUR PRANKS~
HEH HEH! YOU WERE ALWAYS PRETTY MISCHIEVOUS, YOTSUBA.
WHAT ARE YOU TALKING ABOUT?

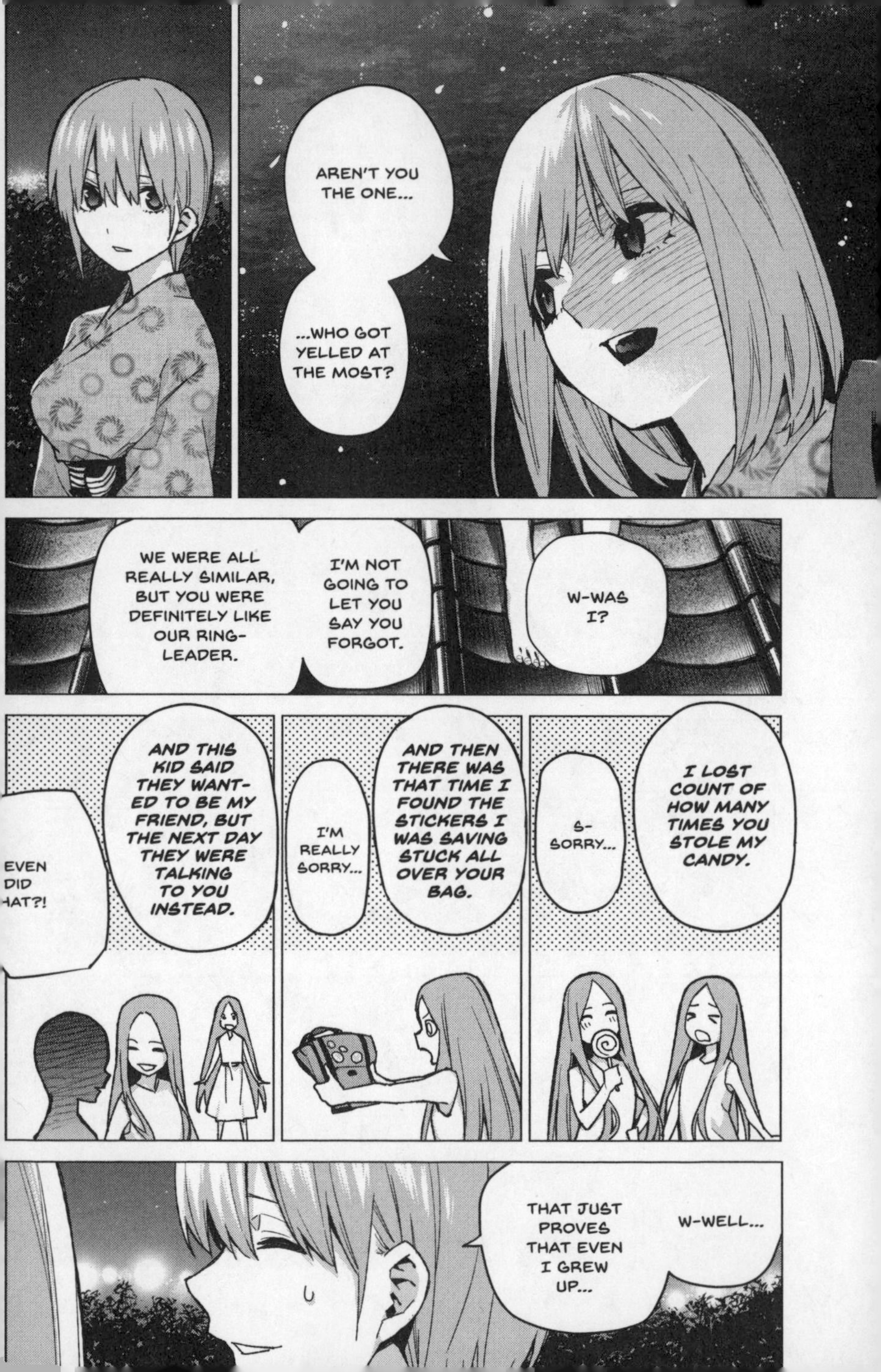
AREN'T YOU THE ONE...
...WHO GOT YELLED AT THE MOST?
W-WAS I?
I'M NOT GOING TO LET YOU SAY YOU FORGOT.
WE WERE ALL REALLY SIMILAR, BUT YOU WERE DEFINITELY LIKE OUR RING-LEADER.
I LOST COUNT OF HOW MANY TIMES YOU STOLE MY CANDY.
S-SORRY...
AND THEN THERE WAS THAT TIME I FOUND THE STICKERS I WAS SAVING STUCK ALL OVER YOUR BAG.
I'M REALLY SORRY...
AND THIS KID SAID THEY WANTED TO BE MY FRIEND, BUT THE NEXT DAY THEY WERE TALKING TO YOU INSTEAD.
EVEN DID HAT?!
W-WELL...
THAT JUST PROVES THAT EVEN I GREW UP...

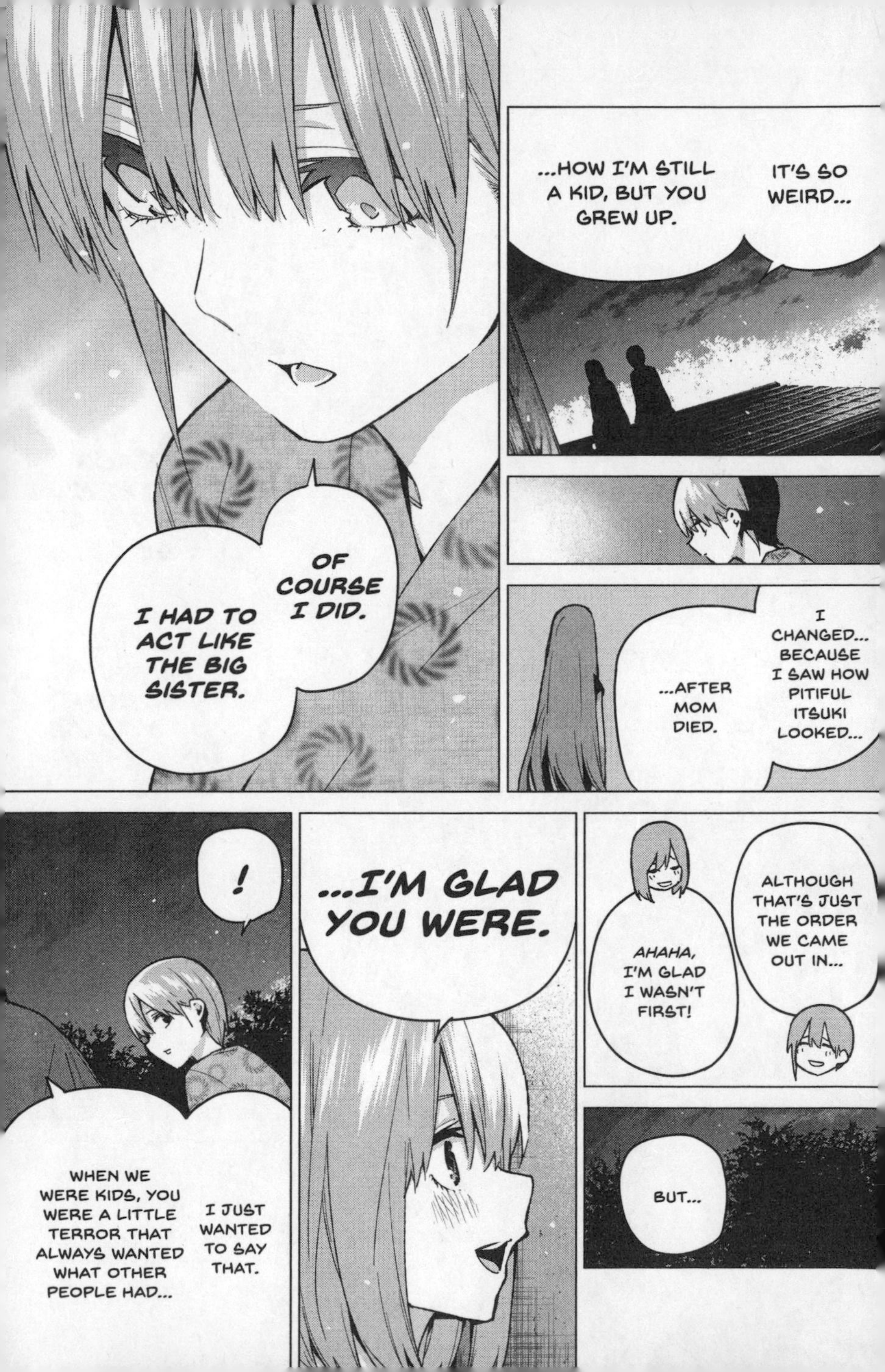
IT'S SO WEIRD...
...HOW I'M STILL A KID, BUT YOU GREW UP.
I CHANGED... BECAUSE I SAW HOW PITIFUL ITSUKI LOOKED...
...AFTER MOM DIED.
OF COURSE I DID.
I HAD TO ACT LIKE THE BIG SISTER.
ALTHOUGH THAT'S JUST THE ORDER WE CAME OUT IN...
AHAHA, I'M GLAD I WASN'T FIRST!
BUT...
...I'M GLAD YOU WERE.
!
WHEN WE WERE KIDS, YOU WERE A LITTLE TERROR THAT ALWAYS WANTED WHAT OTHER PEOPLE HAD...
I JUST WANTED TO SAY THAT.

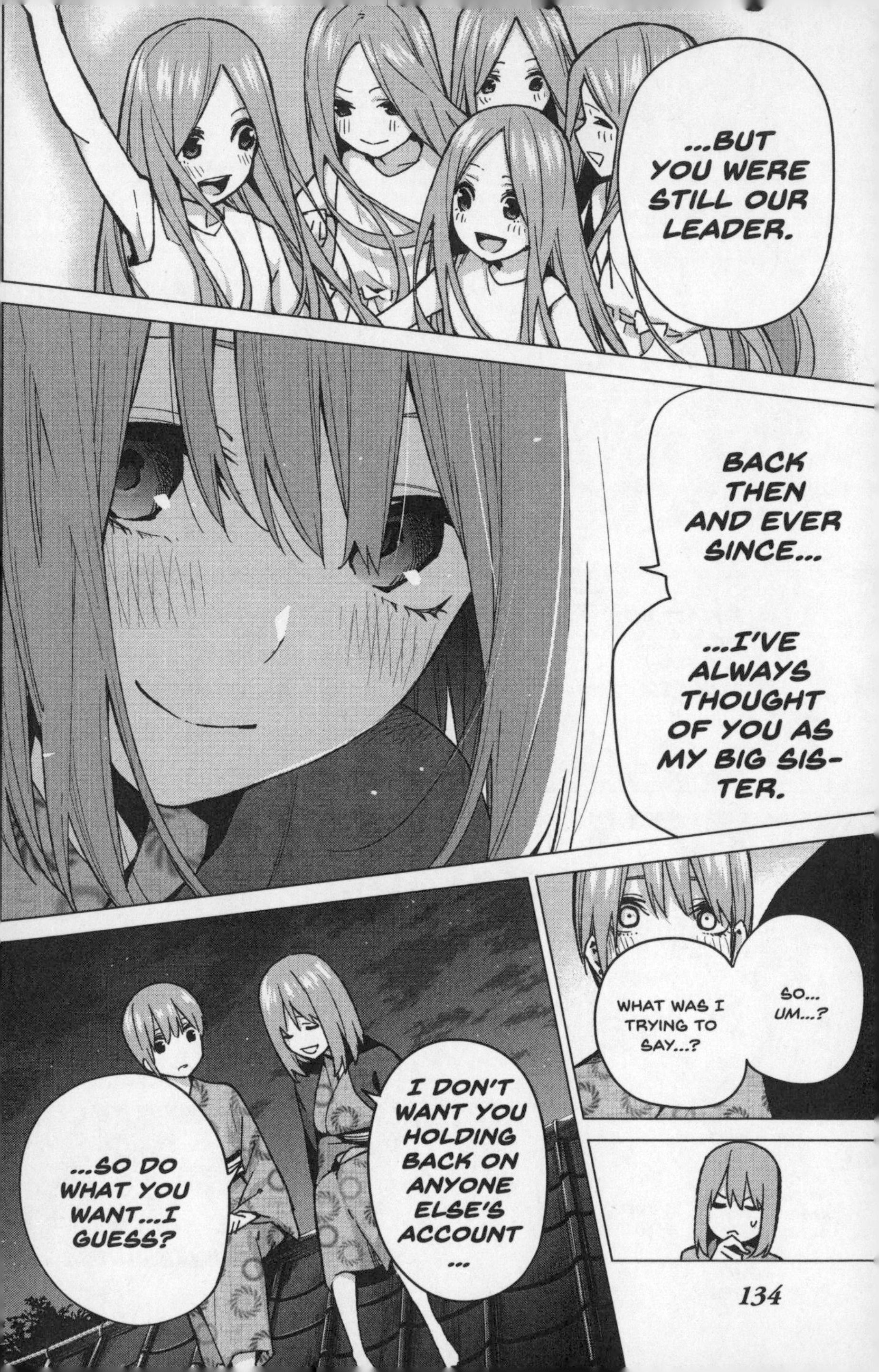
...BUT YOU WERE STILL OUR LEADER.
BACK THEN AND EVER SINCE...
...I'VE ALWAYS THOUGHT OF YOU AS MY BIG SIS-TER.
SO... UM...?
WHAT WAS I TRYING TO SAY...?
I DON'T WANT YOU HOLDING BACK ON ANYONE ELSE'S ACCOUNT ...
...SO DO WHAT YOU WANT...I GUESS?

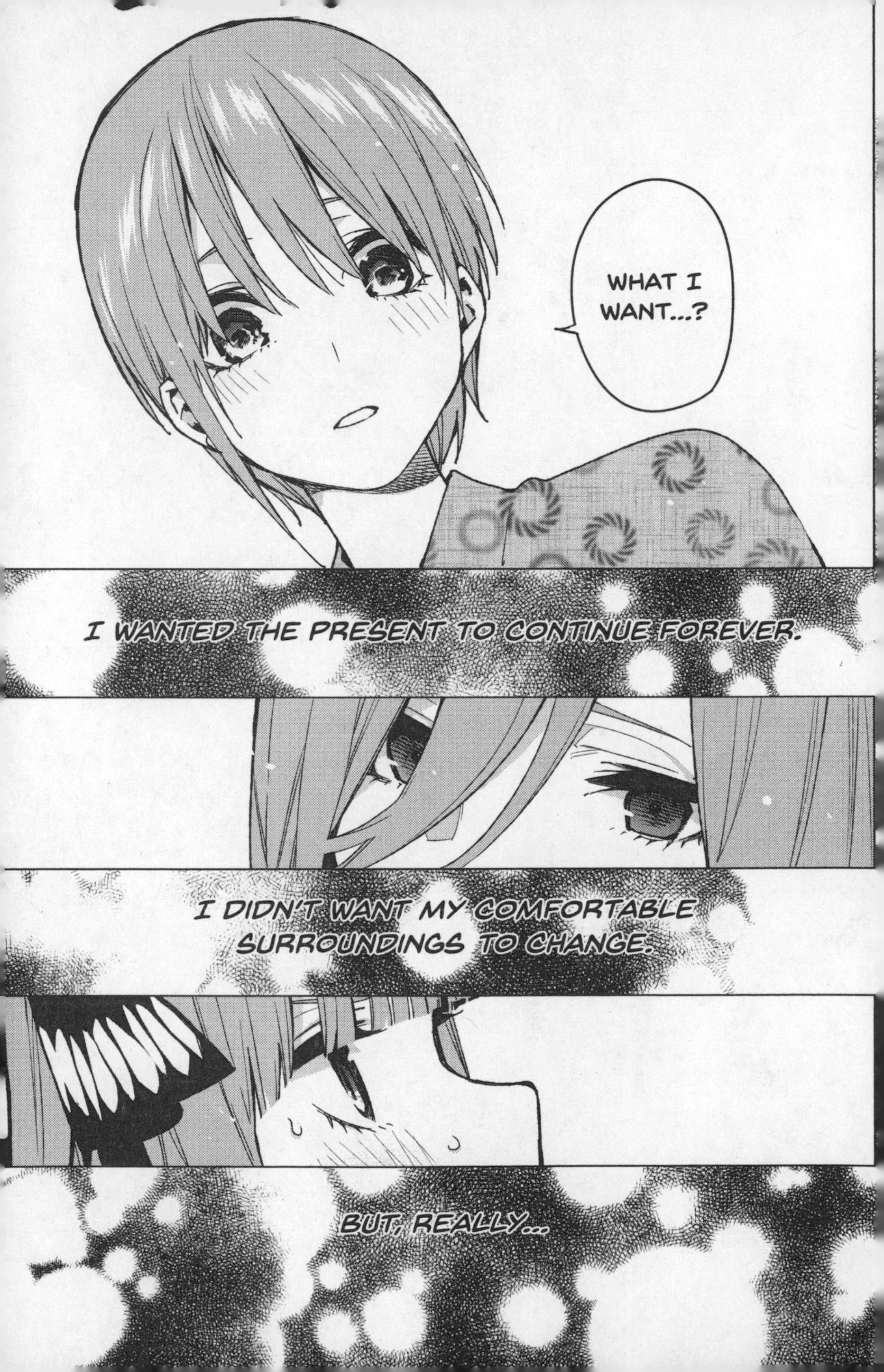
WHAT I WANT...?
I WANTED THE PRESENT TO CONTINUE FOREVER.
I DIDN'T WANT MY COMFORTABLE SURROUNDINGS TO CHANGE.
BUT, REALLY...

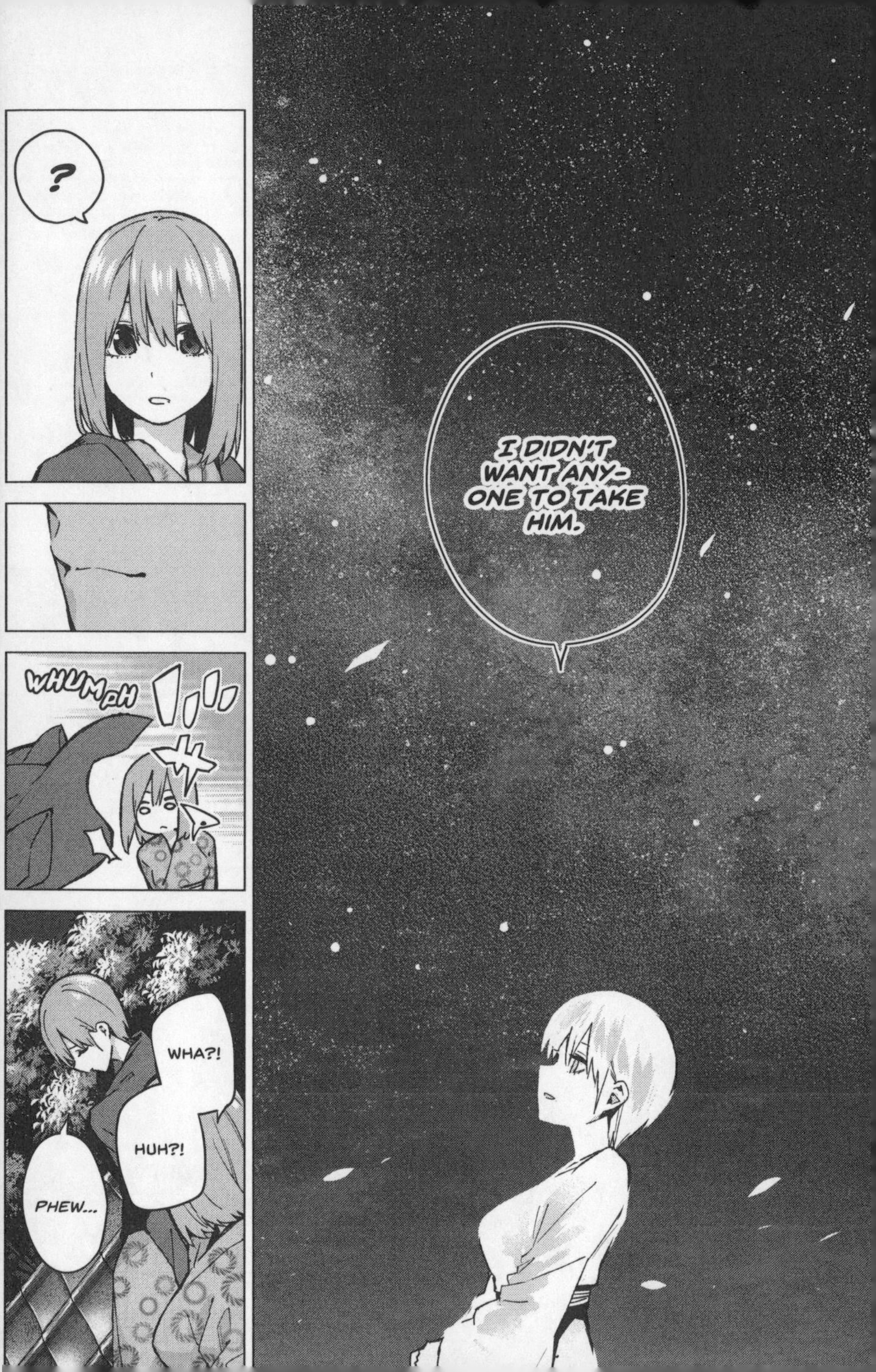
I DIDN'T WANT ANY-ONE TO TAKE HIM.
?
WHUMPH
WHA?!
HUH?!
PHEW...

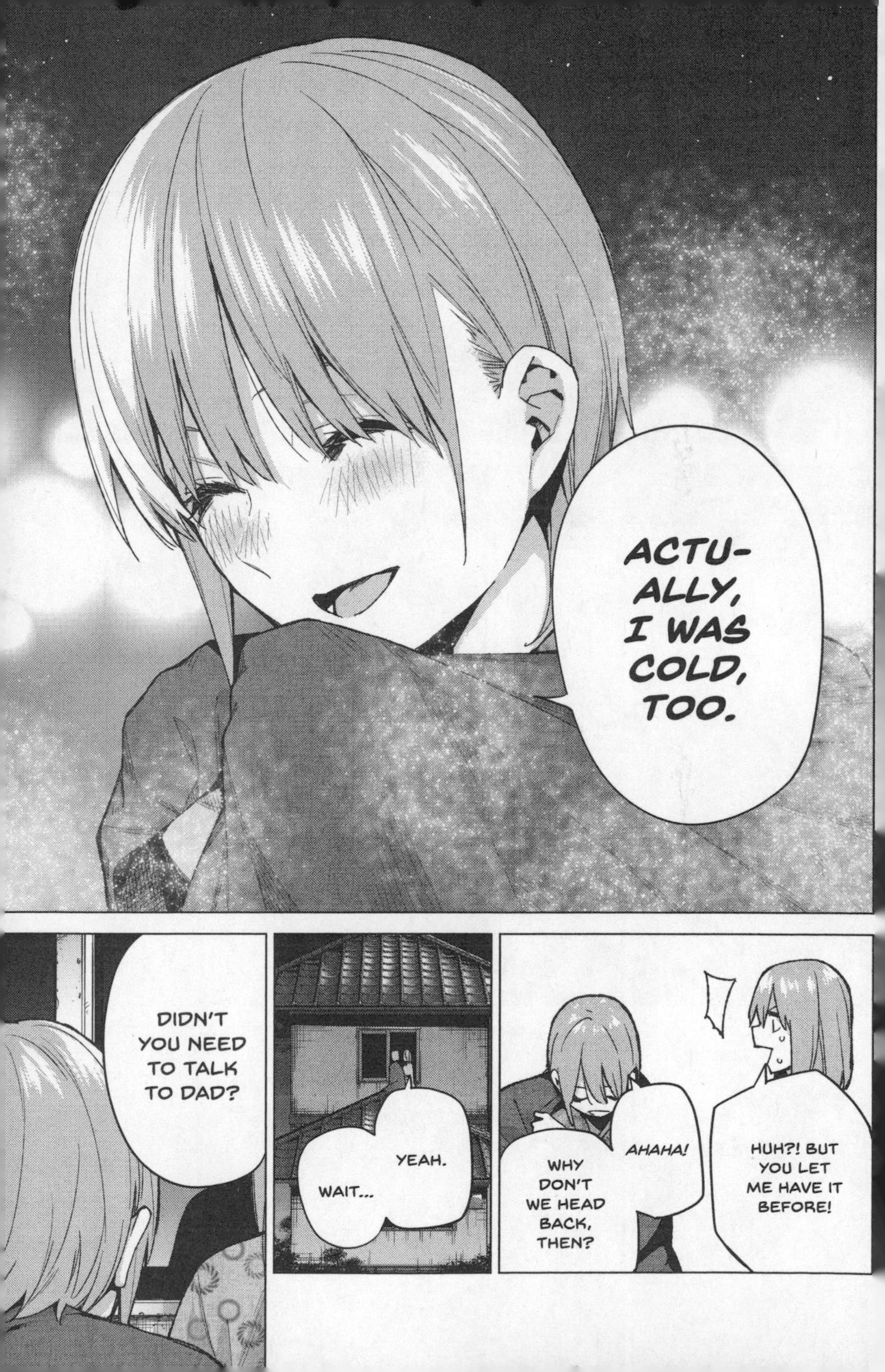
ACTU-ALLY, I WAS COLD, TOO.
HUH?! BUT YOU LET ME HAVE IT BEFORE!
AHAHA!
WHY DON'T WE HEAD BACK, THEN?
YEAH.
WAIT...
DIDN'T YOU NEED TO TALK TO DAD?

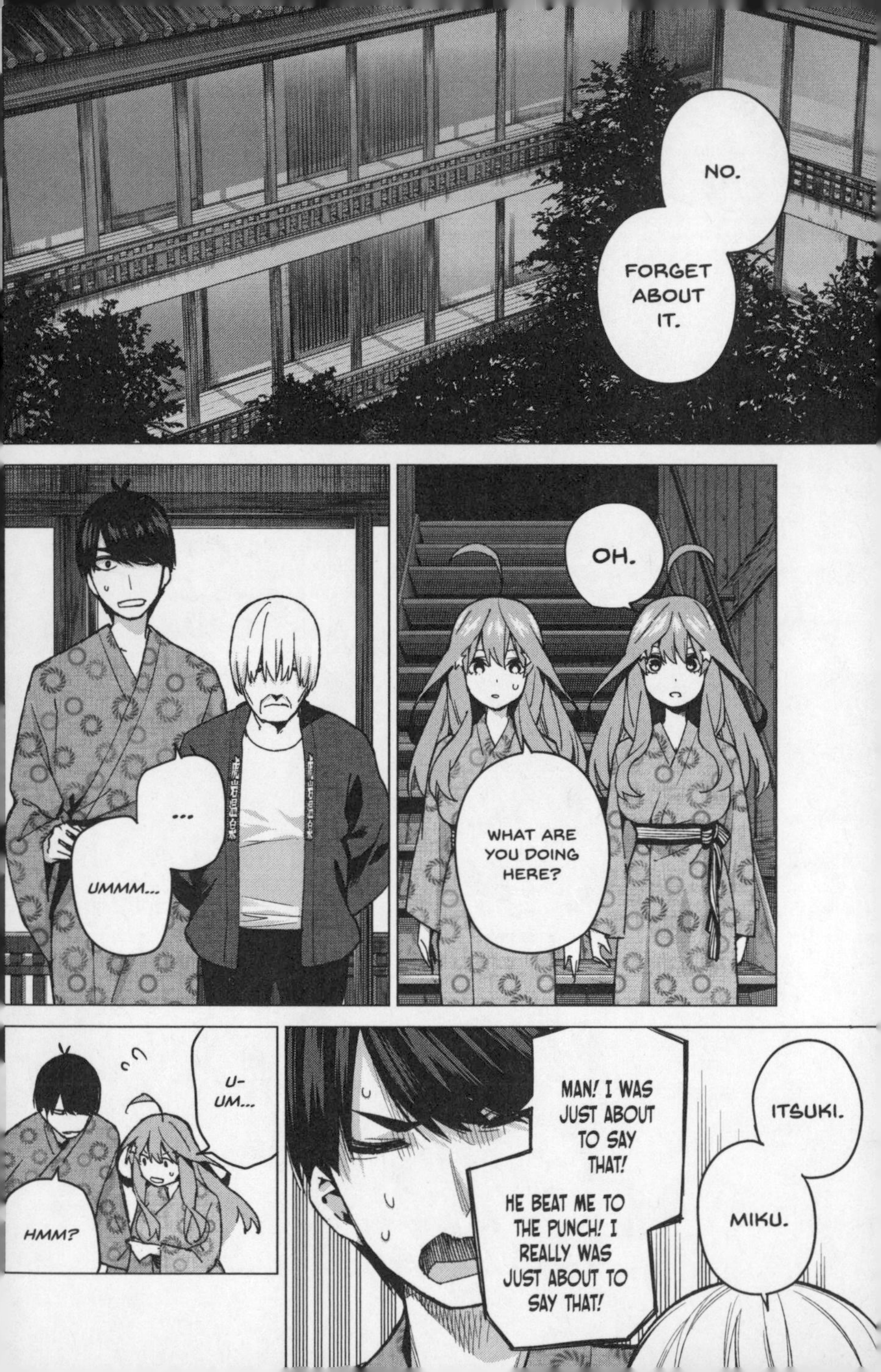
NO.
FORGET ABOUT IT.
OH.
WHAT ARE YOU DOING HERE?
...
UMMM...
ITSUKI.
MIKU.
MAN! I WAS JUST ABOUT TO SAY THAT!
HE BEAT ME TO THE PUNCH! I REALLY WAS JUST ABOUT TO SAY THAT!
U-UM...
HMM?

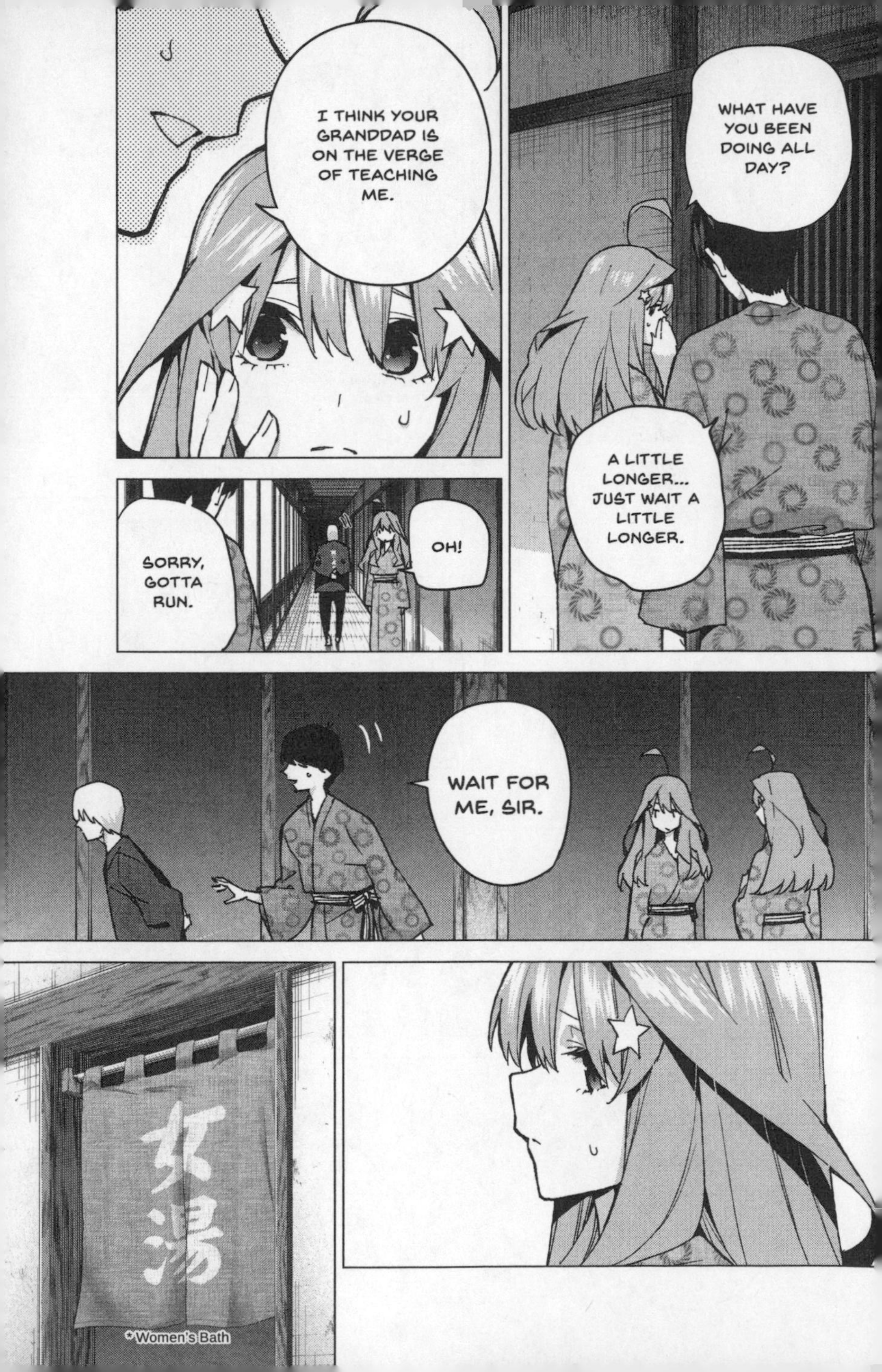
WHAT HAVE YOU BEEN DOING ALL DAY?
A LITTLE LONGER... JUST WAIT A LITTLE LONGER.
I THINK YOUR GRANDDAD IS ON THE VERGE OF TEACHING ME.
OH!
SORRY, GOTTA RUN.
WAIT FOR ME, SIR.
女湯
*Women's Bath

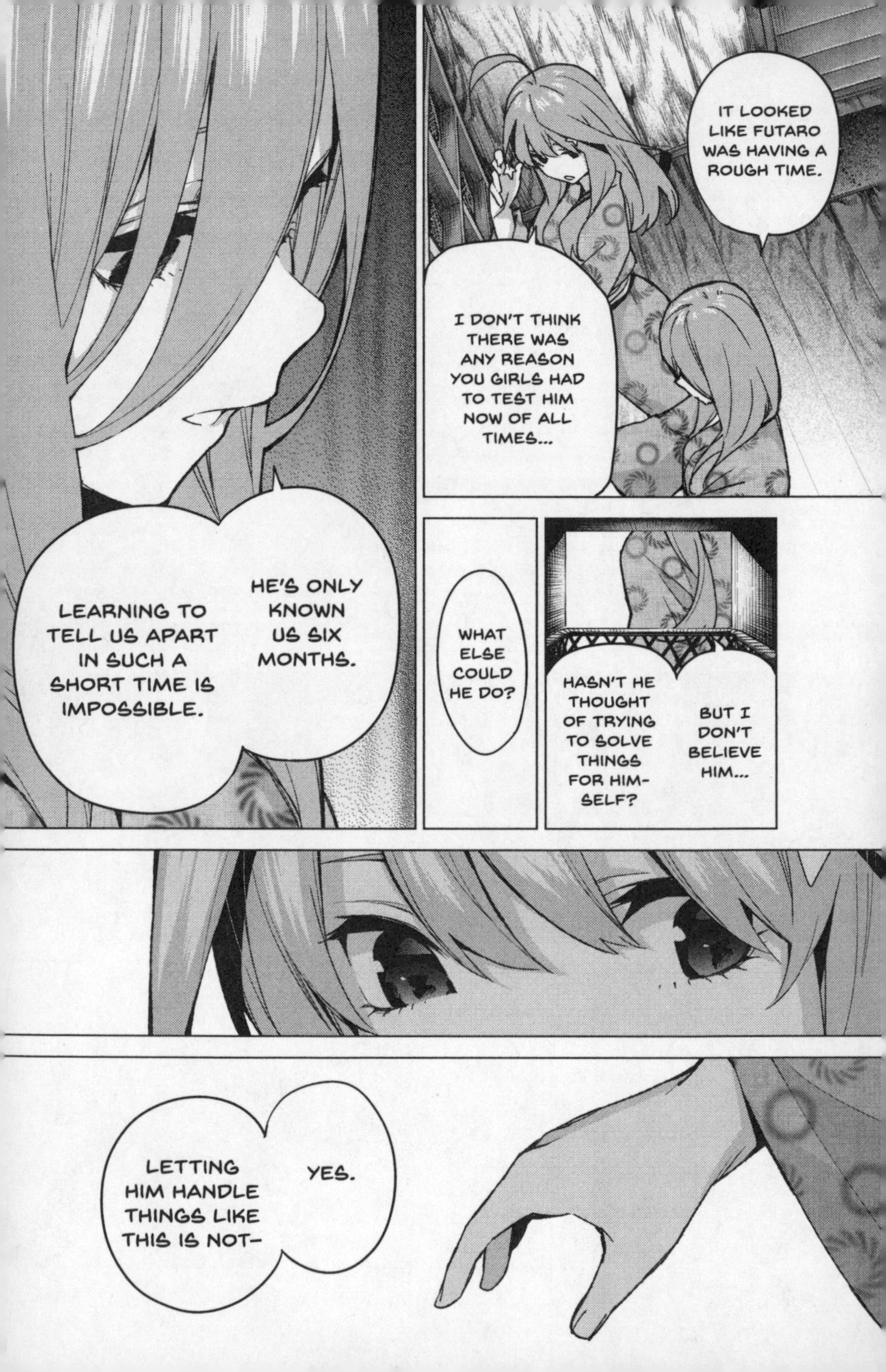
IT LOOKED LIKE FUTARO WAS HAVING A ROUGH TIME.
I DON'T THINK THERE WAS ANY REASON YOU GIRLS HAD TO TEST HIM NOW OF ALL TIMES...
BUT I DON'T BELIEVE HIM...
HASN'T HE THOUGHT OF TRYING TO SOLVE THINGS FOR HIM-SELF?
WHAT ELSE COULD HE DO?
HE'S ONLY KNOWN US SIX MONTHS.
LEARNING TO TELL US APART IN SUCH A SHORT TIME IS IMPOSSIBLE.
YES.
LETTING HIM HANDLE THINGS LIKE THIS IS NOT-

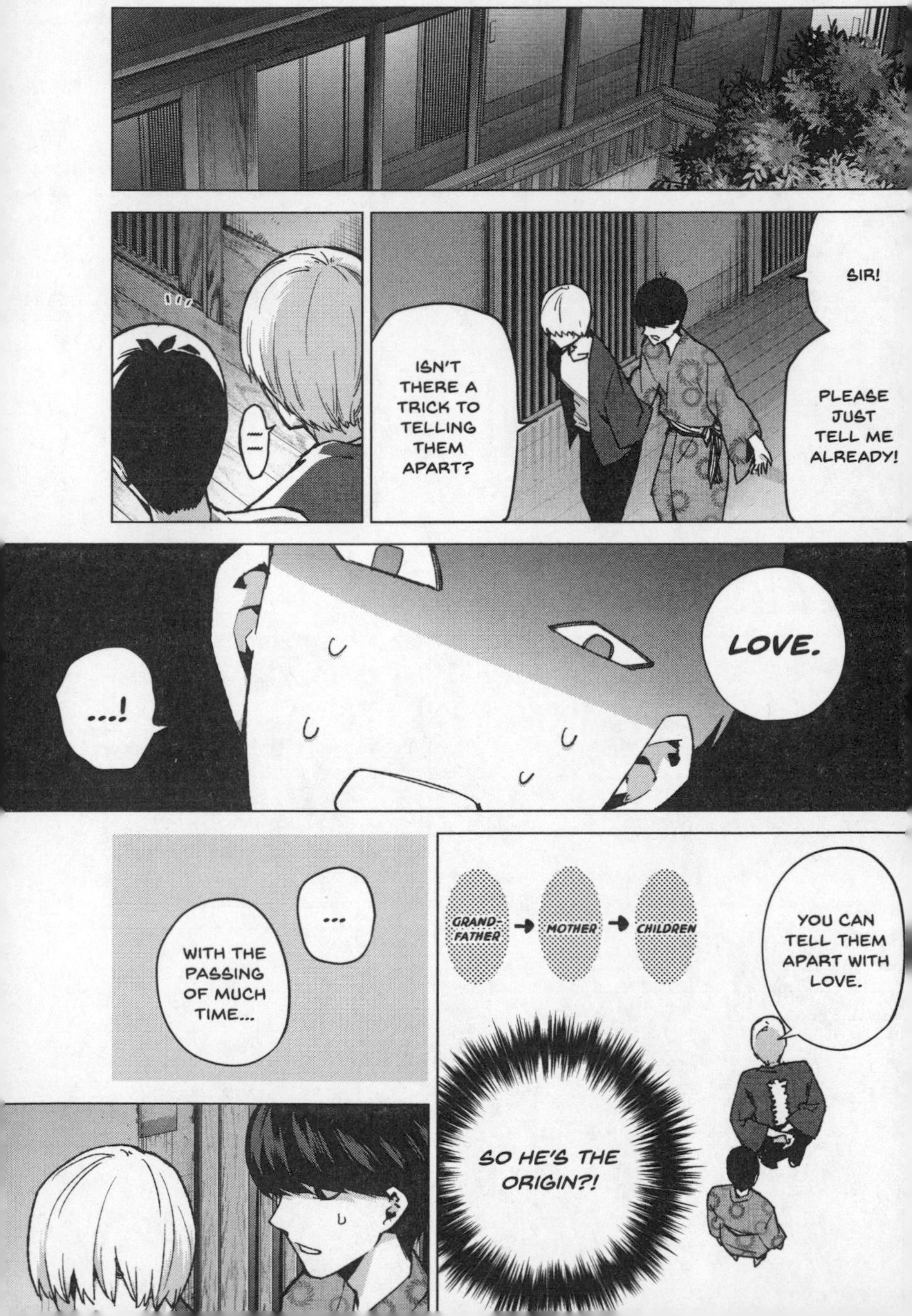
SIR!
PLEASE JUST TELL ME ALREADY!
ISN'T THERE A TRICK TO TELLING THEM APART?
——
LOVE.
...!
YOU CAN TELL THEM APART WITH LOVE.
GRAND-FATHER
MOTHER
CHILDREN
SO HE'S THE ORIGIN?!
...
WITH THE PASSING OF MUCH TIME...

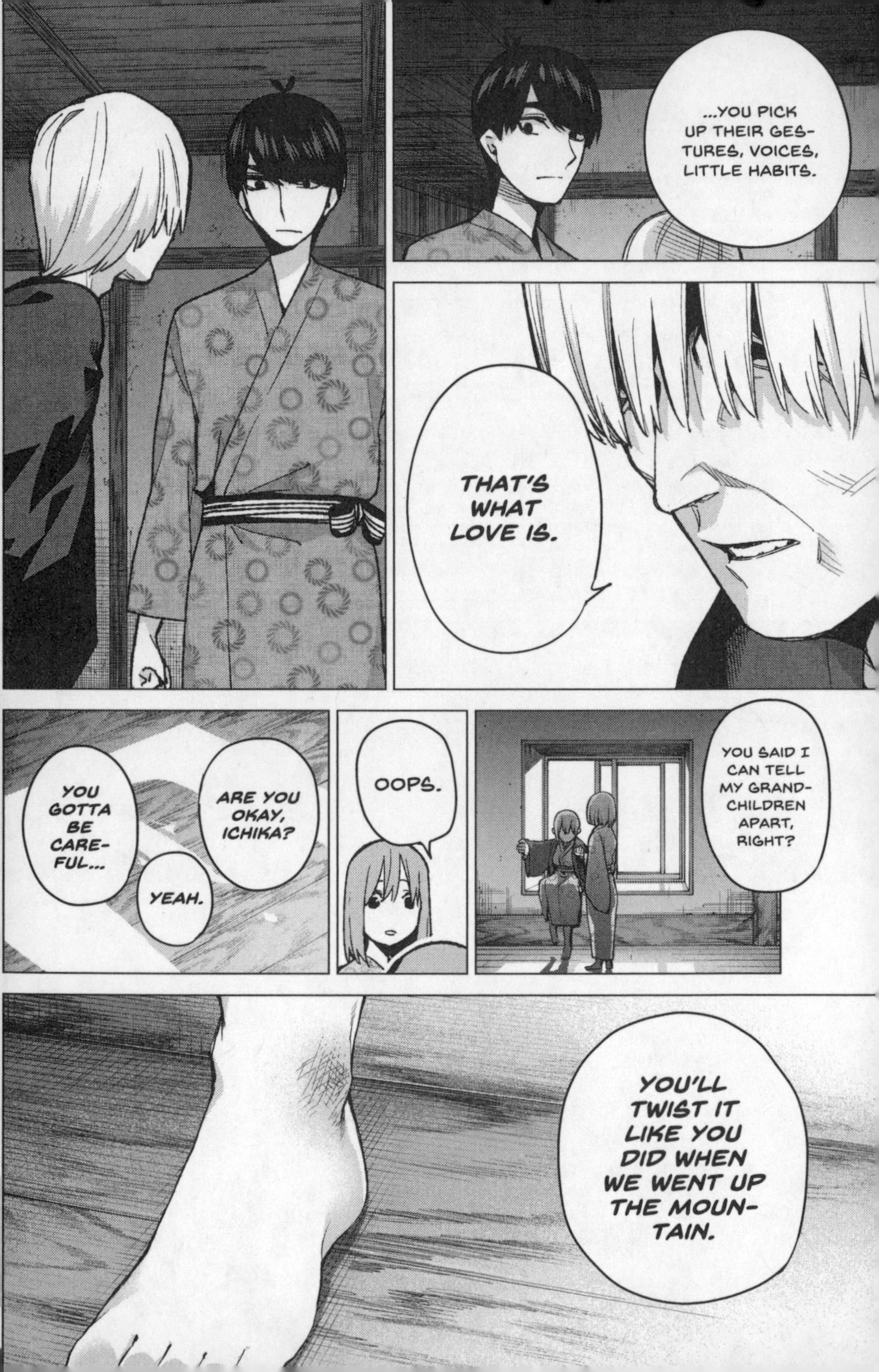
...YOU PICK UP THEIR GES-TURES, VOICES, LITTLE HABITS.
THAT'S WHAT LOVE IS.
YOU SAID I CAN TELL MY GRAND-CHILDREN APART, RIGHT?
OOPS.
ARE YOU OKAY, ICHIKA?
YOU GOTTA BE CARE-FUL...
YEAH.
YOU'LL TWIST IT LIKE YOU DID WHEN WE WENT UP THE MOUN-TAIN.

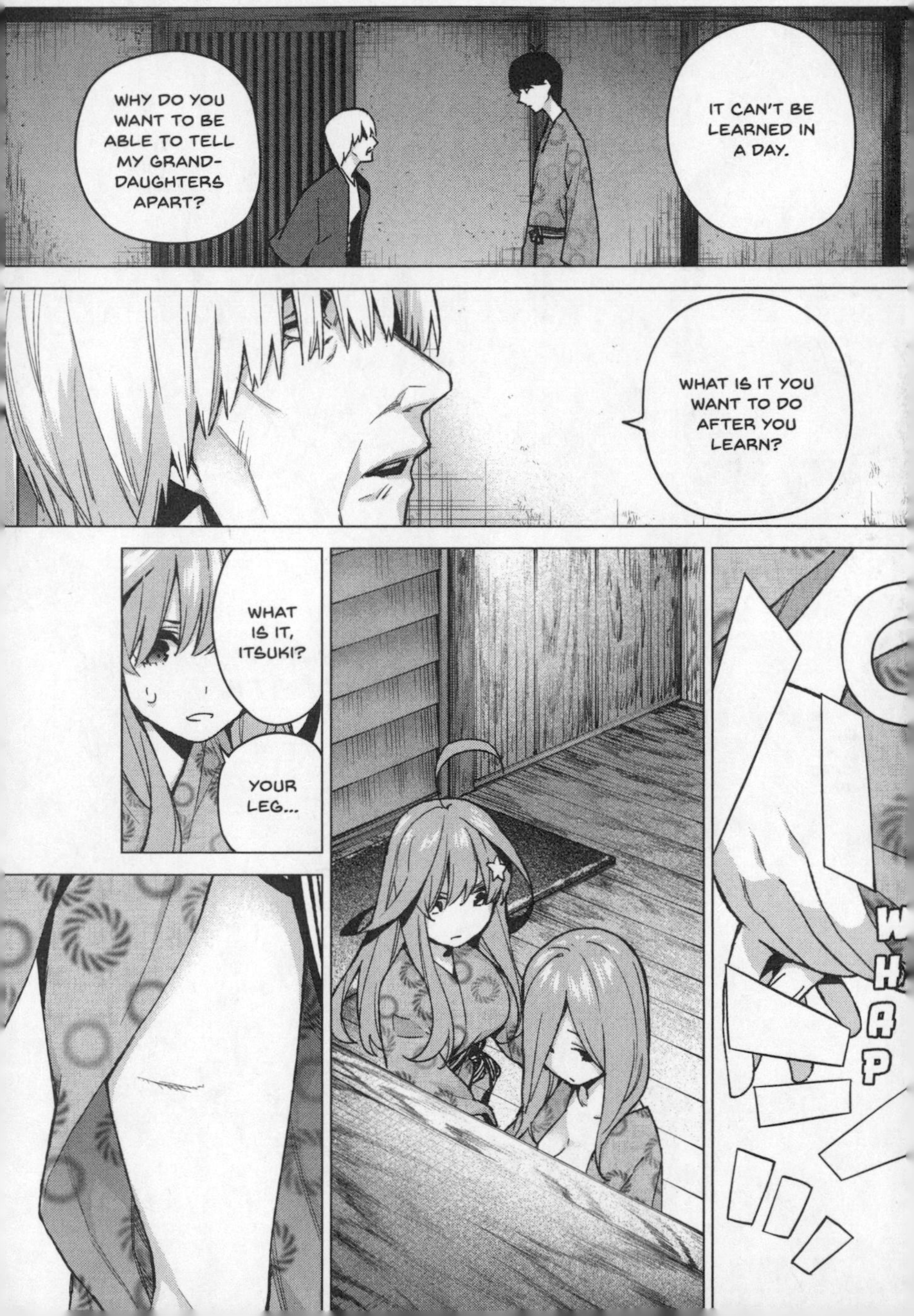
IT CAN'T BE LEARNED IN A DAY.
WHY DO YOU WANT TO BE ABLE TO TELL MY GRAND-DAUGHTERS APART?
WHAT IS IT YOU WANT TO DO AFTER YOU LEARN?
WHAP
WHAT IS IT, ITSUKI?
YOUR LEG...

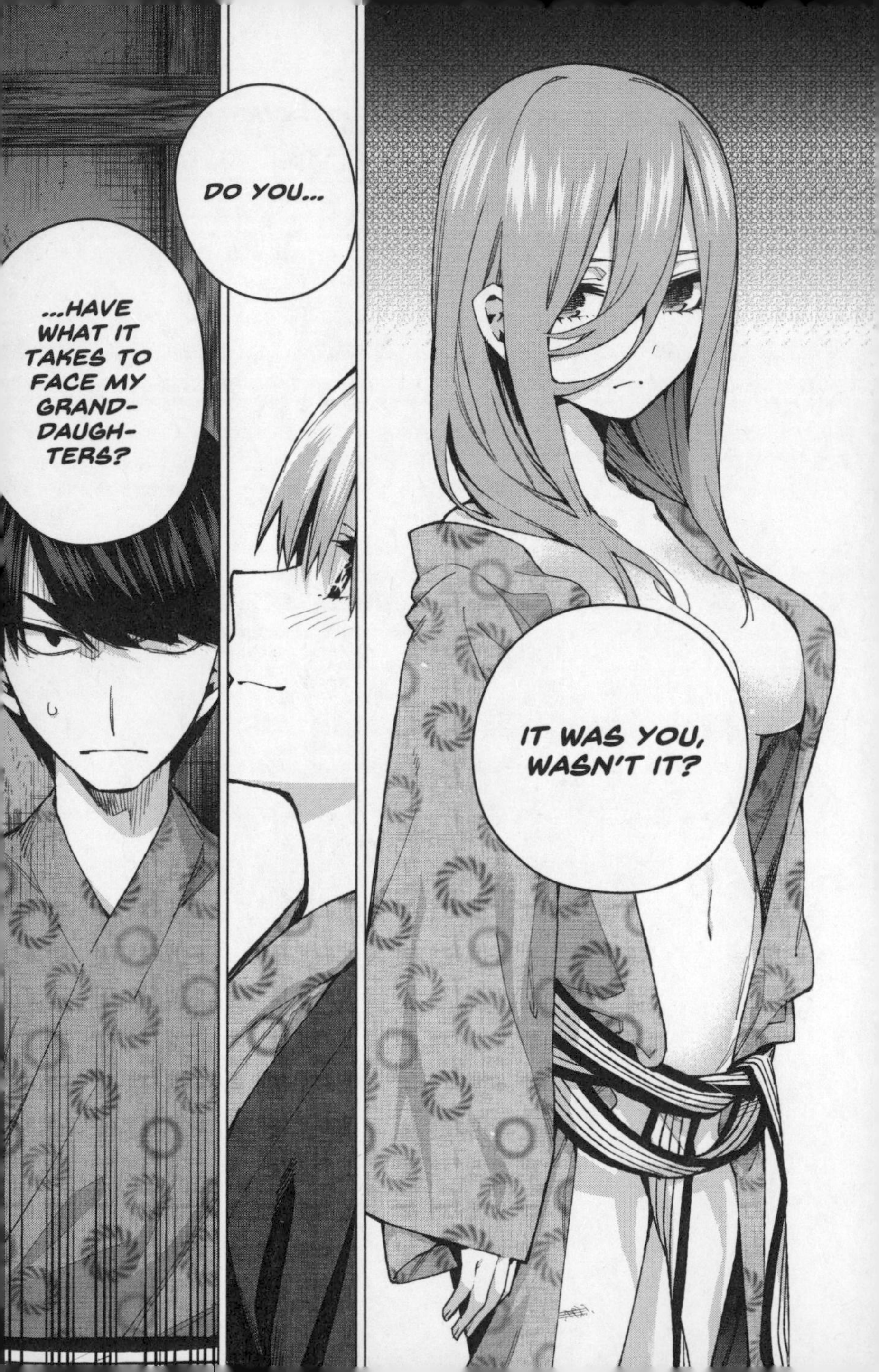
IT WAS YOU, WASN'T IT?
DO YOU...
...HAVE WHAT IT TAKES TO FACE MY GRAND-DAUGH-TERS?

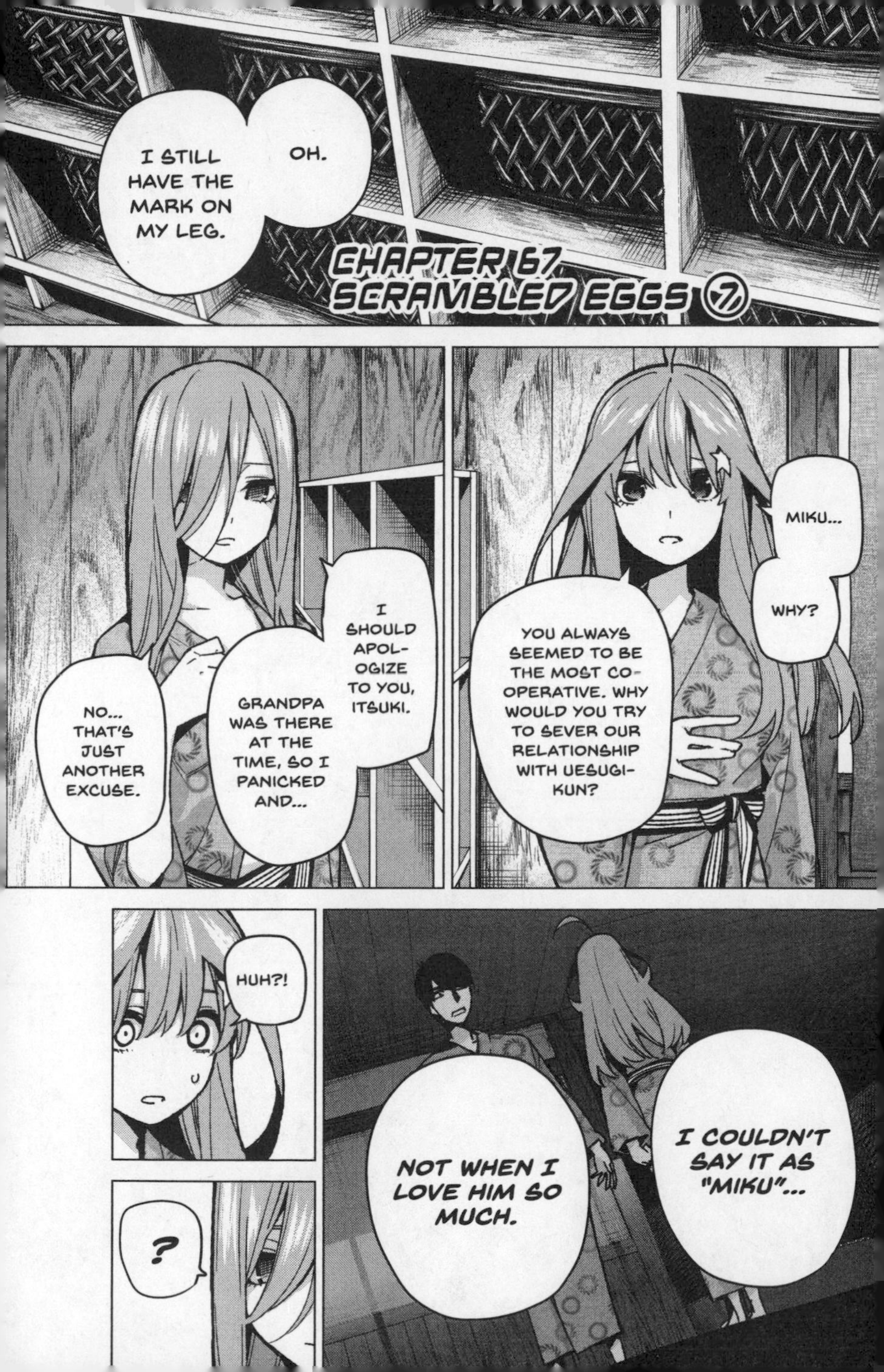
OH.
I STILL HAVE THE MARK ON MY LEG.
CHAPTER 67 SCRAMBLED EGGS ⑦
MIKU...
WHY?
YOU ALWAYS SEEMED TO BE THE MOST CO-OPERATIVE. WHY WOULD YOU TRY TO SEVER OUR RELATIONSHIP WITH UESUGI-KUN?
I SHOULD APOLOGIZE TO YOU, ITSUKI.
GRANDPA WAS THERE AT THE TIME, SO I PANICKED AND...
NO... THAT'S JUST ANOTHER EXCUSE.
I COULDN'T SAY IT AS "MIKU"...
NOT WHEN I LOVE HIM SO MUCH.
HUH?!
?

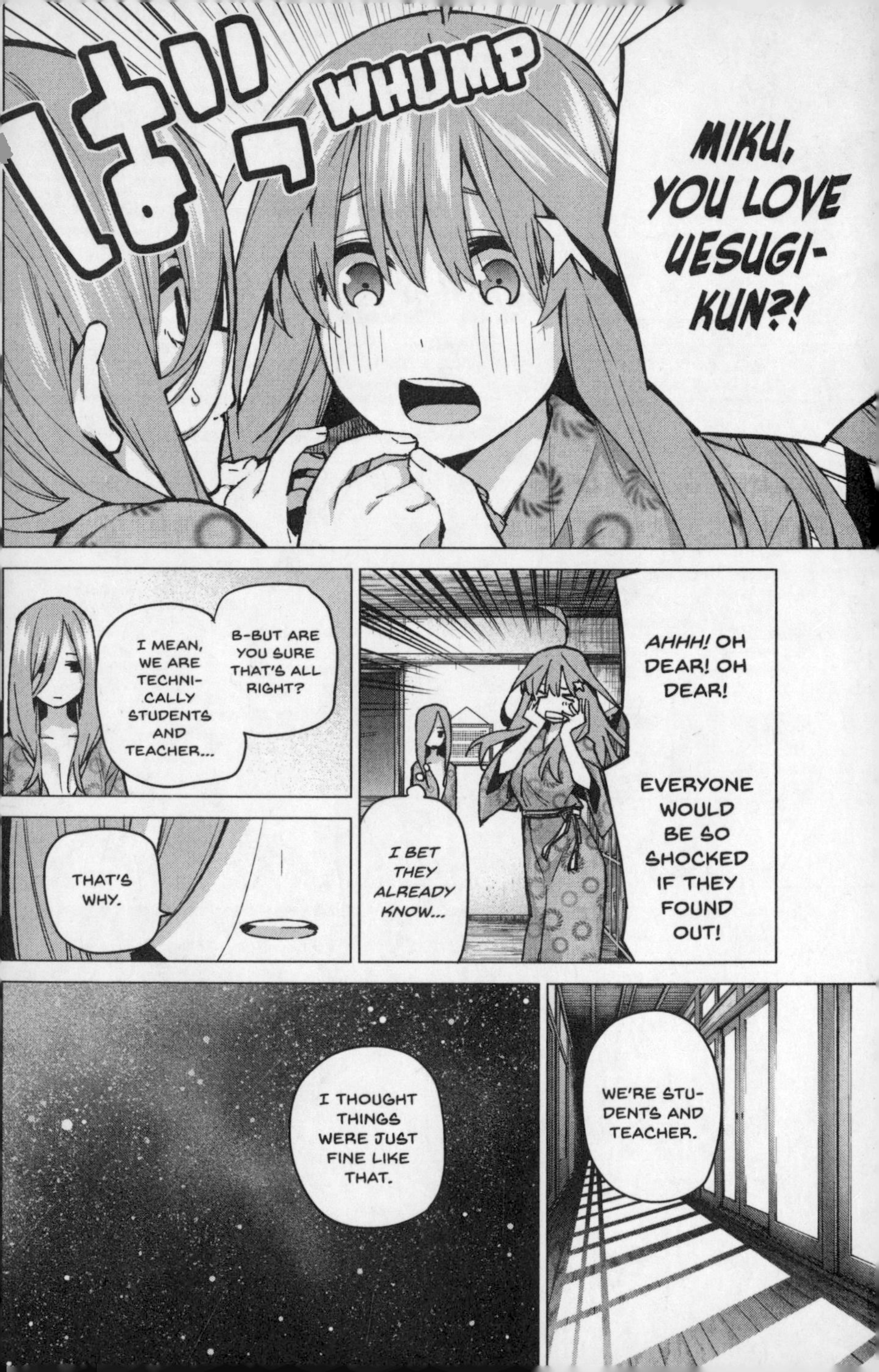
MIKU, YOU LOVE UESUGI-KUN?!
WHUMP
AHHH! OH DEAR! OH DEAR!
EVERYONE WOULD BE SO SHOCKED IF THEY FOUND OUT!
I BET THEY ALREADY KNOW...
B-BUT ARE YOU SURE THAT'S ALL RIGHT?
I MEAN, WE ARE TECHNI-CALLY STUDENTS AND TEACHER...
THAT'S WHY.
WE'RE STU-DENTS AND TEACHER.
I THOUGHT THINGS WERE JUST FINE LIKE THAT.

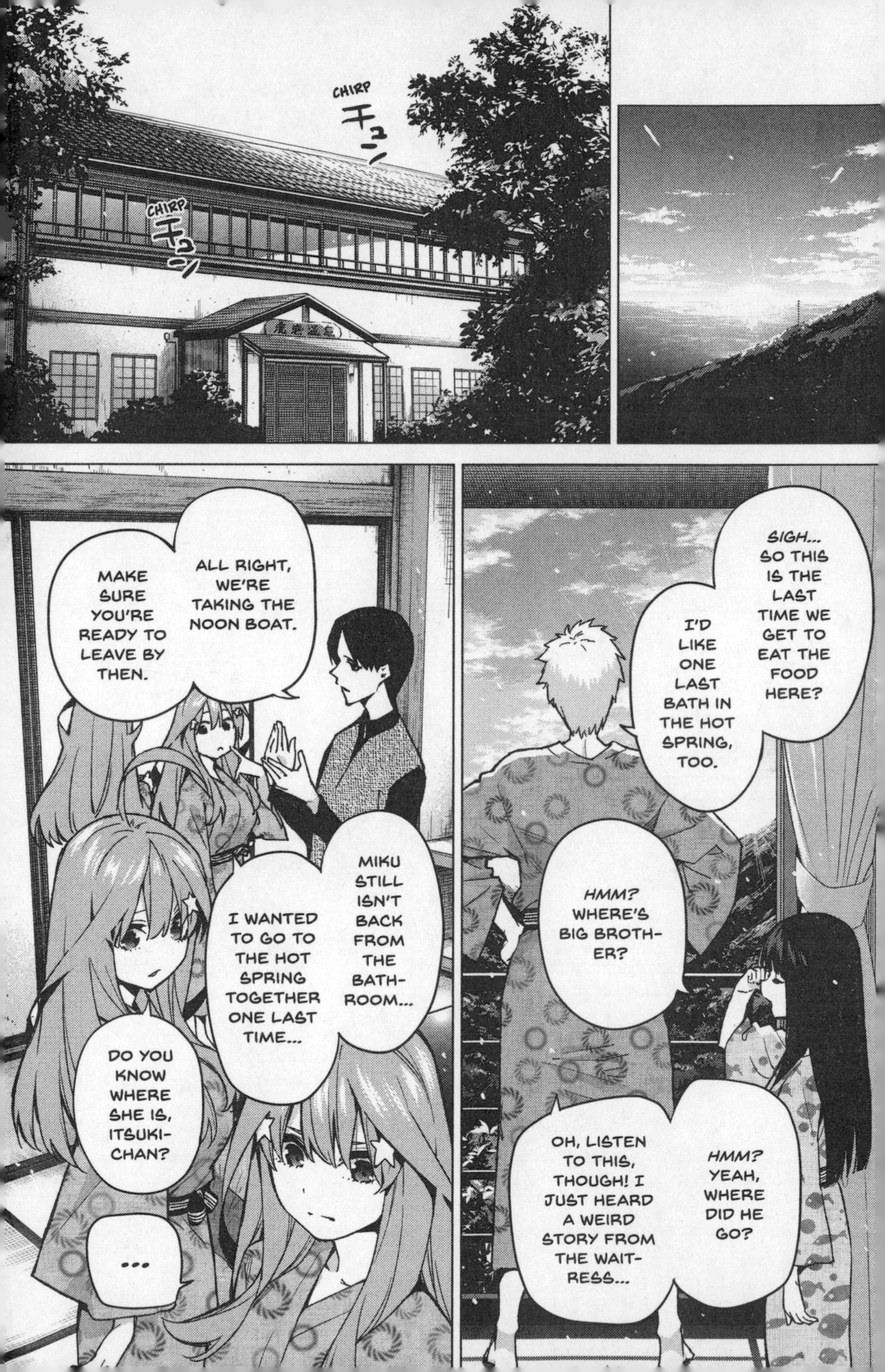
CHIRP
CHIRP
SIGH... SO THIS IS THE LAST TIME WE GET TO EAT THE FOOD HERE?
I'D LIKE ONE LAST BATH IN THE HOT SPRING, TOO.
HMM? WHERE'S BIG BROTH-ER?
HMM? YEAH, WHERE DID HE GO?
OH, LISTEN TO THIS, THOUGH! I JUST HEARD A WEIRD STORY FROM THE WAIT-RESS...
ALL RIGHT, WE'RE TAKING THE NOON BOAT.
MAKE SURE YOU'RE READY TO LEAVE BY THEN.
MIKU STILL ISN'T BACK FROM THE BATH-ROOM...
I WANTED TO GO TO THE HOT SPRING TOGETHER ONE LAST TIME...
DO YOU KNOW WHERE SHE IS, ITSUKI-CHAN?
...

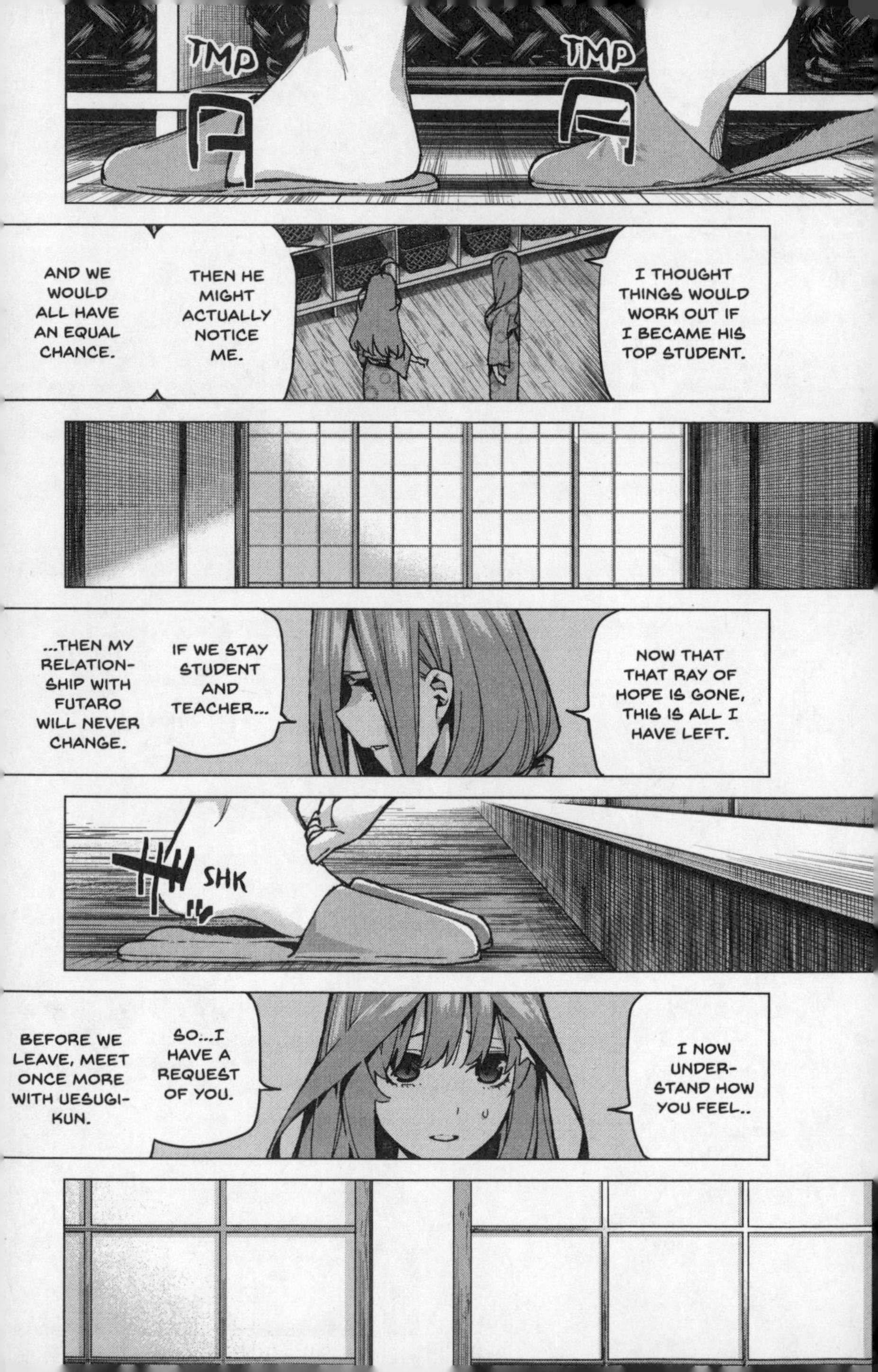
TMP
TMP
I THOUGHT THINGS WOULD WORK OUT IF I BECAME HIS TOP STUDENT.
THEN HE MIGHT ACTUALLY NOTICE ME.
AND WE WOULD ALL HAVE AN EQUAL CHANCE.
NOW THAT THAT RAY OF HOPE IS GONE, THIS IS ALL I HAVE LEFT.
IF WE STAY STUDENT AND TEACHER...
...THEN MY RELATION-SHIP WITH FUTARO WILL NEVER CHANGE.
SHK
I NOW UNDER-STAND HOW YOU FEEL..
SO...I HAVE A REQUEST OF YOU.
BEFORE WE LEAVE, MEET ONCE MORE WITH UESUGI-KUN.

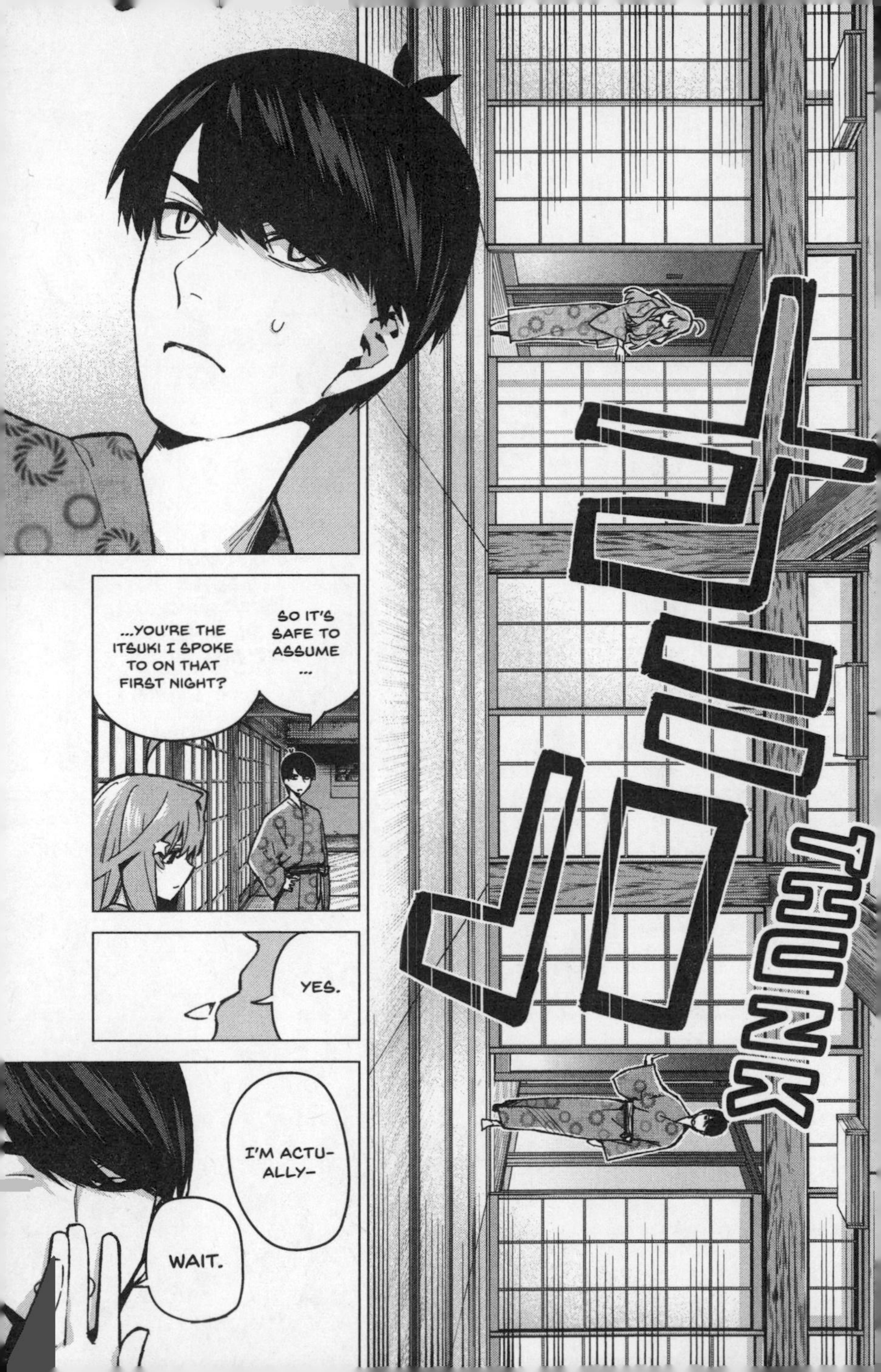
THUNK
SO IT'S SAFE TO ASSUME ...
...YOU'RE THE ITSUKI I SPOKE TO ON THAT FIRST NIGHT?
YES.
I'M ACTU-ALLY-
WAIT.

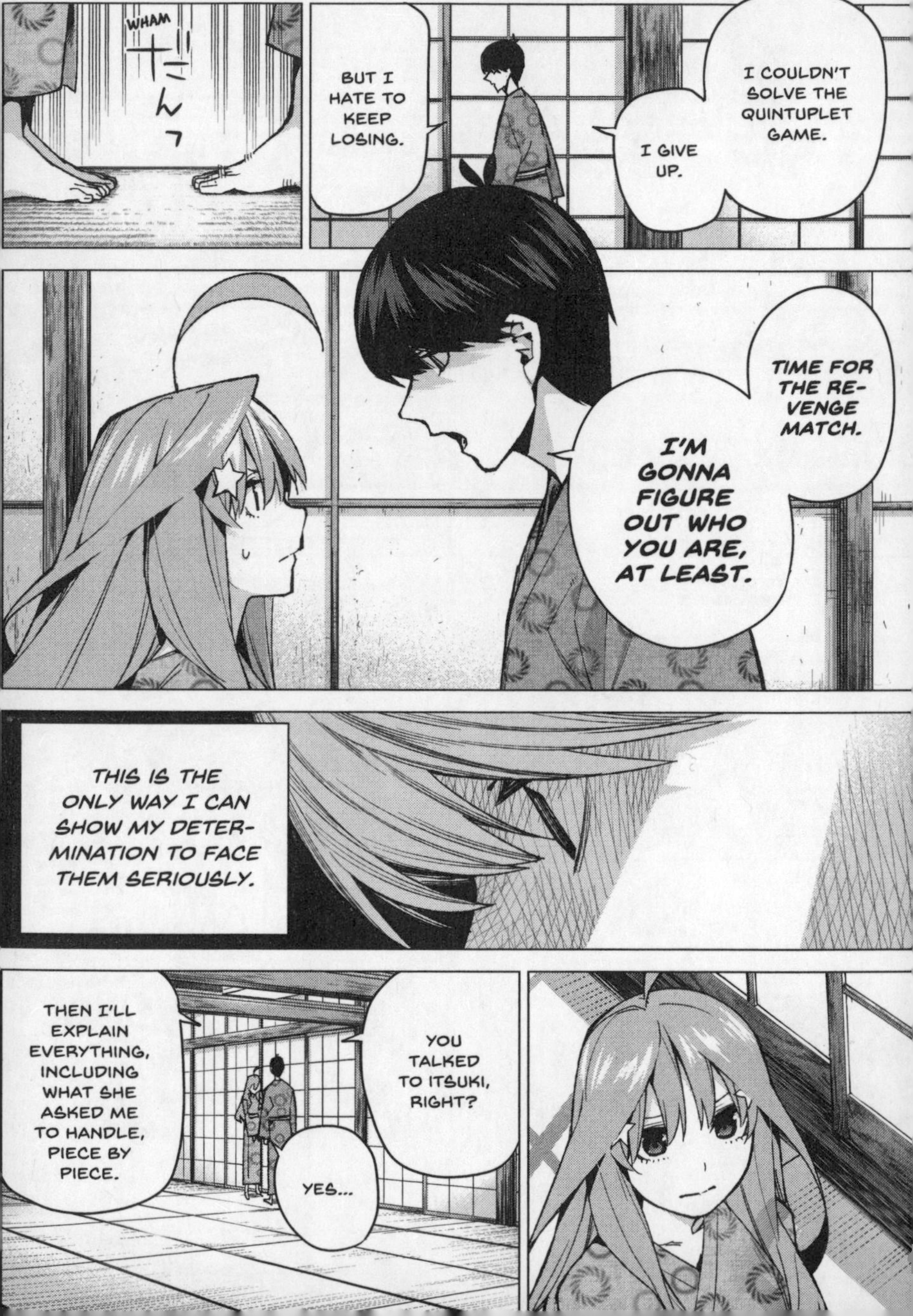
I COULDN'T SOLVE THE QUINTUPLET GAME.
I GIVE UP.
BUT I HATE TO KEEP LOSING.
WHAM
TIME FOR THE RE-VENGE MATCH.
I'M GONNA FIGURE OUT WHO YOU ARE, AT LEAST.
THIS IS THE ONLY WAY I CAN SHOW MY DETER-MINATION TO FACE THEM SERIOUSLY.
YOU TALKED TO ITSUKI, RIGHT?
YES...
THEN I'LL EXPLAIN EVERYTHING, INCLUDING WHAT SHE ASKED ME TO HANDLE, PIECE BY PIECE.

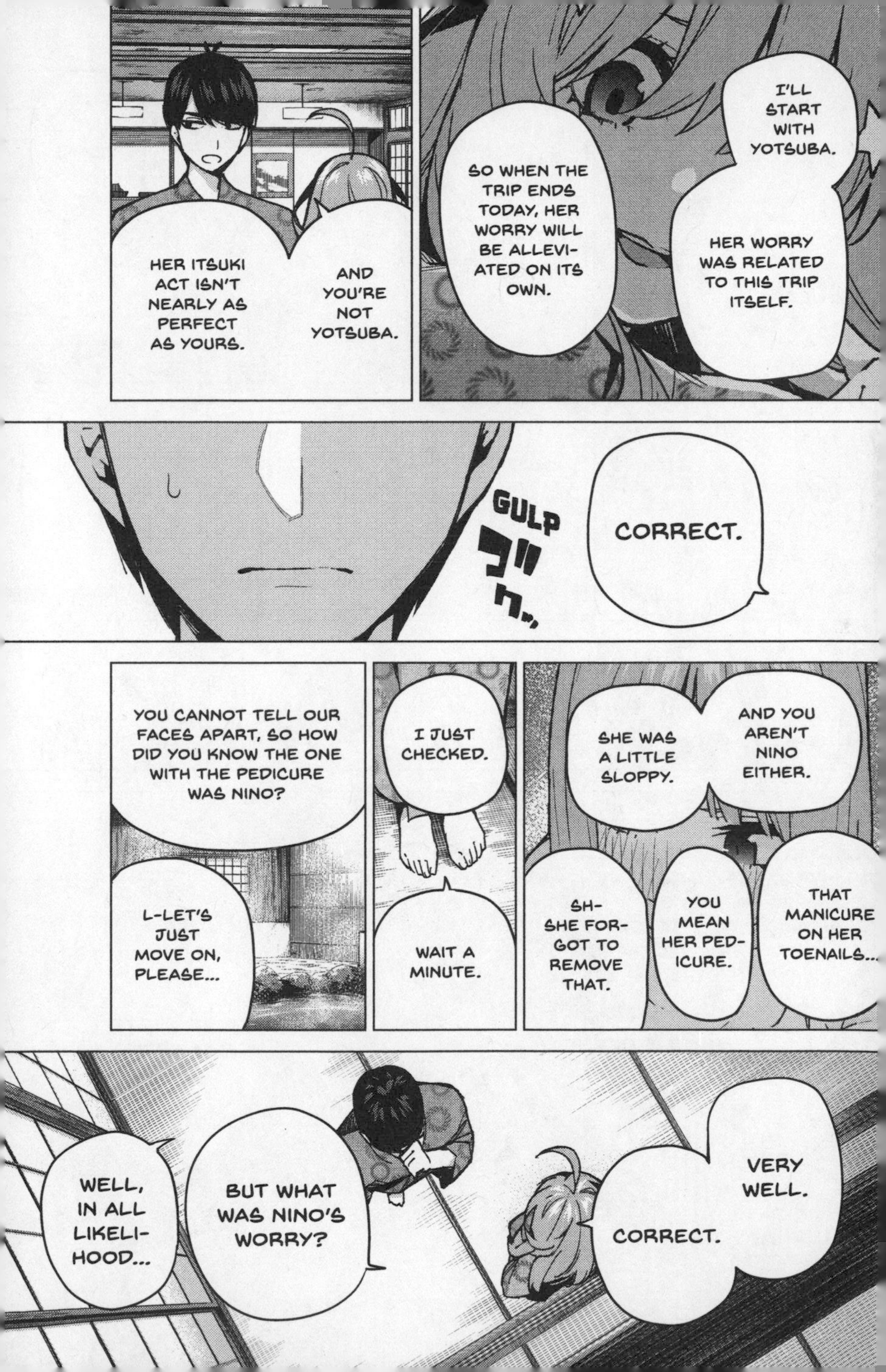
I'LL START WITH YOTSUBA.
HER WORRY WAS RELATED TO THIS TRIP ITSELF.
SO WHEN THE TRIP ENDS TODAY, HER WORRY WILL BE ALLEVIATED ON ITS OWN.
AND YOU'RE NOT YOTSUBA.
HER ITSUKI ACT ISN'T NEARLY AS PERFECT AS YOURS.
CORRECT.
GULP
ゴクッ
AND YOU AREN'T NINO EITHER.
SHE WAS A LITTLE SLOPPY.
THAT MANICURE ON HER TOENAILS...
YOU MEAN HER PEDICURE.
SH-SHE FORGOT TO REMOVE THAT.
I JUST CHECKED.
WAIT A MINUTE.
YOU CANNOT TELL OUR FACES APART, SO HOW DID YOU KNOW THE ONE WITH THE PEDICURE WAS NINO?
L-LET'S JUST MOVE ON, PLEASE...
VERY WELL.
CORRECT.
BUT WHAT WAS NINO'S WORRY?
WELL, IN ALL LIKELIHOOD...

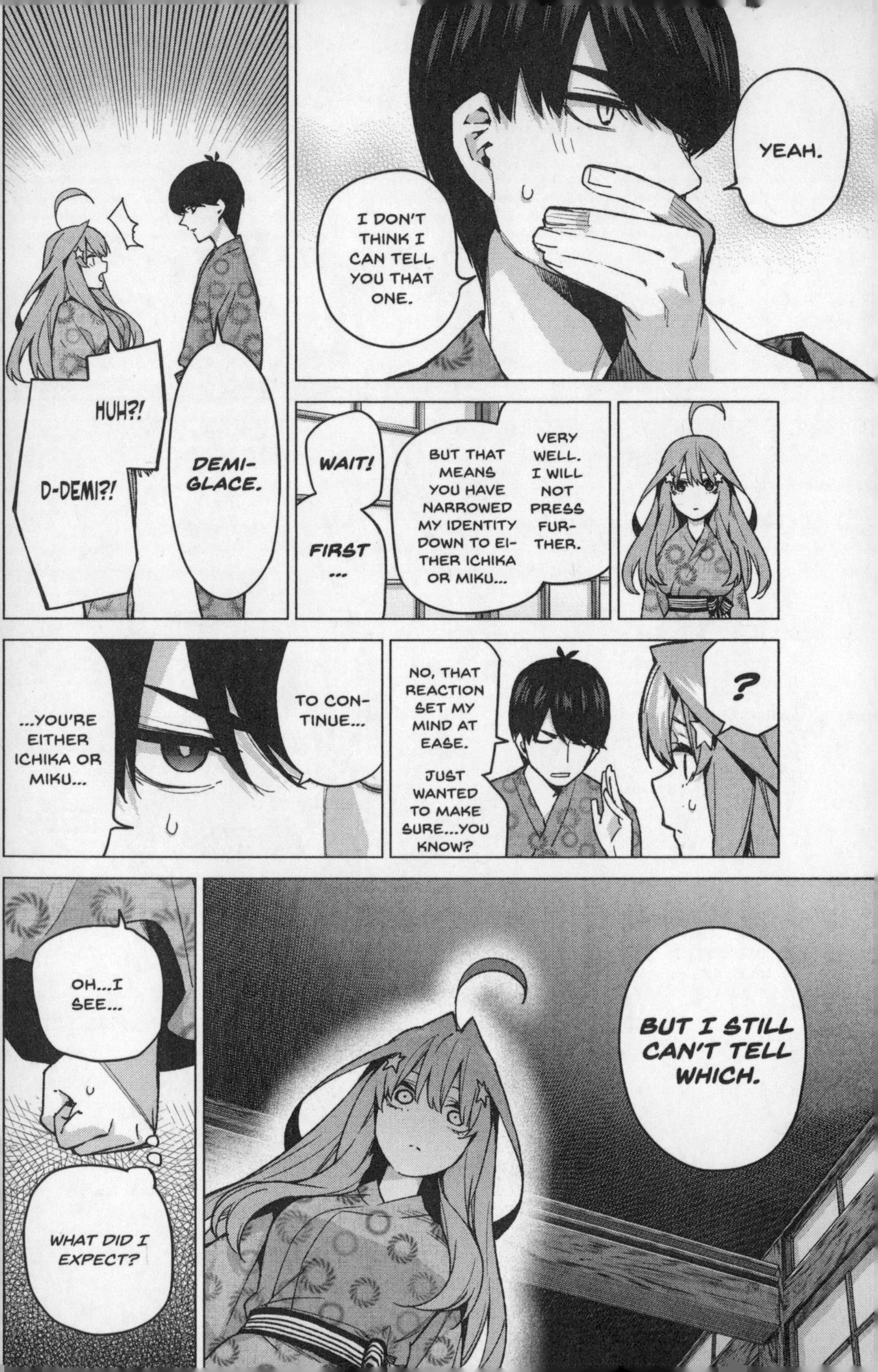
YEAH.
I DON'T THINK I CAN TELL YOU THAT ONE.
VERY WELL. I WILL NOT PRESS FURTHER.
BUT THAT MEANS YOU HAVE NARROWED MY IDENTITY DOWN TO EITHER ICHIKA OR MIKU...
WAIT!
FIRST...
DEMI-GLACE.
HUH?!
D-DEMI?!
?
NO, THAT REACTION SET MY MIND AT EASE.
JUST WANTED TO MAKE SURE...YOU KNOW?
TO CONTINUE...
...YOU'RE EITHER ICHIKA OR MIKU...
BUT I STILL CAN'T TELL WHICH.
OH...I SEE...
WHAT DID I EXPECT?

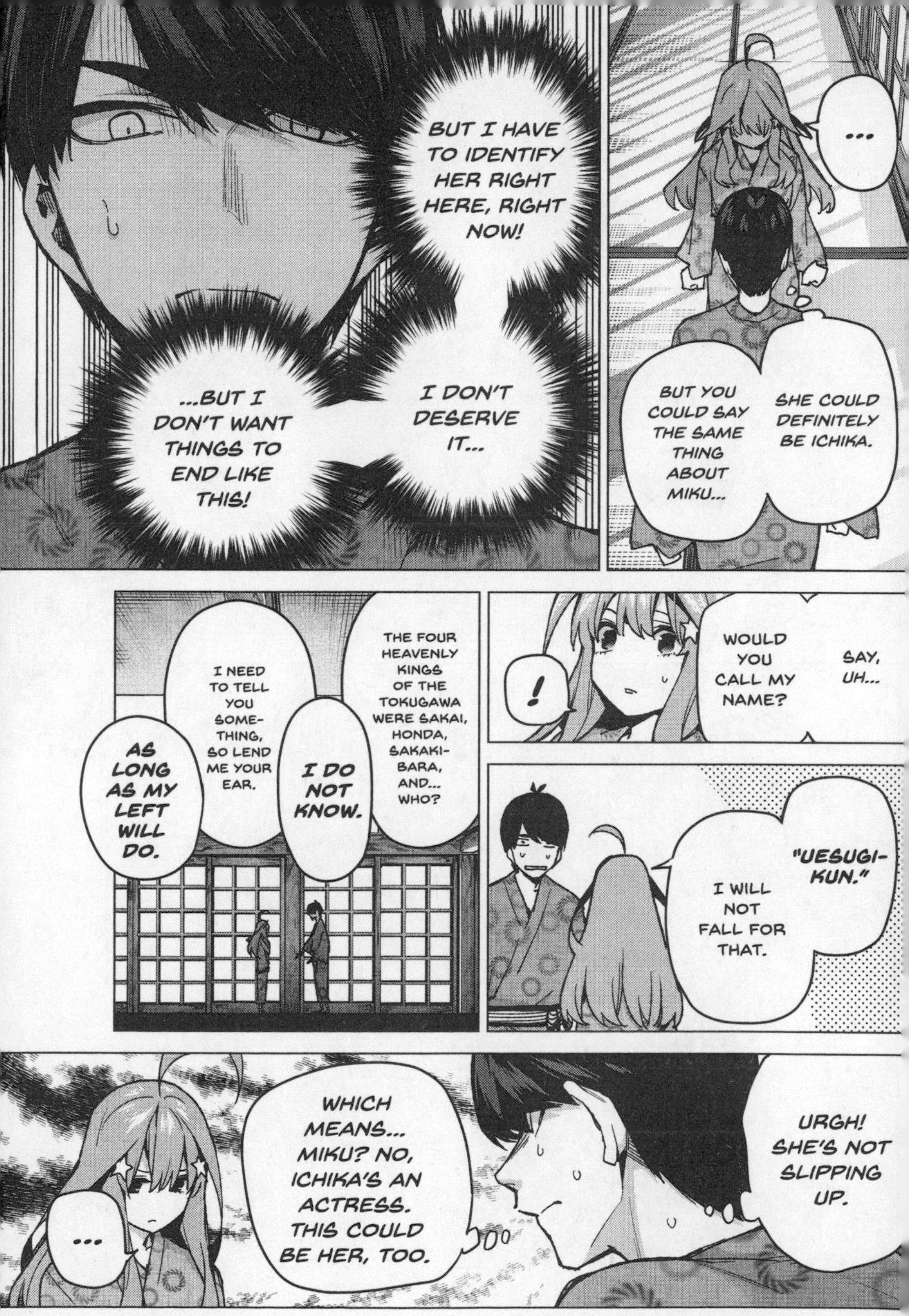
...
SHE COULD DEFINITELY BE ICHIKA.
BUT YOU COULD SAY THE SAME THING ABOUT MIKU...
BUT I HAVE TO IDENTIFY HER RIGHT HERE, RIGHT NOW!
I DON'T DESERVE IT...
...BUT I DON'T WANT THINGS TO END LIKE THIS!
SAY, UH...
WOULD YOU CALL MY NAME?
!
"UESUGI-KUN."
I WILL NOT FALL FOR THAT.
THE FOUR HEAVENLY KINGS OF THE TOKUGAWA WERE SAKAI, HONDA, SAKAKI-BARA, AND... WHO?
I DO NOT KNOW.
I NEED TO TELL YOU SOME-THING, SO LEND ME YOUR EAR.
AS LONG AS MY LEFT WILL DO.
URGH! SHE'S NOT SLIPPING UP.
WHICH MEANS... MIKU? NO, ICHIKA'S AN ACTRESS. THIS COULD BE HER, TOO.
...

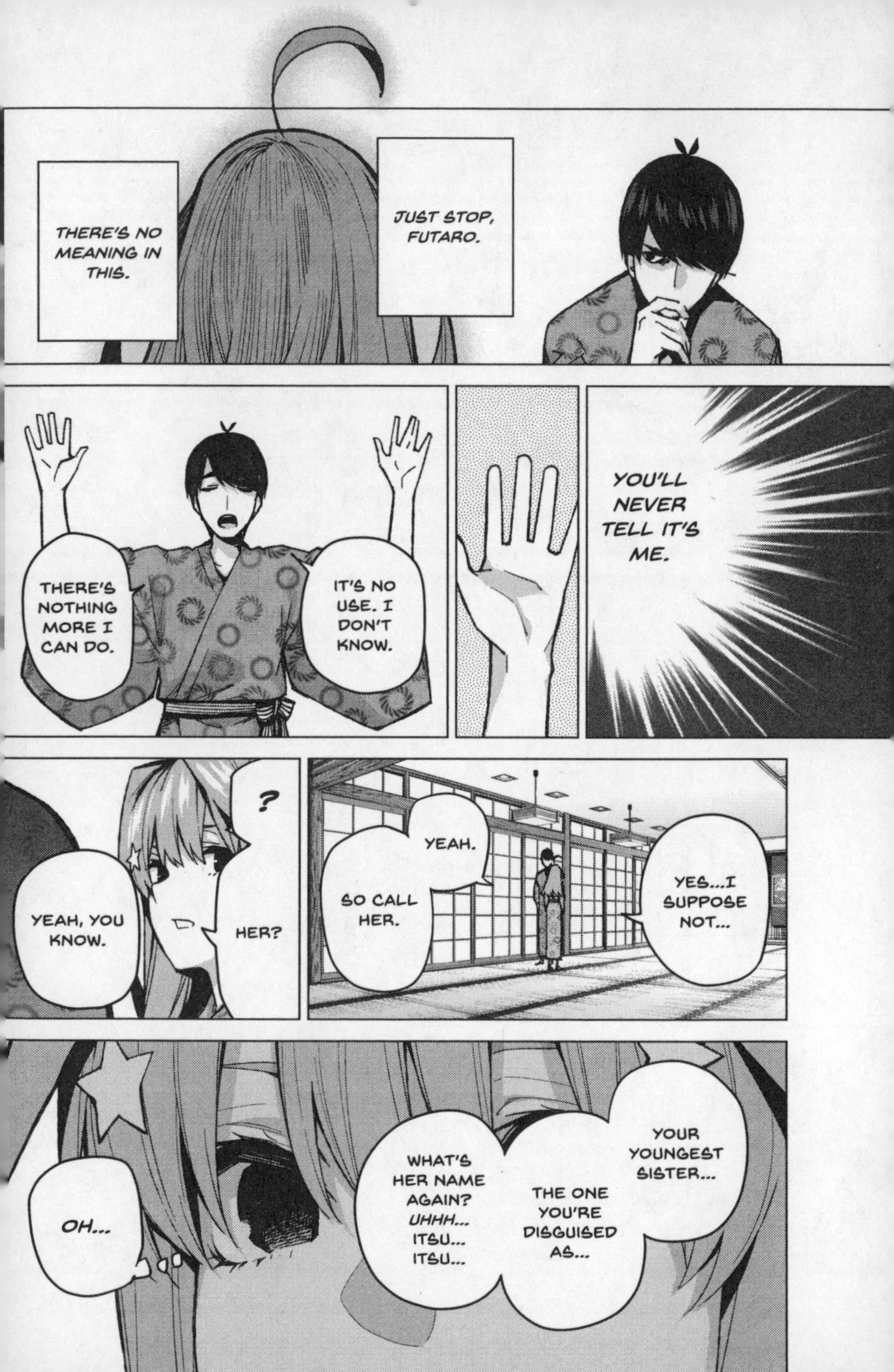
JUST STOP, FUTARO.
THERE'S NO MEANING IN THIS.
YOU'LL NEVER TELL IT'S ME.
IT'S NO USE. I DON'T KNOW.
THERE'S NOTHING MORE I CAN DO.
YES...I SUPPOSE NOT...
YEAH.
SO CALL HER.
?
HER?
YEAH, YOU KNOW.
YOUR YOUNGEST SISTER...
THE ONE YOU'RE DISGUISED AS...
WHAT'S HER NAME AGAIN? UHHH... ITSU... ITSU...
OH...

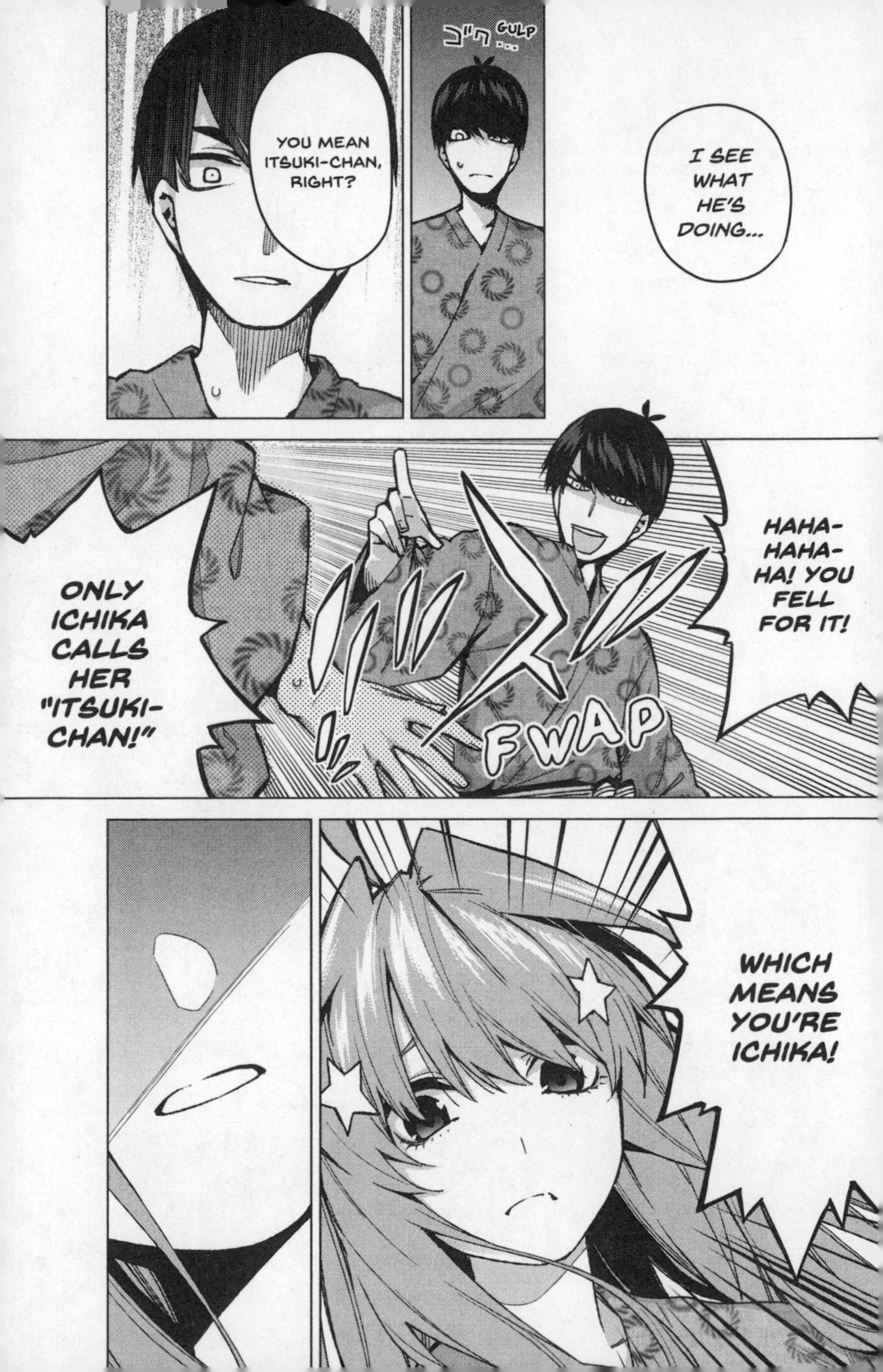
I SEE WHAT HE'S DOING...
ゴクッ GULP...
YOU MEAN ITSUKI-CHAN, RIGHT?
HAHA-HAHA-HA! YOU FELL FOR IT!
FWAP
ONLY ICHIKA CALLS HER "ITSUKI-CHAN!"
WHICH MEANS YOU'RE ICHIKA!

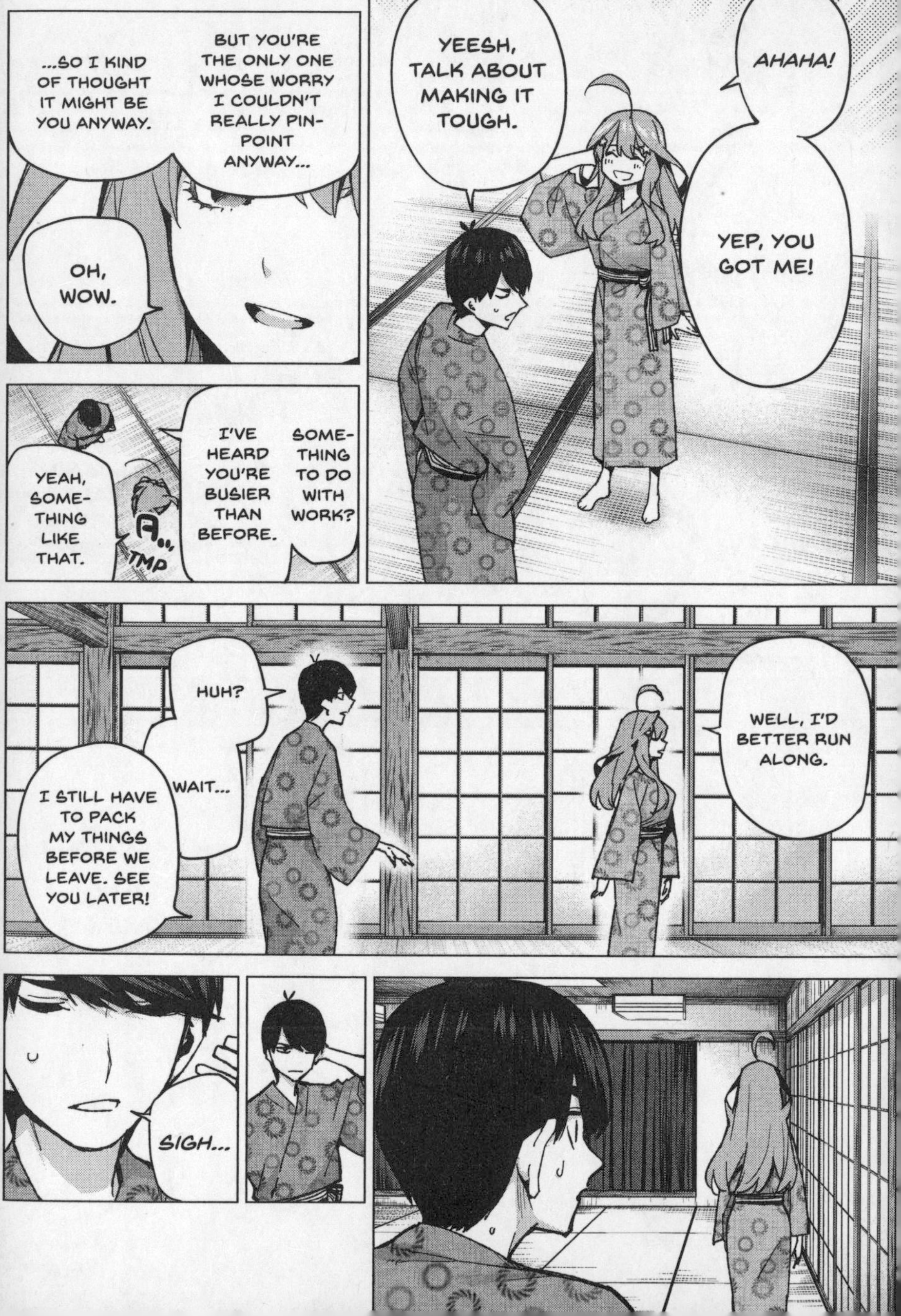
AHAHA!
YEP, YOU GOT ME!
YEESH, TALK ABOUT MAKING IT TOUGH.
BUT YOU'RE THE ONLY ONE WHOSE WORRY I COULDN'T REALLY PIN-POINT ANYWAY...
...SO I KIND OF THOUGHT IT MIGHT BE YOU ANYWAY.
OH, WOW.
SOME-THING TO DO WITH WORK?
I'VE HEARD YOU'RE BUSIER THAN BEFORE.
TMP
YEAH, SOME-THING LIKE THAT.
WELL, I'D BETTER RUN ALONG.
HUH?
WAIT...
I STILL HAVE TO PACK MY THINGS BEFORE WE LEAVE. SEE YOU LATER!
SIGH...

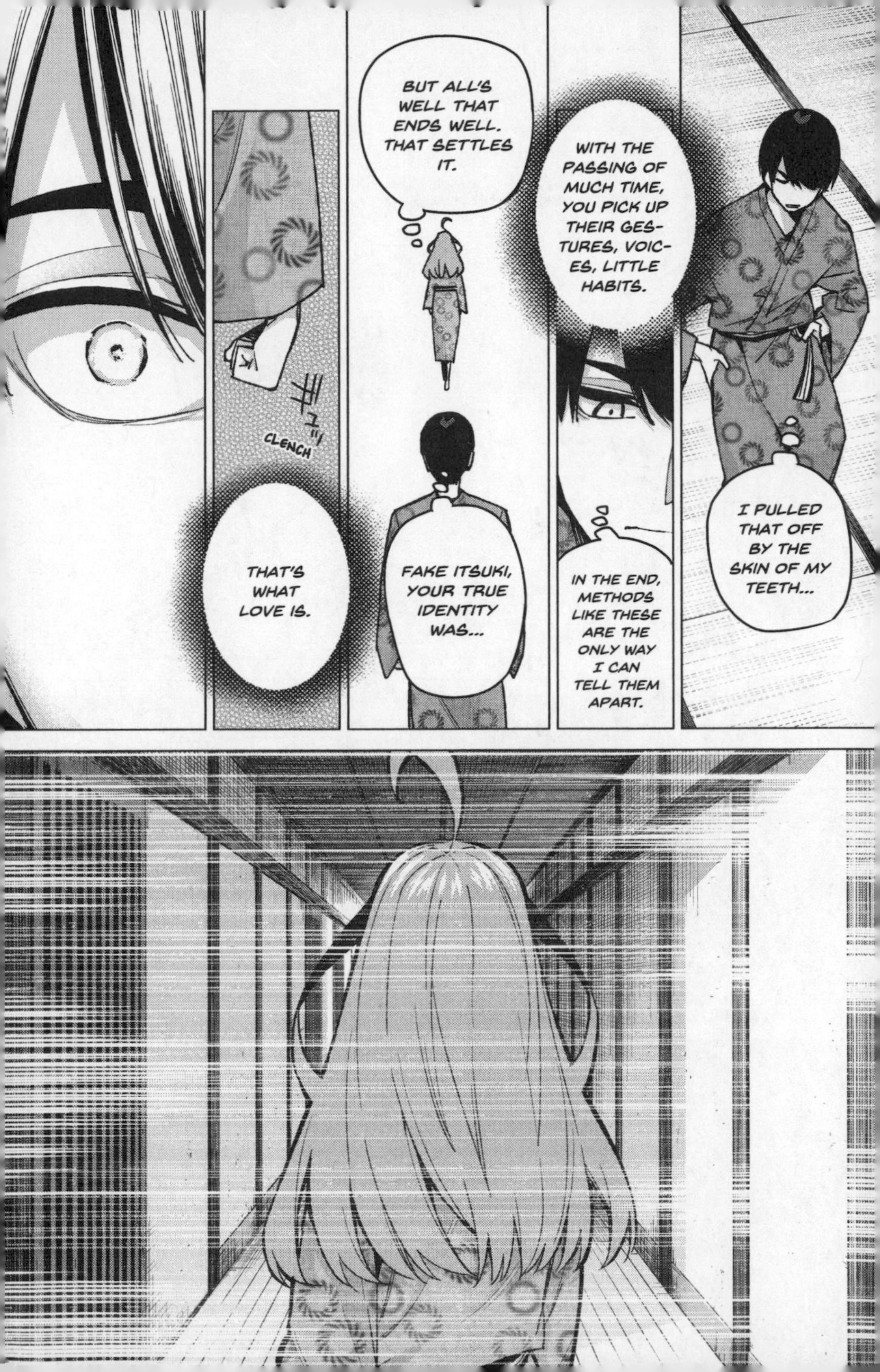

I PULLED THAT OFF BY THE SKIN OF MY TEETH...
WITH THE PASSING OF MUCH TIME, YOU PICK UP THEIR GESTURES, VOICES, LITTLE HABITS.
IN THE END, METHODS LIKE THESE ARE THE ONLY WAY I CAN TELL THEM APART.
BUT ALL'S WELL THAT ENDS WELL. THAT SETTLES IT.
FAKE ITSUKI, YOUR TRUE IDENTITY WAS...
CLENCH
THAT'S WHAT LOVE IS.

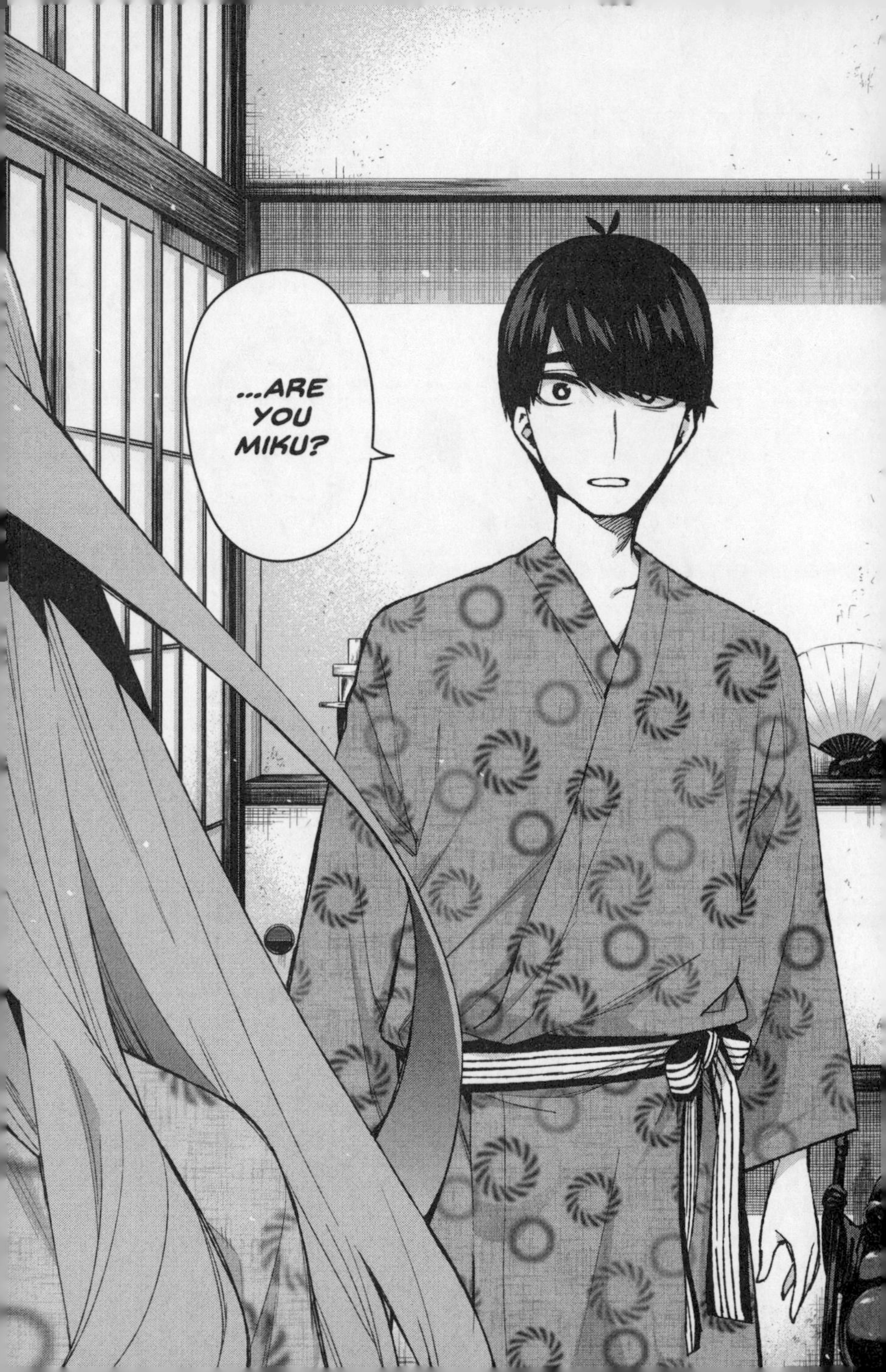
...ARE YOU MIKU?

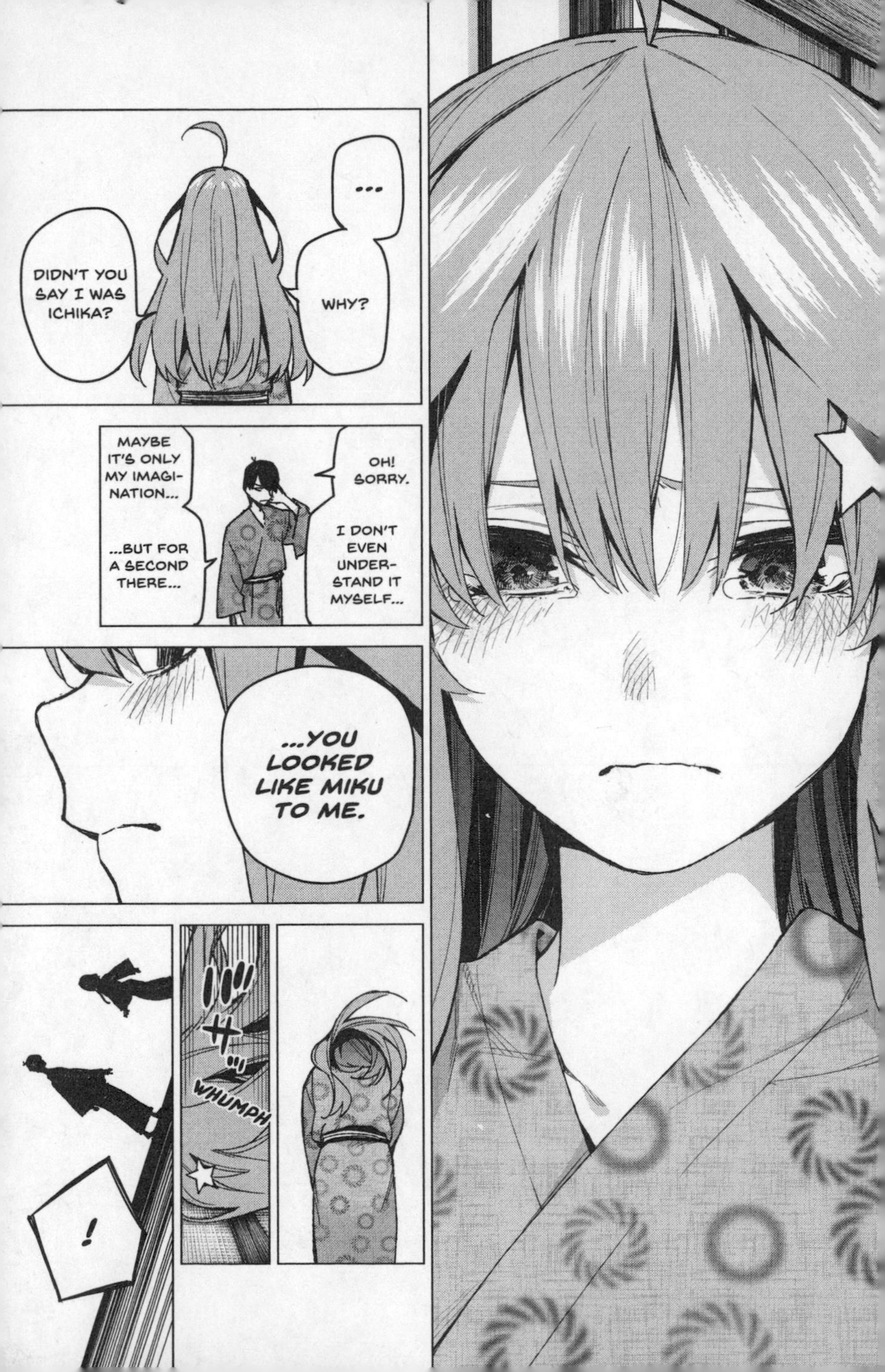
...
WHY?
DIDN'T YOU SAY I WAS ICHIKA?
OH! SORRY.
I DON'T EVEN UNDERSTAND IT MYSELF...
MAYBE IT'S ONLY MY IMAGINATION...
...BUT FOR A SECOND THERE...
...YOU LOOKED LIKE MIKU TO ME.
WHUMPH
!

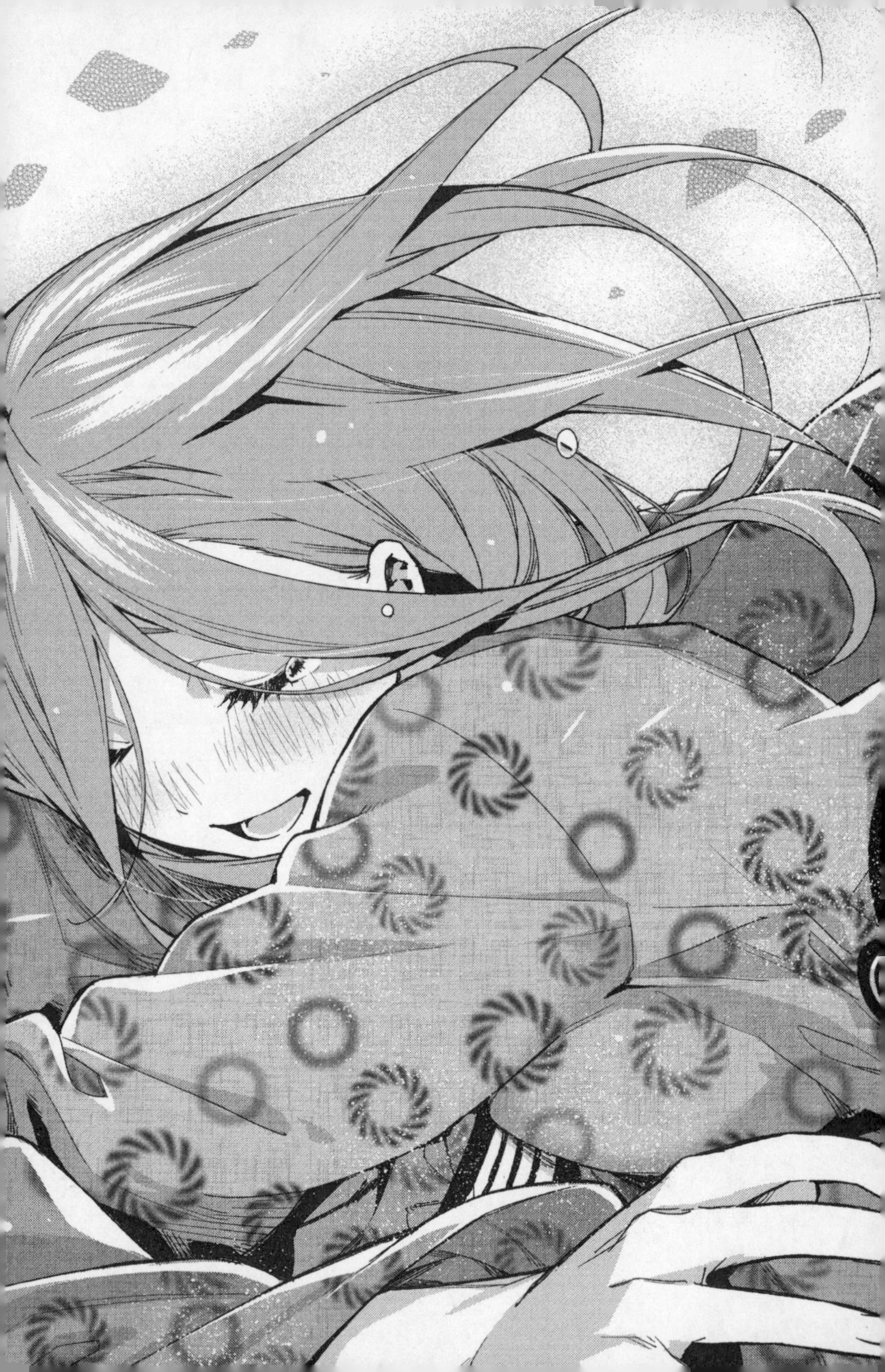

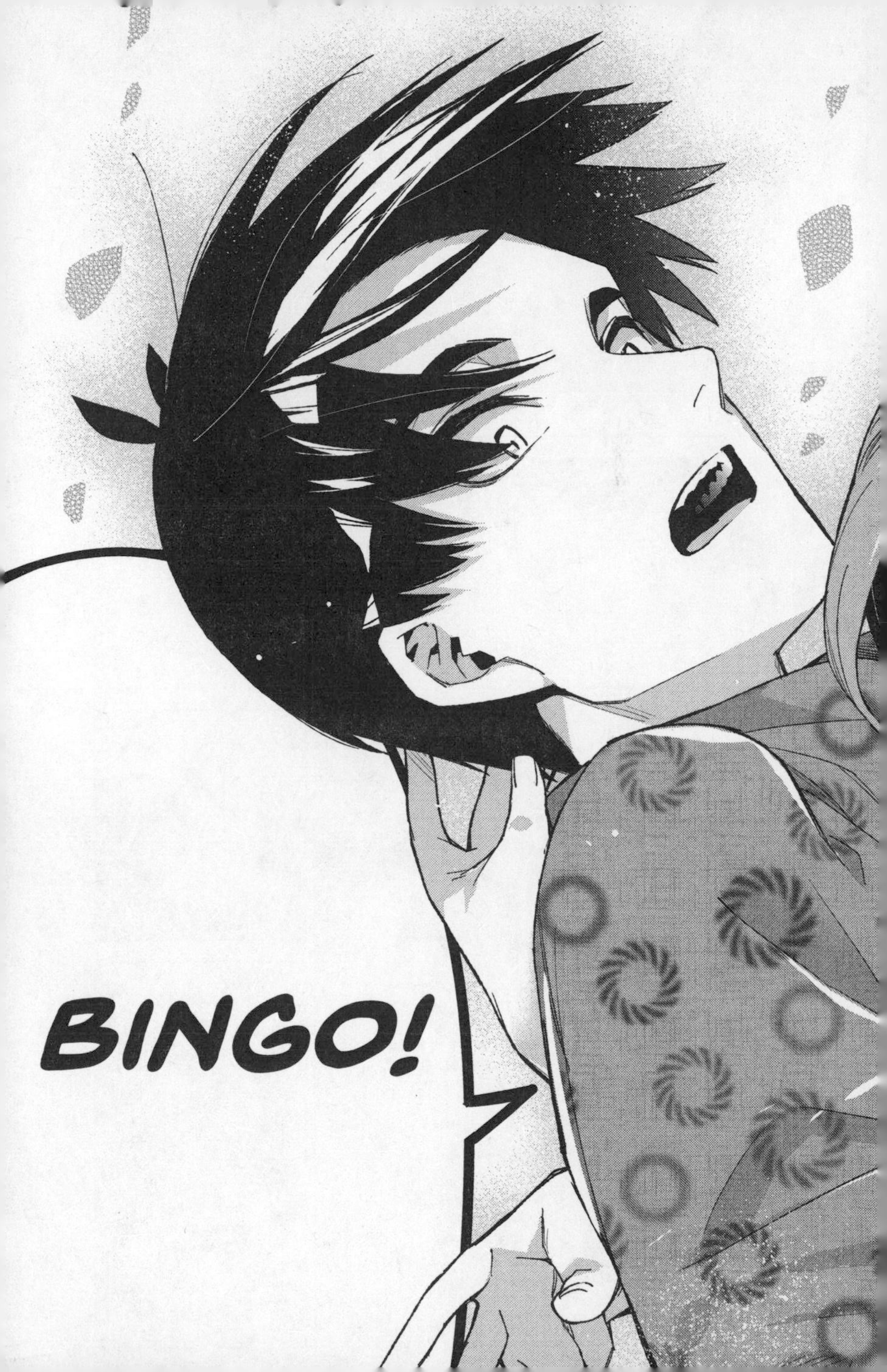
BINGO!

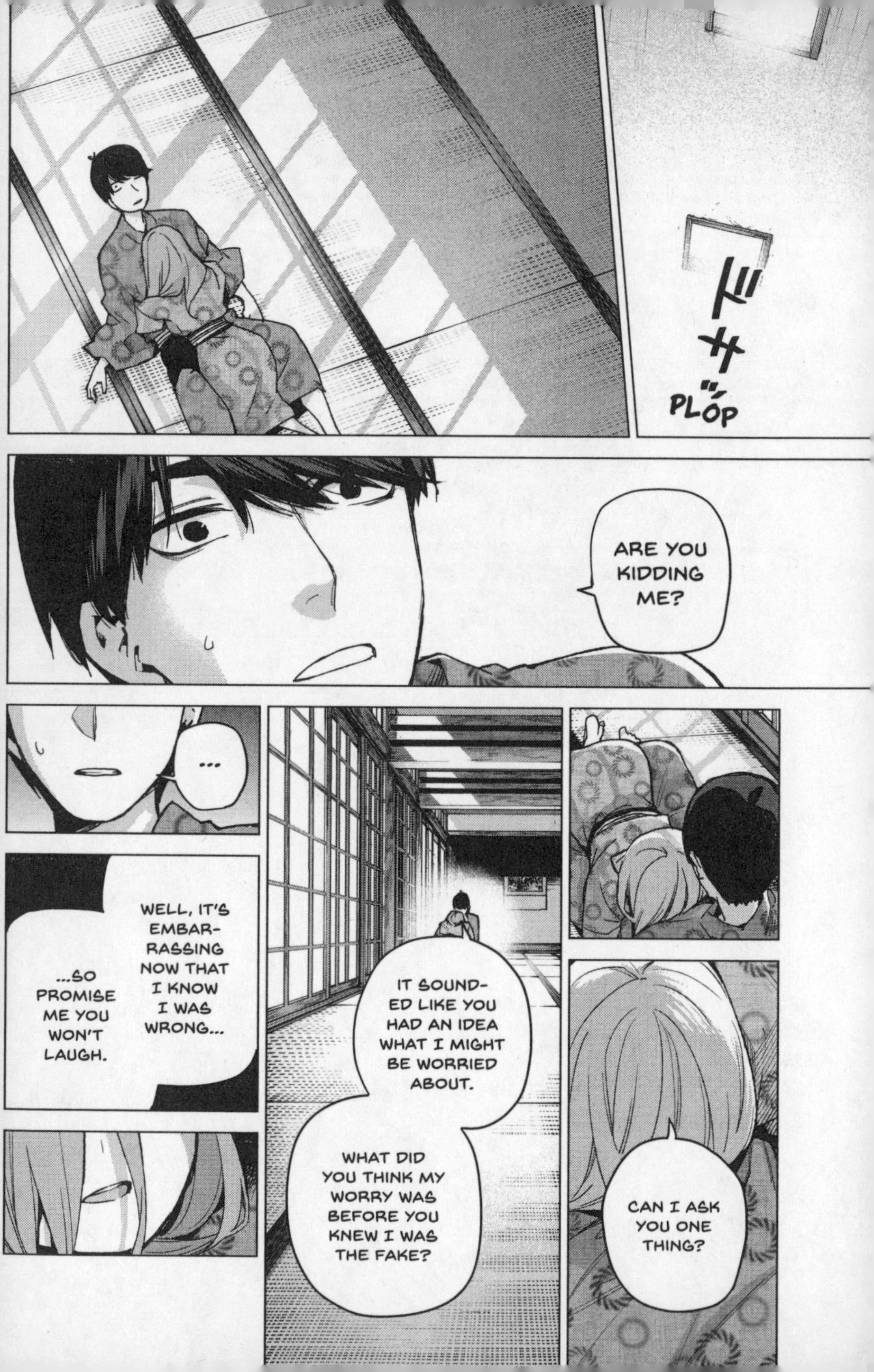
ドサ
PLOP
ARE YOU KIDDING ME?
CAN I ASK YOU ONE THING?
IT SOUND-ED LIKE YOU HAD AN IDEA WHAT I MIGHT BE WORRIED ABOUT.
WHAT DID YOU THINK MY WORRY WAS BEFORE YOU KNEW I WAS THE FAKE?
...
WELL, IT'S EMBAR-RASSING NOW THAT I KNOW I WAS WRONG...
...SO PROMISE ME YOU WON'T LAUGH.

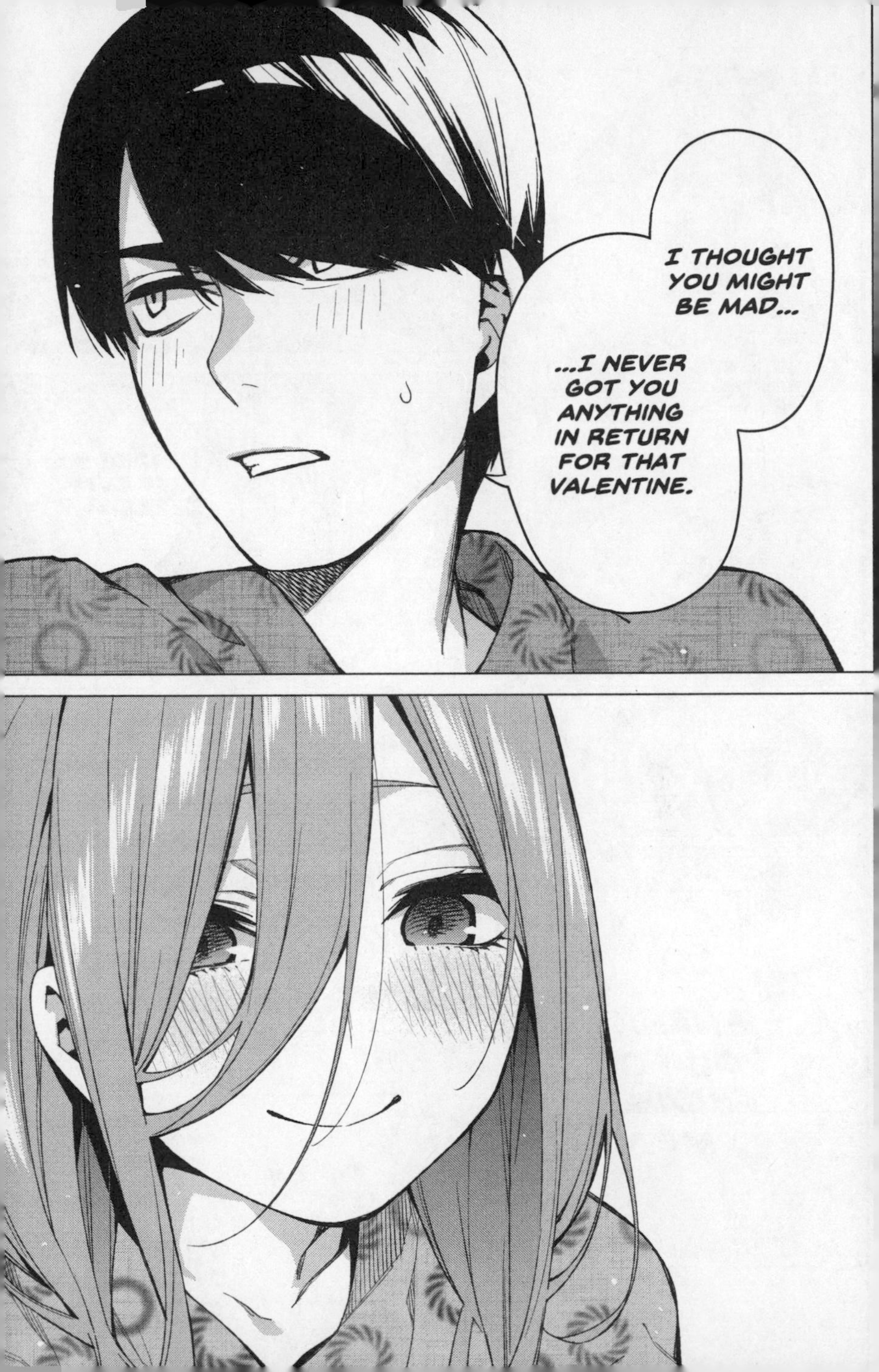
I THOUGHT YOU MIGHT BE MAD...
...I NEVER GOT YOU ANYTHING IN RETURN FOR THAT VALENTINE.

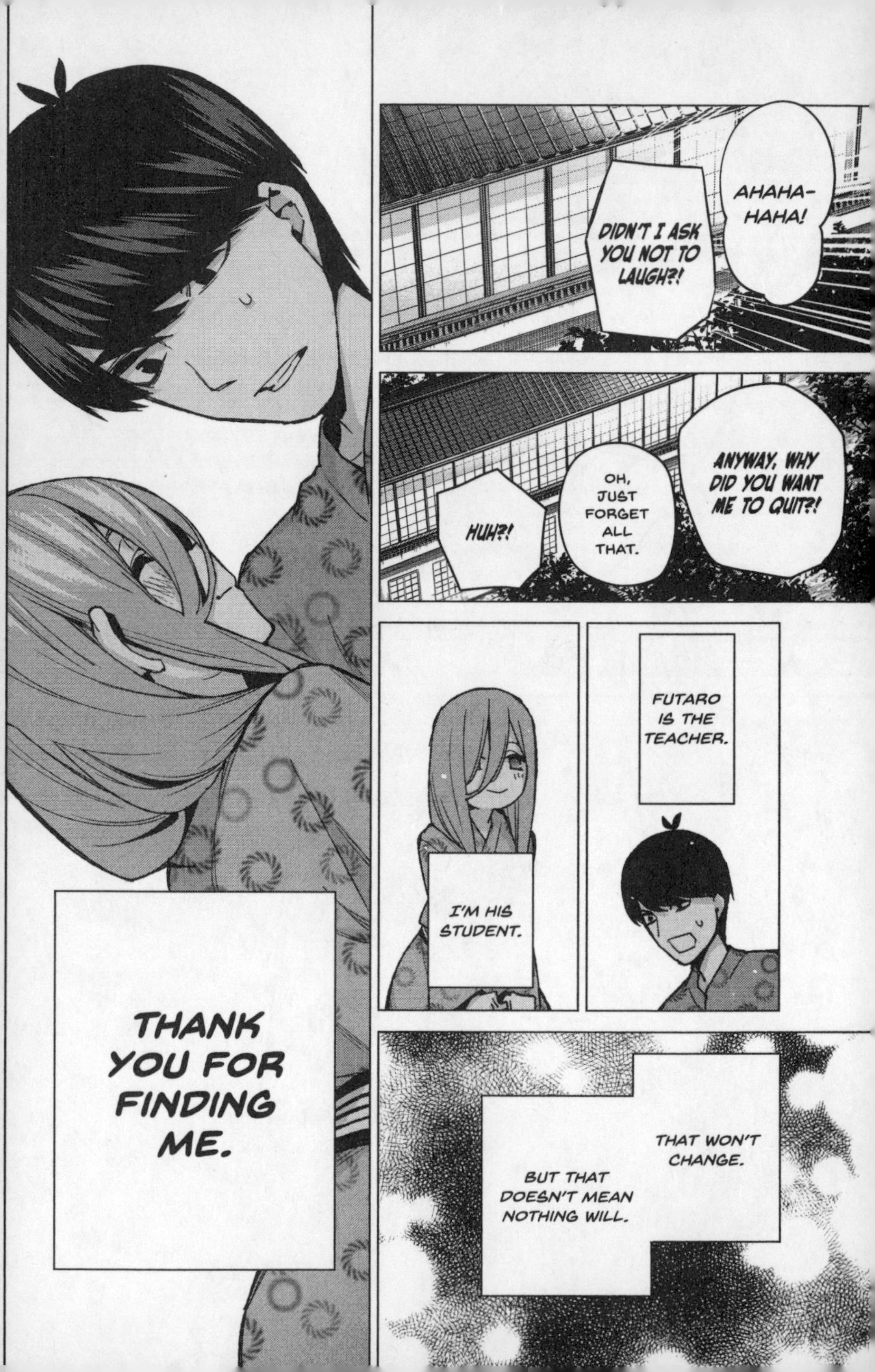
AHAHA-HAHA!
DIDN'T I ASK YOU NOT TO LAUGH?!
ANYWAY, WHY DID YOU WANT ME TO QUIT?!
OH, JUST FORGET ALL THAT.
HUH?!
FUTARO IS THE TEACHER.
I'M HIS STUDENT.
THAT WON'T CHANGE.
BUT THAT DOESN'T MEAN NOTHING WILL.
THANK YOU FOR FINDING ME.

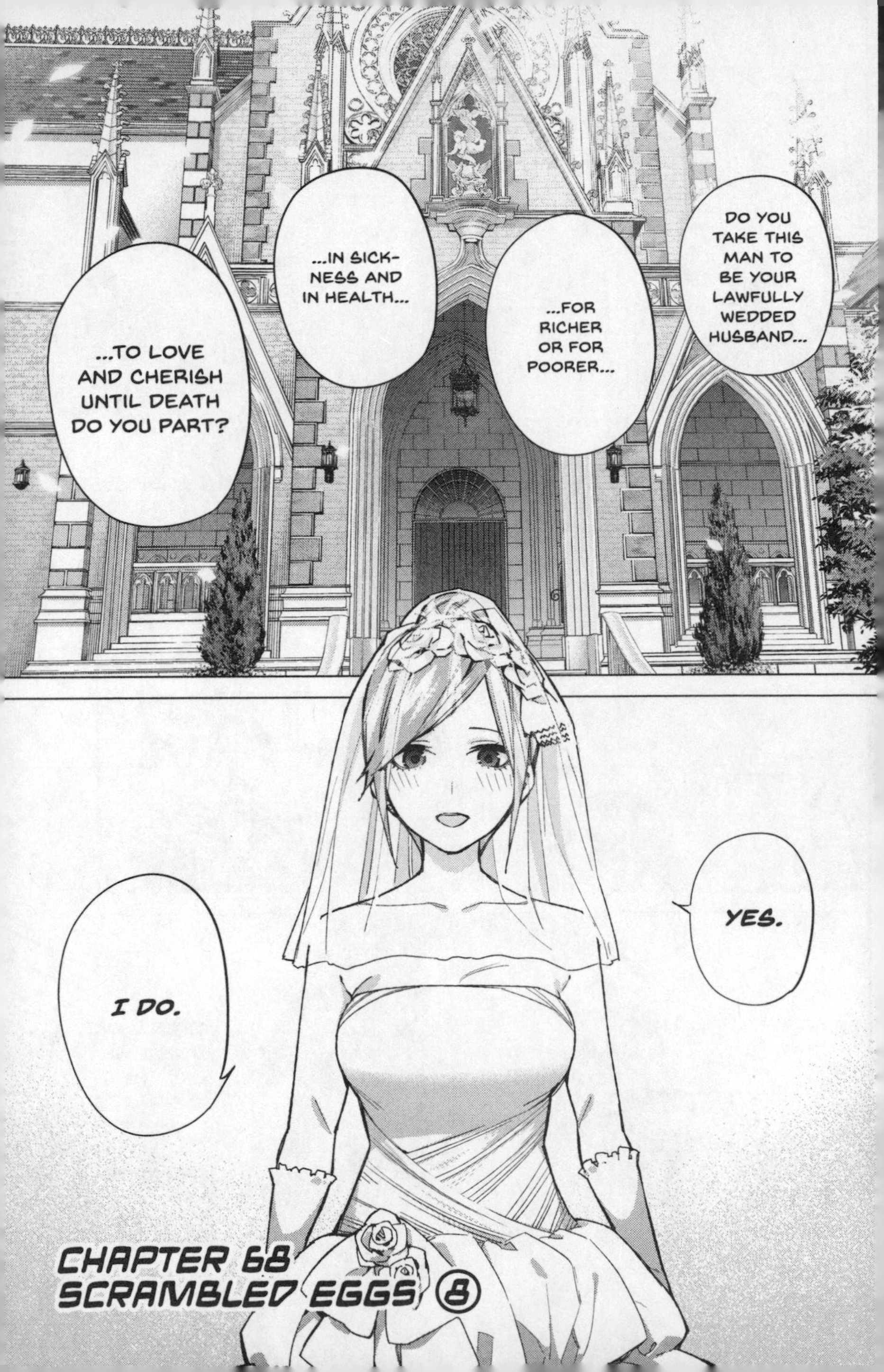
DO YOU TAKE THIS MAN TO BE YOUR LAWFULLY WEDDED HUSBAND...
...FOR RICHER OR FOR POORER...
...IN SICKNESS AND IN HEALTH...
...TO LOVE AND CHERISH UNTIL DEATH DO YOU PART?
YES.
I DO.
CHAPTER 68
SCRAMBLED EGGS ⑧

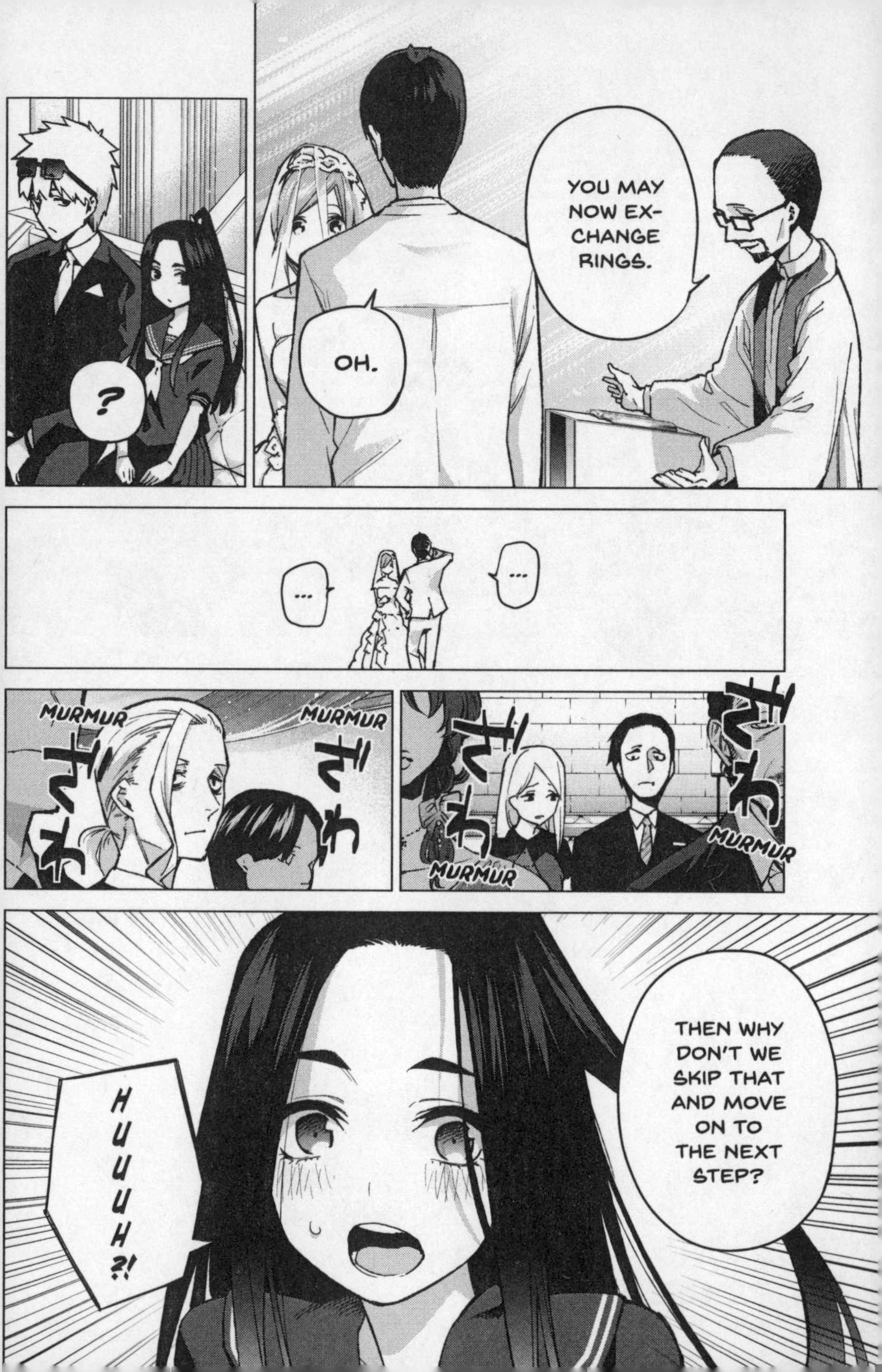
YOU MAY NOW EX-CHANGE RINGS.
OH.
?
...
...
ざわ
MURMUR
ざわ
MURMUR
MURMUR
ざわ
MURMUR
ざわ
THEN WHY DON'T WE SKIP THAT AND MOVE ON TO THE NEXT STEP?
HUUUH?!

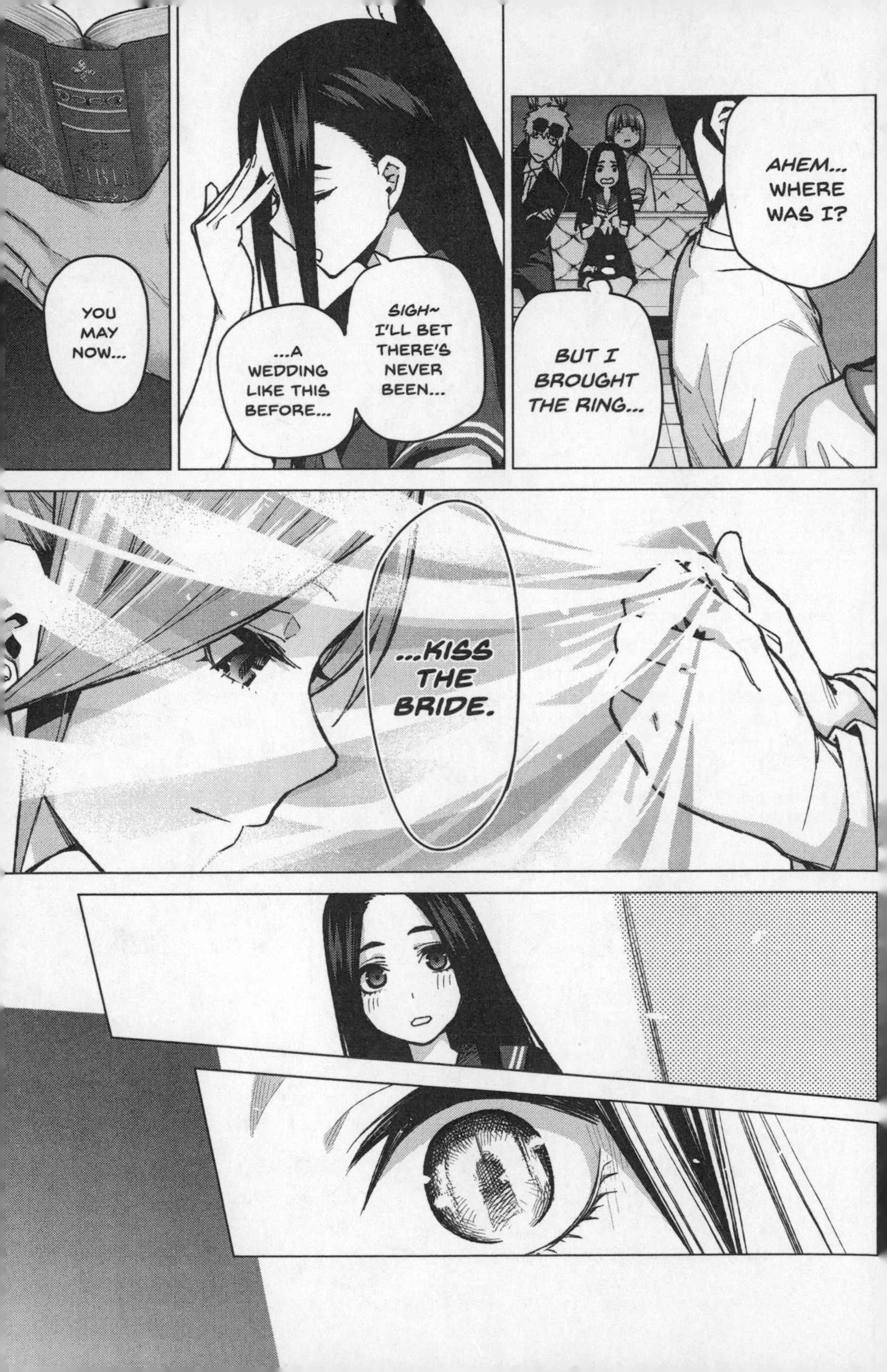
AHEM... WHERE WAS I?
BUT I BROUGHT THE RING...
SIGH~ I'LL BET THERE'S NEVER BEEN...
...A WEDDING LIKE THIS BEFORE...
YOU MAY NOW...
...KISS THE BRIDE.

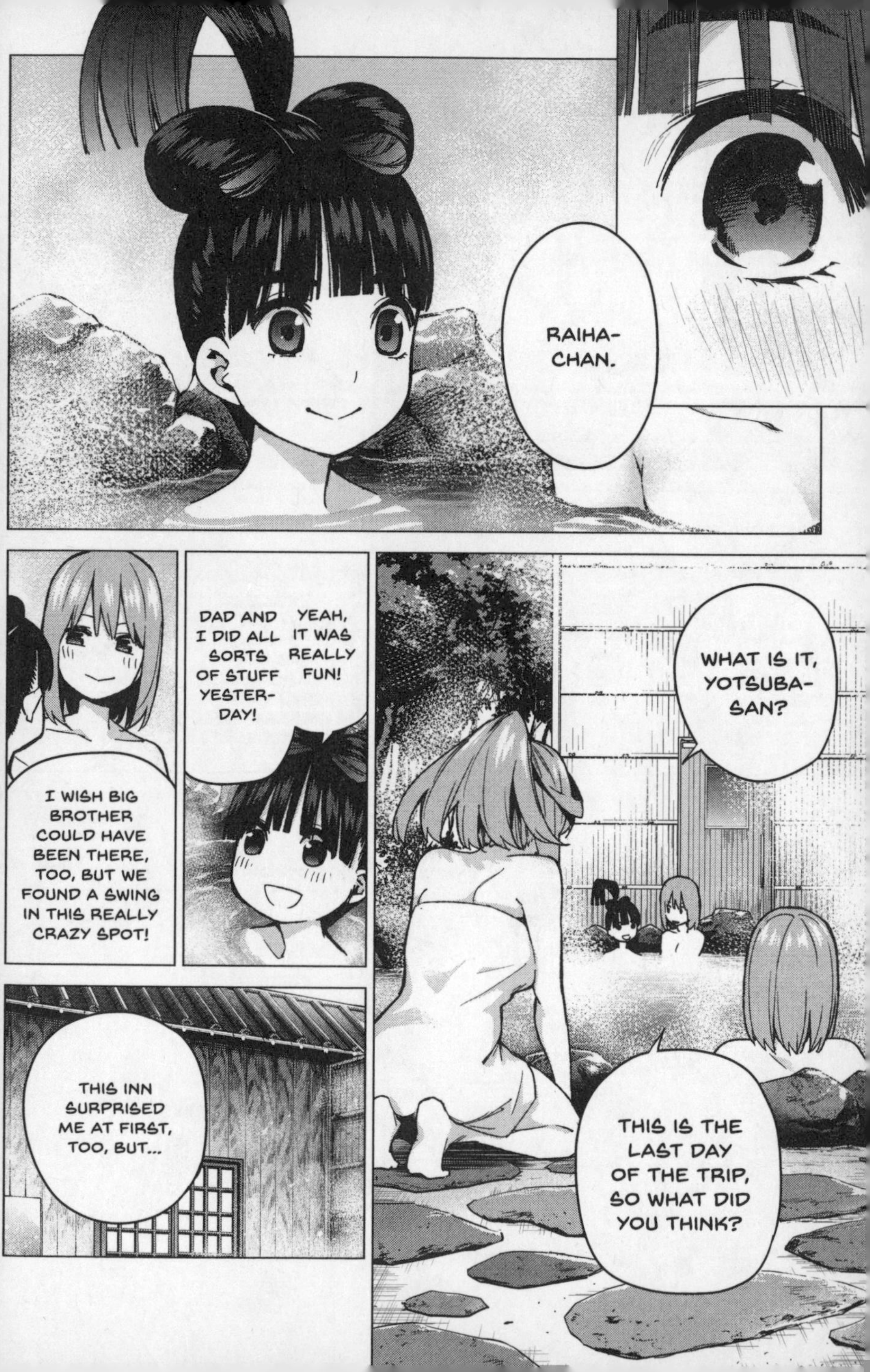
RAIHA-CHAN.
WHAT IS IT, YOTSUBA-SAN?
THIS IS THE LAST DAY OF THE TRIP, SO WHAT DID YOU THINK?
YEAH, IT WAS REALLY FUN!
DAD AND I DID ALL SORTS OF STUFF YESTER-DAY!
I WISH BIG BROTHER COULD HAVE BEEN THERE, TOO, BUT WE FOUND A SWING IN THIS REALLY CRAZY SPOT!
THIS INN SURPRISED ME AT FIRST, TOO, BUT...

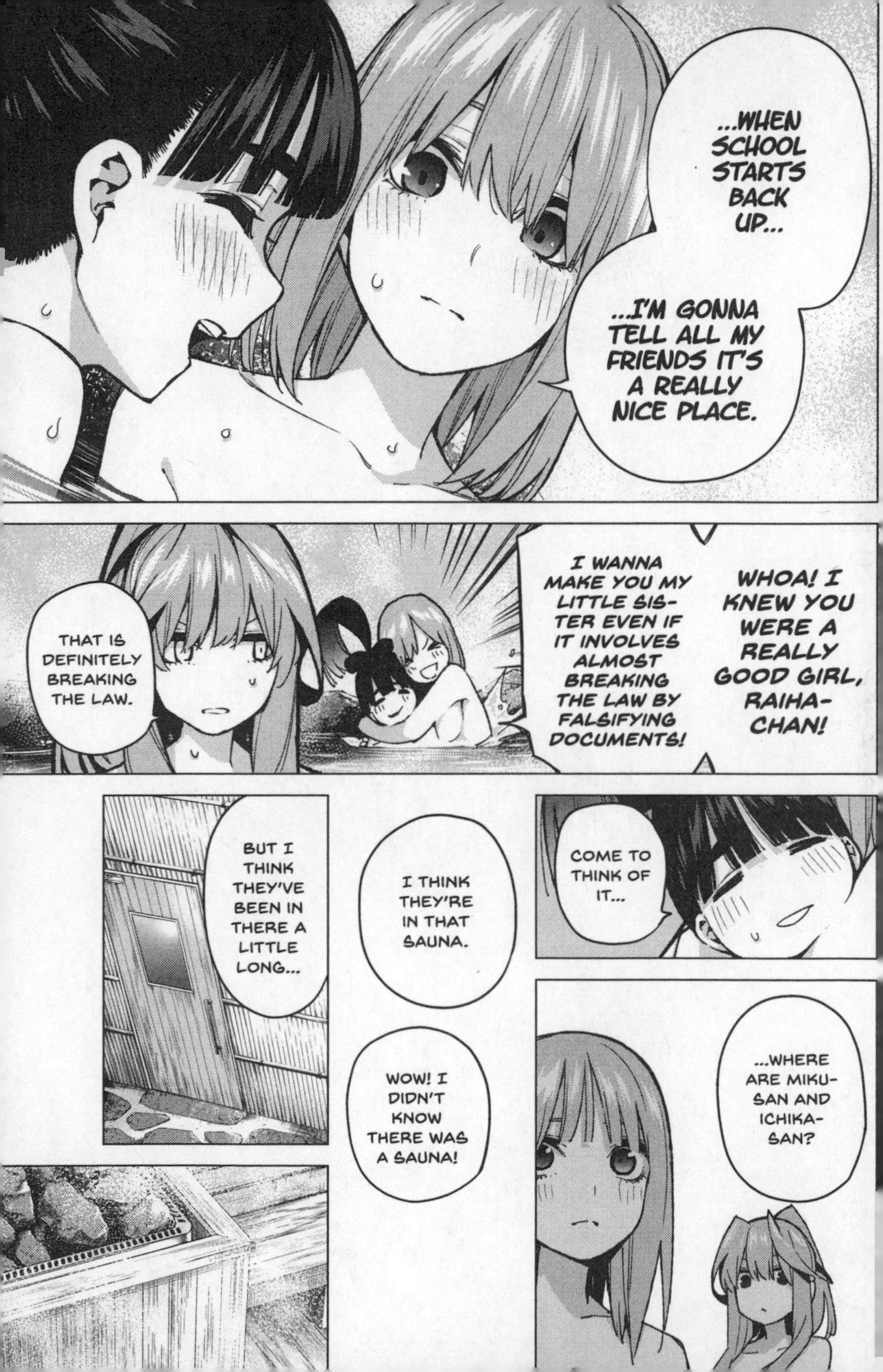
...WHEN SCHOOL STARTS BACK UP...
...I'M GONNA TELL ALL MY FRIENDS IT'S A REALLY NICE PLACE.
WHOA! I KNEW YOU WERE A REALLY GOOD GIRL, RAIHA-CHAN!
I WANNA MAKE YOU MY LITTLE SIS-TER EVEN IF IT INVOLVES ALMOST BREAKING THE LAW BY FALSIFYING DOCUMENTS!
THAT IS DEFINITELY BREAKING THE LAW.
COME TO THINK OF IT...
...WHERE ARE MIKU-SAN AND ICHIKA-SAN?
I THINK THEY'RE IN THAT SAUNA.
WOW! I DIDN'T KNOW THERE WAS A SAUNA!
BUT I THINK THEY'VE BEEN IN THERE A LITTLE LONG...

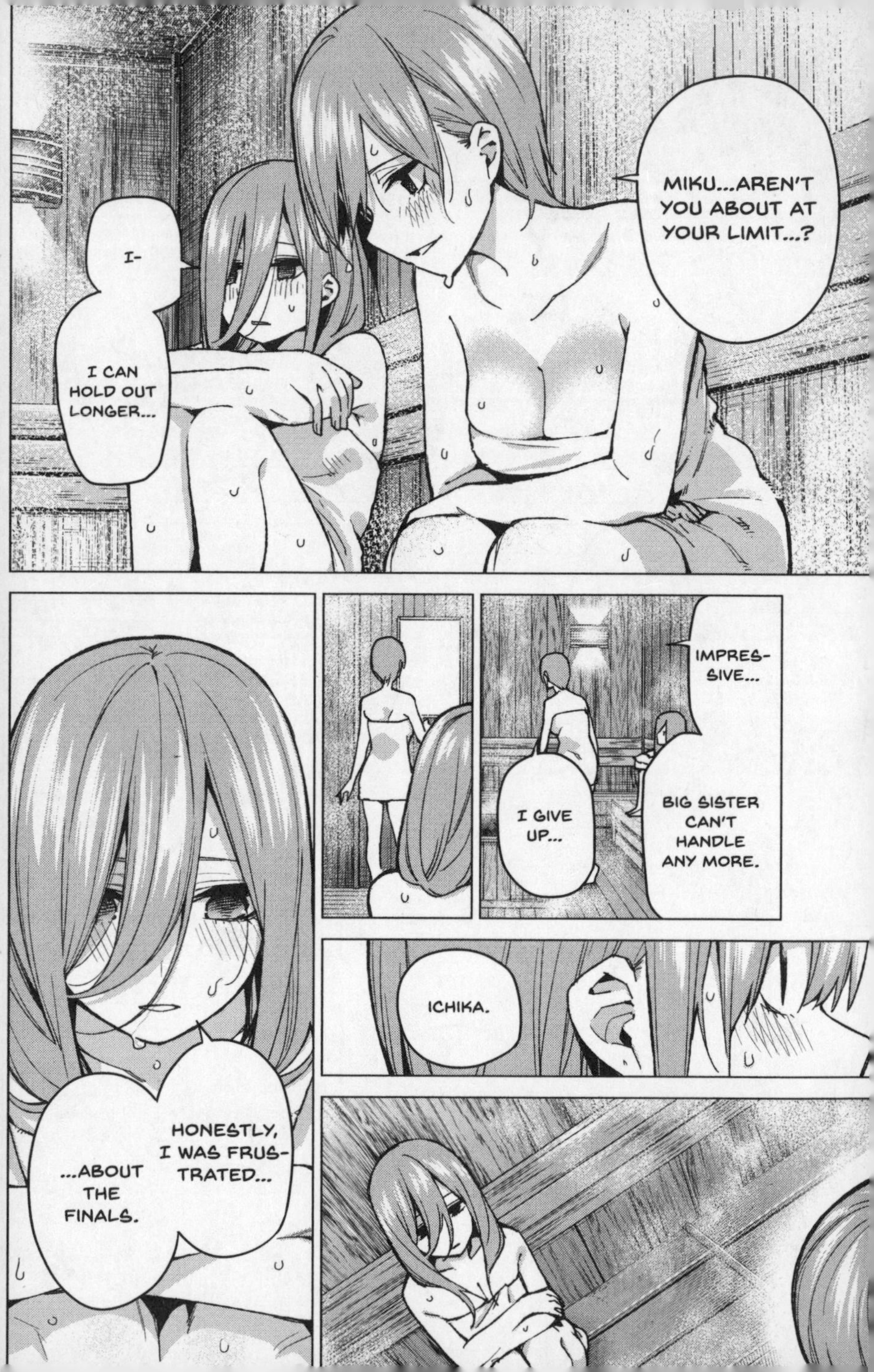
MIKU...AREN'T YOU ABOUT AT YOUR LIMIT...?
I-
I CAN HOLD OUT LONGER...
IMPRES-SIVE...
I GIVE UP...
BIG SISTER CAN'T HANDLE ANY MORE.
ICHIKA.
HONESTLY, I WAS FRUS-TRATED...
...ABOUT THE FINALS.

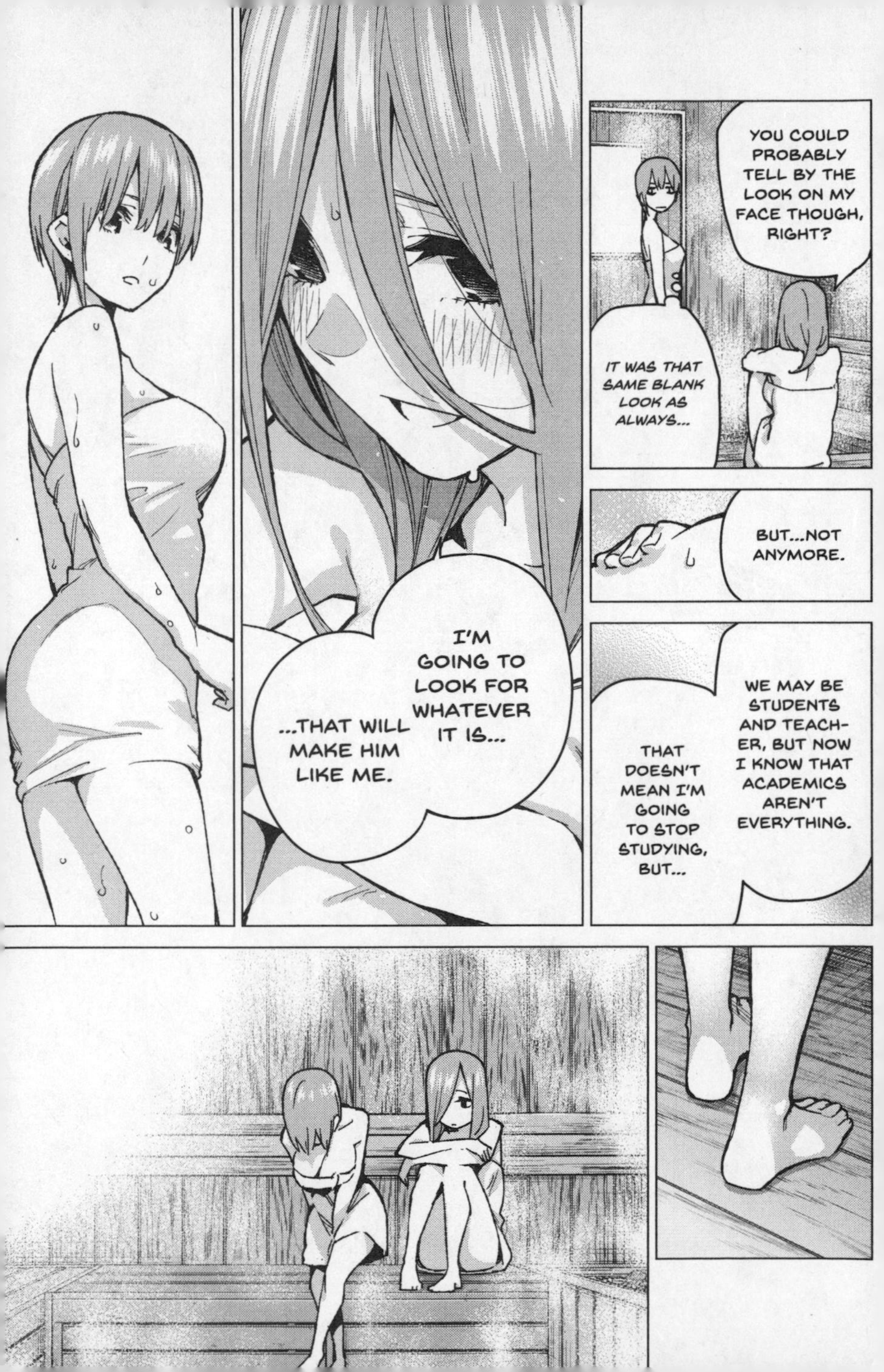
YOU COULD PROBABLY TELL BY THE LOOK ON MY FACE THOUGH, RIGHT?
IT WAS THAT SAME BLANK LOOK AS ALWAYS...
BUT...NOT ANYMORE.
WE MAY BE STUDENTS AND TEACH-ER, BUT NOW I KNOW THAT ACADEMICS AREN'T EVERYTHING.
THAT DOESN'T MEAN I'M GOING TO STOP STUDYING, BUT...
I'M GOING TO LOOK FOR WHATEVER IT IS...
...THAT WILL MAKE HIM LIKE ME.

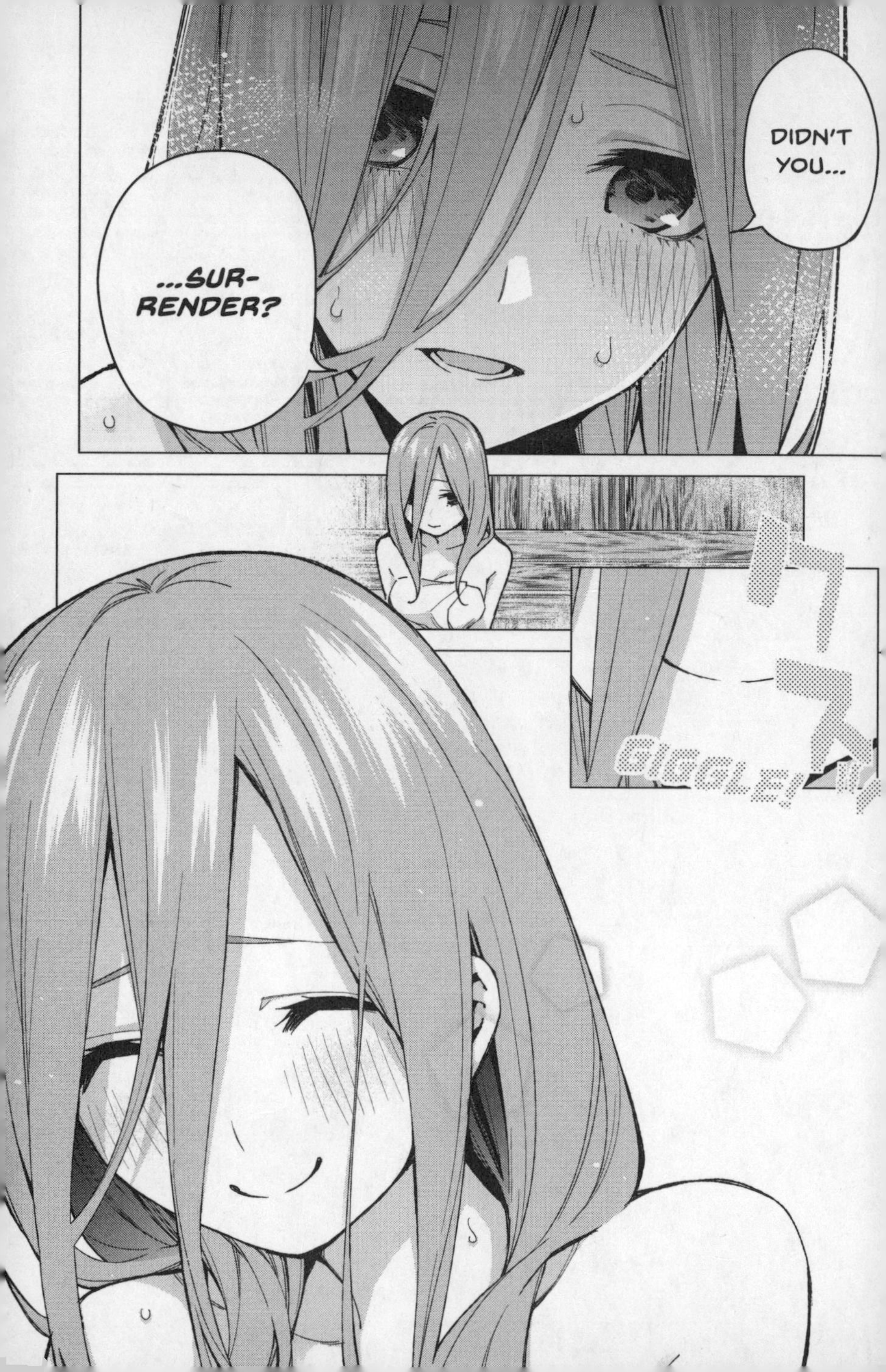
DIDN'T YOU...
...SUR-RENDER?
GIGGLE!

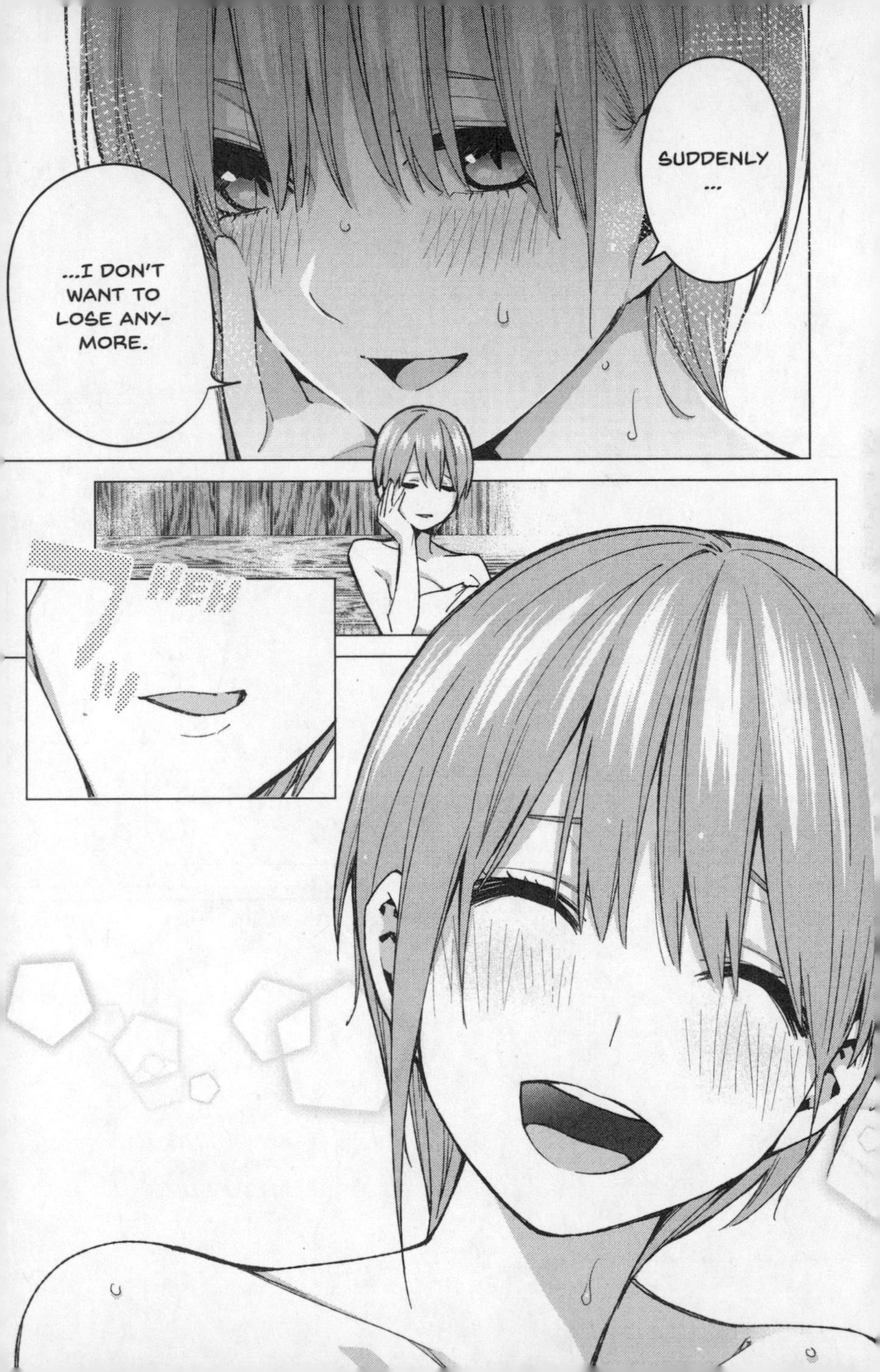
SUDDENLY ...
...I DON'T WANT TO LOSE ANY-MORE.
HEH

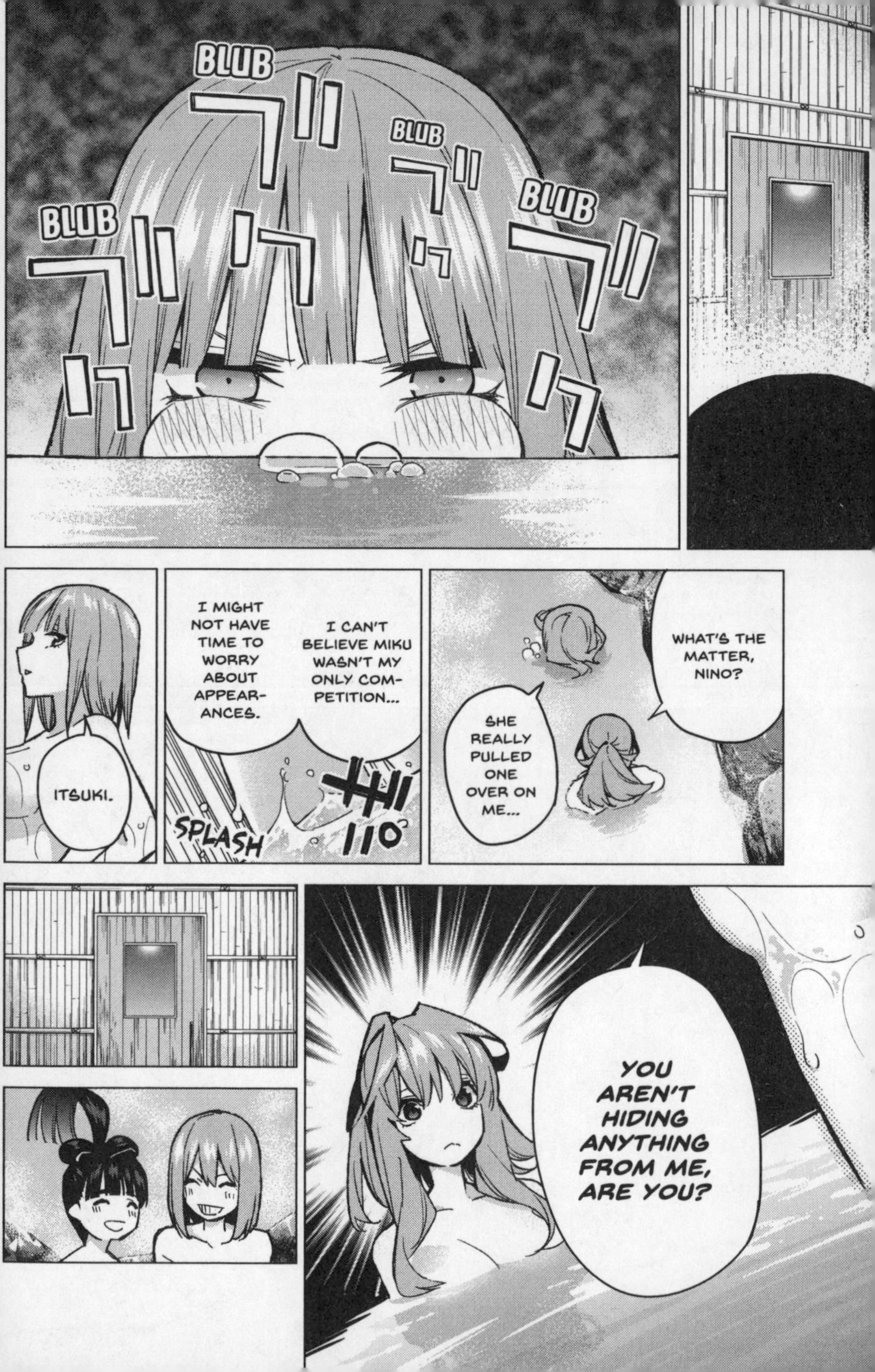
BLUB
BLUB
BLUB
BLUB
WHAT'S THE MATTER, NINO?
SHE REALLY PULLED ONE OVER ON ME...
I CAN'T BELIEVE MIKU WASN'T MY ONLY COMPETITION...
I MIGHT NOT HAVE TIME TO WORRY ABOUT APPEARANCES.
SPLASH
ITSUKI.
YOU AREN'T HIDING ANYTHING FROM ME, ARE YOU?

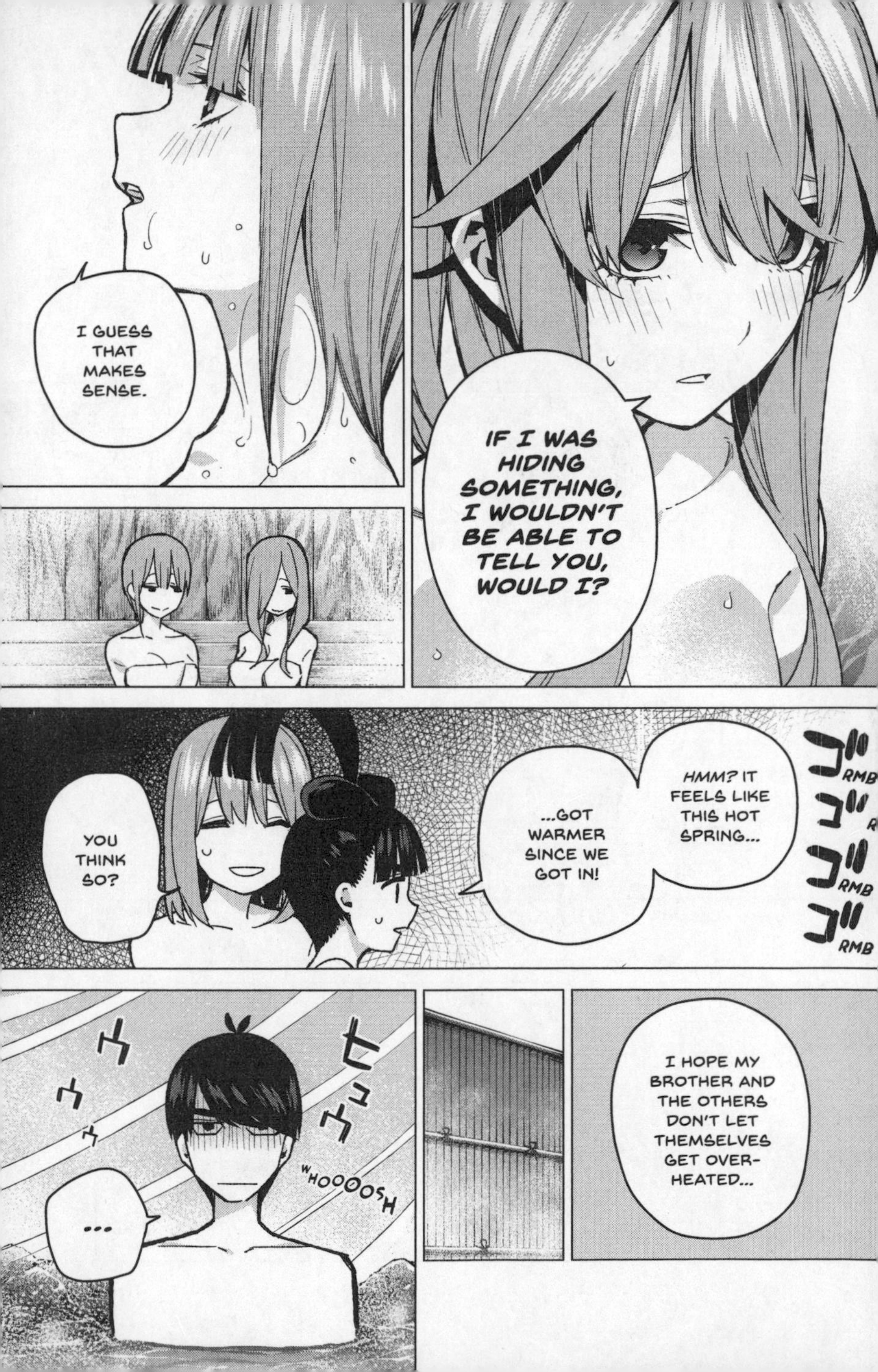
IF I WAS HIDING SOMETHING, I WOULDN'T BE ABLE TO TELL YOU, WOULD I?
I GUESS THAT MAKES SENSE.
ゴゴゴゴ
RMB RMB RMB RMB
HMM? IT FEELS LIKE THIS HOT SPRING...
...GOT WARMER SINCE WE GOT IN!
YOU THINK SO?
I HOPE MY BROTHER AND THE OTHERS DON'T LET THEMSELVES GET OVER-HEATED...
ヒュウウウ
WHOOOOSH
...

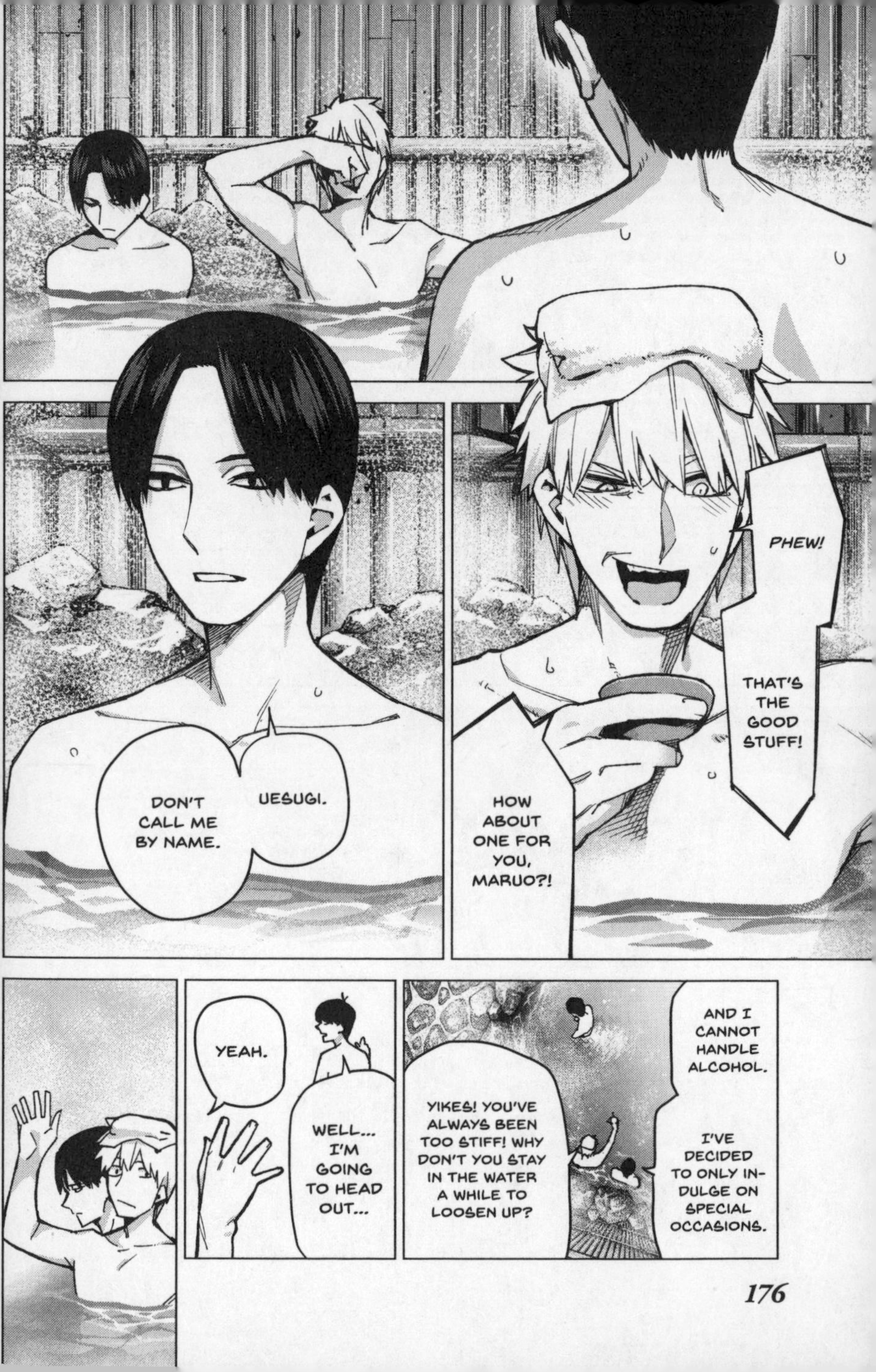
PHEW!
THAT'S THE GOOD STUFF!
HOW ABOUT ONE FOR YOU, MARUO?!
UESUGI.
DON'T CALL ME BY NAME.
AND I CANNOT HANDLE ALCOHOL.
I'VE DECIDED TO ONLY IN-DULGE ON SPECIAL OCCASIONS.
YIKES! YOU'VE ALWAYS BEEN TOO STIFF! WHY DON'T YOU STAY IN THE WATER A WHILE TO LOOSEN UP?
WELL... I'M GOING TO HEAD OUT...
YEAH.

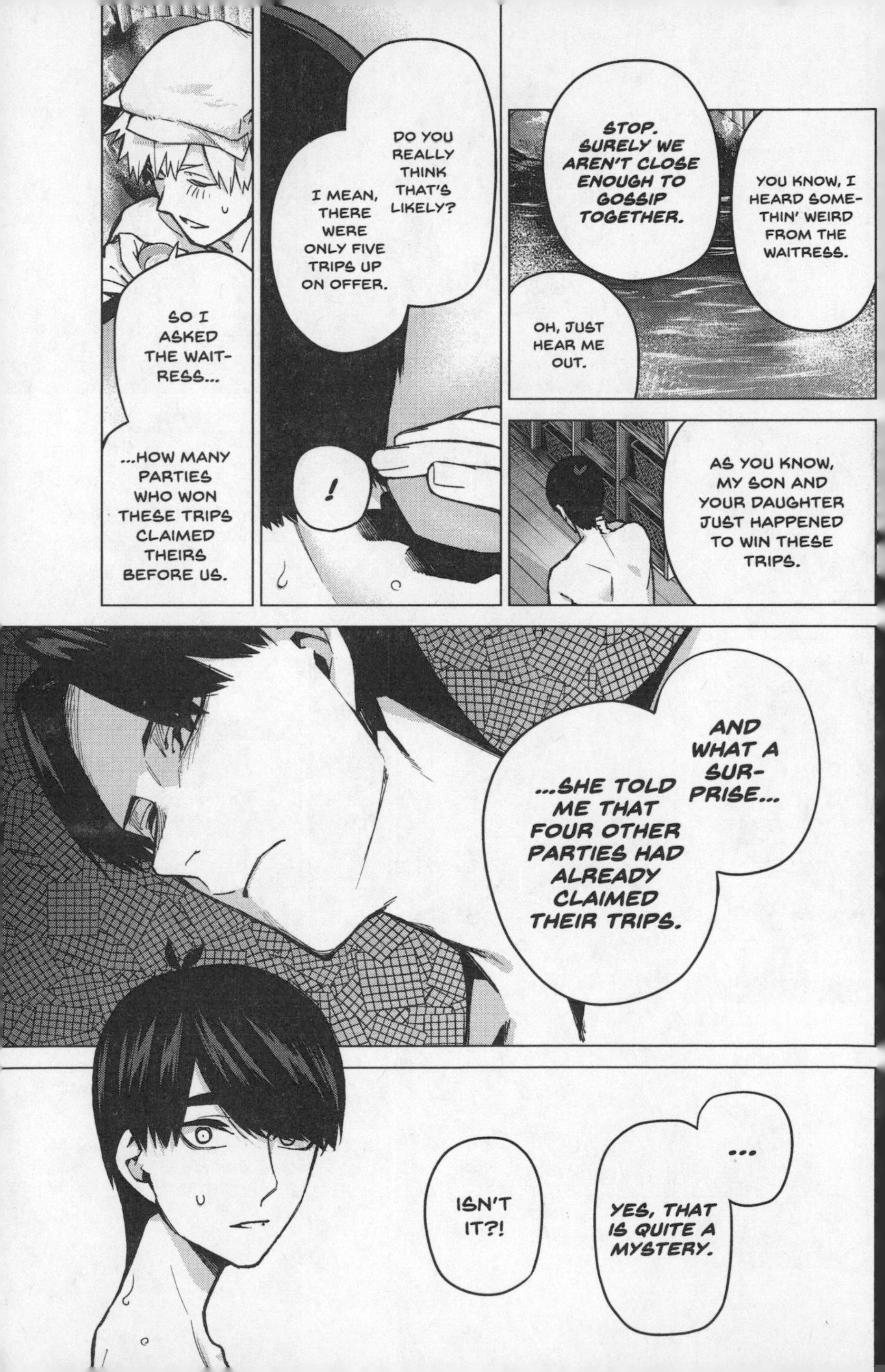
YOU KNOW, I HEARD SOME-THIN' WEIRD FROM THE WAITRESS.
STOP. SURELY WE AREN'T CLOSE ENOUGH TO GOSSIP TOGETHER.
OH, JUST HEAR ME OUT.
AS YOU KNOW, MY SON AND YOUR DAUGHTER JUST HAPPENED TO WIN THESE TRIPS.
DO YOU REALLY THINK THAT'S LIKELY?
I MEAN, THERE WERE ONLY FIVE TRIPS UP ON OFFER.
!
SO I ASKED THE WAIT-RESS...
...HOW MANY PARTIES WHO WON THESE TRIPS CLAIMED THEIRS BEFORE US.
AND WHAT A SUR-PRISE...
...SHE TOLD ME THAT FOUR OTHER PARTIES HAD ALREADY CLAIMED THEIR TRIPS.
...
YES, THAT IS QUITE A MYSTERY.
ISN'T IT?!

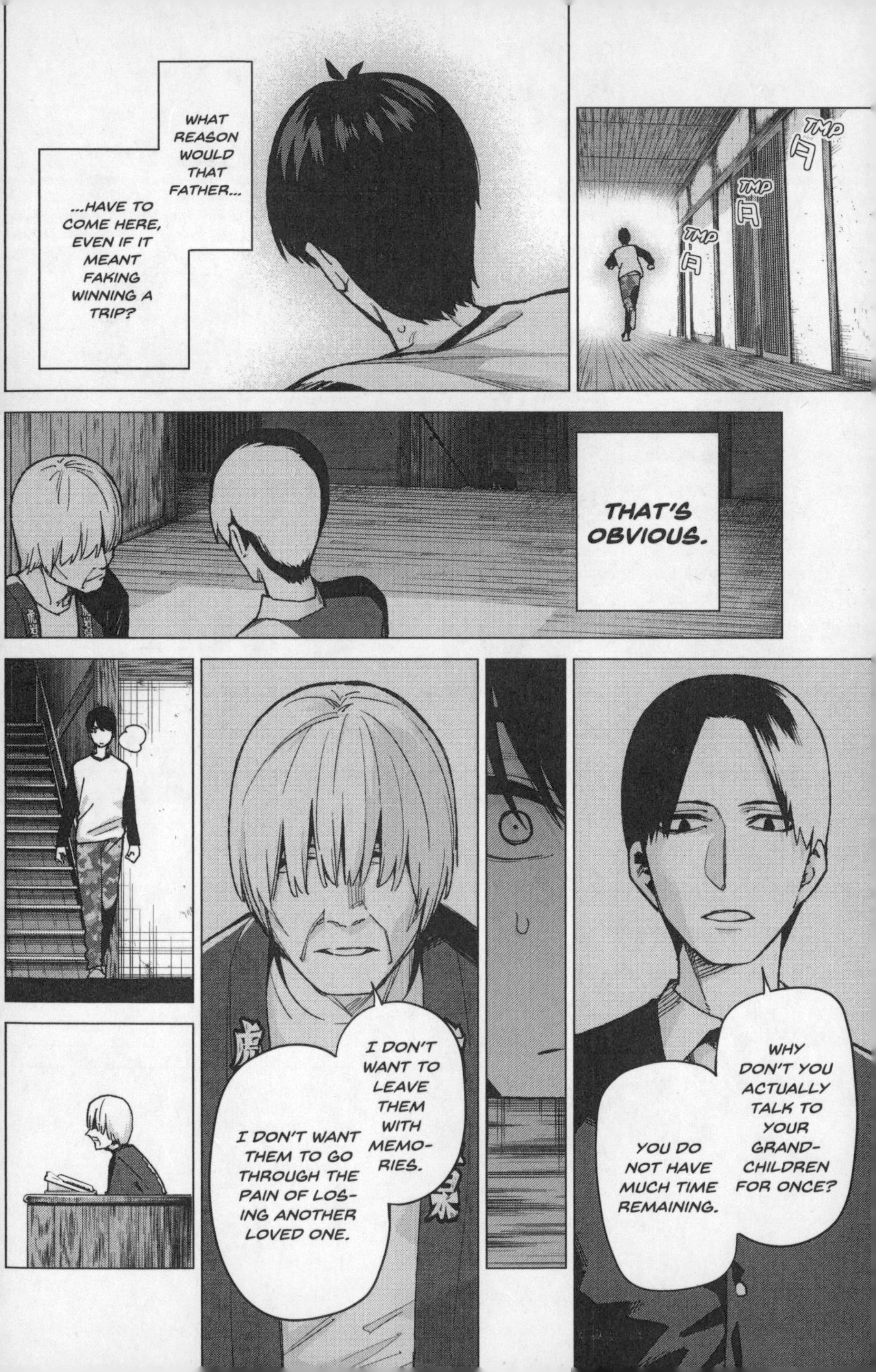
TMP
TMP
TMP
WHAT REASON WOULD THAT FATHER...
...HAVE TO COME HERE, EVEN IF IT MEANT FAKING WINNING A TRIP?
THAT'S OBVIOUS.
WHY DON'T YOU ACTUALLY TALK TO YOUR GRAND-CHILDREN FOR ONCE?
YOU DO NOT HAVE MUCH TIME REMAINING.
I DON'T WANT TO LEAVE THEM WITH MEMO-RIES.
I DON'T WANT THEM TO GO THROUGH THE PAIN OF LOS-ING ANOTHER LOVED ONE.

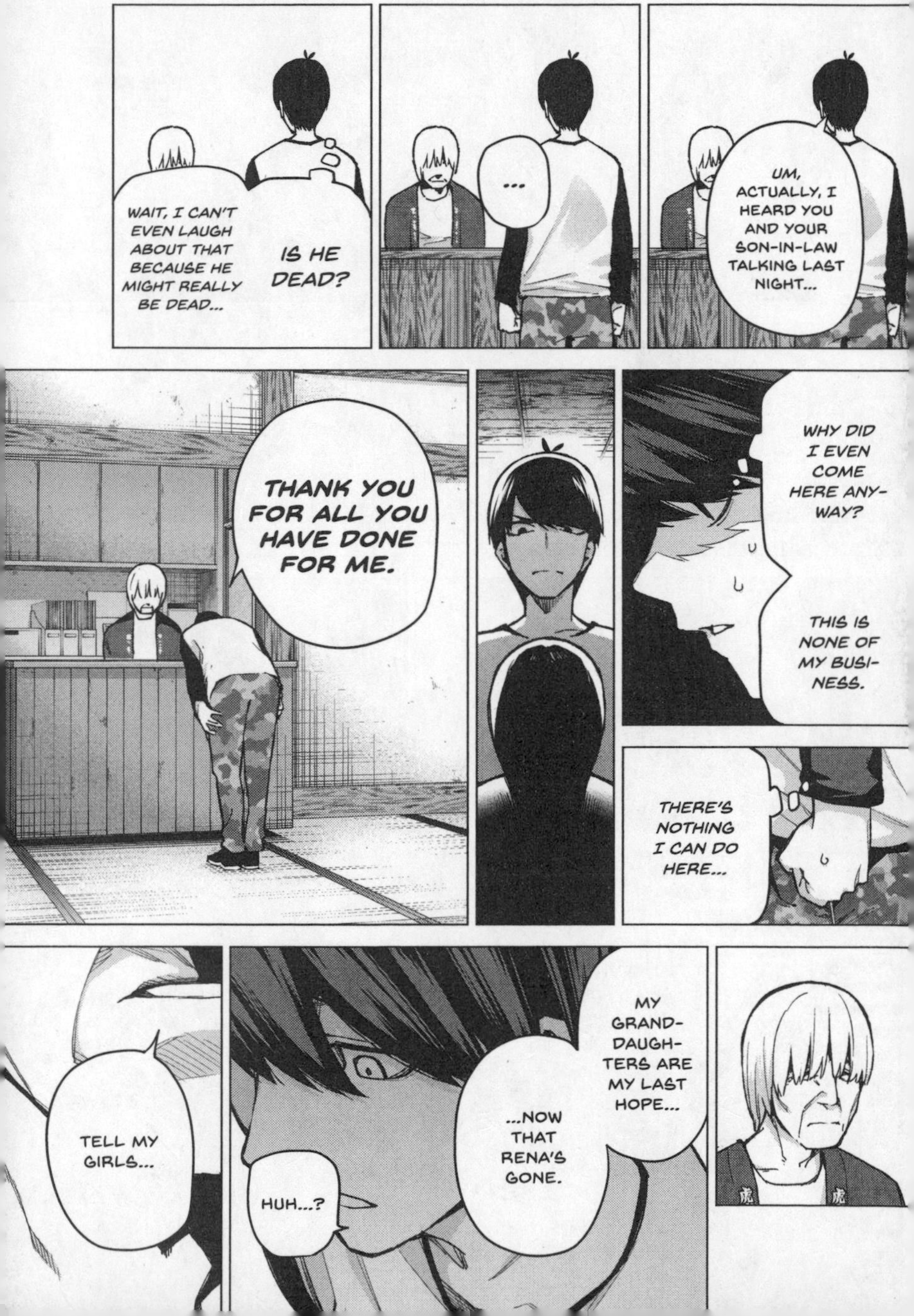
UM, ACTUALLY, I HEARD YOU AND YOUR SON-IN-LAW TALKING LAST NIGHT...
...
IS HE DEAD?
WAIT, I CAN'T EVEN LAUGH ABOUT THAT BECAUSE HE MIGHT REALLY BE DEAD...
WHY DID I EVEN COME HERE ANYWAY?
THIS IS NONE OF MY BUSINESS.
THERE'S NOTHING I CAN DO HERE...
THANK YOU FOR ALL YOU HAVE DONE FOR ME.
MY GRANDDAUGHTERS ARE MY LAST HOPE...
...NOW THAT RENA'S GONE.
HUH...?
TELL MY GIRLS...

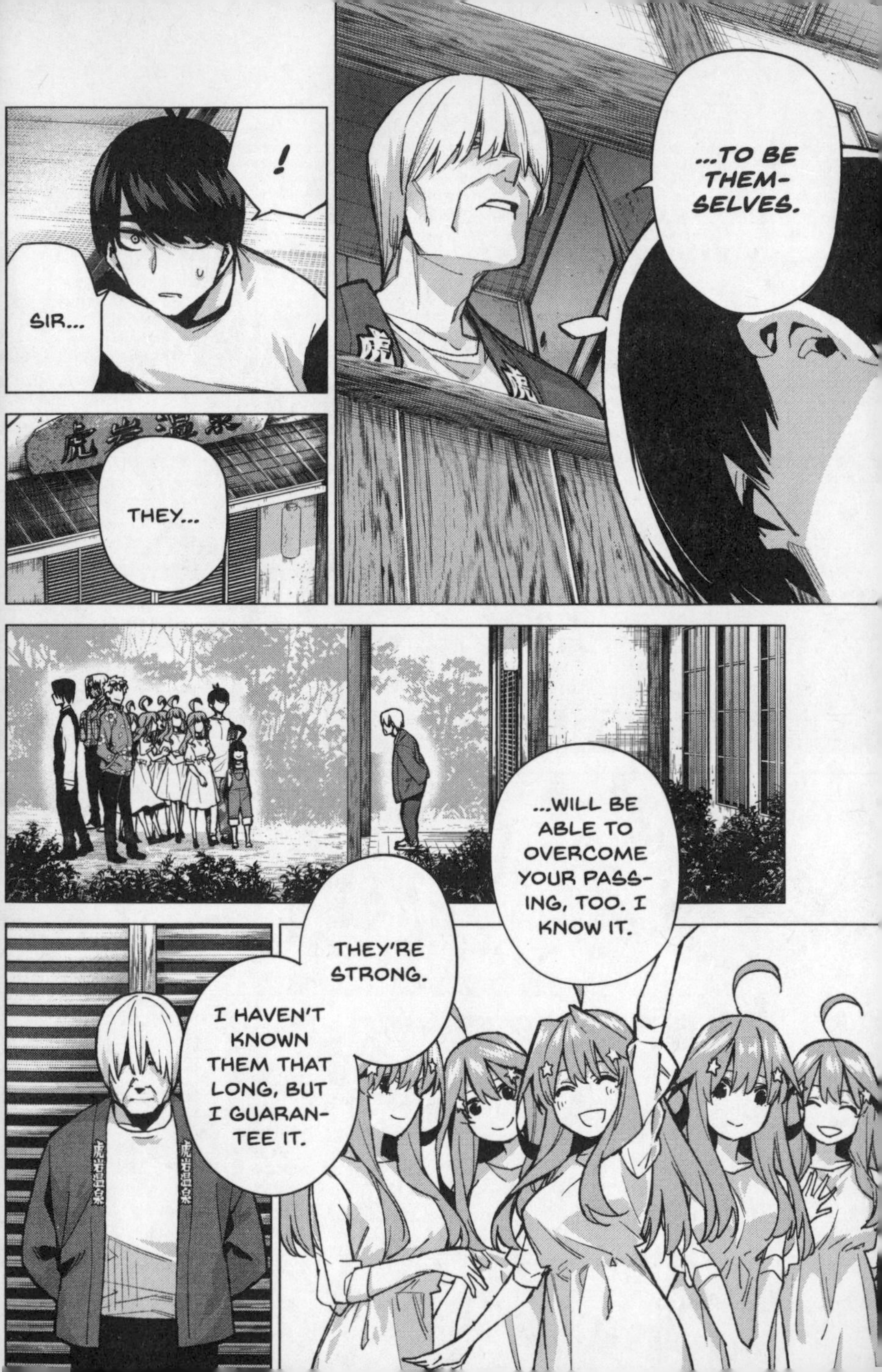
...TO BE THEM-SELVES.
!
SIR...
THEY...
...WILL BE ABLE TO OVERCOME YOUR PASS-ING, TOO. I KNOW IT.
THEY'RE STRONG.
I HAVEN'T KNOWN THEM THAT LONG, BUT I GUARAN-TEE IT.

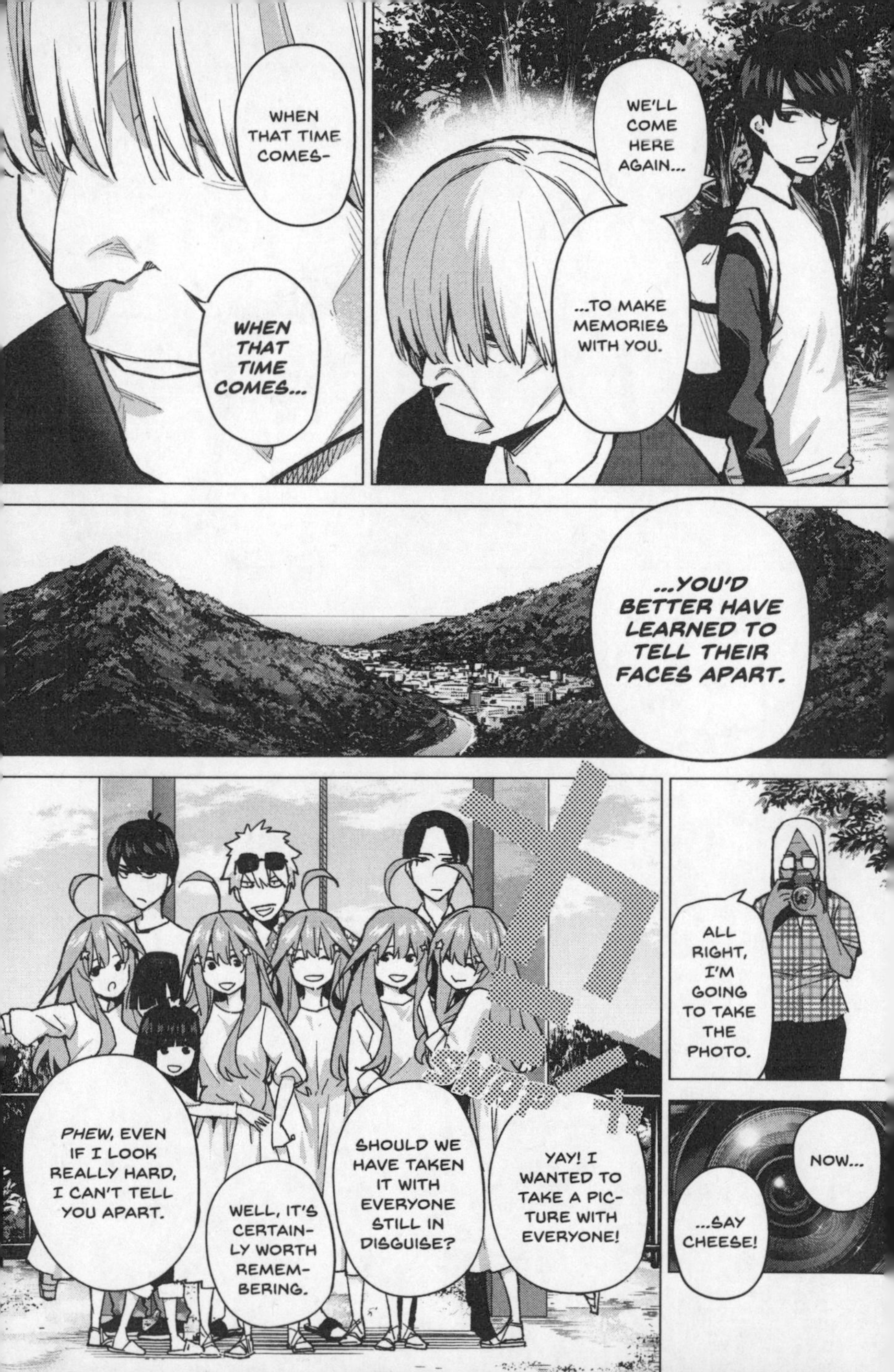
WE'LL COME HERE AGAIN...
...TO MAKE MEMORIES WITH YOU.
WHEN THAT TIME COMES-
WHEN THAT TIME COMES...
...YOU'D BETTER HAVE LEARNED TO TELL THEIR FACES APART.
ALL RIGHT, I'M GOING TO TAKE THE PHOTO.
NOW...
...SAY CHEESE!
YAY! I WANTED TO TAKE A PIC-TURE WITH EVERYONE!
SHOULD WE HAVE TAKEN IT WITH EVERYONE STILL IN DISGUISE?
WELL, IT'S CERTAIN-LY WORTH REMEM-BERING.
PHEW, EVEN IF I LOOK REALLY HARD, I CAN'T TELL YOU APART.

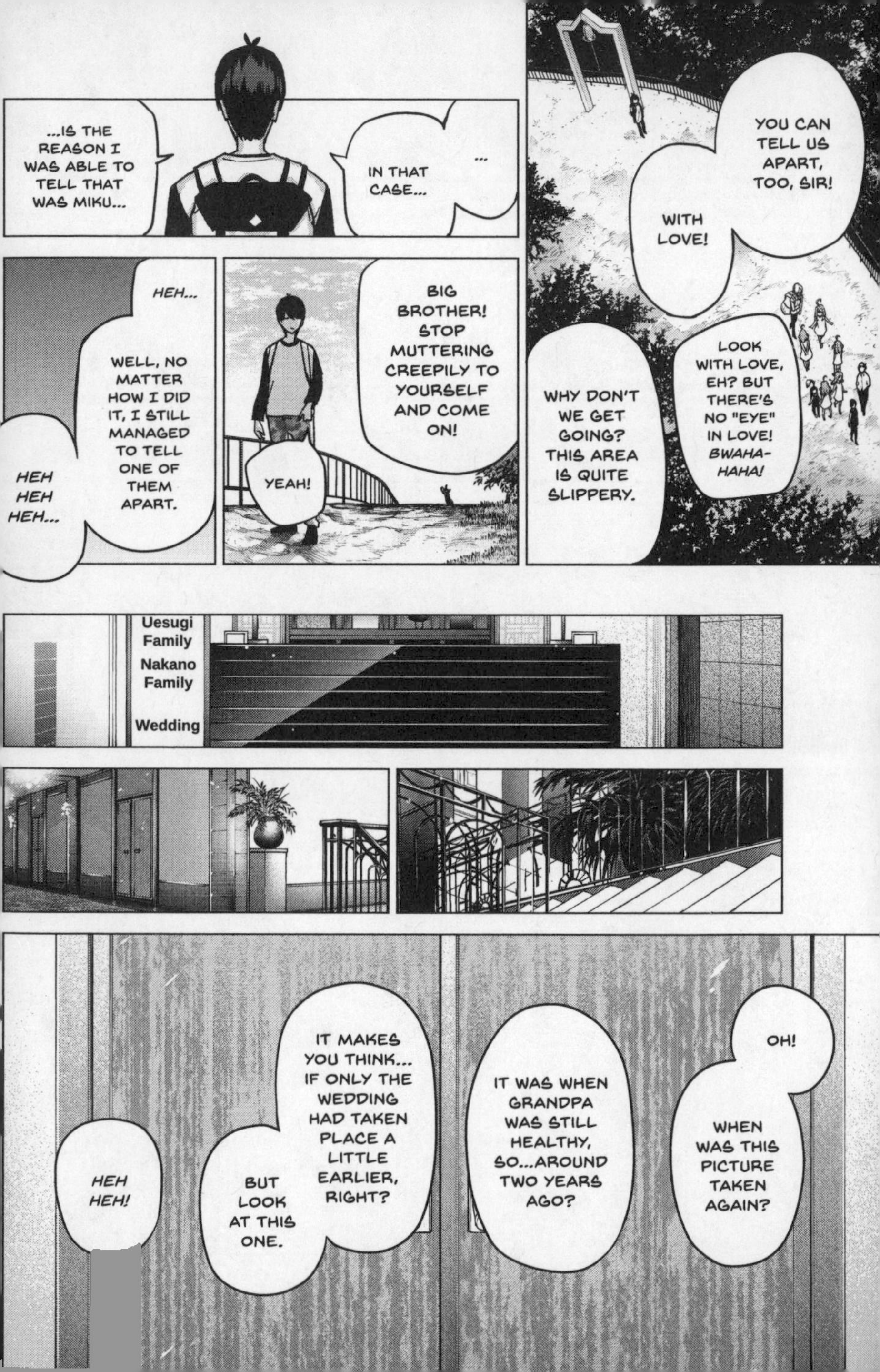
YOU CAN TELL US APART, TOO, SIR!
WITH LOVE!
LOOK WITH LOVE, EH? BUT THERE'S NO "EYE" IN LOVE! BWAHA-HAHA!
WHY DON'T WE GET GOING? THIS AREA IS QUITE SLIPPERY.
...
IN THAT CASE...
...IS THE REASON I WAS ABLE TO TELL THAT WAS MIKU...
BIG BROTHER! STOP MUTTERING CREEPILY TO YOURSELF AND COME ON!
YEAH!
HEH...
WELL, NO MATTER HOW I DID IT, I STILL MANAGED TO TELL ONE OF THEM APART.
HEH HEH HEH...
Uesugi Family
Nakano Family
Wedding
OH!
WHEN WAS THIS PICTURE TAKEN AGAIN?
IT WAS WHEN GRANDPA WAS STILL HEALTHY, SO...AROUND TWO YEARS AGO?
IT MAKES YOU THINK... IF ONLY THE WEDDING HAD TAKEN PLACE A LITTLE EARLIER, RIGHT?
BUT LOOK AT THIS ONE.
HEH HEH!

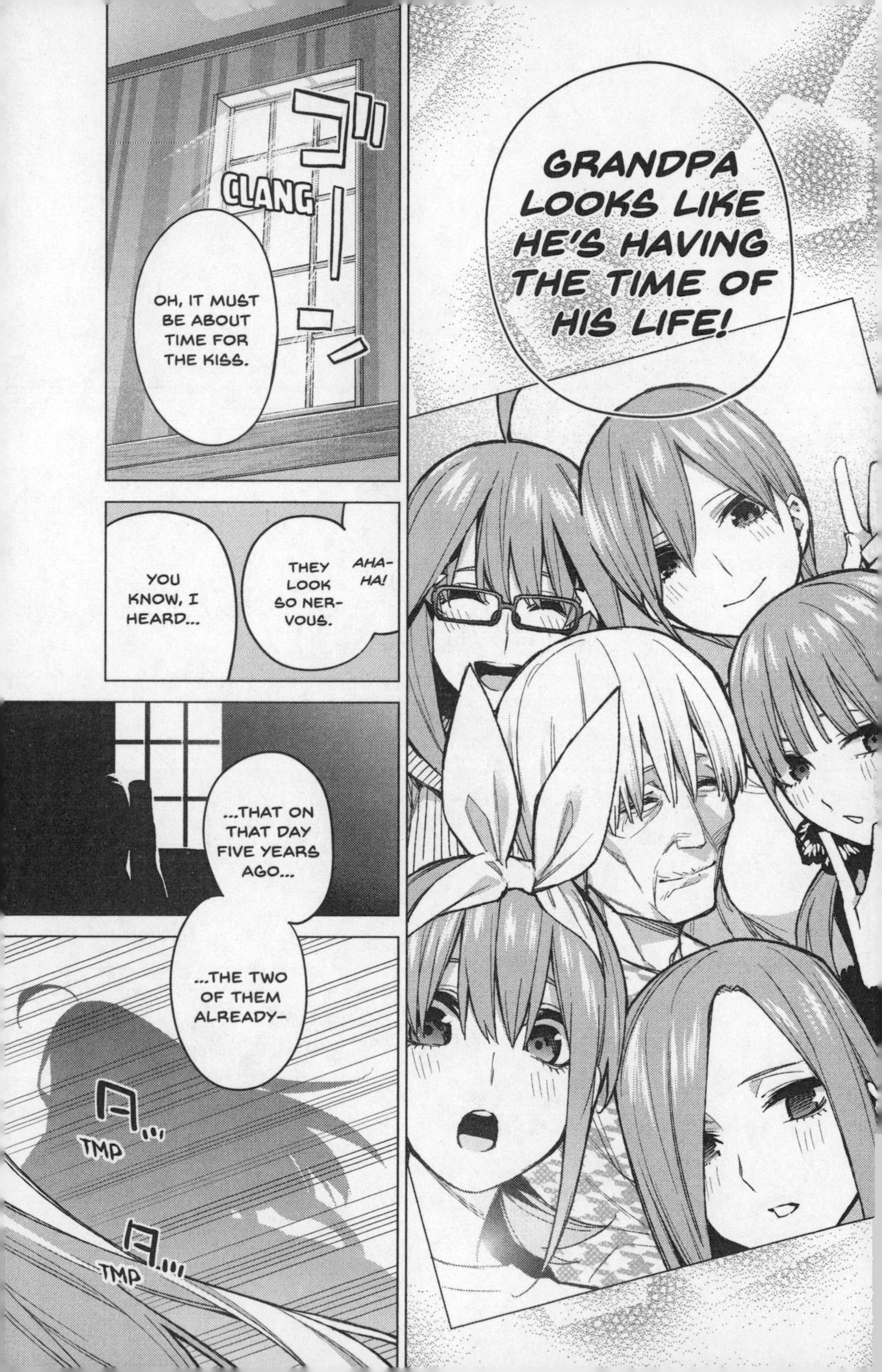
GRANDPA LOOKS LIKE HE'S HAVING THE TIME OF HIS LIFE!
CLANG
OH, IT MUST BE ABOUT TIME FOR THE KISS.
AHA-HA!
THEY LOOK SO NER-VOUS.
YOU KNOW, I HEARD...
...THAT ON THAT DAY FIVE YEARS AGO...
...THE TWO OF THEM ALREADY–
TMP
TMP

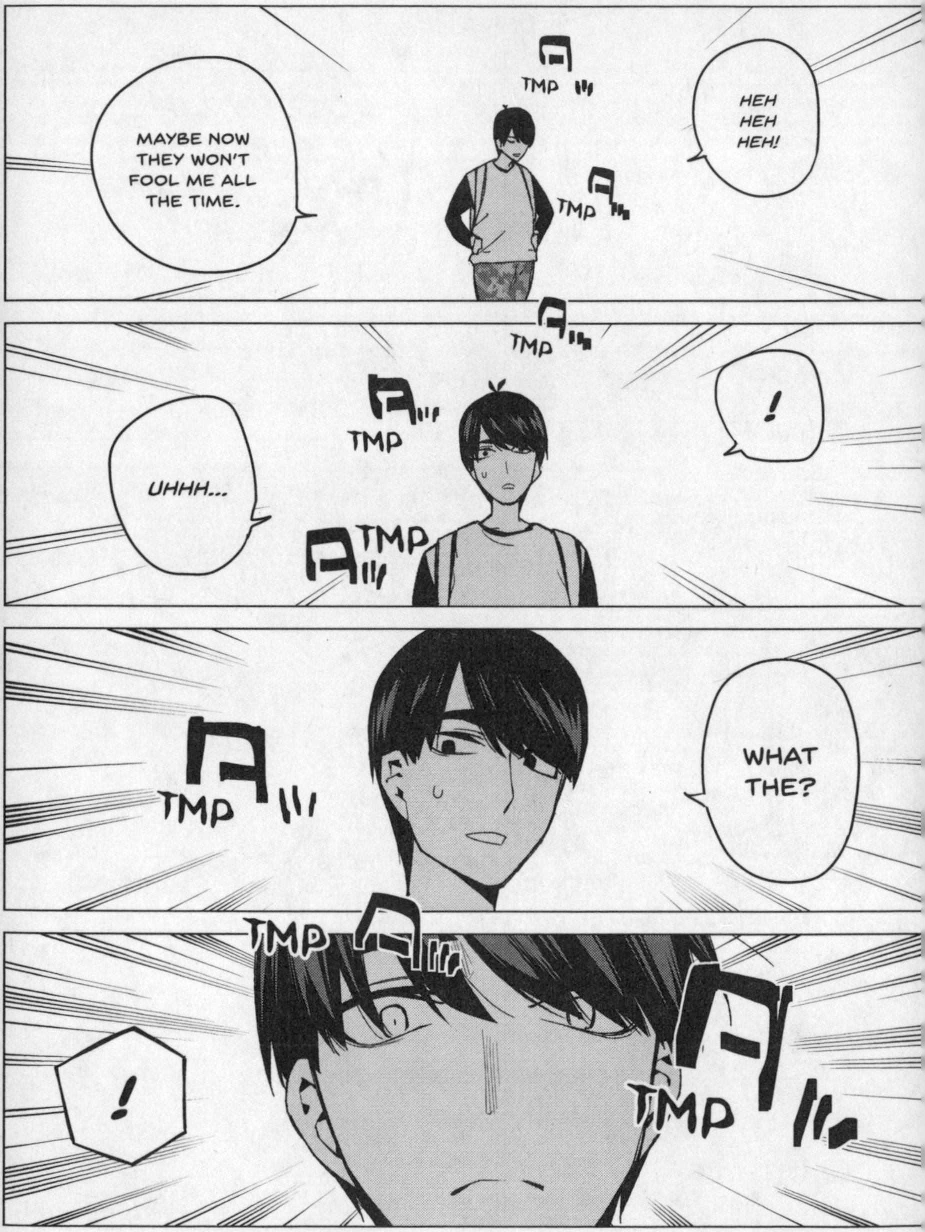

HEH HEH HEH!
TMP
TMP
MAYBE NOW THEY WON'T FOOL ME ALL THE TIME.
TMP
!
TMP
UHHH...
TMP
WHAT THE?
TMP
TMP
TMP
!

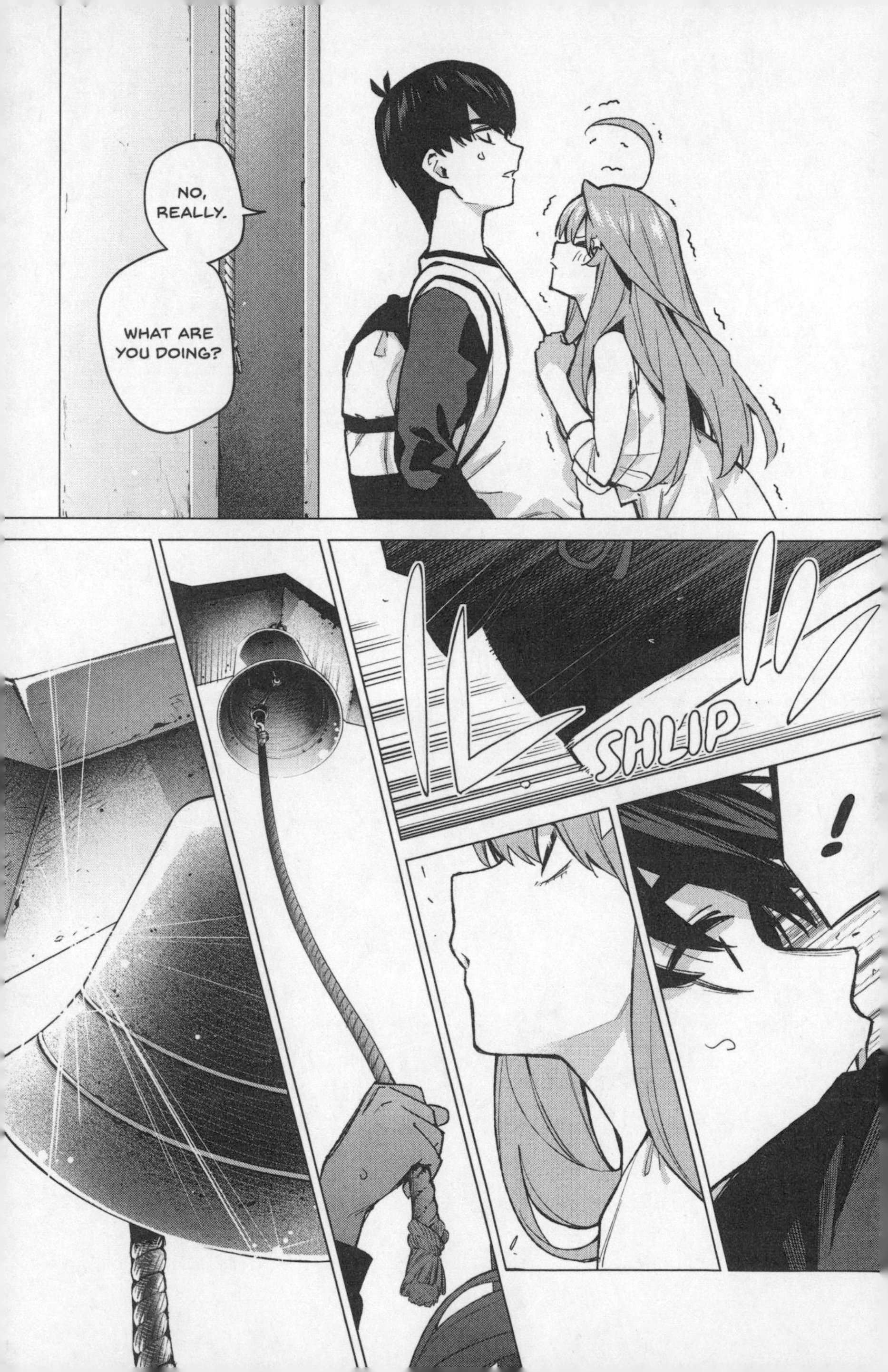
NO, REALLY.
WHAT ARE YOU DOING?
SHLIP
!

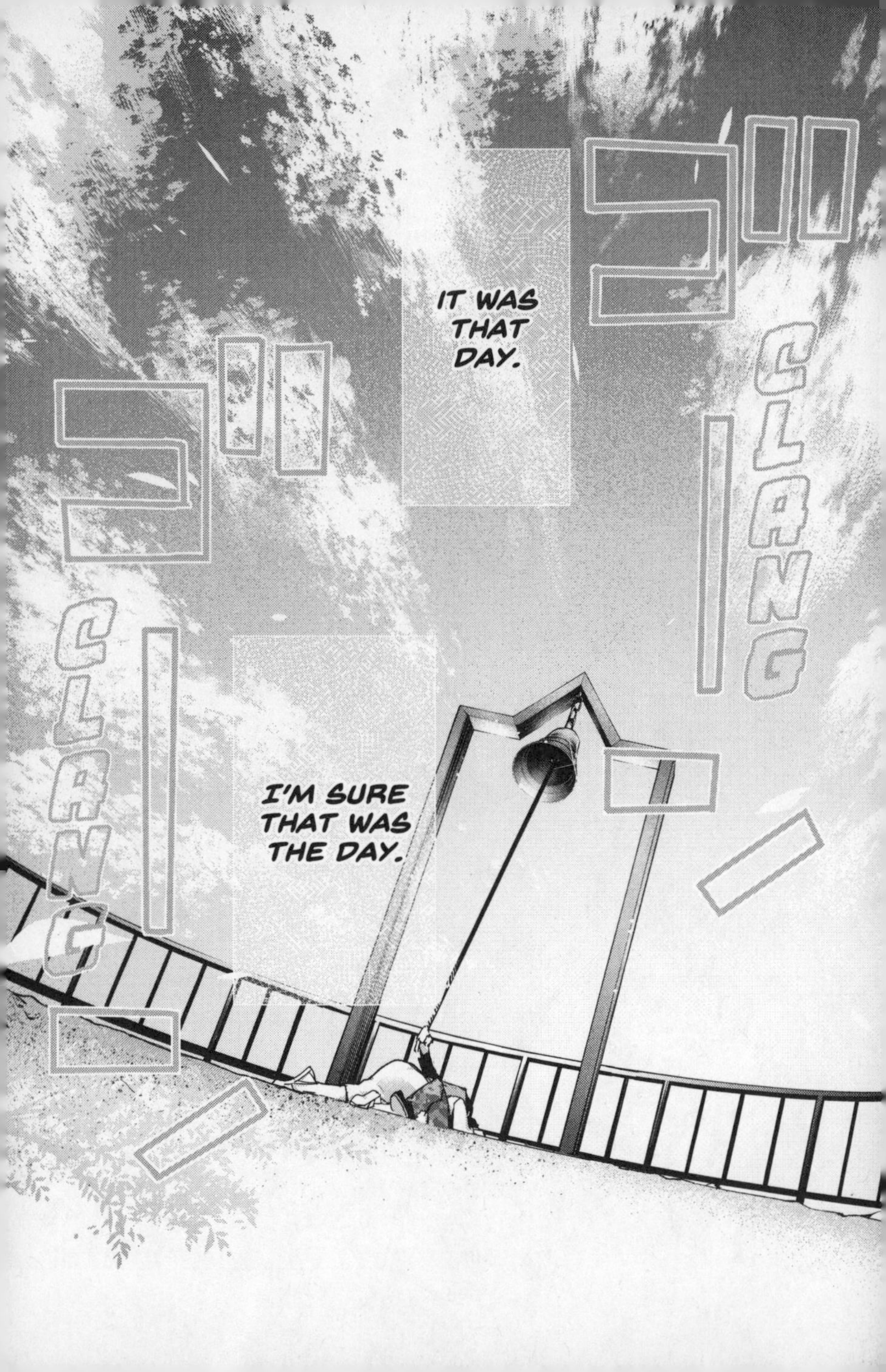
CLLANG
IT WAS THAT DAY.
CLLANG
I'M SURE THAT WAS THE DAY.

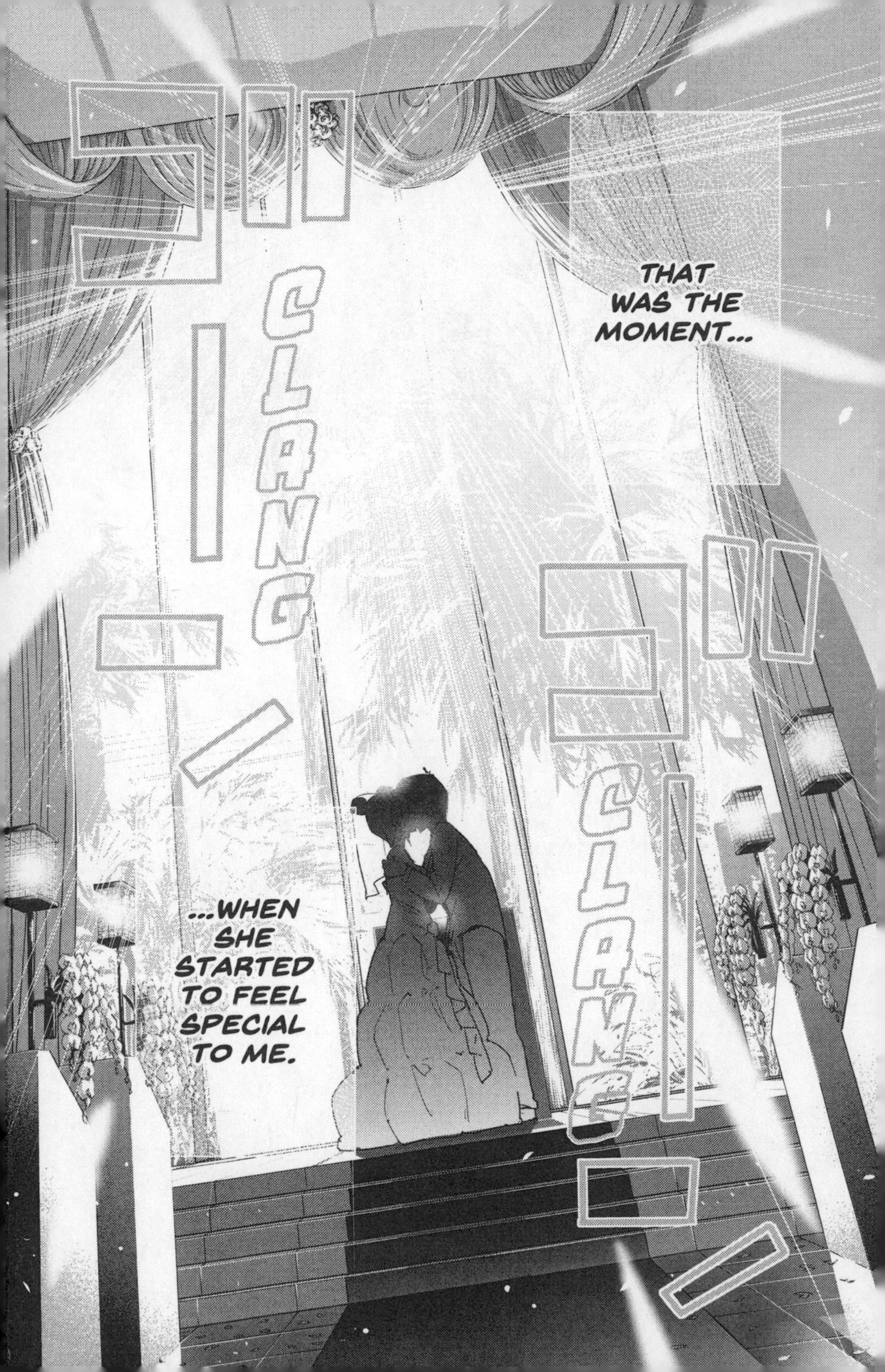
THAT WAS THE MOMENT...
CLANG
CLANG
...WHEN SHE STARTED TO FEEL SPECIAL TO ME.

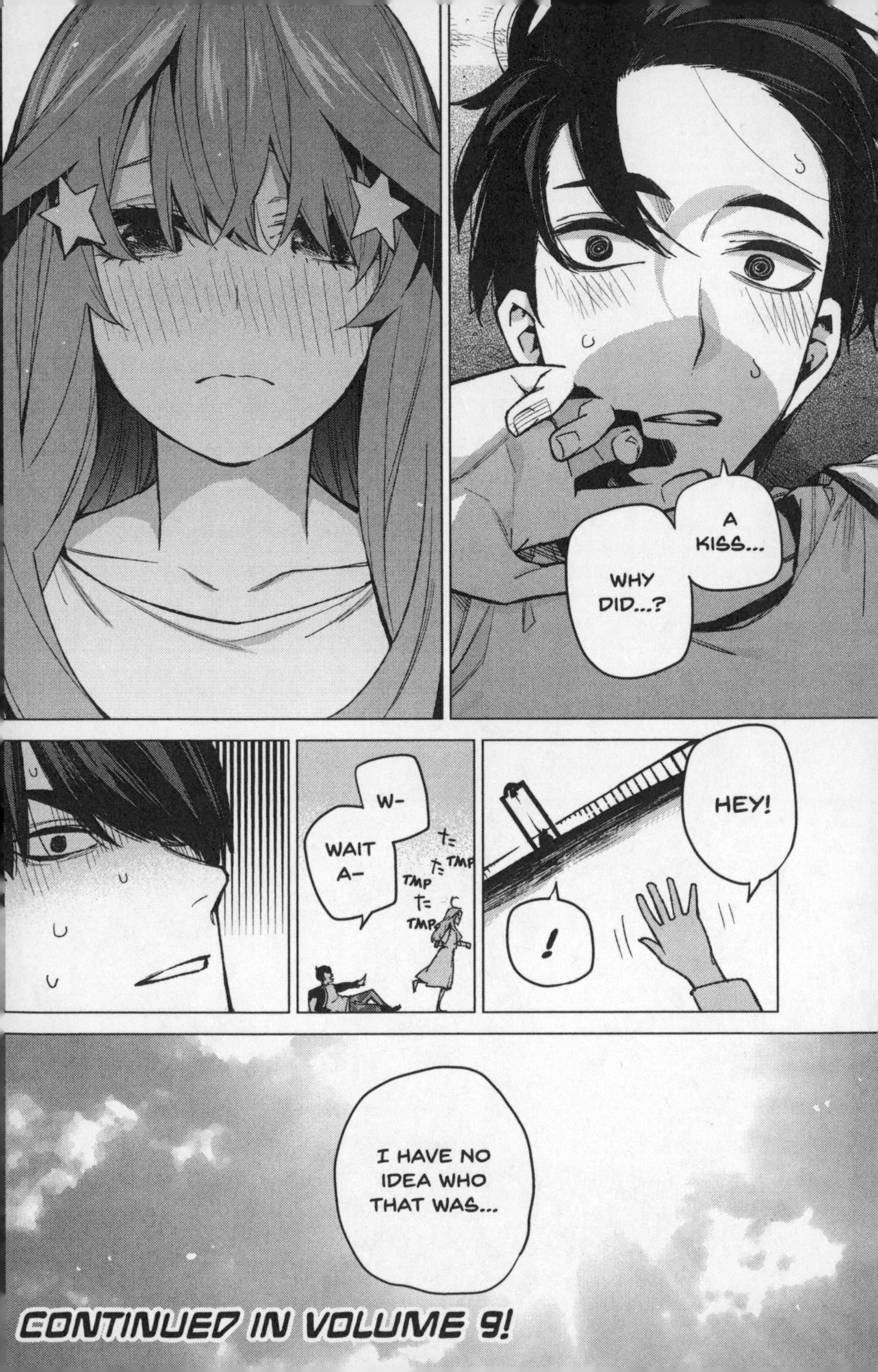
A KISS...
WHY DID...?
HEY!
!
W-
WAIT A-
TMP
TMP
TMP
I HAVE NO IDEA WHO THAT WAS...
CONTINUED IN VOLUME 9!

THE QUINTUPLETS CANNOT SHARE A FUTON

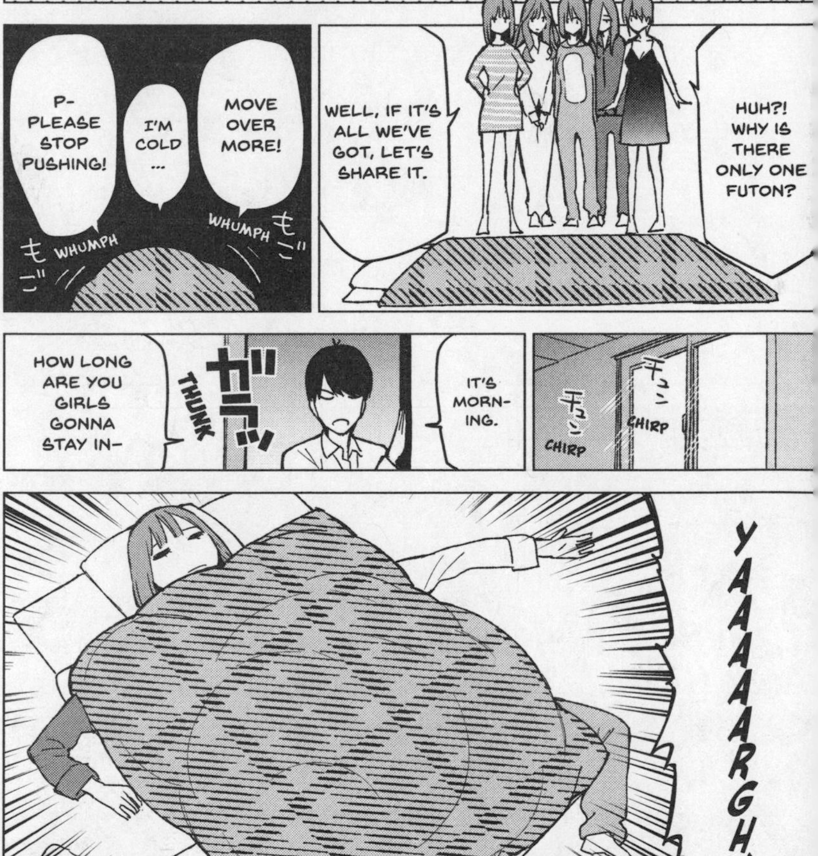
HUH?! WHY IS THERE ONLY ONE FUTON?
WELL, IF IT'S ALL WE'VE GOT, LET'S SHARE IT.
MOVE OVER MORE!
WHUMPH
I'M COLD ...
P-PLEASE STOP PUSHING!
WHUMPH
CHIRP
CHIRP
IT'S MORNING.
THUNK
HOW LONG ARE YOU GIRLS GONNA STAY IN-
YAAAAAARGH!

Staff Ueno Hino Cho Erimura

Princess Jellyfish

Akiko Higashimura

ALSO AN ANIME!

"One of the best manga for beginners!"
—*Kotaku*

Tsukimi Kurashita is fascinated with jellyfish. She's loved them from a young age and has carried that love with her to her new life in the big city of Tokyo. There, she resides in Amamizukan, a safe-haven for geek girls where no boys are allowed. One day, Tsukimi crosses paths with a beautiful and fashionable woman, but there's much more to this woman than her trendy clothes...!